FIRST DAY
COVER
CATALOGUE
& CHECKLIST

BY MICHAEL A. MELLONE

Complete
Up-to-date Catalogue

VICE PRESIDENT/PUBLISHER .... **Stuart J. Morrissey**
EDITOR .... **James E. Kloetzel**
ASSOCIATE EDITOR .... **William W. Cummings**
VALUING EDITOR .... **Martin J. Frankevicz**
NEW ISSUES EDITOR .... **David C. Akin**
COMPUTER CONTROL COORDINATOR .... **Denise Oder**
EDITORIAL ASSISTANTS .... **Judith E. Bertrand, Beth Brown**
ART/PRODUCTION DIRECTOR .... **Janine C. S. Apple**
PRODUCTION ARTIST .... **Nancy S. Martin**
SALES/MARKETING DIRECTOR .... **William Fay**
ADVERTISING .... **Sabrina D. Morton**
CIRCULATION/PRODUCT PROMOTION MANAGER ...... **Tim Wagner**

CONTENTS

5A

ACKNOWLEDGEMENTS

Appreciation and gratitude go to the following individuals who have assisted us in preparing information included in this catalogue. These individuals have generously shared their knowledge with others through the medium of this work. Those whose names follow have provided information that is in addition to the many dealer price lists and advertisements, as well as auction results, which were used in producing the Scott U.S. First Day Catalogue. Support from these people goes beyond data leading to catalogue values, for they also are key to editorial changes: Alan Berkun, Larry Graf, Scott Pelcyger, William Geijsbeek, Edward Siskin, Ken Kribbs and Carl Swain.

THE "COVERS" ON THE "COVER"

The front cover of this catalog shows three winners from the 1997 American First Day Cover Society Cachetmakers Contest. The top two covers tied for the Top Cachet Award of 1997. Above is a cachet made by Florence Villasenor featuring a WWII B-17 pilot Roy Test. In the center is a cachet made by Blossom Brower. The Bogart cachet is the work of Herb Barré. It was judged the Best "Computer Generated Cachet."

The back cover of this catalog shows 6 more winning covers from the 1997 AFDCS Cachetmakers Contest. Starting at the top, the Hanukkah FDC by Camille Randal won the Rookie of the Year category. Next is the Year of the Ox cachet by Kendal Bevil, which is the "Best Handpainted/Printed from Original Art Work." The center cover is a Mars Rover cachet made by Dave Bennett, judged the "Best Printed Art in two or more colors." Next is the Year of the Ox cachet by S&T, which is the "Best Handpainted/Printed from Clip Art." Shown at the bottom of the row of five cachets is the "Best Event Cachet" made by Florence Villasenor.

Shown to the right is a Bugs Bunny cachet made by Dave Bennett, maker of Bennett Cachetoons, judged the "Best Esoteric Cover." The Esoteric Cover Category is for FDCs made with material or methods not usually found on FDCs. This cover pays tribute to cartoon illustrator Jack Bradbury, an illustrator since 1934, who worked for Disney and later Warner Brothers. The work space is printed on the envelope. A piece of multicolored "cel art" in cartoon style slides into four corner mounts on the envelope to inhabit the work space.

You can learn more about First Day Cover collecting by joining the American First Day Cover Society. The Annual AFDCS Cachetmakers Contest is just one of many services and programs sponsored by the society. For more information about the AFDCS or the Annual Cachetmakers Contest, contact Mrs. S. Monte Eiserman, 14359 Chadbourne, Houston, TX 77079.

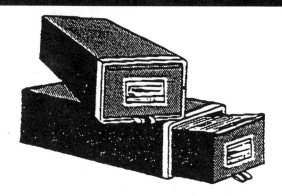

11A

HOW TO USE THIS CATALOGUE

Sample Listing and Headings

SCOTT NUMBER	DESCRIPTION	UNCACHETED SINGLE BLOCK	CACHETED SINGLE BLOCK	CERM PROG

1923

☐ 610   2c **Warren G. Harding**, 9/1/23, DC..30.00 ..35.00
☐   Marion, OH (5,000) ....20.00 ..22.50
☐   Brooklyn, NY; Mt. Rainier, MD;
        Caledonia, OH (Unofficial cities) 37.50
☐   **Pre-date**, 8/31/23, DC,(1known) 250.00
☐   1st George W. Linn cachet
        (1st modern cachet) 800.00

    The first number is the Scott catalogue number. This is followed by the denomination and subject. Next is the official first day (FD) date, 9/1/23, and the official FD city, Washington, D.C. which normally is listed only as "DC."

    Marion, Ohio is another official FD city. Some issues have more than one official FD city. The number after Marion, Ohio, is the approximate number of covers canceled there on the FD. There's no number after the Washington, D.C. listing because it is not known.

    Listed next is "Caledonia, Ohio, unofficial." This listing is for a cover postmarked on the first day of issue in Caledonia, Ohio, which was not an official FD city. Often collectors have purchased stamps in the official FD city and taken them to other cities to create "unofficial" FDCs.

    Unofficial cities from which cancellations are obtained on the FD normally add to the value of the FDC, when the value is compared to that of the official city. Often a special slogan cancel, related to the new stamp, will be available on the FD. Even when these are from the official city, they are valued as unofficials on FDCs since 1940.

    A Pre-dated FDC or Pre-FDC is a stamp or stamps on cover with a postmark before the official first day of issue

A 1st Cachet is simply the first cachet that a particular cachet maker has produced. Only the most prominent are listed in this catalogue. The total number could exceed 2,000.

First day ceremony programs (CERM PROG) are produced and distributed at ceremonies dedicating a new stamp. The programs normally are produced by either the U.S. Postal Service or a local sponsoring group.

Formats of the programs vary greatly. They can be as simple as a single sheet of paper or an elaborate work of graphic art. A common element is that most programs contain the words "First Day Ceremony Program" and contain a listing of the ceremony order of events.

13A

CATALOGUE VALUES

Catalogue Values shown in this book are retail prices. A value represents what you could expect to pay for the cover. The values listed are a reference which reflects recent actual dealer selling prices drawn from retail lists and auction realizations.

A catalogue value in italics suggests that not enough information was available to establish a firm value, and the italicized number is as close an estimate as we could ascertain.

Use this catalogue as a guide in your own buying and selling. The actual price you pay for a cover may be higher or lower than the catalogue value because of one or more of the following: the amount of personal service a dealer offers, increased interest in the cachet maker or time period when the stamp was issued, whether an item is a "loss leader," part of a special sale, or otherwise is being sold for a short period of time at a lower price, or if at a public auction you are able to obtain a cover inexpensively because of little interest in the cover at that time.

Minimum catalogue value

The minimum value for an item in this catalogue is one dollar. For items where the stamp or item of postal stationery has a face value of 25 cents or more, the minimum value is $1.25. In all cases, the minimum value is designed to reflect the cost of purchasing a single item from a dealer.

Values by year range

Values for pre-1920 first day covers (FDCs) are for uncacheted FDCs with single stamps, unless otherwise stated. Many early FDCs or earliest known use (EKU or eku) covers are unique. A dash in the value column means that FDCs are seldom found in these categories, or that no market value has been determined through recent sales of the covers.

Before 1920, stamps were not regularly released with an official first day of issue observance. In many of these cases, the catalogue shows the earliest known postal use of the stamp.

Regular issues of 1922-26, Scott 551-600, are valued as uncacheted FDCs with singles and blocks of four stamps or as singles and pairs of stamps.

During the issues of 1923-35, Scott 610-771, cachets on FDCs first appeared. Values are arranged in four columns, giving values for singles and blocks both as uncacheted and cacheted FDCs. FDCs with plate blocks from this period sell for two to three times the price for singles.

From 1935 to date, values are given for common cacheted FDCs with singles, blocks, and plate blocks. Coils are valued as common cacheted FDCs with singles, and pairs (Pr), line pairs (Lp), and plate number coils (PNCs) where appropriate. **Uncacheted covers sell for about 10-15 percent of the catalogue value of common cacheted covers.**

Cacheted FDCs, 1950 (Scott 987) to date values, are for clean unaddressed FDCs with printed cachets. **Addressed FDCs usually sell for about 50-75 percent of catalogue value.**

Values for Cacheted FDCs in this catalogue are for common mass-produced commercial cachets. Specific cachets may sell for several times catalogue value. Values for many various cachets can be found in our Cachet Valuing Calculator section of this book.

Values for Ceremony Programs

Values for material from 1940-1957, unless otherwise stated, are for programs without stamps and first-day cancels. Programs containing stamps and first-day cancels usually sell for twice the stated value.

Values for material from 1958 to date, unless otherwise stated, are for programs with stamps and first-day cancels. Programs without stamps and first-day cancels usually sell for half the stated value.

17A

cover box

10.5"

4.25"   7.5"

Keep your collection organized in this handsome
and durable cover box. Box will hold hundreds
of covers. Available in classic marble styling.

Item	Description	Retail
CVBOX	Marble Cover Box	$6.95

INTRODUCTION TO FDC COLLECTING

This introductory material is presented as a grouping of individual essays.

• First is a nuts-and-bolts discussion of
First Day Covers,
including definitions and concepts.

• Following is the classic
Cram Course
by the late Prof. Earl Planty, which will get you in a proper frame of mind to enjoy this hobby.

• Next is B. Wayne Caldwell's article,
"How to Make Your Own First Day Covers."
Completing this introduction is an "Introduction to Cachet Collecting"

and the
"Cachet Calculator"

WHAT IS A FIRST DAY COVER?

When a new stamp is issued by the U.S. Postal Service (USPS), it is offered for sale in (usually) only a single city on one day and then throughout the country on the second day and thereafter. That date of sale in a single city is designated as the "official" First Day of Issue. It is permissible to purchase stamps at that official city and have the stamps canceled elsewhere on that day, which lead to "unofficial" first day cancellations.

The USPS requires that cancellations may be applied only to those covers which contain enough postage to at least meet the current First Class Mail rate. For newly issued stamps which individually do not meet that rate, multiples of that stamp to "make rate" or that stamp coupled with other stamps to reach the minimum are required.

Figure 1. The first official First Day of Issue machine cancel used for the Ordinance of 1787 commemorative (Scott 795) issue July 13, 1937, in Marietta, Ohio, and New York, New York.

A special cancel is applied to the new stamp in the official city. These cancellations can never again be duplicated after the grace period allowed by the USPS to secure such postal markrags.

In the 1920's and 1930's, FDCs were canceled with everyday working postmarks. The post office first used an official FD postmark with the words "First Day of Issue," in killer bars, for the 1937 Ordinance of 1787 Commemorative (Scott 795). An official "First Day of Issue" machine cancel has been supplied for almost every new issue since.

An official "First Day of Issue" hand cancel was first

used for the first stamps released in the Famous Americans Series, the 1-cent and 2-cent Authors, Washington Irving and James Fenimore Cooper (Scott 859-860), both issued January 29, 1940.

Figure 2. The first official First Day of Issue hand cancel used for the 1-cent and 2-cent Famous Americans Authors (Scott 859-860), issued in Cooperstown or Tarrytown, New York, on January 29, 1940.

Figure 3. The first official pictorial First Day of Issue cancel used for the Horticulture commemorative (Scott 1100) issued on March 15, 1958, in Ithaca, New York.

A third type of official FD cancel has been available for many U.S. new issues. In the 1940's and 1950's this third type of cancel was a short-bar hand cancel. Now it is a bull's eye, which is usually identical to the town machine cancel, without the killer bars or "First Day of Issue" slogan.

Sometimes the stamp with FD postmark can be found on some other object: postcard, souvenir, piece of wood, bark, or cloth, or anything that will accept a stamp and postmark.

Most often an FDC is an envelope. Some are just plain white envelopes. Some bear elaborate and attractive cachets.

WHAT IS A CACHET?
(pronounced ka-SHAY)
A cachet is a design of words and/or pictures which refers specifically to the new stamp on the FDC. Designs

are usually found on the front, left side of the envelope. They can be printed, rubber stamped, individually hand created, or pasted-on. The purpose of a cachet is to enhance the meaning and appearance of the cover.

WHY COLLECT CACHETED FDCs?

For a long time, collectors wanted an example of every stamp issue on an FDC. They did not really care if the FDC was uncacheted or cacheted, or who made the cachet. If they could find one with an attractive cachet, all the better, but any FDC to fill the space in the collection would do.

Today, many (if not most) collectors don't want just any FDC. They are looking for cacheted FDCs. There are several reasons for this.

Information about cachet collecting has been published and promoted in many places and in many ways. The American First Day Cover Society has promoted FDCs through its magazine First Days for more than 25 years. More recently, several cover-oriented columns have appeared in the philatelic press, helping to generate additional interest. And, there has been a steady upsurge in mass-produced FDCs offered on a subscription basis, each with its own cachet series.

The real reason for the great increase in interest is the collector himself. Collectors have become much more knowledgeable about FDC cachets. They have been captured by the quest for new cachets and information about them.

WHAT TO SEEK WHEN BUYING FDCs

When you are buying an FDC, look at the whole cover. It should be in good condition, without tears, wrinkles, stains, or wear. The stamp should not be torn or damaged. The postmark should be legible and it should have the correct FD date.

Many collectors prefer unaddressed FDCs because they are perceived as neater and more attractive. Often the specialist will want to see an address on a cover because it can sometimes help identify the cachet or the servicer of the cover. Occasionally collectors put their own name on previously unaddressed FDCs.

Just because this catalog emphasizes cacheted FDCs does not mean that uncacheted FDCs are not collectible. A number of the important early FDC servicers, — Adam Bert, C.E. Nickles, and Edward Worden — made many uncacheted FDCs which remain valuable.

Only a small percentage of all pre-1930 FDCs that exist are cacheted, because most collectors and dealers of that period were happy enough to have an uncacheted FDC. Some collectors today prefer uncacheted FDCs because they look more like legitimate pieces of mail than elaborately cacheted covers. Thus, the choice is left to the collector.

When buying cacheted FDCs, seek unusual looking cachets when you can. You will always be able to find the mass-produced commercial cachets for your collection. If you bypass an unusual cachet, however, you may not ever see that cachet offered for sale again.

If you generally collect one of the mass-produced commercial cachets, the same rule applies. Keep your eyes open for unusual color or text varieties.

WHAT ARE THE SPECIALISTS COLLECTING?

Specialists collect in many ways: by cachet maker, by issue, by set, by years or periods of years, and by topic. They collect first cachets, combination FDCs, unofficial FDCs, and hand painted cachets.

If you find a cachet maker whose work you particularly like, you can try to put together an entire run of FDCs. For example, Anderson, Artcraft, and House of Farnam all started producing cachets before 1940. While you may not have too much trouble finding most of the cachets, it will be a challenge to fill in some of the early cachets of any of these three makers. It will be particularly hard to find some of the early cachet color varieties of Anderson and Artcraft.

Some specialists pick out a particular issue or set that they like and try to make a complete collection of cachet varieties. This can be a modern issue, such as a space issue, a Kennedy issue, or an older issue that is of special interest to you. Pick out a stamp issued in your home state, or issued for your profession, or one that is related to one of your other hobbies.

Check the new issue information in any of the stamp periodicals. If there is a new stamp for which the first day of issue is near your home, you might enjoy going to a FD ceremony, collecting all the cachets you can find on that issue, and perhaps producing a cachet for that stamp that you design yourself.

Figure 4. An example of a combination FDC.

Collectors sometimes seek groupings: all FDC cachets of the 3-cent purple-colored stamps of the late 1930's, all cachets of the 28 stamps issued in 1948, and so on. Some specialists collect early uncacheted regular issues or commemoratives by set or for FD postmark varieties.

People also collect by topic - masonic, military, or

professional topics, women's history, national or local history, sesquicentennials, bicentennials, or just about anything else that interests them.

First Cachet collecting has become very popular with FDC specialists. A "first cachet" is simply the initial effort a particular cachet maker has produced. First cachets have been researched, documented, and firmly established for hundreds of cachet makers.

For other cachet makers, the search for the first cachet is still going on. First-cachet collecting is just one of many areas in FDC collecting where the knowledgeable collector can find desirable cachets in dealers' boxes. Very often first cachets are priced the same as the more common mass-produced commercial cachets because the former are not recognized for what they are.

Listings for many first cachets appear under the appropriate Scott number in this catalogue.

A combination FDC is one which has other stamps or labels along with the new stamp. Together the stamps help to tell a more complete story about the new issue.

The stamps or labels should be related thematically, usually by the history or topic of the stamp. For example, a stamp with a bird on it could be accompanied by other U.S. or foreign stamps with birds, or perhaps a wildlife conservation label.

A new stamp issued for an anniversary of statehood could be used in combination with older issues related to the state's history, or other stamps that had FDs in the state. The possibilities are only limited by imagination.

An unofficial FDC is one canceled on the official FD date, but not in the official FD city. An unofficial FDC can be canceled in any city as long as it has a postmark showing the FD date. An unofficial FDC is more meaningful when the city is related to the new issue. These relationships may be historically significant or by name only.

In 1926, Edward Worden prepared a truly classic unofficial FDC for the 13-cent Harrison stamp (Scott 622). He took 500 stamps from Indianapolis, Indiana, one of the official FD cities, to North Bend, Ohio, Harrison's home town.

On the Battle of Fallen Timbers stamp of 1929 (Scott 680), unofficial FDCs are known postmarked in Fallen Timbers, Pennsylvania. The only connection here between the stamp and the unofficial FDC is the town name. There are a number of issues from the 1920's and 1930's which have 50 or more unofficial FDCs known. While all of these unofficials are not related to the new issue, they are still eagerly collected.

A semi-official FDC is canceled in the official city, but with something other than the usual first-day-of-issue slogan or bull's eye cancels. Often these are pictorial cancels, perhaps from a stamp show where the show cancel is used rather than the FD cancel.

Hand-painted cachets are collected because they often have attractive and colorful original artwork. Each FDC represents a lot of time, effort and talent on the part of the cachet maker. Hand-painted FDCs are often difficult to find in dealers' boxes, because they are usually produced in limited quantities. Some of the well-known commercial cachet designers also make handpainted cachets. Ralph Dyer, who designed cachets for Artcraft during the 1930's, produced hand-painted cachets for several decades after that.

HOW TO LEARN MORE ABOUT FDCs

The best way to learn about FDCs is to be in touch with other FDC collectors. Visit them or write to them to exchange information and opinions on covers.

Join the American First Day Cover Society (AFDCS), which publishes the journal First Days eight times per year. The journal contains new issue information, free cover exchange ads, several columns on modern FDCs, and detailed research articles on cachet makers.

The AFDCS also has regular FDC auctions, an annual convention, periodic regional get-togethers, an FDC Expertizing Committee and numerous slide shows on FDCs available on loan. For additional information write AFDCS, P.O. Box 65960-S, Tucson, AZ 85728.

HOW TO ACQUIRE CURRENT FDCs

There are several ways that a collector can obtain current FDCs. The collector may service his own FDCs by sending envelopes to the FD city postmaster as new stamps are released. Different unserviced cacheted envelopes can be purchased from local or mail order cover dealers. Or the collector may choose to join a cover club or service offered by many cover dealers, and automatically receive each new FDC.

HOW TO SERVICE YOUR OWN FDCs

Many collectors believe that servicing their own FDCs is what FDC collecting is all about. There is a tremendous feeling of involvement and accomplishment. You may service your own FDCs by purchasing the new stamp when it is available at your local post office, affixing the stamp to your envelope and forwarding the envelope for servicing to the FD post office within 30 days of the issue date.

Your local post office has bulletins on upcoming stamps, their date of issue, and FD city, along with an illustration of the new stamp.

A detailed procedure for servicing your FDCs is outlined below:

Method 1: You affixing your stamps

1. Purchase the new stamp at your local post office as soon as it becomes available, which usually will be one or two days after the FD date. If you cannot obtain the

stamp at your local post office, you may need to visit your nearest post office with a Philatelic Center.

2. Affix the stamp(s) to the upper right corner of the envelope, 1/4-inch from the top and 1/4-inch from the right edge. Pencil address your cover or affix an addressed peelable label near the bottom of the envelope.

3. Send your cover(s) in an outer envelope to the FD city within 30 days after the first day of issue. No payment is necessary.

Method 2: How to join an FDC service

A more convenient method of obtaining current FDCs is to join an FDC new issue service, usually that of a cachet maker, or purchase the FDCs separately from dealers. By subscribing to a service, there is no chance of missing upcoming issues due to oversight. Uncacheted First Day Covers are now available through the USPS Philatelic Fulfillment Service Center.

The postal service will no longer affix stamps to envelopes sent in to FC cities.

There are over 200 different cachet makers who sell their cacheted FDCs for current issues. Some cachet makers produce individually hand-painted cachets in very limited quantities. Also, there are "comic" cachets, "silks" and many others. Some collectors purchase current FDCs from several different cachet makers, adding variety to their collections.

Most cachet makers stock FDCs of past issues, allowing you to add to your collection.

For a booklet of cachetmakers, send $4.00 and a SASE to: Michael Mellone, Cachetmakers List, P.O. Box 206, Stewartsville, NJ 08886.

CRAM COURSE IN FIRST DAY COVERS
by Professor Earl Planty & Michael Mellone

Introduction

To meet the needs of newcomers to First Day Cover (FDC) collecting, we have produced this very simple cram course on getting started in, and enjoying, FDCs. There is plenty of research and writing by and for advanced collectors. There is an abundance of giant advertisements designed to hard sell a particular cover or set of expensive covers, mostly aimed at beginners and laymen. But little exists to guide the new collector before, and even after, he starts buying.

It tells simply what the first day cover pros have learned over years of experience, and it is knowledge which has been held a little tightly among the pros, or at least not written and published extensively.

Lesson I
Getting To Know FDCs

Your first step in all this is to visit local and nearby stamp dealers. Include all of them within a reasonable radius of your city, or further out if you are isolated in a small town or city. Visit them on business trips and vacations, too.

Make up a list of dealers from the telephone yellow pages. Then check off each stop as your visit there is completed—perhaps, with notes on the dealer's stock, how you were received, etc.

Visit each dealer several times. Stock changes from day to day. I have found some of my best covers in cupboards that were bare in my previous stop. Perhaps phone before going out to learn what first-day stock the dealer has and his open hours.

Once in the store, ask to see the dealer's stocks of first-days, those in his boxes, albums, collections and even good single covers from the safe.

Handle them very gently, study them, stare at them. Look at the details of the cachet and its workmanship, color, message and total impact upon you.

Then study the stamp, the envelope, the cancel, corner card, address and backstamp, if any.

At the store, don't hurry; instead, browse, linger, browse some more and compare. Look at a multitude of covers—at least 10,000 during this course.

But don't tie up a busy dealer. Come back at a slower time. Talk with the dealer. Make up and take along a list of questions for him.

Get answers from all whom you visit. Note the variety of their responses. Recognize that the field of first days is still growing and expanding rapidly.

Collecting practices are not yet firmly fixed and not wholly agreed upon. You will learn this from the variety and even contradictions among dealers' responses.

So, don't look for final answers. Expose yourself to many viewpoints and then decide for yourself which path and preference you wish to follow.

If a dealer asks what you want to see, be bold. Reply firmly, "Covers from 1940 to 1950, or recents." The 1940s are easily available, moderately priced and of great variety and interest.

They are starting to move up in price, too, but are still available at two to three dollars. But restrain yourself. You have not completed the course yet and have not graduated.

You are not a competent buyer or collector now. You will buy later, when you are more prepared. But perhaps you could buy a very few just to feel the thrill of purchase and possession, and to actually start you on collecting.

While in the shops with the covers and their cachets before you, appreciate them, feel for them as you would paintings in a gallery. These cachets are really little pictures to be understood and treated as such.

Note that a visit to them is free with no admission charge to these philatelic galleries. It's great for beginners or even seniors who are short on enough bread and bucks to buy in today's inflated market.

On your monopoly of the dealer's time: you'll repay him in a few weeks when you are an established collector, having fun with the hobby and spending money freely with him.

Lesson II
Learning At Bourses & Shows

The next assignment in this course takes you to shows, expositions, bourses and flea markets. At these places, dealers and collectors rent booths and tables and display stock for sale. These are mostly held on weekends.

Many shows are advertised in the classified sections of city newspapers, placed near the antique and hobby columns.

The pace may be a little fast and crowded here, but stock is good and often cheaper than at established dealers who have high rents and taxes.

Besides, at shows and bourses, dealers come to sell, to clean up remainders and overstocks. They price accordingly. Bargaining is in order, too. At the shows and bourses, repeat the learning exercises previously described for your searching in dealers' shops.

Linn's Stamp News, Box 29, Sidney, OH 45365, and other publications list upcoming shows and bourses faithfully for you each week, sometimes even six months in advance.

To find where and when to go, use these publications at

your local library, or buy a copy from a local dealer until you learn the publications to which you wish to subscribe.

Lesson III
Contacting FDC Mail Order Dealers

The next lesson in this cram course is a postcard campaign to mail-order dealers in first days. Buy 25 cards and request from those dealers their very helpful, educational, regularly issued lists and catalogs. Many mail-order dealers have advertisements in this publication.

This is particularly useful to collectors who live in places isolated from dealers. Some mail-order dealers may be small, relatively new and committed to collector services as well as their own profit.

Large or small, mail-order dealers usually are well-stocked, helpful, service-oriented and moderate in price. Their educational catalogs describe, picture and price their offerings.

Begin your collection of first-day literature by obtaining and saving these catalogs and lists for future reference.

Buy a few covers, too, and more as you advance in knowledge and confidence.

Lesson IV
Collecting The Newer FDCs

Probably, you have asked by now about servicers. FDC servicers are those who will, for a moderate deposit, send you one or more FDCs, issue by issue, as they are released. No fuss, no bother, they just keep you up to date. Servicing is for those who want recents. Most collectors eventually prefer earlier issues, as it is with collectors of coins, books and automobiles. Use of servicers is neat, assuredly regular, easy and almost effortless on the beginning collector's part.

Did we say "collectors?" Well hardly. Buying is not collecting. Collecting means searching out, finding, discover-

ing, choosing from a great many, negotiating and
then buying.

In servicing, you go through the buying process only
once. You buy for 10 to 50 future issues at once. You also
miss the pleasant practice of hunting bargains and negotiating on price.

Your range of cachets is usually very limited. Mostly, you
choose from two to six cachets that the dealer services—a
few offer up to a dozen different ones.

Buy from them for a wider choice among cachets, of
which 50 to 75 different are usually made for each issue.
If you buy a service, rotate cachet makers until you have
bought and seen them all.

There is a wide variety of cachets available. A cachet
can be very beautiful, educational or even comical.

Servicers as well as individual cachetmakers are well
advertised in the classified and display sections of the philatelic press, and in "First Days" Magazine, the Journal of
the American First Day Cover Society.

The servicers fill a good need for some. They help beginners who do not have time or inclination to follow this
cram course or who do not have access to it.

They also serve those who have a casual interest, who
want to see a little of what's regularly coming out in first
day covers, but nothing more.

There are many good and great cachets too numerous to
mention. Of the most heavily advertised cachets, perhaps
60,000 to 150,000 are issued per stamp. But some cachet
makers restrict their issues to 2,000 or 3,000 copies.
Others, especially hand-painted to 100 or less.

As you graduate here and move on to upper levels of
instruction, you will hunt out these limited producers, if
scarcity and advancement potential interest you.

Some servicers sell postally unused, cacheted envelopes
for future stamp issues. The collector buys these and services them himself.

The process is simple and rewarding. It gets you into the act a little more than merely buying a service. But service a variety of cachets for each issue so you may learn about different cachets and choose among them for concentration.

The current edition of the "Directory of Cachet Makers" is available from the American First Day Cover Society for a SASE. The address is Box 65960, Tucson, AZ 85728.

This directory lists all known current participating cachet makers' names and addresses, where to write to purchase their cachets and the number of issues they produce.

Lesson V
Starting With The Currents, and Working Your Way Back

To the degree that you are not interested in profit making or even getting your money back, collecting of recents that come out in such great numbers becomes more attractive.

Surely, the current cachets, disregarding age and romance of the earlies, are more professional than in the classic period. And, if you start on currents, you can easily work back to earlier ones. Most collectors do. Visit the local dealer and stamp shows first just to get oriented to the field.

Will you have to choose between earlies and recents? Handling both to any degree of completeness is costly in time and money. But you could easily carry both for a year or two while you are making a choice. The recents are easier because they are easily available. The early ones have to be hunted, i.e. collected.

What will you do for an album? Nothing. It's too early yet. Albums tie down and imprison your covers. You can't handle them, rearrange them and shuffle them in an album.

You can't hand a cover to a friend to be felt physically as well as psychologically. Go to a haberdasher. Get empty shirt or shoe boxes for your files.

Do encase your covers promptly in glassine or poly envelopes costing a few cents each and regularly advertised in the philatelic press.

Keep a record. Make up a marketing code to tell you what you paid for each cover. Mark the price lightly in pencil on the back. In a marketing code, letters stand for numbers thus: B (1) U (2) Y (3) I (4) N (5) G (6) F (7) D (8) C (9) S (0) (BUYING FDCS). Thus, a cover costing $1.75 would be marked $B.FN.

Lesson VI
Deciding Upon And Buying Catalogs

You'll need a First Day catalog. It is a guidebook and road map to the territory you will travel. The definitive first day catalog (the one you have in your hand now) debuted at the American Stamp Dealer's Association's 1979 show.

The book originally was called *Discovering the Fun in First Day Covers,* by Michael Mellone. It lists and prices all FDCs from the start of United States stamps in 1847 to date. It's was the poor man's first-day Bible, listing everything in first days. This had never been done in one volume.

In 1983, that publication was retitled *Scott's U.S. First Day Cover Catalogue and Checklist.*

Also available is a *Photo Encyclopedia of Cacheted First Day Covers,* in 10 volumes. The encyclopedia covers the years 1901-39 and pictures, numbers, describes, and prices all known first day cachets on U.S. covers of that period. Some of these varieties may be unknown in your own collection and unidentified in dealers' boxes you will be searching.

The *Encyclopedia* also identifies hundreds of cachet

makers never known before. It also does the same for more than 1,000 cachet maker's and their first cachets. The encyclopedia also is a Bible on what to collect, where to find it, how much to pay for it and how to appreciate it fully. The encyclopedia was 50 years in the making but the first printing sold out in eight months.

Other specialized photo cachet catalogues cover the period from 1940-69 in seven volumes, consisting of over 15,000 photos of FDCs and values. For descriptive information send a SASE to the publisher of this catalogue. The address of which is printed on the title page.

Lesson VII
Specializing in various FDC Specialties

You begin to specialize a little bit now. Various collecting interests include cachets on the recently issued Marilyn Monroe stamp; cachets on stamps of various states; baseball cachets; and cachets on larger than standard-size envelopes.

In first days, there are over 200 different specialties, enough to fit each collector's whim or fancy. A few include all the covers of a particular year or decade; all cachets of two or three preferred makers; all airmails; special deliveries; registered; booklet panes; sets; back of the book; regular issues; or commemoratives.

Some collectors like to collect only hand-painted cachets. There are many beautiful hand-painted cachets produced today. Some are illustrated on the cover of this catalogue.

There are stamps and first-day cachets dealing with law, agriculture, science, education, environment, minorities, flowers, animals, state, presidents, space, military, polar, ships, railroads, transportation, art, books, music, Olympics, major historical events, opening of the country, emancipation and the Old West.

Explore these topics freely in dealers' boxes. Pick a few specialties that please you.

When is graduation? When does the course end? Like education, it never does. You continue learning doing the same things discussed in this section, but you also may wish to join the American First Day Cover Society. The membership address is Box 65960-S, Tucson, AZ 80728. Ask for membership information. Your membership includes a free subscription to the award-winning Journal, *"First Days."*

Lesson VIII
Graduation

When is spring training over and time for the game to begin? When may we buy a little more freely? You may begin to buy when you feel you don't know as much about the game as you thought you did. Buy when you are a little cautious, perhaps confused by it all. Confused enough to be careful about what you buy or sign up to buy.

When you see a glimmer of an attractive path ahead, an area and a direction in first days that fits your purse and personality, move on more freely.

When you just can't get enough to read or find enough shows to attend, then open your pocket and spend a little more—discreetly. Then you are a graduate and this Cram Course pedagogy is behind you.

Good luck, and happy collecting. Enjoy this fascinating hobby of ours.

HOW TO MAKE YOUR OWN FIRST DAY COVERS
by B. Wayne Caldwell

A great deal of the fun I have with First Day Covers is
making my own limited edition FDCs. While this information is presented to help you prepare your own cachets for
the first day of issue of a stamp, the process also is valid for
any event for which you would like a postal cancellation as
a commemoration. Two of my favorite FDCs are the
Barrymores (Scott 2012), issued June 8, 1982, and the
Knoxville World's Fair (Scott 2006-2009), issued April 29,
1982.

Here are the steps I follow:
1. First decide how many FDCs you want to make. I
prefer to make 100. You may want to do more or less.
There are no requirements here. I have chosen 100 as a
base because at that level I have found average cost per
cover to be reasonable.
   The USPS charges for canceling more than 50 covers at a
time with handstamp cancels. You may wish to investigate
this charge if you choose to prepare covers in such a
quantity.

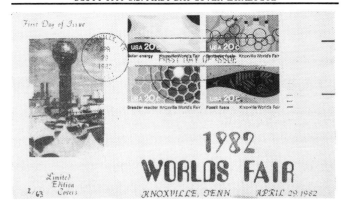

2. Buy a box of No. 6 3/4 envelopes. A nice quality envelope can be purchased reasonably at a paper company or an office supply store.

3. When you purchase the stamps you will be using on the envelopes, be sure to buy a few more than you will need. You may not want to break up the plate number block or any of the other marginal blocks.

4. Make arrangements to have the envelope stamped (you can request this) on the day and in the city where the event took place. If you are not able to attend the event personally, you can provide a return envelope for all the covers you are having canceled. Explain that you want to print on them and do not want any smudges or stains on them.

If you are not able to have the covers returned in a single package, you will need to use a peel off label on each prepared cover with your return address on it. These can be purchased from a stamp shop or office supply store or ordered through the classified ads of the philatelic newspapers.

5. While you are waiting for the envelopes to be returned, decide what you want as the envelope cachet. You are free to use whatever means you want, q.v., commercial printing, hand drawing (color if you want), collage, or even a computer-generated piece of art or art and text. I recommend that you number your "limited-edition" covers, which adds to the later appeal.

6. If you choose to go with a commercial printer, or

even a hobbyist with a printing press, you will need to make your arrangements while the envelopes are being canceled. (Of course, if you prefer, you may wish to have the cachet prepared far enough in advance to send the finished envelope for cancellation. Before committing to a commercial printer, be certain he is able to print on the canceled envelopes. Most of the printers I talked to assure me they can.

When you have completed all of these steps, you will have a group of cachets for your own collection, to trade with others, or to sell. An increasing number of FDC collectors are choosing this route to having an enjoyable time with First Day Covers.

INTRODUCTION TO CACHET COLLECTING

As more and more FDC collectors turn to collecting FDCs by cachet varieties, the question is asked, "Who makes this cachet?" Included in this introduction to cachet collecting is a mini-identifier, with several popular cachet makers of the past 40 years.

Sixty cachet makers are identified and priced in *The Cachet Identifier,* available for $7.95 from FDC Publishing, Box 206D, Stewartsville, NJ 08886, or from your local dealer.

C. Stephen Anderson

C. Stephen Anderson produced cachets for every issue between 1933 and 1979. Anderson cachets are easy to identify. They usually are signed "C. Stephen Anderson" or "CSA" and contain an illustration and some historical information in the text. His cachets are usually one color, with the earliest ones printed in black. Later purple, and then other color varieties, were printed. Many cachets were printed in several different colors.

Figure AND-1
THE FIRST ANDERSON CACHET was prepared for the Oglethorpe Issue of 1933. Anderson cachets can usually be identified by the lettering style and use of scrolls. Most are signed "C. Stephen Anderson" or "CSA."

41A

Artcraft Leo August - Washington Stamp Exchange

Leo August of Washington Stamp Exchange traces the history of Artcraft cachets back to the World's Fair Issue of 1939. The earliest Artcraft cachets were not signed, but can be identified by their usual high quality engraving. Some early Artcraft cachets exist both unsigned and signed with the familiar Artcraft pallet with brush trademark. Most Artcraft FDC cachets since 1940 are signed.

The first Artcraft cachet is not the first cachet produced by Leo August. August started to service FDCs in the late 1920's, and he started producing cachets in the early 1930's. Washington Stamp Exchange cachets of the 1930's were designed by J.W. Clifford, John Coulthard and Ralph Dyer. Many of these cachets are signed by the cachet artist, and occasionally with "WSE."

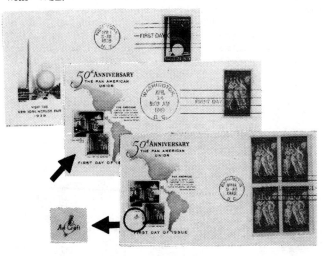

Figure ARC-1
THE FIRST ARTCRAFT CACHET was prepared for the New York World's Fair commemorative issue. This is an engraved cachet, printed in blue. Also shown are two Artcraft varieties for the 1940 Pan American Union commemorative. As with a number of early Artcraft FDCs, the cachet exists both with and without the Artcraft trademark.

Artmaster

Artmaster cachets have been created by Robert Schmidt of Louisville, Kentucky, since 1946. The firm is currently owned and operated by his nephew, Mike Zoeller. The first Artmaster cachet was prepared for the Honorable Discharge Emblem commemorative.

Artmaster cachets can be easily identified because they are high quality engravings signed "Artmaster."

Figure ARM-1
The first Artmaster cachet

W.G. Crosby

A typical Crosby cachet has a small photo pasted on the cover. Crosby thermographed the text and frames found around the photos, which resulted in an unmistakably heavy raised printing. Crosby often produced several cachets for each issue, and occasionally produced cachets without a photo. Crosby cachets without photos can be identified by a similarity in text and cachet design. Crosby cachet photos are not to be confused with Ioor's, since Crosby's are actual photos that have been pasted onto the envelopes after the cachet was printed, and Ioor's are printed on the envelopes.

A few of Crosby's covers are signed. The trick is to see his name, which he had printed in the upper right-hand corner, right where the stamp is affixed. To see his name, one must hold the cover up to a bright light.

Crosby made cachets for ship covers in the early 1930's. He died in 1947, but his wife continued to make the Crosby covers through the Annapolis Tercentenary issue of 1949.

Figure WC-1
Most Crosby covers contain a pasted-on photo, making them easy to identify.

It was not uncommon for Crosby to have more than one cachet for a stamp issue. There are some issues where he created as many as 20 different designs.

Notice that one of the cachets for this issue does not contain a photo. However, the cachet does contain the same familiar raised print.

Figure WC-2
A few Crosby cachets are signed with a fine-line Crosby advertising imprint. This imprint is found in the upper right-hand corner of the envelope or, occasionally, on the back.

House of Farnam

House of Farnam cachets have been produced for nearly every issue since the TIPEX Souvenir sheet of 1936. Many Farnam cachets are signed 'HF" or "House of Farnam." The early unsigned Farnams are usually small, simple, one-color designs found in the upper left-hand corner of the envelope. They are printed from steel-die engravings with slightly raised printing.

Figure HF-1
THE FIRST FARNAM CACHET is an unsigned design prepared for the 1936 TIPEX Souvenir sheet. Also shown is a typical unsigned early Farnam and a signed Farnam from the 1980's.

Dr. Harry Ioor (pronounced EYE-or)

Dr. Ioor's cachet career spanned the period from 1929 to 1951. His cachet designs fall into three different patterns.

Figure OR-1
Two early Ioor's, including the first Ioor cachet prepared for the George Rogers Clark commemorative of 1929. Notice that both cachets contain fine line drawings.

Early Ioor cachets (1929-1933) followed no particular pattern except that many are fine line drawings. Several are printed in black and light pink ink. In some cases the covers are addressed to Ioor, which allows for easy identification.

Figure OR-2
From 1934-1940 Ioor's covers followed a definite pattern. Almost all of them contained a printed photo as part of the cachet. These photos are printed on the envelopes and are not to be confused with Crosby's cachets, where the photos are pasted on the envelope. During this period, Ioor often produced several cachet varieties, using different black and white photos, with different colors around them.

Figure OR-3
Harry Ioor died before the completion of the Famous American series of 1940. His sister completed the series and then continued to produce cachets with a different design pattern. This particular period of Ioor is easy to identify since most of the covers are signed.

F.R. Rice

Rice cachets are undoubtedly one of the easiest cachets to identify. Most are signed and have a definite and consistent style. Rice's career spanned from 1932 to 1940.

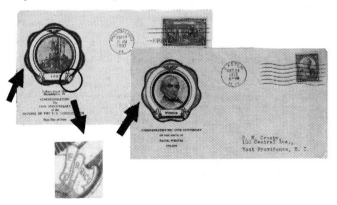

Figure RI-1
Rice used different illustrations or text inside this common border for about 75 percent of his cachets.

48A

CACHETMAKER'S DIRECTORY

CACHET CALCULATOR

As discussed in the introduction, values in this catalogue are for an average market FDC. Many FDCs, depending on the cachet, sell for many times the catalogue value, while others may sell for much less.

Below is a list of cachet makers, the dates they serviced FDCs and a multiplier. By taking the multiplier range listed below and multiplying it by the catalogue value for a cacheted FDC *single*, you will get the approximate catalogue value of the specific cacheted FDC.

First cachets of all makers are in great demand and usually sell for a substantial premium.

Cachet Maker Dates	Pricing Multiplier	Cachet Maker Dates	Pricing Multiplier
Adelphia Stamp Shop		**Andrews**	
1932-1939	2 times	1978	6 times
Aero Print		1979-1982	2 times
1931-1932	2 to 3 times	**Animated (Ellis) Covers**	
1933-1934	1 to 2 times	1968-1969	6 times
Apage Cachets		1970-date	3 to 4 times
1984-date	5 times	**Annis, D. R.**	
Albers Cache		1938-1939	2 to 4 times
1966-1974	2 times	**Ardee Covers**	
Alexander, George A.		1975-date	3 to 4 times
1981-1984	6 to 12 times	**Aristocrat**	
America		1936-1937	.4 to 4 1/2 times
1975-1980	3 times	1938-1940	1 to 2 times
1981-1988	2 to 3 times	1941-date	1/2 to 1 time
Anagram hand colored Cachets		**Artcraft**	
1987-date	6 times	1939	4 times
Anderson, C.		1940-1945	1 1/2 times
1933-1934	1 1/2 to 2 times	1946-date	1 time
1935-date	1/2 to 1 time	**Artique**	
		1974-date	3 to 4 times

Cachet Maker Dates	Pricing Multiplier	Cachet Maker Dates	Pricing Multiplier
Artmaster		**Beverly Hills**	
1946-1950	...1 to 1 1/2 times	1933-1937	.......2 to 3 times
1951-1986	...............1 time	**Bi-Color Craft**	
1989-date	..........1 1/2 times	1945-1947	.......3 to 4 times
Artopages		**Bickford, C.L.**	
1962-1969	.... 4 times	1931-1932	...............2 times
1970-date	.........2 to 3 times	**Bill Ressl Cachets**	
Aubry		1977-date	.........2 to 3 times
1936-1938	...............2 times	**Bittings**	
Ayerst Laboratories		1979-date	................2 times
(Artcraft variety)		**Black Heritage**	
1965-circa		1978-1984	...............4 times
1970's	......................5 times	**Boerger (ABC)**	
Barcus, Norman		1952-date	.........2 to 3 times
1931-1939	...............5 times	**Border Craft**	
Baxter, James H.		1966-1968	.....8 to 12 times
1929-1932	.......2 to 3 times	**Broadway Stamp Co.**	
Bazaar		(Max Sage)	
1971-1972	...............2 times	1923-1929	...............5 times
1973-date	..1 to 1 1/2 times	1930-1937	.......4 to 5 times
Beardsley, Waiten S.		**Brookhaven**	
1933-1939	.......4 to 5 times	1933-1938	.......5 to 6 times
Beazell, R.		**Buchanan, Bradie**	
1929-1934	.............15 times	1927-1939	.......1 to 2 times
1935-1937	.............25 times	**Burfeind, George H.**	
Beck Printing Co. Inc.		1928-1934	...............3 times
1930-1931	.......2 to 3 times	**Burroughs, E.L.**	
Bert, Adam		1940-1941	.......2 to 3 times
1929-1933	.1 1/2 to 2 times	**Cachet Craft**	
Bennett, Ira		Pre-1950	..........1 to 2 times
1948-1949	... 10 to 15 times	1950-1972	.......2 to 3 times
Bernet Egon & Fred		**Calhoun Collectors Soc.-Gold**	
1929-1941	.......4 to 5 times	1978	.......................3 times
Bernet-Reid W. Sheetlets		1979-1986	.......1 to 2 times
1938-1939	...............3 times	**Carrollton**	
1940-1945	...............4 times	1977-date	................2 times
Betts W.W.		**Cascade Cachet**	
1928-1931	..1 1/2 to 2 times	1958-1968	.......2 to 4 times

Cachet Maker Dates	Pricing Multiplier	Cachet Maker Dates	Pricing Multiplier
Chambers Gold Bond 1935-1953	4 times	**Cuscaden** 1978-date	2 times
Clifford, J 1936-1944	2 times	**Czubay, W.** 1936-1954	6 times
Clinton Classics 1984-date	2 to 3 times	**DRC hand painted** 1979-1984	8 to 15 times
Collins, F., hand painted 1978-date	8 to 20 times	**DYS** 1978-date	2 to 3 times
Colonial 1974	5 times	**David "C" Cachets, hand painted**	
1975-1983	1 to 2 times	1966-1980	7 to 8 times
Colorano "silks" 1971-1973	15 to 20 times	1980-date	5 times
1974-1976	4 to 5 times	**DeRosset hand painted** 1986-date	12 times
1977-date	3 to 4 times	**Doak Ernest L.** 1978-1950	5 to 8 times
Com Cut 1932-1939	1 to 2 1/2 times	**Dome** 1983-date	5 to 8 times
1940-1948	2 to 3 times	**Doris Gold Cachets** 1977-date	2 to 4 times
Combo Cover Co. 1975-date	2 times	**Double A** 1981-1987	3 to 5 times
Comic Cachets 1977-1982	2 times	**Dragon Card** 1983	2 to 3 times
Copecrest Woven Cachets 1969-1974	6 to 8 times	1984-date	3 times
Cos-Art Covers 1944-1950	1 to 2 times	**Dyer R.** 1928-1938	1 1/2 to 2 times
Coulson Cachet 1972-1977	2 times	**Dyer, R hand painted** 1950-date	80-125 times
Coulthard, John 1936-1948	2 to 3 times	**Dynamite Cover** 1994-date	4-6 times
Cover Craft 1964-1966	5 times	**Dysinger, M.** 1975-1979	2 times
1967-date	1 1/2 to 2 times	**Eagle Cover Service** 1933-1936	1 to 2 times
Covered Wagon 1931-1934	3 to 4 times	**Eastern Covers** 1983-date	2 to 5 times
Crosby, W. Pre-1939	6 times	**Edgerly, Robert K.** 1932-1948	2 to 4 times
1940-1948	6 to 10 times		

Cachet Maker Dates	Pricing Multiplier	Cachet Maker Dates	Pricing Multiplier
Edken		**Fluegel, I.**	
1989-date	3 to 6 times	1945-1959	6 to 8 times
Egolf		1960-1964	10 to 15 times
1928-1931	2 to 3 times	**Folio-Print**	3 to 4 times
Edminston, Florence, hand painted		**Fox Jack**	
1936-1939	10 to 20 times	1928-1930	2 to 4 times
Elliott		**Fulton Stamp Co.**	
1929-1931	2 to 3 times	1947-1949	1 1/2 to 2 times
Emblem Cachet		**Gamm**	
1982-date	2 to 3 times	1977	8 to 10 times
Emeigh		1978-date	4 to 6 times
1929-1930	1 to 3 times	**Geerling hand painted**	
Emerson		1984-date	20 to 30 times
1925-1932	2 to 4 times	**George, C. W.**	
Espenshade		1927-1931	3 to 4 times
1935-1942	2 times	1931-1950	2 to 3 times
Evans, C. M.		**Gilbert, John C.**	
1929-1932	2 to 3 times	1937-1939	2 to 3 times
Evans, Glen L.		**Gill John**	
1935-1942	3 to 4 times	1932-1933	2 times
Fairway		**Gill Craft**	
1931-1940	1 to 2 times	1980	10 times
Fawcett, James W.		1981-date	2 to 5 times
1934-1936	2 to 4 times	**Glen**	
Ferryman F.R.		1974	3 times
1938-1940	4 times	1975-date	1 1/2 times
Fidelity Stamp Co.		**Glory**	
1937-1950	1 to 1 1/2 times	1962-1963	3 to 4 times
First Rank First Day Covers		**Gold Bond**	
1979-date	2 to 3 times	1935-1950	3 to 5 times
Fleetwood		**Goldcraft**	
1941-1947	3 to 6 times	1959-date	1 1/2 to 2 times
1948-1960	2 to 3 times	**Gorham, A.**	
1961-date	1 to 1 1/2 times	1932-1938	2 to 3 times
Flok		**Grandy, W.**	
1954-1955	6 to 10 times	1935-date	2 to 4 times
		Griffin, H. H.	
		1926-1933	3 to 4 times

57A

Cachet Maker Dates	Pricing Multiplier	Cachet Maker Dates	Pricing Multiplier
Grimsland, H.		**Horseshoe hand painted**	
1932-1934	.1 1/2 to 2 times	1983-1987	.......3 to 6 times
1935-1952	.......1 to 2 times	**Hubbard**	
Gundel, T.		1935-1937	.......2 to 3 times
1929-1941	.......6 to 7 times	**Hunt Harris R.**	
Guy Mannino (GM)		1927-1930	.......3 to 4 times
1984-date	.....10 to 25 times	**HUX**	
HM Cachets		1928-1950	.1 1/2 to 2 times
1977-date	.......6 to 10 times	**Imperial**	
HS Color Tint		1934-1940	.......4 to 5 times
1954-circa		**Info Cachets**	
1960's	..............2 to 4 times	1992-date	.........3 to 8 times
Habbert, George Lewis		**Info Handpainted**	
1927-1929	...............5 times	1993-date	.......8 to 15 times
Hacker, E.		**Info Gold**	
1931-1938	.......4 to 5 times	1996	........................5 times
Halvorsen, Ejgil J. S.		**Intercity Stamp Co.**	
1926-1930	.......2 to 4 times	1939-1948	.......3 to 5 times
Hammond Maxi		**Ioor, H.**	
1957-1972	.......2 to 4 times	1929-1931	.......3 to 4 times
HAM hand painted Cachets		1932-1939	......1/2 to 1 time
1977-1978	.............80 times	1940 & later	....1 to 2 times
1979-date	......15 to 30 times	**Jackson, Gladys**	
Heartland FDC		1948-date	.........2 to 3 times
1984-date	................2 times	**Janis, C. W.**	
Heritage Cachets		1935-1936	.......3 to 4 times
1994 to date	.........5-8 times	**Jeweled Envelopes**	
Hist-O-Card		1935-1939	.......2 to 3 times
1952-circa		1940-1948	.......4 to 6 times
1970's	..............2 to 4 times	**Joseph, N.**	
Hobby Cover Service		1929-1933	.......4 to 6 times
1932-1933	.......2 to 3 times	**Judith Fogt hand painted**	
Hobby Life-WCO		1982- date	..............15 times
1945-1950	.......2 to 3 times	**Justice Covers**	
House of Farnam		1979-date	..........1 1/2 times
1936-1939	...............3 times	**Kapner**	
1940-1960	.1 to 1 1/2 times	1934-1937	.1 to 1 1/2 times
1960-1977	................1 time		
1978-date	................2 times		

Cachet Maker Dates	Pricing Multiplier	Cachet Maker Dates	Pricing Multiplier
Kee Ed		**Linto, Williams S.**	
1933-1935	1 to 2 times	1937-1940	8 to 10 times
Kirk Kover		1940-1959	10 to 15 times
1947-1949	4 to 7 times	**Ludwig, Oswald A.**	
Klotzbach		1937-1949	2 to 3 times
1929-1935	2 to 3 times	**Marg**	
KMC Venture		1962-1964	6 times
1978	10 times	1965-date	2 times
1979-date	2 1/2 times	**Mauck**	
Knapp, Dorothy, hand painted		1927-1930	2 to 3 times
1941-1945	300 to 400 times	**Minkus, J.**	
1945-1952	200 to 300 times	1940-date	1 time
Knoble, Dr. Ross M. hand painted		**Munprint**	
1952		1936-1941	2 to 4 times
1960's	15 to 25 times	**Nickles, C. E.**	
Kolor Kover		1925-1929	1 time
1948	10 times	**Nix**	
1949-1960	8 times	1934-1958	3 to 5 times
1960-1973	7 times	**Nu-art**	
Kraft B, hand painted		1945-1946	3 to 5 times
1982-date	4 times	**Orbit Covers**	
Kribb's HD/HP Kovers/Kards		1962-1967	3 to 10 times
1978	15 times	**Overseas Mailers**	
1979-date	5-8 times	1953-1977	6 to 10 times
Kurkjian, S.S.		**Panda Cachets**	
1927-1929	3 to 4 times	1982-date	5 to 8 times
LEB Cachets		**Parsons, Albert B.**	
1981-date	3 to 6 times	1933-1936	2 to 4 times
LRC Cachets		**Paslay Classic hand painted**	
1975-date	3 to 6 times	1982-date	10 to 20 times
Laird		**Pavois**	
1935-1937	1 to 2 times	1937-1940	1 time
Linprint		**Pent Arts**	
1932-1941	1 time	1943-1958	1 to 11/2 times
		Phoenix Insurance Overprint	
		1937-1956	2 to 5 times

Cachet Maker Dates	Pricing Multiplier	Cachet Maker Dates	Pricing Multiplier
Pilgrim		**Rothblum**	
1937-1941	6 to 10 times	1929-1934	2 to 3 times
Plimpton		**Roy J.A.**	
1936-1939	1 time	1934-1937	2 to 3 times
Plotz David O.		**S & T (black & white)**	
1926-1927	2 to 3 times	1990-date	2 to 4 times
Pontiac Press		**S & T (color)**	
1944		1991-date	4 to 8 times
1960's	3 to 10 times	**Sadworth G.V.**	
Post/Art Engraved		1940-1952	2 to 8 times
1980-1981	5 times	**Sanders, Michael**	
1982-1986	3 times	1933-1939	2 to 3 times
Post/Art hand painted		1940-1952	2 to 5 times
1983-1985	10 to 20 times	**Sarzin Metallic**	
Postmasters of America		1964-1970	5 to 8 times
1976	3 times	1970-1977	4 to 6 times
1977-date	1 time	**Scatchard, Norwood B.**	
Pugh hand painted Cachets		1935-1938	3 to 6 times
1979-date	15 to 25 times	**Scenic Craft**	
Quadracolorplus		1940-1948	3 to 6 times
1977-1987	3 to 5 times	**Serug Cachet**	
Raley		1944	2 to 3 times
1932-1938	2 to 3 times	**Shockley**	
Rank II (flocked)		1929-1930	1 time
1955-1959	5 to 10 times	**Sidenius**	
Riemann		1932-1939	2 to 3 times
1947-1986	10 to 15 times	**Smartcraft**	
Rice, F. R.		1942-1952	.1 to 1 1/2 times
1932-1941	1 to 3 times	**Softones**	
Risko Art		1978-1980	2 to 3 times
1935-1938	10 to 15 times	**Spartan**	
Roessler, A. C.		1948-1950	3 to 4 times
1925-1931	2 times	**Spectrum**	
1932-1938	2 to 3 times	1977	6 times
Ross Foil		1978-1983	2 to 3 times
1971-date	2 to 3 times	**Steelcraft**	
		1952-1953	2 times

cover sleeves

Protect your covers with 2 mil crystal clear
polyethylene sleeves. (Sold in packages of 100.)

U.S. Postal Cards

Item		Retail
CV005	5 7/8" x 3 3/4"	$3.95

U.S. First Day Cover #6

Item		Retail
CV006	6 3/4" x 3 3/4"	$3.95

Continental Postcard

Item		Retail
CV007	6 1/4" x 4 1/4"	$4.95

European Standard Envelope

Item		Retail
CV008	7 1/4" x 4 5/8"	$4.95

European FDC

Item		Retail
CV009	7 " x 5 3/8"	$4.95

#10 Business Envelope

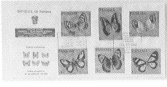

Item		Retail
CV010	10 1/8" x 4 1/2"	$5.95

SCOTT

P.O. Box 828 Sidney OH 45365-0828

to order call 1-800-572-6885

Cachet Maker Dates	Pricing Multiplier	Cachet Maker Dates	Pricing Multiplier
Sudduth 1936-1937	.1 to 1 1/2 times	**Velvatone** 1951-1970	.....5 to 10 times
Sun Craft 1947-1948	..2 times	**Von Ohlen, William J.** 1937-1945	................3 times
Texture Craft 1955-1957	.......4 to 6 times	1945-1969	................5 times
TM Historical Covers (black &white) 1977-1983	..............10 times	**WCO** 1946-1949	.......3 to 7 times
TM Historical Covers (color) 1977-1983	.......15-20 times	**Wanstead & Co.** 1935-1937	.......2 to 4 times
Top Notch 1934-1937	.1 1/2 to 2 times	**Warneford** 1937-1940	.......2 to 3 times
Tri-Color 1958-1960	.......2 to 4 times	**Washington Stamp Exchange** 1931-1939	.......3 to 6 times
Truby 1931-1934	.......5 to 6 times	**Weaver, Howard M.** 1928-1934	.......2 to 3 times
Tudor House 1977	......................3 times	**Weddle, T. M.** 1977-1981	...15 to 25 times
1978-date	............11/2 times	1981-date	..............10 times
Uladh Covers 1977-date	.........2 to 3 times	**Western Silk Cachets** 1978	......................4 times
Ulrich Frank J., hand painted 1960-1968	...15 to 50 times	1979-1983	.......2 to 3 times
Urie, C. W. 1926-1929	.......2 to 3 times	**Wright, William N. hand painted** 1945-1950	...40 to 75 times
Vaughn Hord hand painted Cachets 1983-date	......20 to 30 times	1951-1959	.............40 times
		Zaso 1977	......................6 times
		1978-1983	.1 1/2 to 2 times

Cachetmakers

Editors Note:
Cachetmakers wishing to be listed in the cachet calculator should send three samples of their work along
with current price list/auction showing the value of
their work on the secondary market. Send information to the editor at Box 206, Stewartsville, NJ 08886.

COMMEMORATIVES AND REGULAR ISSUES

Editor's Note:

All listings prior to Scott 551 are considered 'Earliest Known Uses' (EKUs), unless otherwise specified as a 'First Day Cover'. An EKU is defined as a cover that has either received a valid certificate of authenticity from a recognized expertizing service, or has been examined by acknowledged experts in the field.

The editor wishes to thank Edward J. Siskin for his help in compiling the earliest-known use (EKU) dates.

Since EKUs can change as new discoveries are made, with a few exceptions, no prices are given for these covers. As a general rule, an EKU is worth a premium over the 'on cover' price found in the 'Scott Specialized Catalogue of United States Stamps', published by Scott Publishing Company. Collectors are urged to document covers with earlier dates than those listed here, and share their discoveries with the editors, so that we may update future listings.

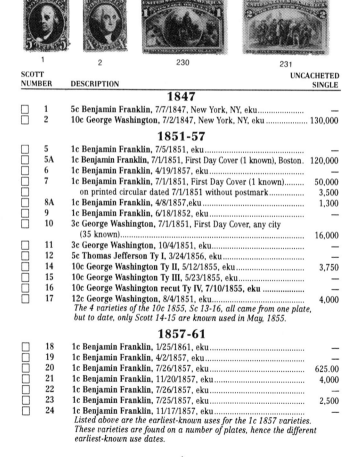

SCOTT NUMBER	DESCRIPTION	UNCACHETED SINGLE
	1847	
☐ 1	5c Benjamin Franklin, 7/7/1847, New York, NY, eku.....................	—
☐ 2	10c George Washington, 7/2/1847, New York, NY, eku	130,000
	1851-57	
☐ 5	1c Benjamin Franklin, 7/5/1851, eku..	—
☐ 5A	1c Benjamin Franklin, 7/1/1851, First Day Cover (1 known), Boston.	120,000
☐ 6	1c Benjamin Franklin, 4/19/1871, eku..	—
☐ 7	1c Benjamin Franklin, 7/1/1851, First Day Cover (1 known)........	50,000
	on printed circular dated 7/1/1851 without postmark...............	3,500
☐ 8A	1c Benjamin Franklin, 4/8/1857,eku..	1,300
☐ 9	1c Benjamin Franklin, 6/18/1852, eku..	—
☐ 10	3c George Washington, 7/1/1851, First Day Cover, any city	
	(35 known)..	16,000
☐ 11	3c George Washington, 10/4/1851, eku...	—
☐ 12	5c Thomas Jefferson Ty I, 3/24/1856, eku....................................	—
☐ 14	10c George Washington Ty II, 5/12/1855, eku..............................	3,750
☐ 15	10c George Washington Ty III, 5/23/1855, eku.............................	—
☐ 16	10c George Washington recut Ty IV, 7/10/1855, eku	—
☐ 17	12c George Washington, 8/4/1851, eku...	4,000
	The 4 varieties of the 10c 1855, Sc 13-16, all came from one plate, but to date, only Scott 14-15 are known used in May, 1855.	
	1857-61	
☐ 18	1c Benjamin Franklin, 1/25/1861, eku..	—
☐ 19	1c Benjamin Franklin, 4/2/1857, eku..	—
☐ 20	1c Benjamin Franklin, 7/26/1857, eku..	625.00
☐ 21	1c Benjamin Franklin, 11/20/1857, eku..	4,000
☐ 22	1c Benjamin Franklin, 7/26/1857, eku..	—
☐ 23	1c Benjamin Franklin, 7/25/1857, eku..	2,500
☐ 24	1c Benjamin Franklin, 11/17/1857, eku..	—
	Listed above are the earliest-known uses for the 1c 1857 varieties. These varieties are found on a number of plates, hence the different earliest-known use dates.	

1

☐ 25	3c George Washington, 2/28/1857, eku..	—
☐ 26	3c George Washington, 9/15/1857, eku..	—
☐ 26a	3c George Washington, 7/11/1857, eku..	6,500
☐ 27	5c Thomas Jefferson Ty I, 10/6/1858, eku......................................	—
☐ 28	5c Thomas Jefferson Ty I, 8/23/1857, eku......................................	2,300
☐ 28A	5c Thomas Jefferson Ty I, 3/31/1858, eku......................................	—
☐ 29	5c Thomas Jefferson Ty I, 4/4/1859, eku..	—
☐ 30	5c Thomas Jefferson Ty II,5/8/1861, eku..	—
☐ 30A	5c Thomas Jefferson Ty II, 5/14/1860, eku.....................................	—
☐ 31	10c George Washington, 9/21/1857, eku..	6,500
☐ 32	10c George Washington, 7/27/1857, eku..	—
	The four varieties of the 10c 1857, Scott 31-34, all come from one plate, but to date, only Scott 32 is known postmarked July 27, 1857.	
☐ 35	10c George Washington, 4/29/1859, eku..	—
☐ 36	12c George Washington, 7/30/1857, eku..	—
☐ 36b	12c George Washington, 12/3/1859, eku..	—
☐ 37	24c Benjamin Franklin, 7/7/1860, eku..	—
☐ 38	30c Benjamin Franklin, 8/8/1860, eku..	—
☐ 39	90c Benjamin Franklin, 9/11/1860, eku..	—

1861-66

☐ 62B	10c George Washington, 9/17/1861, New York, NY, eku	—
☐ 64b	3c George Washington, 8/17/1861, First Day Cover 1 known........	21,000
☐ 65	3c George Washington, 8/19/1861, eku..	1,100
☐ 67	5c Thomas Jefferson, buff, 8/19/1861, eku	—
☐ 67a	5c Thomas Jefferson, (brown-yellow), 8/21/1861,eku	1,300
☐ 68	10c George Washington, 8/20/1861, eku..	—
☐ 69	12c George Washington, 8/20/1861, eku..	475.00
☐ 70	24c George Washington, 1/7/1862, eku..	3,750
☐ 70c	24c George Washington, 8/20/1861, eku..	13,000
☐ 71	30c Benjamin Franklin, 8/20/1861, eku..	1,000
☐ 72	90c George Washington, 11/27/1861, eku..	—
☐ 73	2c Andrew Jackson, 7/6/1863, eku..	—
☐ 75	5c Thomas Jefferson, 1/2/1862, eku	—
☐ 76	5c Thomas Jefferson, 2/3/1863, eku	—
☐ 77	15c Abraham Lincoln, 4/14/1866, eku..	5,000
☐ 78	24c George Washington, 2/20/1863, eku..	—
☐ 78b	24c George Washington, 10/20/1862, eku..	2,600

1867 Grilled Issue

☐ 79	3c George Washington, A Grill, 8/13/1867, eku............................	2,000
☐ 83	3c George Washington, (grill), 11/19/1867, eku	1,000

1869

☐ 112	1c Benjamin Franklin, 3/27/1869, eku..	10,000
☐ 113	2c Post Horse & Rider, 3/20/1869, eku..	—
☐ 114	3c Locomotive, 3/27/1869, eku	—
☐ 115	6c Washington, 4/26/1869, eku	1,450
☐ 116	10c Shield & Eagle, 4/1/1869, eku	—
☐ 117	12c S.S. Adriatic, 4/1/1869, eku	—
☐ 118	15c Landing of Columbus Ty I, 4/2/1869, eku	1,700
☐ 119	15c Landing of Columbus Ty II, 4/26/1869, eku	—
☐ 120	24c Declaration of Independence, 4/7/1869, eku	—
☐ 121	30c Shield, Eagle & Flags, 5/22/1869, eku....................................	—

1870-71

☐	133	1c Buff Re-issue, 11/28/1880, eku	3,500
☐	134	1c Franklin, 4/9/1870, eku	—
☐	135	2c Jackson, 9/1/1870, eku	—
☐	136	3c Washington, 3/25/1870, eku	—
☐	137	6c Lincoln, 7/31/1870, eku	—
☐	138	7c Stanton, 2/12/1871, eku	—
☐	139	10c Jefferson, 6/11/1870, eku	—
☐	140	12c Clay, 2/9/1872, eku	—
☐	141	15c Webster, 6/2/1870, eku	5,000
☐	143	30c Hamilton, 8/?/70, eku	—
☐	145	1c Franklin, 7/18/1870, eku	—
☐	146	2c Jackson, 6/11/1870, eku	—
☐	147	3c Washington, 3/13/1870, eku	—
☐	148	6c Lincoln, 3/28/1870, eku	—
☐	149	7c Stanton, 5/11/1871, eku	—
☐	150	10c Jefferson, 5/29/1870, eku	—
☐	151	12c Clay, 7/9/1870, eku	—
☐	152	15c Webster, 9/24/1870, eku	—
☐	153	24c Scott, 11/18/1870, eku	—
☐	154	30c Hamilton, 1/31/1871, eku	—
☐	155	90c Perry, 9/1/1872, eku	—

1873

☐	156	1c Franklin, 8/22/1873, eku	—
☐	157	2c Jackson, 7/12/1873, eku	—
☐	158	3c Washington, 7/17/1873, eku	—
☐	159	6c Lincoln, 7/24/1873, eku	—
☐	160	7c Stanton, 10/5/1873, eku	—
☐	161	10c Jefferson, 8/2/1873, eku	—
☐	162	12c Clay, 1/3/1874, eku	—
☐	163	15c Webster, 7/22/1873, eku	—
☐	165	30c Hamilton, 10/30/1874, eku	—
☐	166	90c Perry, ?/?/1875, eku	—

1875

☐	178	2c Jackson, 7/17/1875, eku	—
☐	179	5c Taylor, 7/12/1875, eku	—

1879

☐	182	1c Franklin, 4/25/1879, eku	—
☐	183	2c Jackson, 2/4/1879, eku	325.00
☐	184	3c Washington, 2/7/1879, eku	—
☐	185	5c Taylor, 5/12/1879, eku	—
☐	186	6c Lincoln, 7/1/1879, eku	—
☐	187	10c Jefferson, 9/5/1879, eku	—
☐	188	10c Jefferson (w/secret mark), 2/21/1879, eku	—
☐	189	15c Webster, 1/20/1879, eku	—
☐	190	30c Hamilton, 8/8/1882, eku	—
☐	191	90c Perry, 6/17/1880, eku	—

1881-88

☐	205	5c Garfield, 2/18/82, eku..	—
		The designated first day for Scott 205 was 4/10/1882, but stamps were legitimately sold as early as 2/18. Curiously, no 4/10 covers are currently known.☐	
☐	206	1c Franklin, 12/5/1881, eku..	500
☐	207	3c Washington, 7/16/1881, eku	—
☐	208	6c Lincoln, 9/27/1882, eku...	—
☐	209	10c Thomas Jefferson, 5/11/1882, eku.............................	—
☐	210	2c Washington, 10/1/1883, any city, First Day Cover (60-80 known)	2,000
☐	211	4c Andrew Jackson, 10/1/1883, First Day Cover, no solo usage known	—
☐		Scott 210 & 211 on one cover (1 known)	32,500
☐	212	1c Franklin, 7/28/1887, eku..	—
☐	213	3c Washington, 9/21/1887, eku	—
☐	214	3c Washington, 10/3/1887, eku	—
☐	215	4c Jackson, 7/11/1889, eku...	—
☐	216	5c Garfield, 4/7/1888, eku..	—
☐	217	30c Andrew Jackson, 9/22/1888, eku................................	8,000

1890

☐	219	1c Franklin, 4/19/1890, eku..	—
☐	219D	2c Washington, 2/22/1890, First Day Cover (1 known)	14,500
☐	220	2c Washington, 5/31/1890, eku	—
☐	221	3c Jackson, 7/1/1890, eku...	—
☐	222	4c Lincoln, 10/22/1890, eku...	—
☐	223	5c Grant, 6/14/1890, Haddonfield NJ, eku........................	—
☐	224	6c Garfield, 5/30/1890, eku..	—
☐	225	8c Sherman, 5/21/1893, eku	—
☐	226	10c Webster, 4/30/1890, eku..	—
☐	227	15c Clay, 7/21/1891, eku..	—
☐	228	30c Jefferson, 7/30/1892, eku..	—
☐	229	90c Perry, 6/10/1892, eku..	—

1893

☐	230	1c Columbian, 1/1/1893, First Day Cover	4,000
☐	231	2c Columbian, 1/1/1893, First Day Cover	4,000
☐	232	3c Columbian, 1/1/1893, First Day Cover	6,000
☐	233	4c Columbian, 1/1/1893, First Day Cover	9,000
☐	234	5c Columbian, 1/1/1893, First Day Cover	14,500
☐	235	6c Columbian, 1/2/1893, First Day Cover	18,000
☐	236	8c Columbian, 3/3/1893, eku	18,000
☐	237	10c Columbian, 1/1/1893, First Day Cover	7,500
☐	238	15c Columbian, 1/26/1893, eku..	—
☐	239	30c Columbian, 2/8/1893, eku..	—
☐	240	50c Columbian, 2/8/1893, eku..	—
☐	241	$1 Columbian, 1/21/1893, eku..	—
☐	242	$2 Columbian, 1/2/1893, First Day Cover	52,500
☐	243	$3 Columbian, 4/4/1893, eku..	—
☐	244	$4 Columbian, 7/14/1893, eku..	—
☐	245	$5 Columbian, 1/6/1893, eku..	—

Since Jan. 1, 1893 was a Sunday, few post offices were open. January 1st and January 2nd are both collected as First Day Covers. Several values are known with Dec. 30 or Dec. 31, 1892 pre-dates.

1894-95

☐	246	1c Franklin (ultramarine), 10/24/1894, eku	—
☐	247	1c Franklin (blue), 11/11/1894, eku	—
☐	248	2c Washington, 10/20/1894, eku	—
☐	249	2c Washington, 10/11/1894, eku	—
☐	250	2c Washington, 10/17/1894, eku	600.00
☐	251	2c Washington, 2/18/1895, eku	—
☐	252	2c Washington, 10/11/1894, eku	—
☐	253	3c Jackson, 1/5/1895, eku	—
☐	254	4c Lincoln, 1/5/1895, eku	—
☐	255	5c Grant, 11/22/1894, eku	—
☐	256	6c Garfield, 8/11/1894, eku	—
☐	257	8c Sherman, 9/15/1895, eku	—
☐	258	10c Webster, 11/19/1894, eku	—
☐	259	15c Clay, 2/20/1895, eku	—
☐	260	50c Jefferson, 1/15/1895, eku	—
☐	261A	$1 Perry (Ty II), 3/22/1895, eku	—
☐	262	$2 Madison, 7/6/1896, eku	—
☐	263	$5 John Marshall unwatermarked dark green, 7/16/1896, (not known on cover) eku	—
☐	264	1c Franklin watermarked blue, 5/16/1895, eku	—
☐	265	2c Washington watermarked carmine Type I, 5/2/1895, First Day Cover	9,500
☐	266	2c Washington watermarked carmine Type II, 7/13/1895, eku	—
☐	267	2c Washington watermarked carmine Type III,6/1/1895, eku on cover	—
☐	268	3c Andrew Jackson watermarked purple, 2/18/1896, eku	—
☐	269	4c Lincoln watermarked dark brown, 9/25/1895, eku	—
☐	270	5c Grant watermarked chocolate, 9/14/1895, eku	—
☐	271	6c Garfield watermarked dull brown, 9/14/1895, eku	—
☐	272	8c Sherman watermarked violet brown, 12/24/1895, eku	—
☐	273	10c Daniel Webster watermarked dark green, 9/23/1895 eku	—
☐	274	15c Henry Clay watermarked dark blue, 2/27/1897, eku	—
☐	275	50c Jefferson watermarked orange, 2/27/1897, eku	—
☐	276	$1 Commodore Perry unwatermarked black Type I, 9/15/1898, eku	—
☐	276A	$1 Commodore Perry watermarked black Type II, 5/6/1896, eku	—

1897-98

☐	279	1c Franklin, 2/2/1898, eku	—
☐	279B	2c Washington (Ty IV), 1/16/1898, eku	—
☐	280	4c Lincoln, 12/12/1898, eku	—
☐	281	5c Grant, 3/19/1898, eku	—
☐	282	6c Garfield, 5/30/1899, eku	—
☐	282C	10c Webster (Ty I), 3/24/1899, eku	—
☐	283	10c Webster (Ty II), 3/13/1899, eku	—
☐	284	15c Clay, 5/1/1899, eku	—
☐	285	1c Marquette on the Mississippi, 6/17/1898, First Day Cover, DC, NY	10,000
☐	286	2c Farming in the West, 6/17/1898, First Day Cover, DC, & NY, Baltimore, Omaha, NB	12,000
		Pittsburgh, PA	7,000
☐	286	6/16/1898, eku, Harrisburg, PA or Camden, NJ	13,000
☐	287	4c Indian Hunting Buffalo, 6/17/1898, First Day Cover, DC	25,000
☐	288	5c Fremont on the Rocky Mountains, 6/17/1898, First Day Cover, DC	25,000

☐	289	8c Troops Guarding Trains, 6/17/1898, First Day Cover, DC, NY ..	25,000
☐	290	10c Hardships of Emigration, 6/17/1898, First Day Cover	25,000
☐		Scott 285-290 on one cover , 6/17/1898 one known..................	50,000
☐	291	50c Western Mining Prospector, 6/17/1898, First Day Cover,	
		1 known	30,000
☐	292	$1 Western Cattle in a Storm, 6/17/1898, First Day Cover,	
		1 known	35,000
☐	293	$2 Mississippi River Bridge, 6/24/1898, eku.............................	—
☐		Scott 285, 287-288 on 1 cover, 6/17/1898, First Day Cover, DC	15,000

1901

☐	294	1c Fast Lake Navigation, 5/1/1901, First Day Cover (10 known)...	4,800
☐	295	2c "Empire State Express", 5/1/1901, First Day Cover	
		(50-60 known)	2,500
☐	296	4c Electric Automobile, 5/1/1901, First Day Cover	7,500
☐		Scott 296, 298 on one cover, 5/1/1901, First Day Cover............	11,000
☐	297	5c Bridge at Niagara Falls, 5/1/1901, First Day Cover	9,000
☐		Scott 294, 295, 297 on one cover, 5/1/1901, First Day Cover........	8,500
☐		294, 296, 297 on one cover, 5/1/1901	22,500
☐	298	8c Soo Locks, 5/1/1901, First Day Cover	10,000
☐	299	10c Fast Ocean Navigation, 5/1/1901, First Day Cover.................	10,000
☐		Scott 294-299, complete set of 6 on one cover, 5/1/01 (9 known)..	30,000

1902-08 (Regular Issue)

☐	300	1c Franklin, 2/8/03, eku	—
☐	301	2c Washington, 1/17/03, eku	—
☐	302	3c Jackson, 3/21/03, eku..	—
☐	303	4c Grant, 4/13/03, eku	—
☐	304	5c Lincoln, 1/28/03, eku	—
☐	305	6c Garfield, 5/8/03, eku	—
☐	306	8c Martha Washington, 12/27/02, eku	—
☐	307	10c Webster, 3/12/03, eku...	—
☐	308	13c Harrison, 11/22/02, eku	—
☐	309	15c Clay, 9/24/03, eku	—
☐	310	50c Jefferson, 02/17/04, eku..	—
☐	311	$1 Farragut, 1/23/03, eku	—
☐	312	$2 Madison, 2/17/04, eku	—
☐	313	$5 Marshall, 2/17/04, eku	—
☐	314	1c Franklin (imperf), 2/12/07, eku	—
☐	315	5c Lincoln (imperf pair), 9/15/08, eku	—
☐	319	2c Washington, 11/19/03, eku	—
☐	320	2c Washington (imperf), 11/6/06, eku..	—

1904

☐	323	1c Livingston, 4/30/04, First Day Cover (6 known)	5,000
☐	324	2c Jefferson, 4/30/04, First Day Cover (10-15 known)...................	6,000
		pre-dates exist as early as 4/20/04	
☐	325	3c Monroe, 4/30/04, First Day Cover (5 known)	6,000
☐		323, 324, 325 pre-dates on one cover..	15,000
☐	326	5c McKinley, 4/30/04, First Day Cover (approx. 5 known)	21,000
☐	327	10c Map of Louisiana Purchase, 4/30/04, First Day Cover	
		(2 known)...	22,000
		Scott 323-327 on one cover, 4/30/04 (1 known)	90,000

Notice was sent to postmasters that this set was being shipped from Washington on Apr. 21, but could not be sold to the public before Apr. 30, 1904. Because of these instructions, any cover dated before Apr. 30, 1904, is considered a pre-dated cover.

1907

☐	328	1c Capt. John Smith, 4/26/07, First Day Cover (6 known)	6,000
☐	329	2c Founding of Jamestown, 4/26/07, First Day Cover (2 known) ..	9,000
☐	330	5c Pocahontas, 5/10/07, Norfolk VA, eku (3 known)	10,000

1908-09 (Regular Issue)

☐	331	1c Franklin, 12/1/08, eku	—
☐	331a	1c Franklin (booklet single), 12/2/08, First Day Cover (1 known).	18,000
☐	332	2c Washington, 12/4/08, eku	—
☐	332a	2c Washington (booklet single), 11/16/08, First Day Cover	
		(1 known)...	35,000
☐	333	3c Washington (Ty I), 1/12/09, eku..	—
☐	334	4c Washington, 1/12/09, eku...	—
☐	335	5c Washington, 1/12/09, eku...	—
☐	336	6c Washington, 1/6/09, eku...	—
☐	337	8c Washington, 1/9/09, eku...	—
☐	338	10c Washington, 2/1/09, eku (2 known)	1,000
☐	339	13c Washington, 3/5/09, eku...	—
☐	340	15c Washington, 3/12/09, eku...	—
☐	341	50c Washington, 10/23/09, eku...	—
☐	343	1c Franklin (imperf), 2/11/09, eku...	—
☐	344	2c Washington (imperf), 2/1/09, eku..	—
☐	345	3c Washington (Ty I, imperf), 2/13/09, eku	—
☐	346	4c Washington (imperf), 3/13/09, eku..	—
☐	347	5c Washington (imperf), 3/4/09, eku..	—
☐	348	1c Franklin (coil), 1/25/09, eku	—
☐	349	2c Washington (coil), 5/16/09, eku	—
☐	351	5c Washington (coil), 9/21/09, eku	1,050
☐	352	1c Franklin (coil), 3/30/09, eku	1,050
☐	353	2c Washington (coil), 10/6/09, eku	—
☐	354	4c Washington (coil), 6/9/09, eku	1,650
☐	355	5c Washington (coil), 10/25/09, eku	1,650
☐	356	10c Washington (coil), 3/9/09, eku	1,650
☐	357	1c Franklin (blue paper), 2/22/09, eku	—
☐	358	2c Washington (blue paper), 3/25/09, eku....................................	—
☐	364	10c Washington (blue paper), 2/3/10,eku	15,000

1909

☐	367	2c Lincoln, 2/12/09, any city, First Day Cover (503 known)	500.00
☐		on Lincoln-related post-card..	600.00
☐		pre-dated covers exist as early as 2/8/09 (20 known)	700.00
☐	368	2c Lincoln (imperf), 2/12/09, First Day Cover (6 known)..............	13,000
☐	369	2c Lincoln (blue paper), 2/27/09, eku	
		Feb. 12, 1909 was designated as the official First Day of the Lincoln stamp.	
		A total of 277 different cities from 42 states and Puerto Rico are known on	
		Scott 367's FDCs, with Boston, MA and Canton, OH being the most common.	
☐	370	2c Alaska-Yukon, 5/29/09, First Day Cover (57 known)................	5,000
☐		on expo-related post-card (approx. 15 known).............................	7,500
☐		covers dated 6/1/09, ...	2,000
☐	371	2c Alaska-Yukon (imperf), 6/7/09, Richmond, VA, (4 known), eku.	—
☐	372	2c Hudson-Fulton, 9/25/09, and city, First Day Cover	
		(152 known)..	1,000
☐		9/25/09, Lancaster PA, on 2-part Hudson-Fulton post-card..........	1,500
		Pre-dates exist as early as 9/23/09 (2 known) and 9/24/09 (33 known).	
		A total of 29 different cities in 10 states are known for this issue.	

☐	373	2c Hudson-Fulton (imperf), 9/25/09, First Day Cover, Poughkeepsie, NY (1 known)	7,500
☐	374a	1c Franklin Booklet pane stamp, 7/1/1911, eku	700.00

1911-13

☐	390	1c Franklin (endwise coil), 10/22/11, eku	—
☐	391	2c Washington (endwise coil), 5/3/11, eku	—
☐	392	1c Franklin (sidewise coil), 3/24/11, eku	1,650
☐	393	2c Washington (sidewise coil), 12/27/10, eku	550.00
☐	394	3c Washington (sidewise coil), 9/18/11, Orangeburg, NY, eku	550.00
☐	395	4c Washington (sidewise coil), 6/21/12, eku	1,650
☐	396	5c Washington (sidewise coil), 5/20/13, eku	950.00

1913-15

☐	397	1c Balboa (perf 12), 1/1/13, First Day Cover .... (10-15 known)	5,000
☐	398	2c Pedro Miguel Locks (perf 12), 1/17/13, eku	425.00
☐	399	5c Golden Gate (perf 12), 1/1/13, First Day Cover (1 known)........	19,000
☐	400	10c San Francisco Bay (perf 12, orange-yellow), 1/1/13, First Day Cover, (2 known)	10,000
☐		Scott 397, 399 & 400 on one cover, 1/1/13, San Francisco CA	9,000
☐	400A	10c San Francisco Bay (perf 12, orange), 12/18/13, eku.............	—
☐	401	1c Balboa (perf 10), 12/21/14, eku.......................................	—
☐	402	2c Pedro Miguel Locks (perf 10), 1/13/15, eku........................	880.00
☐	403	5c Golden Gate (perf 10), 2/6/15, eku...................................	6,250
☐	404	10c San Francisco Bay (perf 10), 8/27/15, eku	—

1912-15 (Regular Issue)

☐	405	1c Washington, 2/23/12, eku	950.00
☐	405b	1c Washington (booklet), 4/1/12, eku.....................................	—
☐	406	2c Washington, 2/23/12, eku	—
☐	406a	2c Washington (booklet), 6/6/12, eku.....................................	—
☐	407	7c Washington, 5/1/14, eku (probably a first day cover)...............	—
☐		Scott 407, 415, 419, 420 & 421 on one cover, 5/1/14	15,000
☐	408	1c Washington (imperf), 3/27/12, eku.....................................	—
☐	408	1c Washington (Kansas City Roulette perfs), 11/25/14, eku.........	—
☐	409	2c Washington (imperf), 4/15/12, eku.....................................	—
☐	409	2c Washington (w/Schermack III perfs), 5/14/12, eku.................	—
☐	409	2c Washington (Kansas City Roulette perfs), 12/10/14, eku.........	—
☐	410	1c Washington (endwise coil), 7/5/12, eku	—
☐	411	2c Washington (endwise coil), 5/31/12, eku	—
☐	412	1c Washington (sidewise coil), 5/31/12, eku	—
☐	413	2c Washington (sidewise coil), 5/13/12, eku	—
☐	414	8c Franklin, 4/20/12, eku...	—
☐	415	9c Franklin, 5/1/14, eku (probably a first day cover)	—
☐	416	10c Franklin, 5/11/12, eku	—
☐	417	12c Franklin, 6/2/14, eku	—
☐	418	15c Franklin, 5/17/13, eku	—
☐	419	20c Franklin, 5/1/14, eku (probably a first day cover)	—
☐	420	30c Franklin, 5/1/14, eku (probably a first day cover)	—
☐	421	50c Franklin (sng line wmrk), 5/1/14, eku (probably a first day cover)	—
☐	422	50c Franklin (dbl line wmrk), 7/15/15, eku	—
☐	423	$1 Franklin (dbl line wmrk), 7/15/15, eku...............................	—
☐	424	1c Washington, 11/30/14, eku	—
☐	424a	1c Washington (perf 12x10), 1/8/14, eku................................	—
☐	424	1c Washington (coil waste), 8/2/15, First Day Cover	5,000

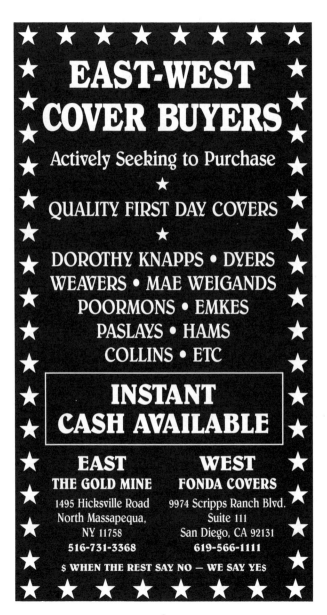

		UNCACHETED SINGLE
☐ 424d	1c Washington (booklet single), 12/20/13, eku	—
☐ 425	2c Washington, 12/2/14, eku	—
☐ 425e	2c Washington (booklet single), 1/6/14, eku	450.00
☐ 426	3c Washington, 11/26/14, eku	—
☐ 427	4c Washington, 1/19/15, eku	—
☐ 428	5c Washington, 1/29/15, eku	—
☐ 428a	5c Washington (perf 12x10), 4/14/15, eku	—
☐ 429	6c Washington, 2/6/15, eku	—
☐ 431	8c Franklin, 7/15/15, eku	—
☐ 433	10c Franklin, 11/13/14, eku	—
☐ 434	11c Franklin, 10/8/15, eku	—
☐ 435	12c Franklin, 4/24/15, eku	—
☐ 438	20c Franklin, 11/28/14, eku	—
☐ 439	30c Franklin, 2/13/15, eku	—
☐ 441	1c Washington (endwise coil), 2/16/15, eku	—
☐ 442	2c Washington (endwise coil), 7/22/14, eku	475.00
☐ 443	1c Washington (sidewise coil), 6/24/14, eku	1,650
☐ 444	2c Washington (sidewise coil), 5/28/14, eku	1,650
☐ 445	3c Washington (sidewise coil), 7/1/16, eku	—
☐ 446	4c Washington (sidewise coil), 8/4/15, eku	—
☐ 448	1c Washington (endwise coil), 4/30/16, eku	—
☐ 449	2c Washington Ty I (endwise coil), 10/29/15, eku	—
☐ 450	2c Washington Ty III (endwise coil), 12/21/15, eku	1,650
☐ 452	1c Washington (sidewise coil), 3/22/15, eku	—
☐ 453	2c Washington Ty I (sidewise coil), 11/14/14, eku	—
☐ 454	2c Washington Ty II (sidewise coil), 7/7/15, eku	—
☐ 455	2c Washington Ty III (sidewise coil), 2/4/16, eku	—
☐ 456	3c Washington (sidewise coil), 4/13/16, eku	—
☐ 457	4c Washington (sidewise coil), 11/5/15, eku	770.00
☐ 458	5c Washington (sidewise coil), 5/15/17, eku	1,650
☐ 460	$1 Franklin, 5/25/16, eku	—
☐ 461	2c Washington (perf 11), 7/19/15, eku	—

1916-17

☐ 462	1c Washington, 10/25/16, eku	—
☐ 463	2c Washington, 11/1/16, eku	—
☐ 464	3c Washington, 6/6/17, eku	—
☐ 465	4c Washington, 2/18/17, eku	—
☐ 466	5c Washington, 12/18/16, eku	—
☐ 467	5c Washington carmine (color error), 5/25/17, eku	—
☐ 470	8c Franklin, 10/17/17, eku	—
☐ 472	10c Franklin, 12/29/16, eku	—
☐ 473	11c Franklin, 4/13/17, eku	—
☐ 474	12c Franklin, 10/13/16, eku	—
☐ 475	15c Franklin, 3/2/17, eku	—
☐ 477	50c Franklin, 8/31/17, eku	—
☐ 478	$1 Franklin, 11/9/17, eku	—
☐ 479	$2 Madison, 8/31/17, eku	—
☐ 480	$5 Marshall, 8/31/17, eku	—
☐ 481	1c Washington (imperf), 11/17/16, eku	800.00
☐ 482	2c Washington (imperf), 1/9/17, eku	—
☐ 482A	2c Washington (Ty Ia, imperf w/Schermack III perfs), 2/17/20, eku	20,000
☐ 483	3c Washington (Ty I, imperf), 11/8/17, eku	—
☐ 484	3c Washington (Ty II, imperf), 4/30/18, eku	—

STAMP COLLECTORS

1916-22

☐	486	1c Washington (endwise coil), 6/30/18, eku	—
☐	489	3c Washington Ty I (endwise coil), 2/16/17, eku	—
☐	490	1c Washington (sidewise coil), 3/30/17, eku	—
☐	491	2c Washington Ty II (sidewise coil), 2/2/17, eku	1,650
☐	492	2c Washington Ty III (sidewise coil), 2/17/17, eku	—
☐	493	3c Washington Ty I (sidewise coil), 11/2/17, eku	1,650
☐	494	3c Washington Ty II (sidewise coil), 5/29/18, eku	—
☐	497	10c Washington (sidewise coil), 1/31/22, First Day Cover, DC	4,500
		Only seen serviced by Henry Hammelman (15-20 known)	

1917-19

☐	498	1c Washington, 4/19/17, eku	—
☐	498e	1c Washington (booklet), 6/22/17, eku	—
☐	498f	1c Washington (AEF booklet single), 8/15/17, eku	—
☐	499	2c Washington, 3/27/17, eku	—
☐	499e	2c Washington (booklet), 10/30/17, eku	—
☐	499f	2c Washington (AEF booklet single), 8/12/17, eku (probably a first day cover)	8,000
☐	500	2c Washington Ty Ia, 12/15/19, eku	1,000
☐	501	3c Washington Ty I, 7/3/17, eku	—
☐	501b	3c Washington Ty I (booklet), 2/8/18, eku	—
☐	502c	3c Washington Ty II (imperf between), 5/7/22, eku	—
☐	503	4c Washington, 7/17/1917, eku	—
☐	504	5c Washington, 6/18/1917, eku	—
☐	506	6c Washington, 6/26/1917, eku	—
☐	507	7c Washington, 8/1/1917, eku	—
☐	508	8c Franklin, 7/17/1917, eku	—
☐	509	9c Franklin, 10/2/1917, eku	—
☐	510	10c Franklin, 3/27/17, eku	—
☐	511	11c Franklin, 12/1/1917, eku	—
☐	512	12c Franklin, 10/13/1917, eku	—
☐	513	13c Franklin, 2/4/19, eku	—
☐	514	15c Franklin, 12/7/1917, eku	—
☐	515	20c Franklin, 9/17/1918, eku	—
☐	517	50c Franklin, 12/28/1917, eku	—
☐	518	$1 Franklin, 12/13/17, eku	—
☐	519	2c Washington, 10/10/1917, eku	—

1918-20

☐	523	$2 Franklin, 12/17/18, eku	—
☐	525	1c Washington, 12/24/18, eku	—
☐	526	2c Washington Ty IV, 3/15/20, First Day Cover (50-75 exist)	900.00
☐	527	2c Washington Ty V, 4/20/20, eku	—
☐	528A	2c Washington Ty VI, 7/30/20, eku	—
☐	528B	2c Washington Ty VII, 11/10/20, eku	—
☐	529	3c Washington Ty III, 4/24/18, eku	—
☐	530	3c Washington Ty IV, 6./30/18, eku	—
☐	533	2c Washington Ty V (imperf), 6/30/20, eku	—
☐	534B	2c Washington Ty VII (imperf), 11/3/20, eku, probably a first day cover	4,000
☐	535	3c Washington Ty IV (imperf), 10/5/18, eku	625.00

1919

☐	536	**1c Washington,** 8/15/19, First Day Cover (2 known) 4,000
☐	537	**3c Victory Issue,** 3/3/19, First Day Cover (75-100 known)............ 800.00
☐	539	**2c Washington** rotary carmine Type II, 6/30/19, eku 30,000
☐	541	**3c Washington,** 6/14/19, eku .... —

1920

☐	542	**1c Washington,** 5/26/20, First Day Cover (40-50 known)............... 2,000
☐	543	**1c Washington,** 5/26/21, eku .... —
☐	548	**1c The Mayflower,** 12/21/20, First Day Cover (30-50 exist) 1,000
☐	549	**2c Landing of the Pilgrims,** 12/20/20, First Day Cover (3 known). 5,000
☐		covers dated 12/21/20 (50-75 exist) 750.00
☐	550	**5c Signing the Compact,** 12/21/20, First Day Cover (5-10 known) 2,500
		full set of three on one cover, 12/21/20 (15-20 known) 3,500
☐		Scott 548-550 predate 12/18/20, Plymouth, MA 1,600
☐		Pre-dates for 12/20/20 from Plymouth, MA (3 known) 1,200
☐		Blocks of four on 548-550 12/21/20, DC First Day Cover 2,200

1922-26

☐	551	**1/2c Nathan Hale,** 4/4/25, DC...18.00
☐		New Haven, CT..25.00
☐		Unofficial city (20-30 known) 150.00
☐		Scott 551 & 576 (1/2c Hale & 1 1/2c Harding imperf.)
		on one cover, DC...150.00
☐	552	**1c Benjamin Franklin,** 1/17/23, DC, pair.............................25.00 30.00
☐		Philadelphia, PA..45.00 60.00
☐		Norristown, PA 50.00
☐		Unofficial city (7 known) 100.00
☐	553	**1 1/2c Warren G. Harding,** 3/19/25, DC, pair.......................30.00 35.00
☐		Scott 553, 582, 598 on Scott U482......................................175.00
☐		Scott 553 on Scott U481 Plate Block combination,
		First Day Cover..500.00
☐		Unofficial city, (7 known) 150.00
☐	554	**2c George Washington,** 1/15/23, DC....................................40.00 50.00
☐		Unofficial city Alexandria, VA, Allentown, PA....................300.00
☐		Scott 554 & 556, Scott 554 & 561, Scott 554 & 562
		on one cover 250.00
☐	555	**3c Abraham Lincoln,** 2/12/23, DC..40.00 50.00
☐		Hodgenville, KY..250.00 375.00
☐		Unofficial city (9 known)..200.00 —
☐	556	**4c Martha Washington,** 1/15/23, DC....................................60.00 100.00
☐		Scott 556 & 561 combination...250.00
☐		Scott 556 unofficial city (1 known).....................................300.00
☐	557	**5c Theodore Roosevelt,** 10/27/22, DC 125.00 175.00
☐		New York, NY..200.00 300.00
☐		Oyster Bay, NY...1,400. 1,800
☐	558	**6c James A. Garfield,** 11/20/22, DC....................................225.00 300.00
☐	559	**7c William McKinley,** 5/1/23, DC.......................................175.00 200.00
☐		Niles, OH..200.00 300.00
☐		Scott 559-560 on one cover...400.00
☐	560	**8c U.S. Grant,** 5/1/23, DC...175.00 200.00

551

552, 581,
597, 604

553, 576, 582,
598, 605, 631

557

562

565

567

571

572

573

1st George W. Linn cachet

610, 611, 612

614

615

616

617

1st Guy Atwood Jackson cachet

618

619

1st Ernest J. Weschcke cachet

1st Albert C. Roessler cachet

620

621

622

623

14

			SINGLE	BLOCK
☐	561	9c Thomas Jefferson, 1/15/23, DC	175.00	200.00
☐		Scott 561 on Scott U420	200.00	
☐	562	10c James Monroe, 1/15/23, DC	175.00	200.00
☐		Scott 554, 556, 561, 562 on one cover	2,500.	
☐	563	11c Rutherford B. Hayes, 10/4/22, DC	600.00	775.00
☐		Fremont, OH (51 known)	2,600.	
☐	564	12c Grover Cleveland, 3/20/23, DC	175.00	200.00
☐		Boston, MA (Philatelic Exhibition)	175.00	200.00
☐		Caldwell, NJ	200.00	225.00
☐	565	14c American Indian, 5/1/23, DC	400.00	600.00
☐		Muskogee, OK	1,000.	6,500.
☐		Scott 565 and 560 on one cover, DC	2,200.	
☐	566	15c Statue of Liberty, 11/11/22, DC	600.00	
☐	567	20c Golden Gate, 5/1/23, DC	600.00	
☐		San Francisco, CA	1,200.	
☐		Oakland, CA, unofficial city (5 known)	7,500.	
☐	568	25c Niagara Falls, 11/11/22, DC	675.00	1,000.
☐	569	30c Buffalo, 3/20/23, DC	825.00	1,350.
☐		Scott 569 and 564 on one cover, DC (1 known)	4,000.	
☐	570	50c Arlington Amphitheater, 11/11/22, DC	1,500.	1,650.
☐		Scott 566, 568, 570 on one cover	4,000.	
☐	571	$1 Lincoln Memorial, 2/12/23, DC	6,000.	
☐		Springfield, IL (17 known)	6,000.	10,000.
☐		Scott 571,555 on one cover, DC	7,500.	
		1 exists - legal size		
☐	572	$2 U.S. Capitol, 3/20/23, DC	17,000.	
☐	573	$5 Head of Freedom Statue, 3/20/23, DC	30,000.	
☐	576	1 1/2c Warren G. Harding, 4/4/25, DC	45.00	60.00
☐	581	1c Benjamin Franklin, unprecanceled 10/17/23, DC (1 known)	7,000.	
☐	582	1 1/2c Warren G. Harding, 3/19/25, DC	50.00	65.00
☐	583	2c George Washington, 4/14/24, New York, NY, earliest known use	—	—
☐	583a	George Washington, booklet pane of 6, 8/27/26, DC	1500.	
☐	584	3c Abraham Lincoln, 8/1/25, DC	65.00	90.00
☐	585	4c Martha Washington, 4/4/25, DC	65.00	90.00
☐		Unofficial city (3 known)	100.00	
☐	586	5c Theodore Roosevelt, 4/4/25, DC	70.00	90.00
☐		Unoffcial city (3 known)	100.00	
☐	587	6c James A. Garfield, 4/4/25, DC	70.00	110.00
		Covers exist with Scott 585-587 and Scott 585-586 from DC official), NYC and Philadelphia, RPO (unofficial)		
☐	588	7c William McKinley, 5/29/26, DC	75.00	120.00
☐	589	8c U.S. Grant, 5/29/26, DC	90.00	135.00
☐	590	9c Thomas Jefferson, 5/29/26, DC	90.00	135.00
☐		Scott 588, 589, 590 on one cover	300.00	
☐	591	10c James Monroe, 6/8/25, DC	110.00	170.00

1923-29 Coils

☐	597	1c Benjamin Franklin, 7/18/23, DC	600.00	700.00
☐	598	1 1/2c Warren G. Harding, 3/19/25, DC	60.00	80.00
☐	599	2c George Washington, Type I, 1/15/23, DC (37 known)	1,400.	
☐		Lancaster, PA, 1/10/23 (1 known)	3,500.	
☐		South Bend, IN, 1/11/23 (1 known)	1,400.	

☐   St. Louis, MO, 1/13/23 (1 known).....................1,400.
      Note: January 10, 1923 is the earliest known use of Scott
      599. Philip Ward prepared 37 covers on January 15, 1923,
      the earliest known use in Washington, DC.

☐	599A	2c George Washington, Type II, 3/29/29, earliest known use.....—	—
☐	600	3c Abraham Lincoln, 5/10/24, DC..........100.00	110.00
☐	602	5c Theodore Roosevelt, 3/5/24, DC..........100.00	130.00
☐	603	10c James Monroe, 12/1/24, DC..........100.00	150.00
☐	604	1c Benjamin Franklin, 7/19/24, DC..........90.00	
☐	605	1 1/2c Warren G. Harding, 5/9/25, DC..........80.00	
☐	606	2c George Washington, 12/31/23, DC..........150.00	

1923

☐	610	2c Warren G. Harding, 9/1/23, DC..........30.00	35.00		
☐		Marion, OH (5,000).....................20.00	22.50		
☐		Brooklyn, NY; Mt. Rainier, MD;			
		Caledonia, OH (Unofficial cities).........37.50			
☐		Pre-date, 8/31/23, DC, (1 known).........250.00			
☐		1st George W. Linn cachet (1st modern			
		cachet).....................................800.00			
☐	611	2c Warren G. Harding, imperf. 11/15/23,			
		DC.....................................90.00	110.00		
☐		Pair.....................................100.00			
☐		Pair or Block with line.........110.00	160.00		
☐		Center line block.........................	165.00		
☐		Unofficial city.........................100.00	110.00		
☐	612	2c Warren G. Harding, perf 10, 9/12/23,			
		DC.....................................100.00	110.00		

1924

☐	614	1c Huguenot-Walloon Tercentenary,			
☐		5/1/24, pair, DC.....................40.00	45.00		
☐		Albany, NY.........................40.00	45.00		
☐		Allentown, PA.........................40.00	45.00		
☐		Charleston, SC.........................40.00	45.00		
☐		Jacksonville, FL.........................40.00	45.00		
☐		Lancaster, PA.........................40.00	45.00		
☐		Mayport, FL.........................40.00	45.00		
☐		New Rochelle, NY.........................40.00	45.00		
☐		New York, NY.........................40.00	45.00		
☐		Philadelphia, PA.........................40.00	45.00		
☐		Reading, PA.........................40.00	45.00		
☐		Unofficial city.........................65.00			
☐	615	2c Huguenot-Walloon Tercentenary, 5/1/24, DC..60.00	65.00		
☐		Albany, NY.........................60.00	65.00		
☐		Allentown, PA.........................60.00	65.00		
☐		Charleston, SC.........................60.00	65.00		
☐		Jacksonville, FL.........................60.00	65.00		
☐		Lancaster, PA.........................60.00	65.00		
☐		Mayport, FL.........................60.00	65.00		
☐		New Rochelle, NY.........................60.00	65.00		
☐		New York, NY.........................60.00	65.00		

17

1st Charles E. Nickles cachet

627

628

1st Herbert H. Griffin cachet

1st James H. Baxter cachet

1st Scott Stamp & Coin Co. cachet

629, 630

643

1st Joshua R. Gerow Jr. cachet

1st Haris R. Hunt cachet

1st Bradie Buchanan cachet

644

645

18

☐		Philadelphia, PA...60.00	65.00	
☐		Reading, PA 60.00	65.00	
☐		Unofficial city 80.00		
☐	616	5c Huguenot-Walloon Tercentenary, 5/1/24, DC.80.00	85.00	
☐		Albany, NY 80.00	85.00	
☐		Allentown, PA 80.00	85.00	
☐		Charlestown, SC...80.00	85.00	
☐		Jacksonville, FL 80.00	85.00	
☐		Lancaster, PA 80.00	85.00	
☐		Mayport, FL 80.00	85.00	
☐		New Rochelle, NY 80.00	85.00	
☐		New York, NY 80.00	85.00	
☐		Philadelphia, PA..80.00	85.00	
☐		Reading, PA 80.00	85.00	
☐		Unofficial city 125.00		
☐		Scott 614-616, set of three on one cover,		
		any official city 175.00	300.00	
		Values are for neat, clean covers.		

1925

☐	617	1c Lexington-Concord, 4/4/25, pair, DC 30.00	40.00	
☐		Boston, MA 30.00	40.00	125.00
☐		Cambridge, MA..25.00	40.00	100.00
☐		Concord, MA 27.50	40.00	100.00
☐		Concord Junction, MA 30.00	40.00	
☐		Lexington, MA...30.00	40.00	125.00
☐		Unofficial city 45.00		
☐		1st Guy Atwood Jackson cachet (on any value)		150.00
☐	618	2c Lexington-Concord, 4/4/25, DC...................35.00	40.00	
☐		Boston, MA 35.00	40.00	125.00
☐		Cambridge, MA..35.00	40.00	125.00
☐		Concord, MA 35.00	40.00	125.00
☐		Concord Junction, MA 35.00	40.00	
☐		Lexington, MA...45.00	75.00	125.00
☐		Unofficial city 50.00		
☐	619	5c Lexington-Concord, 4/4/25, DC...................80.00	110.00	
☐		Boston, MA 80.00	110.00	150.00
☐		Cambridge, MA..80.00	110.00	150.00
☐		Concord, MA 80.00	110.00	150.00
☐		Concord Junction, MA 80.00	110.00	150.00
☐		Lexington, MA...80.00	110.00	150.00
☐		Unofficial city 80.00		
☐		Scott 617-619 Set on one cover, Concord		
		Junction or Lexington 175.00	250.00	
☐		Scott 617-619 Set on one cover, any		
		other official city 140.00	250.00	
☐		Scott 617-619 Set on one cover,		
		unofficial city...200.00	300.00	
☐		Scott 551,576, 585-587, 617-619 on one		
		cover ....*2,500.*		
		Values are for neat, clean covers.		
☐	620	2c Norse-American, 5/18/25, DC 20.00	25.00	
☐		Algona, IA 20.00	25.00	
☐		Benson, MN 20.00	25.00	
☐		Decorah, IA...20.00	25.00	

☐		Minneapolis, MN	20.00	25.00	
☐		Northfield, MN	20.00	25.00	
☐		St.Paul, MN	20.00	25.00	
☐		Unofficial city	50.00		
☐	621	5c Norse-American, 5/18/25, DC	30.00	45.00	
☐		Algona, IA	30.00	45.00	
☐		Benson, MN	30.00	45.00	
☐		Decorah, IA	30.00	45.00	
☐		Minneapolis, MN	30.00	45.00	
☐		Northfield, MN	30.00	45.00	
☐		St.Paul, MN	30.00	45.00	
☐		Unofficial city	65.00		
☐		Scott 620-621 Set on one cover, any city	50.00	70.00	250.00
☐		1st Ernest J.Weschcke cachet			300.00 —
☐		1st Albert C. Roessler cachet			300.00 —

1925-26

☐	622	13c Benjamin Harrison, 1/11/26, DC	20.00	30.00	— —
☐		Indianapolis, IN	30.00	50.00	— —
☐		North Bend, OH, unofficial city (500)	175.00	325.00	— —
☐		Other unofficial cities	200.00	—	— —

Plate blocks, from this period, sell for two to three times the price of singles.

☐	623	17c Woodrow Wilson, 12/28/25, DC	25.00	27.50	300.00 —
☐		New York, NY	25.00	27.50	300.00 —
☐		Princeton, NJ	25.00	27.50	300.00 —
☐		Staunton, VA	25.00	27.50	300.00 —
☐		Bellefonte, PA, AMF, unofficial city	—	—	300.00 —
☐		Other unofficial cities	30.00	—	— —
☐		1st Charles E. Nickles cachet			300.00

1926

☐	627	2c Sesquicentennial Exposition, 5/10/26,			
		DC	10.00	12.00	70.00 —
☐		Boston, MA	10.00	12.00	70.00 —
☐		Philadelphia, PA	10.00	12.00	70.00 —
☐		Chester, PA, unofficial city	—	—	60.00 —
☐		Valley Forge, PA, unofficial city	15.00	—	70.00 —
☐		Other unofficial cities	18.00	—	55.00 —
☐		1st Herbert H. Griffin cachet			150.00 —
☐		1st Griffin			35.00 —
☐		1st James H. Baxter cachet			100.00

Cacheted Sesquicentennial FDC's are most often found with Chester or Valley Forge, PA, unofficial cancels. Cacheted FDC's on this issue from official FDC cities are worth more than those from most unofficial cities.

☐	628	5c Ericsson Memorial, 5/29/26, DC	30.00	32.00	425.00 —
☐		Chicago, IL	30.00	32.00	425.00 —
☐		Minneapolis, MN	30.00	32.00	425.00 —
☐		New York, NY	30.00	32.00	425.00 —
☐		Unofficial city	35.00	—	— —

The cacheted value given above is for a cachet of two crossed gold bars on a blue envelope. Any other cachet sells for one quarter of the value listed.

21

		UNCACHETED		CACHETED	
		SINGLE	BLOCK	SINGLE	BLOCK
☐☐☐ 629	**2c Battle of White Plains,** New York, NY, 10/18/26 ....6.25		8.50	60.00	—
	New York, NY, International Philatelic Exhibition Agency cancellation 6.25		8.50	60.00	—
☐	White Plains, NY (24,830) 6.25		8.50	60.00	—
☐	DC, 10/28/26 ....3.50		5.00	60.00	—
☐	Unofficial city 3.50		5.00	—	—
☐	10/16/26, pre-date 15.00		30.00	—	—
	1st Scott Stamp & Coin Co. cachet			65.00	—
☐ 630	**2c Battle of White Plains,** souvenir sheet, single or block identifiably from				
	souvenir sheet 7.00		10.00	65.00	75.00
☐	Imprint strip of 10 (top or bottom)........................		50.00	—	
☐	Full sheet, 10/18/26 ....1,800.		—	—	—
☐	Full sheet, official city, 10/18/26.................2,000.		—	—	—
☐	Full sheet, 10/28/26 ....1,000.		—	—	—
☐	Unofficial city, single 50.00		—	—	—
	Values for various cachet makers can be determined by using the Cachet Calculator found on pages 32 to 38.				

1926-34

		UNCACHETED		CACHETED	
		SINGLE	BLOCK	SINGLE	BLOCK
☐ 631	**1 1/2c Warren G. Harding,** imperf, 8/27/26, DC, pair 35.00		40.00	—	—
☐ 632	**1c Benjamin Franklin,** 6/10/27, DC, pair 45.00		55.00	165.00	—
☐ 632a	**Benjamin Franklin,** booklet pane of 6, 11/2/27...3,500.		—	—	—
☐ 633	**1 1/2c Warren G. Harding,** 5/17/27, DC, pair 45.00		55.00	175.00	—
☐ 634	**2c George Washington,** 12/10/26, DC...........50.00		60.00	175.00	—
	Experimental Electric Eye, 3/28/35 ....—		—	1,000.	—
☐ 634A	**2c George Washington,** Type 2, 12/20/28, Chicago, IL...775.00		—	—	—
☐ 635	**3c Abraham Lincoln,** violet, 2/3/27, DC........47.50		57.50	165.00	—
☐ 635a	**3c Abraham Lincoln,** bright violet, 2/7/34, DC 25.00		38.00	50.00	—
☐ 636	**4c Martha Washington,** 5/17/27, DC 50.00		55.00	200.00	—
☐ 637	**5c Theodore Roosevelt,** 3/24/27, DC 50.00		55.00	200.00	—
☐ 638	**6c James A. Garfield,** 7/27/27, DC................60.00		110.00	200.00	—
☐ 639	**7c William McKinley,** 3/24/27, DC 60.00		110.00	200.00	—
☐	Scott 637, 639 on one cover.....................300.00		—	—	—
☐ 640	**8c U.S. Grant,** 6/10/27, DC............................65.00		120.00	225.00	—
☐	Scott 632, 640 on one cover.....................300.00		—	—	—
☐ 641	**9c Thomas Jefferson,** 5/17/27, DC 75.00		150.00	225.00	—
☐	Scott 633, 636, 641on one cover................350.00		—	—	—
☐ 642	**10c James Monroe,** 2/3/27, DC......................90.00		155.00	225.00	—

1927

		UNCACHETED		CACHETED	
		SINGLE	BLOCK	SINGLE	BLOCK
☐ 643	**2c Vermont Sesquicentennial,** 8/3/27, DC......5.00		6.00	55.00	60.00
☐	Bennington, VT (50,000)...............................5.00		6.00	55.00	60.00
☐	Unofficial city 7.50		—	65.00	—
☐	1st Joshua R. Gerow Jr. cachet.............................			250.00	—
☐	1st Haris R. Hunt cachet (Scott 643 or 644)........			90.00	—
☐	1st Bradie Buchanan cachet.................................			50.00	—
☐	1st S.S. Kurkjian cachet.......................................			200.00	

☐ 644	2c Burgoyne Campaign, 8/3/27, DC	12.50	15.00	65.00	70.00
☐	Albany, NY	12.50	15.00	65.00	70.00
☐	Rome, NY	12.50	15.00	65.00	70.00
☐	Syracuse, NY	12.50	15.00	65.00	70.000
☐	Utica, NY	12.50	15.00	65.00	70.00
☐	Oriskany, NY, unofficial city	35.00	—	—	—
☐	Schuylerville, NY, unofficial city	—	—	125.00	—
☐	Other unofficial city	20.00	—	—	—
☐	Scott 643 & 644 on one cover, DC	15.00		100.00	

1928

☐ 645	2c Valley Forge, 5/26/28, DC	4.00	15.00	50.00	55.00
☐	Cleveland, OH (town cancel)	65.00	85.00	150.00	—
☐	Lancaster, PA	4.00	15.00	50.00	55.00
☐	Norristown, PA (25,000)	4.00	15.00	50.00	55.00
☐	Philadelphia, PA	4.00	15.00	50.00	55.00
☐	Valley Forge, PA (70,000)	4.00	15.00	50.00	55.00
☐	West Chester, PA (15,000)	4.00	15.00	50.00	55.00
☐	Cleveland Midwestern Philatelic Sta. cancel	4.00	15.00	50.00	55.00
☐	Other unofficial city	7.50	—	60.00	—
☐	1st Joseph W. Stoutzenberg cachet			225.00	—
☐	1st Howard Davis Egolf cachet			100.00	—
☐	1st Adam K. Bert cachet			75.00	—
☐	1st Howard W. Weaver cachet			80.00	
☐ 646	2c Molly Pitcher, 10/20/28, DC	15.00	20.00	85.00	—
☐	Freehold, NJ (25,000)	15.00	20.00	85.00	—
☐	Red Bank, NJ	15.00	20.00	85.00	—
☐	Unofficial city	15.00	—	90.00	—
☐	1st Ralph Dyer cachet			300.00	—
☐ 647	2c Hawaii Sesquicentennial, 8/13/28, DC	15.00	17.50	75.00	80.00
☐	Honolulu, HI	17.50	20.00	75.00	80.00
☐	Unofficial city	20.00	—	85.00	—
☐ 648	5c Hawaii Sesquicentennial, 8/13/28, DC	22.50	25.00	75.00	80.00
☐	Honolulu, HI	25.00	28.00	75.00	80.00
☐	Unofficial city	30.00	—	—	—
☐	Scott 647, 648 on one cover	40.00	45.00	200.00	—
☐ 649	2c Aeronautics Conference, 12/12/28, Green International Civil Aeronautic Conference slogan	7.00	9.00	40.00	45.00
☐	DC, Black town cancel	9.00	11.00	40.00	45.00
☐	Unofficial city	15.00	—	—	—
☐ 650	5c Aeronautics Conference, 12/12/28, Green International Civil Aeronautic Conference slogan	10.00	12.50	50.00	55.00
☐	DC, Black town cancel	13.50	16.00	50.00	55.00
☐	Unofficial city	20.00	—	—	—
☐	Scott 649-650 on one cover, DC	15.00	—	70.00	—

Cacheted values are for covers with printed cachets. Covers with general purpose rubber stamp cachets sell at the uncacheted value. Rubber stamped Chamber of Commerce cachets sell for 1 1/2 to 2 times the uncacheted value.

1st Joseph W. Stoutzenberg cachet

1st Howard Davis Egolf cachet

1st Adam K. Bert cachet

646

647

648

649

650

651

1st Floyd D. Shockley cachet

1st Harry C. loor cachet

1st Harry E. Klotzbach cachet

653

654, 655, 656

657

1929

☐	651	2c **George Rogers Clark**, Vincennes, IN,			
		2/25/29...6.00	7.50	30.00	32.50
☐		Unofficial city...............................10.00	—	35.00	—
☐		DC, 2/26/29, first day of sale by			
		Philatelic Agency.......................3.00	4.00	22.50	32.50
☐		Charlottesville, VA, 2/26/29 ....7.00	—	30.00	—
☐		1st Floyd D. Shockley cachet....................		25.00	—
☐		1st Harry C. Ioor cachet		150.00	—
☐	653	1/2c **Nathan Hale**, 5/25/29, DC...........—	30.00	—	85.00
☐	654	2c **Electric Light Jubilee**, 6/5/29, Menlo			
		Park, NJ (77,000) 10.00	12.00	40.00	45.00
☐		Orange, NJ, unofficial ....—	—	35.00	—
☐		Other unofficial city..........................—	—	35.00	40.00
☐		DC, 6/6/29, first day of sale by Philatelic			
		Agency...4.00	5.00	16.50	22.50
☐		1st Harry E. Klotzbach cachet..............		175.00	—
☐	655	2c **Electric Light Jubilee**, 6/11/29, DC.....80.00	95.00	200.00	225.00
☐	656	2c **Electric Light Jubilee**, coil, 6/11/29, DC....90.00	110.00	200.00	225.00
☐		Line Pair...—	150.00	—	300.00
☐		Scott 655-656 on one cover.......................150.00	—	400.00	—
☐	657	2c **Sullivan Expedition**, Auburn, NY,			
		6/17/29 (5,000) 4.00	5.00	30.00	32.00
☐		Binghamton, NY (50,000)................4.00	5.00	30.00	32.00
☐		Canajoharie, NY (12,000)................4.00	5.00	30.00	32.00
☐		Canandaigua, NY..........................4.00	5.00	30.00	32.00
☐		Elmira, NY (11,000)......................4.00	5.00	30.00	32.00
☐		Geneseo, NY.................................4.00	5.00	30.00	32.00
☐		Geneva, NY 4.00	5.00	30.00	32.00
☐		Horseheads, NY.............................4.00	5.00	30.00	32.00
☐		Owego, NY...................................4.00	5.00	30.00	32.00
☐		Penn Yan, NY...............................4.00	5.00	30.00	32.00
☐		Perry, NY 4.00	5.00	30.00	32.00
☐		Seneca Falls, NY (8,500) 4.00	5.00	30.00	32.00
☐		Waterloo, NY................................4.00	5.00	30.00	32.00
☐		Watkins Glen, NY (6,500) 4.00	5.00	30.00	32.00
☐		Waverly, NY.................................4.00	5.00	30.00	32.00
☐		Loman, NY, unofficial city...........40.00			
☐		Other Unofficial city.......................6.50	10.00	50.00	55.00
☐		DC, 6/18/29 ....2.00	3.00	20.00	25.00
☐		1st Robert C. Beazell cachet....................		450.00	
☐		1st A.C. Elliot cachet		75.00	
☐		1st R. Roscher cachet		80.00	

1st Robert C. Beazell cachet

1st A.C. Elliott cachet

1st Delf Norona cachet

680

681

682

683

684, 686

685, 687

688

689

1st Denys J. Truby cachet

690

**Values for various cachet makers can be determined
by using the Cachet Calculator which begins on page 52A.**

658, 668   669, 679

Kansas and Nebraska Overprints

The first day of sale for the complete series of 22 Kansas-Nebraska overprints, Scott 658 through 679, was May 1, 1929, at the Philatelic Agency in Washington, D.C.

Stamps of that series also are known canceled in April 1929 from 27 Kansas and 28 Nebraska towns. These are relatively scarce and command a price greater than the May 1, 1929, Washington, D.C., cancels.

Listed below are the earliest known cancels of these stamps at Kansas and Nebraska post offices in April 1929. Only a few of each are known to exist.

☐	658	1c **Kansas**, 5/1/29, DC, pair............................	50.00
☐		Newton, KS, 4/15/29	400.00
☐	659	1 1/2c **Kansas**, 5/1/29, DC, pair	60.00
☐		Colby, KS, 4/16/29	—
☐	660	2c **Kansas**, 5/1/29, DC	60.00
☐		Colby, KS, 4/16/29	—
☐		Dodge City, KS 4/16/29..............................	—
☐		Liberal, KS 4/16/29	—
☐	661	3c **Kansas**, 5/1/29, DC	75.00
☐		Colby, KS, 4/16/29	—
☐	662	4c **Kansas**, 5/1/29, DC	70.00
☐		Colby, KS, 4/16/29	—
		Plate blocks, from this period, sell for two to	
		three times the price of singles.	
☐	663	5c **Kansas**, 5/1/29, DC	100.00
☐		Colby, KS, 4/16/29	—
☐	664	6c **Kansas**, 5/1/29, DC	100.00
☐		Newton, KS, 4/15/29	600.00
☐	665	7c **Kansas**, 5/1/29, DC	1,250.
☐		Colby, KS, 4/16/29	—
☐	666	8c **Kansas**, 5/1/29, DC	125.00
☐		Newton, KS, 4/15/29	600.00
☐	667	9c **Kansas**, 5/1/29, DC	150.00
☐		Colby, KS, 4/16/29	—
☐	668	10c **Kansas**, 5/1/29, DC	200.00
☐		Colby, KS, 4/16/29	—
☐		Scott 658-668 on one cover, DC, 5/1/29......1,300.	
☐		Scott 658, 664, 666, 4/15/29 Newton,KS...750.00	
		April canceled covers with Kansas overprint stamps are	
		also known from Cape Henry, VA; Denver and Pueblo,	
		CO; Kansas City, MO, and Waynesboro, PA.	
☐	669	1c **Nebraska**, 5/1/29, DC, pair.......................	50.00
☐		Beatrice, NE, 4/15/29.................................	400.00
☐	670	1 1/2c **Nebraska**, 5/1/29, DC, pair	50.00
☐		Hartington, NE, 4/15/29.............................	400.00

	671	2c **Nebraska**, 5/1/29, DC	60.00			
		Auburn, NE, 4/15/29	—			
		Beatrice, NE, 4/15/29	—			
		Hartington, NE, 4/15/29	400.00			
	672	3c **Nebraska**, 5/1/29, DC	75.00			
		Beatrice, NE, 4/15/29	250.00			
		Hartington, NE, 4/15/29	250.00			
	673	4c **Nebraska**, 5/1/29, DC	75.00			
		Beatrice, NE, 4/15/29	400.00			
		Hartington, 4/15/29	400.00			
	674	5c **Nebraska**, 5/1/29, DC	75.00		100.00	
		Beatrice, NE, 4/15/29	400.00			
		Hartington, NE, 4/15/29	400.00			
	675	6c **Nebraska**, 5/1/29, DC	100.00			
		Auburn, NE, 4/16/29	400.00			
	676	7c **Nebraska**, 5/1/29, DC	100.00			
		Auburn, NE, 4/17/29	400.00			
	677	8c **Nebraska**, 5/1/29, DC	150.00			
		Humbolt, NE, 4/17/29	250.00			
		Pawnee City, NE, 4/17/29	400.00			
	678	9c **Nebraska**, 5/1/29, DC	150.00			
		Cambridge, NE, 4/17/29	400.00			
	679	10c **Nebraska**, 5/1/29, DC	200.00			
		Tecumseh, NE, 4/18/29	400.00			
		Scott 669-679 on one cover, DC, 5/1/29	1300.			

April canceled covers with Nebraska Overprint stamps are also known from Cleveland, OH; Kansas City, MO; and Washington, DC. There also are 1c and 2c Nebraska overprints canceled April 6, 1929 (pre-date), from Syracuse, NE, known and confirmed genuine by The Philatelic Foundation.

	680	2c **Battle of Fallen Timbers**, Erie, PA,				
		9/14/29	3.50	4.00	35.00	40.00
		Maumee, OH	3.50	4.00	35.00	40.00
		Perrysburg OH	3.50	4.00	35.00	40.00
		Toledo, OH	3.50	4.00	35.00	40.00
		Waterville, OH (18,000)	3.50	4.00	35.00	40.00
		Fallen Timbers, PA	7.00			
		Unofficial city	5.00		40.00	
		DC, 9/16/29	2.00	3.00	20.00	22.00
		1st Eugene Laird cachet			200.00	—
	681	2c **Ohio River**, Cairo, IL, 10/19/29	3.50	4.00	35.00	40.00
		Cincinnati, OH	3.50	4.00	35.00	40.00
		Evansville, IN (30,000)	3.50	4.00	35.00	40.00
		Homestead, PA (55,000)	3.50	4.00	35.00	40.00
		Louisville, KY	3.50	4.00	35.00	40.00
		Pittsburgh, PA (50,000)	3.50	4.00	35.00	40.00
		Wheeling, WV	3.50	4.00	35.00	40.00
		Unofficial city R.P.O.	7.50		45.00	
		R.P.O.10/18/29, pre-date	50.00			
		Other unofficial city			45.00	
		DC, 10/21/29	2.00	2.50	20.00	22.00
		1st Delf Norona cachet			70.00	

**Uncacheted covers, from this period,
sell for about 20% that of cacheted covers.**

1930

☐	682	2c **Massachusetts Bay Colony**, Boston, MA 4/8/30 (60,000)	3.50	4.00	35.00	40.00
☐		Salem, MA	3.50	4.00	35.00	40.00
☐		Unofficial city	6.50		45.00	47.00
☐		DC, 4/11/30	2.00	2.50	20.00	22.00
☐	683	2c **Carolina-Charleston**, Charleston, SC, 4/10/30 (100,000)	3.50	4.00	35.00	40.00
☐		Unofficial city	6.00			
☐		DC, 4/11/30	2.00	1.50	20.00	25.00
☐		682-683 on one cover, DC, 4/11/30	4.00		45.00	
☐	684	1 1/2c **Warren G. Harding**, pair, Marion, OH, 12/1/30	4.50	5.00	45.00	50.00
☐		DC, 12/2/30	2.00	3.00	25.00	30.00
☐	685	4c **William H. Taft**, Cincinnati, OH, 6/4/30	6.00	7.50	55.00	60.00
☐		DC, 6/5/30	3.00	3.50	25.00	30.00
☐	686	1 1/2c **Warren G. Harding**, coil, Marion, OH, 12/1/30	5.00	6.00	50.00	60.00
☐		DC, 12/2/30	3.00	3.50	25.00	30.00
☐		Scott 684, 686 on one cover, Marion, OH, 12/1/30	7.50		65.00	
☐		Scott 684, 686, DC, 12/2/30	3.00		40.00	
☐	687	4c **William H. Taft**, coil 9/18/30, DC	20.00	25.00	75.00	80.00
☐	688	2c **Braddock's Field**, Braddock PA, 7/9/30 (50,000)	4.00	4.50	30.00	32.00
☐		Unofficial city	7.00		50.00	
☐		DC, 7/10/30	2.00	2.50	20.00	21.00
☐	689	2c **Von Steuben**, New York, NY, 9/17/30	4.00	4.50	30.00	32.00
☐		Unofficial city			50.00	
☐		DC, 9/18/30	2.00	2.50	20.00	21.00
☐		Scott 687, 689 on one cover, DC	25.00		75.00	

1931

☐	690	2c **Pulaski**, Brooklyn, NY, 1/16/31	4.00	4.50	30.00	32.00
☐		Buffalo, NY	4.00	4.50	30.00	32.00
☐		Chicago, IL	4.00	4.50	30.00	32.00
☐		Cleveland, OH	4.00	4.50	30.00	32.00
☐		Detroit, MI	4.00	4.50	30.00	32.00
☐		Gary, IN	4.00	4.50	30.00	32.00
☐		Milwaukee, WI	4.00	4.50	30.00	32.00
☐		New York, NY	4.00	4.50	30.00	32.00
☐		Pittsburgh, PA	4.00	4.50	30.00	32.00
☐		Savannah, GA	4.00	4.50	30.00	32.00
☐		South Bend, IN	4.00	4.50	30.00	32.00
☐		Toledo, OH	4.00	4.50	30.00	32.00
☐		Unofficial city	8.50		35.00	
☐		DC, 1/17/31	2.00			
☐		1st Denys J. Truby cachet			90.00	
☐	692	11c **Rutherford B. Hayes**, 9/4/31, DC	125.00	135.00		
☐	693	12c **Grover Cleveland**, 8/25/31, DC	125.00	135.00		
☐	694	13c **Benjamin Harrison**, 9/4/31, DC	125.00	135.00		
☐		Woolrich, PA 9/4/31	500.00			
☐	695	14c **American Indian**, 9/8/31, DC	125.00	135.00		

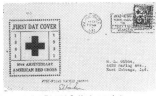

1st Edward G. Hacker cachet

1st Aero Print cachet

1st Covered Wagon cachet

702

703

704

705

706

707

708

709

710

711

712

713

714

715

1st Frederick R. Rice cachet

1st Beverly Hills cachet

1st Linprint cachet

716

717

718

	Scott No.	Description	Uncacheted Single	Block	Cacheted Single	Block
☐	696	15c Statue of Liberty, 8/27/31, DC 125.00	225.00			
☐	697	17c Woodrow Wilson, 7/25/31, Brooklyn,NY .3000.				
☐		DC, 7/27/31 .... 400.00	725.00			
☐	698	20c Golden Gate, 9/8/31, DC 325.00	650.00			
☐		Woolrich, PA, 9/4/31 .... 500.00				
☐	699	25c Niagara Falls, 7/25/31, Brooklyn, NY. ..... 1500.				
☐		DC, 7/27/31 .... 400.00	800.00			
☐		Scott 697 and 699 on one cover,				
☐		Brooklyn, NY .... 3500.				
☐	700	30c Bison, 9/8/31, DC 325.00	550.00			
☐	701	50c Arlington Amphitheater, 9/4/31, DC 450.00	875.00			
☐		Woolrich, PA, 9/4/31 .... 700.00				
☐	702	2c Red Cross, 5/21/31, DC 3.00	3.50	30.00	32.00
☐		Dansville, NY 3.00	3.50	30.00	32.00
☐		Unofficial city 6.00		45.00	
☐		1st Edward G. Hacker cachet		90.00	
☐		1st August (WSE) cachet		40.00	
☐	703	2c Yorktown, 10/19/31, Wethersfield, CT 3.50	4.00	45.00	50.00
☐		Yorktown, VA 3.50	4.00	45.00	50.00
☐		Unofficial city 7.00		55.00	
☐		1st Aero Print cachet		100.00	
☐		1st Walter G. Crosby cachet		450.00	
☐		1st Covered Wagon cachet		75.00	
☐		Washington, DC, 10/20/31 .... 2.00	2.50	20.00	21.00
☐		10/5/31 pre-date Wenatchee, WA (75)				
☐		(AAMS #1146) 400.00				
☐		Any pre-date 10/6/31 through 10/18/31. ..... 25.00		80.00	

The Post Office Department experimented with a new stamp distribution method with the Yorktown stamp. This resulted in a number of pre-dates on this issue. FDC's postmarked in unofficial cities sell for 50 percent to 100 percent more than catalogue value.

1932 Washington Bicentennial

	Scott No.	Description	Uncacheted Single	Block	Cacheted Single	Block
☐	704	1/2c olive brown, 1/1/32, DC ....—	5.00	—	20.00
☐	705	1c green, pair, 1/1/32, DC 4.00	5.00	18.00	20.00
☐	706	1 1/2c brown, pair, 1/1/32, DC 4.00	5.00	18.00	20.00
☐	707	2c carmine rose, 1/1/32, DC 4.00	5.00	18.00	20.00
☐	708	3c deep violet, 1/1/32, DC 4.00	5.00	18.00	20.00
☐	709	4c light brown, 1/1/32, DC 4.00	5.00	18.00	20.00
☐	710	5c blue, 1/1/32, DC 4.00	5.00	18.00	20.00
☐	711	6c red orange, 1/1/32, DC 4.00	5.00	18.00	20.00
☐	712	7c black, 1/1/32, DC 4.00	5.00	18.00	20.00
☐	713	8c olive bister, 1/1/32, DC 4.50	5.75	18.00	20.00
☐	714	9c pale red, 1/1/32, DC 4.50	5.75	18.00	20.00
☐	715	10c orange yellow, 1/1/32, DC 4.50	5.75	18.00	20.00
☐		Scott 704-715 on one cover, DC 60.00		250.00	
☐		1st Plimpton cachet (on any single)		30.00	
☐		1st William T. Raley cachet (on any single)		40.00	
☐		1st Frederick R. Rice cachet (on any single		25.00	

Add 100 percent for unofficial first day cancel on this issue.

	Scott No.	Description	Uncacheted Single	Block	Cacheted Single	Block
☐	716	2c Olympic Winter Games, 1/25/32, Lake				
☐		Placid, NY 6.00	6.50	25.00	30.00
☐		Unofficial city		30.00	
☐		DC, 1/26/32 .... 1.50	2.00	10.00	15.00
☐		1st Beverly Hills cachet		250.00	

719

720, 720b,
721, 722

723

724

725

1st Anderson cachet

1st Henry Grimsland cachet

1st Brookhaven cachet

726

727, 752

728, 730, 766a

729, 731, 767a

733, 735,
753, 768a

732

734

1st Albert B. Parsons cachet

**Values for various cachet makers can be determined
by using the Cachet Calculator which begins on page 52A.**

SCOTT NUMBER	DESCRIPTION	UNCACHETED SINGLE	BLOCK	CACHETED SINGLE	BLOCK
☐ 717	2c Arbor Day, 4/22/32, Nebraska City, NE. 4.00	4.50		15.00	18.00
☐	DC, 4/23/32...1.50	2.00		5.00	6.00
☐	Adams, NY, 4/23/32...6.50			18.00	20.00
☐	1st Linprint cachet			25.00	
☐ 718	3c Olympic Games, 6/15/32, Los Angeles, CA..........6.00	6.50		25.00	30.00
☐	Unofficial...			35.00	
☐	DC, 6/16/32...2.75	3.00		8.00	9.00
☐ 719	5c Olympic Games, 6/15/32, Los Angeles, CA 8.00	8.50		25.00	30.00
☐	Unofficial...			35.00	
☐	DC, 6/16/32...2.75	3.00		8.00	9.00
☐	Scott 718-719 on one cover, Los Angeles, CA..10.00	13.50		35.00	45.00
☐	Scott 718-719 on one cover, DC....................4.50				
☐	Scott 718-719 on one cover, unofficial			50.00	
☐ 720	3c George Washington, 6/16/32, DC 7.50	8.50		40.00	45.00
☐ 720b	George Washington, booklet pane of 6,				
	7/25/32, DC..100.00			200.00	
☐ 720b	George Washington, booklet single 20.00			60.00	

SCOTT NUMBER	DESCRIPTION	UNCACHETED SINGLE	PAIR	CACHETED SINGLE	PAIR
☐ 721	3c George Washington, coil, sideways,				
	6/24/32 ....15.00	20.00		60.00	90.00
☐ 722	3c George Washington, coil, endways,				
	10/12/32 ....15.00	20.00		60.00	90.00
☐ 723	6c James A. Garfield, coil, 8/18/32, Los				
	Angeles, CA...15.00	20.00		60.00	90.00
☐	DC, 8/19/32...4.00	6.00		30.00	35.00

SCOTT NUMBER	DESCRIPTION	UNCACHETED SINGLE	BLOCK	CACHETED SINGLE	BLOCK
☐ 724	3c William Penn, 10/24/32, New Castle, DE 3.25	4.00		20.00	25.00
☐	Chester, PA...3.25	4.00		20.00	25.00
☐	Philadelphia, PA..3.25	4.00		20.00	25.00
☐	Unofficial city..			30.00	
☐	DC, 10/25/32...1.25	1.50		9.00	10.00
☐ 725	3c Daniel Webster, 10/24/32, Franklin, NH 3.25	4.00		20.00	25.00
☐	Exeter, NH..3.25	4.00		20.00	25.00
☐	Hanover, NH (70,000) 3.25	4.00		20.00	25.00
☐	Marshfield, MA, unofficial............................35.00			37.00	
☐	Webster, MA, unofficial			40.00	
☐	Any other unofficial city.................................			30.00	
☐	DC, 10/25/32...1.25	1.50		9.00	12.00
☐	Scott 724-725 on one cover 5.00	6.00		30.00	

1933

SCOTT NUMBER	DESCRIPTION	UNCACHETED SINGLE	BLOCK	CACHETED SINGLE	BLOCK
☐ 726	3c Georgia Bicentennial, 2/12/33,				
	Savannah, GA (200,000).................................3.25	4.00		20.00	25.00
☐	Any Georgia town, 2/13/33 ....3.25			9.00	12.00
☐	DC, 2/13/33...1.50	2.50		8.00	9.00
☐	1st Anderson cachet			150.00	

Because 2/12/33 was a Sunday, second-day covers for Scott 726 were serviced.

1st Torkel Gundel cachet

1st Top-Notch cachet

1st Donald Kapner cachet

1st Louis G. Nix cachet

736

737, 738, 754

739, 755

740, 751, 756, 769a

741, 757

742, 750, 758, 770a

743, 759

745, 761

744, 760

1st Imperial cachet

747, 763

746, 762

748, 764

749, 765

34

SCOTT NUMBER	DESCRIPTION	UNCACHETED SINGLE	BLOCK	CACHETED SINGLE	BLOCK
☐ 727	3c Peace of 1783, 4/19/33, Newburgh, NY				
	(349,571)............3.50	4.00	20.00	25.00	
☐	Unofficial city			30.00	
☐	DC, 4/20/33............1.25	2.00		8.00	9.00
☐	1st Henry Grimsland cachet			300.00	
☐	1st Brookhaven cachet................................			90.00	
☐	1st Eagle Cover Service cachet			75.00	
☐	1st Newburgh Chamber of Commerce................			50.00	
☐ 728	1c Century of Progress, 5/25/33, strip of 3,				
	Chicago, IL............3.00	3.50	20.00	25.00	
☐	Unofficial city			20.00	
☐	DC, 5/26/33............1.00	2.00		9.00	12.00
☐ 729	3c Century of Progress, 5/25/33, Chicago,IL ...3.00	3.50	20.00	25.00	
☐	Chicago Ridge fancy cancel 10.00	12.00	40.00	50.00	
☐	Any other unofficial city........................			20.00	
☐	DC, 5/26/33............1.00	2.00		9.00	12.00
☐	Scott 728-729 on one cover 5.00	6.00	25.00	30.00	
☐	1st Lan W. Kreicker cachet................................			40.00	
	Total FDC's mailed May 25: 232,251.				
☐ 730	1c American Philatelic Society, imperf.				
	pane of 25, 8/25/33, Chicago, IL............100.00			200.00	
☐ 730a	American Philatelic Society, strip of 3 .... 3.25	4.00	20.00	25.00	
☐	DC, 8/28/33............1.25	2.00		9.00	12.00
	Values for various cachet makers can be determined by				
	using the Cachet Calculator found on pages 32 to 38.				
☐ 731	3c American Philatelic Society, imperf.				
	pane of 25, 8/25/33, Chicago, IL................100.00			200.00	
☐ 731a	American Philatelic Society, single 3.25	4.00	20.00	25.00	
☐	DC, 8/28/33............1.25	2.00		9.00	12.00
☐	Scott 730a, 731a on one cover 5.50	6.50	20.00	22.00	
	Total FDC's mailed Aug. 25: 65,218.				
☐ 732	3c National Recovery Act, 8/15/33, DC				
	(65,000)............3.25	4.00	20.00	25.00	
	Nira, IA, 8/17/33 unofficial 2.50	5.00	20.00	22.00	
☐ 733	3c Byrd Antarctic, 10/9/33, DC 7.00	9.00	20.00	22.50	
☐	1st Albert B. Parsons cachet................................			75.00	
☐ 734	5c Kosciuszko, 10/13/33, Boston, MA				
	(23,025)............4.50	6.00	20.00	25.00	
☐	Buffalo, NY (14,981) 5.50	7.00	20.00	25.00	
☐	Chicago, IL (26,306)............4.50	6.00	20.00	25.00	
☐	Detroit, MI (17,792) 5.25	6.00	20.00	25.00	
☐	Pittsburgh, PA (6,282)............32.50	37.50	60.00	70.00	
☐	Kosciuszko, MS (27,093)............5.25	6.00	20.00	25.00	
☐	St. Louis, MO (17,872) 5.25	6.00	20.00	25.00	
☐	DC, 10/14/33............1.60	2.00	20.00	25.00	
☐	Unofficial city 10.00	12.00	40.00	50.00	

1934

☐ 735	3c National Stamp Exhibition, imperf. pane				
	of 6, 2/10/34, New York, NY 40.00			75.00	
☐	DC, 2/19/34............27.50				
☐	1st Minkus cachet			60.00	
☐ 735a	National Stamp Exhibition, single				
	(450,715)............5.00	6.00	20.00	25.00	
☐	DC, 2/19/34............2.75	3.50	10.00	12.00	

772

773

774

1st Winfred Milton Grandy cachet

1st William H. Espenshade cachet

1st Norwood B. Scatchard cachet

775

776

777

778

1st John C. Sidenius cachet

1st Walter Czubay cachet

1st J. W. Clifford cachet

1st House of Farnam cachet

SCOTT NUMBER	DESCRIPTION	UNCACHETED SINGLE	UNCACHETED BLOCK	CACHETED SINGLE	CACHETED BLOCK
☐ 736	3c **Maryland Tercentenary**, 3/23/34, St.				
	Mary's City, MD (148,785).............................1.60	2.00	15.00	20.00	
☐	DC, 3/24/34...1.00	1.00	6.00	7.00	
☐	1st Torkel Gundel cachet		300.00		
☐	1st Top-Notch cachet		40.00		
☐	1st Donald Kapner cachet		40.00		
☐	1st Louis G. Nix cachet		200.00		
☐ 737	3c **Mothers of America**, perf. 11x10 1/2,				
	5/2/34, any city...1.60	2.00	15.00	20.00	
☐ 738	3c **Mothers of America**, perf 11, 5/2/34,				
☐	any city...1.60	2.00	15.00	20.00	
☐	Scott 737-738 on one cover 4.00	5.00	25.00		
	FDC's mailed at Washington May 2: 183,359.				
☐ 739	3c **Wisconsin Tercentenary**, 7/7/34, Green				
	Bay, WI (130,000) 1.10	1.65	15.00	20.00	
☐	DC, 7/9/34...1.00	1.10	5.75	9.50	

National Parks Issue

SCOTT NUMBER	DESCRIPTION	UNCACHETED SINGLE	UNCACHETED BLOCK	CACHETED SINGLE	CACHETED BLOCK
☐ 740	1c **Yosemite**, strip of 3, 7/16/34, Yosemite,				
	CA (60,000) 2.75	3.25	10.00	12.00	
☐	DC, (26,219)...2.25	2.75	7.00	8.00	
☐ 741	2c **Grand Canyon**, pair, 7/24/34, Grand				
	Canyon, AZ (75,000) 2.75	3.25	10.00	12.00	
☐	DC, (30,080)...2.25	2.75	7.00	8.00	
☐ 742	3c **Mt. Rainier**, 8/3/34, Longmire, WA				
	(64,500)..3.00	3.50	10.00	12.00	
☐	DC, (30,114)...2.50	3.00	7.00	8.00	
☐ 743	4c **Mesa Verde**, 9/25/34, Mesa Verde, CO				
	(51,882)..2.75	3.25	10.00	12.00	
☐	DC, (21,729)...2.25	2.75	7.00	8.00	
☐ 744	5c **Yellowstone**, 7/30/34, Yellowstone, WY				
	(87,000)..2.50	3.00	10.00	12.00	
☐	DC (32,150)..2.25	2.75	7.00	8.00	
☐ 745	6c **Crater Lake**, 9/5/34, Crater Lake, OR				
	(45,282)..3.25	3.75	10.00	12.00	
☐	DC (19,161)..3.00	3.50	7.00	8.00	
☐ 746	7c **Acadia**, 10/2/34, Bar Harbor, ME (51,312)..3.25	3.75	10.00	12.00	
☐	DC, (20,163)...3.00	3.50	7.00	8.00	
☐ 747	8c **Zion**, 9/18/34, Zion, UT (43,650) 3.75	4.25	10.00	12.00	
☐	DC (19,001) 3.25	3.75	7.00	8.00	
☐ 748	9c **Glacier Park** 8/27/34, Glacier Park, MT				
	(52,626)...3.75	4.00	10.00	12.00	
☐	1st Imperial cachet		60.00		
☐	DC (16,250) 3.50	4.00	7.00	8.00	
☐ 749	10c **Smoky Mountains**, 10/8/34,				
	Sevierville, TN (39,000) 7.50	8.50	12.50	14.00	
☐	DC (18,368) 6.00	7.00	10.00	12.50	
☐	Smokemont, TN, unofficial		25.00		
☐	Scott 740-749 with park cancels on one cover.....		150.00		
☐ 750	3c **American Philatelic Society**, imperf.				
	pane of 6, 8/28/34, Atlantic City, NJ 40.00		75.00		
☐ 750a	**American Philatelic Society**, single (40,000)...3.25	4.25	10.00	12.00	
☐	DC, 9/4/34...2.00	2.50	8.00	10.00	

782

783

784

1st Historic Art cachet

785

786

787

788

789

790

791

792

793

794

**Values for various cachet makers can be determined
by using the Cachet Calculator which begins on page 52A.**

SCOTT NUMBER	DESCRIPTION	UNCACHETED SINGLE	BLOCK	CACHETED SINGLE	BLOCK
☐ 751	1c Trans-Mississippi Philatelic Exposition, imperf. pane of 6, 10/10/34, Omaha, NE 35.00			65.00	
☐ 751a	Trans-Mississippi Philatelic Exposition, strip of 3 (125,000) 3.25		4.25	10.00	—
☐	DC, 10/15/34..2.00		2.50	6.00	—

1934 Special Printing

Nos. 752-771 issued 3/15/35.

☐ 752	3c Peace of 1783, DC...................................5.00	7.50	35.00	40.00
☐ 753	3c Byrd Antarctic, DC..................................6.00	7.50	35.00	40.00
☐ 754	3c Mothers of America, DC...........................6.00	7.50	35.00	40.00
☐ 755	3c Wisconsin Tercentenary, DC.....................6.00	7.50	35.00	40.00
☐ 756	1c Yosemite, strip of 3, DC............................6.00	7.50	35.00	40.00
☐ 757	2c Grand Canyon, pair, DC............................6.00	7.50	35.00	40.00
☐ 758	3c Mount Rainier, DC....................................6.00	7.50	35.00	40.00
☐ 759	4c Mesa Verde, DC 6.50	7.50	35.00	40.00
☐ 760	5c Yellowstone, DC..6.50	7.50	35.00	40.00
☐ 761	6c Crater Lake, DC..6.50	7.50	35.00	40.00
☐ 762	7c Acadia, DC..6.50	7.50	35.00	40.00
☐ 763	8c Zion, DC 7.50	8.00	35.00	40.00
☐ 764	9c Glacier Park, DC.......................................7.50	8.00	35.00	40.00
☐ 765	10c Smoky Mountains, DC.............................7.50	8.00	35.00	40.00
☐ 766	1c Century of Progress, imperf. pane of 25, imperf, DC...		250.00	
☐ 766a	Century of Progress, strip of 3 ....5.50	7.50	40.00	45.00
☐ 767	3c Century of Progress, imperf. pane of 25, DC		300.00	
☐ 767a	Century of Progress, single............................5.50	7.50	40.00	45.00
☐ 768	3c Byrd, imperf. pane of 6, DC............................		300.00	
☐ 768a	Byrd, single...6.50	8.50	40.00	45.00
☐ 769	1c Yosemite, imperf. pane of 6, DC......................		300.00	
☐ 769a	Yosemite, strip of 3 ....4.00	6.00	40.00	45.00
☐ 770	3c Mount Rainier, imperf. pane of 6, DC.............		300.00	
☐ 770a	Mount Rainier, single 5.00	7.00	40.00	45.00
☐ 771	16c Air Mail Special Delivery, DC.................12.50	16.00	40.00	60.00

SCOTT NUMBER	DESCRIPTION	SINGLE	BLOCK	PLATE BLOCK
☐ 772	3c Connecticut Tercentenary, 4/26/35, Hartford, CT.			
	(217,800) 15.00	16.00	18.00	
☐	DC, 4/27/35 ....1.25	1.75	2.75	
☐	1st Winfred Milton Grandy cachet 30.00			
☐ 773	3c California-Pacific Exposition, 5/29/35,			
	San Diego, CA (214,042) 15.00	16.00	18.00	
☐	DC, 5/31/35 ....1.25	1.75	2.75	
☐	1st William H. Espenshade cachet 35.00			
☐ 774	3c Boulder Dam, 9/30/35, Boulder City, NV			
	(166,180) 15.00	16.00	18.00	
☐	DC, 10/1/35 ....2.00	2.75	3.75	
☐	1st Norwood B. Scatchard cachet 75.00			
☐ 775	3c Michigan Centenary, 11/1/35, Lansing, MI			
	(176,962) 15.00	16.00	18.00	
☐	DC, 11/2/35 ....1.25	1.75	2.00	
☐	1st Risko Art Studio cachet.................... 200.00			

1st Cachet Craft cachet

1st Pilgrim cachet

1st Fidelity Stamp Co. cachet

795

796

798

797

799

800

801

802

804, 839, 848

815, 847

HOW TO USE THIS BOOK

The number in the first column is its Scott number or identifying number. Following that is the denomination of the stamp, description, date of issue, and the value.

1936

	776	3c **Texas Centennial**, 3/2/36, Gonzales, TX			
☐		(319,150) 20.00	22.00	25.00
☐		DC, 3/3/36...1.50	2.00	3.00
☐		1st John C. Sidenius cachet 75.00		
☐		1st Walter Czubay cachet......................75.00		
☐	777	3c **Rhode Island Tercentenary**, 5/4/36, Providence,			
☐		RI (245,400) 15.00	16.00	18.00
☐		DC, 5/5/36...1.25	1.75	2.75
☐		1st J.W. Clifford cachet 35.00		
☐	778	3c **TIPEX**, souvenir sheet, 5/9/36, New York, NY			
☐		(297,194) (TIPEX cancellation) 18.00		
☐		DC, 5/11/36..3.50		
☐		1st House of Farnam cachet 500.00		
☐	**778a-778d** Single from sheet.....................................5.00				
☐	782	3c **Arkansas Centennial**, 6/15/36, Little Rock, AR			
☐		(376,693)...10.00	12.00	18.00
☐		DC, 6/16/36..1.00	1.75	2.75
☐	783	3c **Oregon Territory**, 7/14/36, Astoria, OR (91,110)..8.50	9.50	15.00
☐		Daniel, WY (67,013).........................8.50	9.50	15.00
☐		Lewiston, ID (86,100)........................8.00	9.00	15.00
☐		Missoula, MT (59,883)........................8.50	9.50	15.00
☐		Walla Walla, WA (106,150) 8.00	9.00	15.00
☐		DC, 7/15/36..1.25	1.75	2.75
☐		1st Whitman Centennial Inc. cachet 35.00		
☐	784	3c **Susan B. Anthony**, 8/26/36 DC (178,500) 10.00	12.00	15.00
☐		1st Historic Art cachet......................35.00		
☐		1st Dean Aubry cachet............................30.00		

1936-37

☐	785	1c **Army**, strip of 3, 12/15/36, DC 8.00	9.00	12.00
☐	786	2c **Army**, pair, 1/15/37 ....8.00	9.00	12.00
☐	787	3c **Army**, 2/18/37, DC...8.00	9.00	12.00
☐		1st William J. Von Ohlen cachet 60.00		
☐	788	4c **Army**, 3/23/37, DC...8.00	9.00	12.00
☐	789	5c **Army**, 5/26/37, West Point, NY (160,000) 8.00	9.00	12.00
☐		DC, 5/27/37..1.25	1.75	2.75
☐		Scott 785-789 on one cover 40.00		
☐		1st Pavois cachet....................................20.00		
☐	790	1c **Navy**, strip of 3, 12/15/36, DC 8.00	9.00	12.00
☐	791	2c **Navy**, pair, 1/15/37, DC...............................8.00	9.00	12.00
☐	792	3c **Navy**, 2/18/37, DC...8.00	9.00	12.00
☐	793	4c **Navy**, 3/23/37, DC...8.00	9.00	12.00
☐	794	5c **Navy**, 5/26/37, Annapolis, MD (202,806)................8.00	9.00	12.00
☐		DC, 5/27/37..1.25	1.75	2.75
☐		Scott 790-794 on one cover 40.00		
☐		Scott 785-794 on one cover 80.00		

Covers for both 1c values total 390,749; 2c values total 292,570; 3c values total 320,888; 4c values total 331,000.
Uncacheted covers from this period sell for about 20% that of cacheted covers.

1937

☐	795	3c **Northwest Ordinance Centennial**, 7/13/37,			
		Marietta, OH (130,531) 9.00	10.00	13.00
☐		New York, NY (125,134) 9.00	10.00	13.00

835

836

837

838

1st Artcraft cachet

852

853

854

855

856

858

857

859

864

869

874

879

884

889

HOW TO USE THIS BOOK
The number in the first column is its Scott number or identifying number. Following that is the denomination of the stamp, description, date of issue, and the value.

			SINGLE	BLOCK	PLATE BLOCK
☐		DC, 7/14/37...1.20		1.75	2.75
☐		1st William S. Linto cachet 125.00			
☐		1st Cachet Craft cachet 100.00			
☐	796	5c Virginia Dare, 8/18/37, Manteo, NC (226,730)....10.00		12.00	15.00
☐		Dare, VA, unofficial................................15.00			
☐		DC, 8/19/37..1.50		2.50	3.50
☐	797	10c Society of Philatelic Americans, souvenir sheet,			
		8/26/37, Asheville, NC (164,215)............................10.00			
☐		DC, 8/28/37..1.50			
☐	798	3c Constitution Sesquicentennial, 9/17/37,			
		Philadelphia, PA (281,478)......................................10.00		12.00	14.00
☐		DC, 9/18/37..1.00		1.50	2.50
☐		1st Pilgrim cachet 100.00			
☐		1st Fidelity Stamp Co. cachet................20.00			
☐	799	3c Hawaii, 10/18/37, Honolulu, HI (320,334) 10.00		12.00	14.00
☐		DC, 10/19/37..1.00		1.50	2.50
☐	800	3c Alaska, 11/12/37, Juneau, AK (230,370).............10.00		12.00	14.00
☐		DC, 11/13/37..1.00		1.50	2.50
☐	801	3c Puerto Rico, 11/25/37, San Juan, PR (244,054)..10.00		12.00	14.00
☐		DC, 11/26/37..1.00		1.50	2.50
☐	802	3c Virgin Islands, 12/15/37, Charlotte Amalie, VI			
		(225,469)..10.00		12.00	14.00
☐		DC, 12/16/37..1.00		1.50	2.50
☐		799-802 Set of 4 on one cover 40.00		—	—

1938-54 Presidential Issue

			SINGLE	BLOCK	PLATE BLOCK
☐	803	1/2c Benjamin Franklin, block of 6, 5/19/38,			
		Philadelphia, PA (224,901)..		3.00	3.50
☐		DC, 5/20/38		1.00	1.25
☐	804	1c George Washington, strip of 3, 4/25/38, DC			
		(124,037)..3.00		3.50	6.00
☐	804b	George Washington, booklet pane of 6, 1/27/39,DC 15.00			
☐	805	1 1/2c Martha Washington, pair, 5/5/38, DC			
		(138,339)..3.00		3.50	4.00
☐	806	2c John Adams, pair, 6/3/38, DC (127,806)................2.00		2.50	4.00
☐	806b	John Adams, booklet pane of 6, 1/27/39, DC...........15.00			
☐	807	3c ThomasJefferson, 6/16/38, DC (118,097).............3.00		3.50	4.00
☐	807a	Thomas Jefferson, booklet pane of 6, 1/27/39, DC..18.00			
☐		Scott 804b, 806b, 807a on one cover, 1/27/39, DC..60.00			
☐	808	4c James Madison, 7/1/38 (118,765), DC...................3.00		4.00	5.00
☐	809	4 1/2c White House, 7/11/38, DC (115,820)................3.00		4.00	5.00
☐	810	5c James Monroe, 7/21/38, DC (98,282) 3.00		4.00	5.00
☐	811	6c John Q. Adams, 7/28/38, DC (97,428) 3.00		4.00	5.00
☐	812	7c Andrew Jackson, 8/4/38, DC (98,414)...................3.00		4.00	5.00
☐	813	8c Martin Van Buren, 8/11/38, DC (94,857) 3.00		4.00	5.00
☐	814	9c William H. Harrison, 8/18/38, DC (91,229) 3.00		4.00	5.00
☐	815	10c John Tyler, 9/2/38, DC (84,707) 3.00		4.00	5.00
☐	816	11c James K. Polk, 9/8/38, DC (63,966).....................3.00		4.00	5.00
☐	817	12c Zachary Taylor, 9/14/38, DC (62,935)..................3.00		4.00	5.00
☐	818	13c Millard Fillmore, 9/22/38, DC (58,965)...............3.00		4.00	5.00
☐	819	14c Franklin Pierce, 10/6/38, DC (49,819)................3.00		4.00	5.00
☐	820	15c James Buchanan, 10/13/38, DC (52,209) 3.00		4.00	5.00
☐	821	16c Abraham Lincoln, 10/20/38, DC (59,566)............5.00		6.00	8.00
☐	822	17c Andrew Johnson, 10/27/38, DC (55,024).............5.00		6.00	8.00

☐ 823	18c U.S. Grant, 11/3/38, DC(53,124) 5.00		6.00	8.00
☐ 824	19c Rutherford B. Hayes, 11/10/38, DC (54,124) 5.00		6.00	8.00
☐ 825	20c James A. Garfield, 11/10/38, DC (51,971)...........5.00		6.00	8.00
☐	Scott 824,825 on one cover...................................35.00			
☐ 826	21c Chester A. Arthur, 11/22/38, DC (44,367) 5.00		6.00	8.00
☐	1st Union College cachet.......................................35.00			
☐ 827	22c Grover Cleveland, 11/22/38, DC (44,358).............5.00		6.00	8.00
☐	Scott 826,827 on one cover...................................35.00			
☐ 828	24c Benjamin Harrison, 12/2/38, DC (46,592)...........5.00		6.00	8.00
☐ 829	25c William McKinley, 12/2/38, DC (45,691)..............6.00		7.50	10.00
☐	Scott 828, 829 on one cover..................................35.00			
☐ 830	30c Theodore Roosevelt, 12/8/38, DC (43,528)...........7.50		9.00	14.00
☐ 831	50c William Howard Taft, 12/8/38, DC (41,984)......10.00		12.50	20.00
☐	Scott 830, 831 on one cover 340.00			
☐ 832	$1 Woodrow Wilson, 8/29/38, DC (24,618) 65.00		70.00	80.00
☐ 832c	$1 Woodrow Wilson, dry-printed, 8/31/54, DC			
☐	(20,202) 30.00		40.00	45.00
☐ 833	$2 Warren G. Harding, 9/29/38, DC(19,895).........125.00		175.00	250.00
☐ 834	$5 Calvin Coolidge, 11/17/38, DC (15,615)............200.00		300.00	450.00
☐	803-834 Set of 32 covers, matched cachets.....................550.00		650.00	800.00

1938-42 Presidential Electric Eye Issues

☐ 803	1/2c Benjamin Franklin, block of 6, 9/8/41, DC		11.00	13.00
☐ 804	1c George Washington, strip of 3, 9/8/41, DC...........7.00		11.00	13.00
☐	Scott 803, 804, E 15 on one cover 25.00		40.00	
	Total for Scott 803, 804, and E15 Electric Eye is 22,000.			
☐ 805	1 1/2c Martha Washington, pair, 1/16/41 ....10.00		11.00	13.00
	Total for Scott 805 Electric Eye is less than 10,000.			
☐ 806	2c John Adams, pair, 6/3/38, DC, Type I.................10.00		11.00	13.00
☐ 806	2c John Adams, pair, 4/5/39, DC, Type II.................10.00		11.00	13.00
☐ 807	3c Thomas Jefferson, 4/5/39, DC............................10.00		11.00	13.00
☐	Scott 806, 807 on one cover 12.00		20.00	
	Total for Scott 806 and 807 Electric Eye is 28,500.			
☐ 808	4c James Madison, 10/28/41, DC 15.00		16.00	20.00
☐ 809	4 1/2c White House, 10/28/41, DC 15.00		16.00	20.00
☐ 810	5c James Monroe, 10/28/41, DC.............................15.00		16.00	20.00
☐ 811	6c John Q. Adams, 9/25/41, DC..............................15.00		16.00	20.00
☐ 812	7c Andrew Jackson, 10/28/41, DC...........................15.00		16.00	20.00
☐ 813	8c Martin Van Buren, 10/28/41, DC........................15.00		16.00	20.00
☐ 814	9c William H. Harrison, 10/28/41, DC.....................15.00		16.00	20.00
☐ 815	10c John Tyler, 9/25/41, DC 15.00		16.00	20.00
☐	Scott 811,815 on one cover...................................25.00		35.00	
	Total for Scott 811 and 815 Electric Eye is 7,300.			
☐ 816	11c James K. Polk, 10/8/41, DC 20.00		22.00	25.00
☐ 817	12c Zachary Taylor, 10/8/41, DC............................20.00		22.00	25.00
☐ 818	13c Millard Fillmore, 10/8/41, DC..........................20.00		22.00	25.00
☐ 819	14c Franklin Pierce, 10/8/41, DC...........................20.00		22.00	25.00
☐ 820	15c James Buchanan, 10/8/41, DC 20.00		22.00	25.00
☐	Scott 816-820 on one cover 30.00		47.50	
☐ 821	16c Abraham Lincoln, 1/7/42, DC...........................25.00		28.00	30.00
☐ 822	17c Andrew Johnson, 10/28/41, DC.........................25.00		28.00	30.00
☐	Scott 808-810, 812-814, 822 on one cover............35.00		55.00	
	Total for Scott 808-810 and 812-814, 822 Electric Eye is 16,200.			
☐ 823	18c U.S. Grant, 1/7/42, DC....................................25.00		28.00	30.00

44

SCOTT NUMBER	DESCRIPTION	SINGLE	BLOCK	PLATE BLOCK
☐ 824	19c Rutherford B. Hayes, 1/7/42, DC	25.00	28.00	30.00
☐ 825	20c James A. Garfield, 1/7/42, DC	25.00	28.00	30.00
☐	Scott 824-825 on one cover	30.00	55.00	
☐ 826	21c Chester Arthur, 1/7/42, DC	25.00	28.00	30.00
☐	Scott 821,823-826 on one cover	35.00	55.00	
☐ 827	22c Grover Cleveland, 1/28/42, DC	35.00	40.00	45.00
☐ 828	24c Benjamin H. Harrison, 1/28/42, DC	35.00	40.00	45.00
☐ 829	25c William McKinley, 1/28/42, DC	45.00	50.00	55.00
☐ 830	30c Theodore Roosevelt, 1/28/42, DC	45.00	50.00	55.00
☐ 831	50c William Howard Taft, 1/28/42, DC	50.00	55.00	60.00
☐	Scott 827-831 on one cover	75.00	85.00	

Total for Scott 827-831 Electric Eye is 6,700. These covers must have sheet selvage electric eye markings attached to stamps.

1938

		SINGLE	BLOCK	PLATE BLOCK
☐ 835	3c Constitution Ratification, 6/21/38, Philadelphia, PA (232,873)	10.00	12.00	15.00
☐	DC, 6/16/38	1.00	1.50	2.50
☐ 836	3c Swedish-Finnish Tercentenary, 6/27/38, Wilmington, DE (225,617)	10.00	12.00	15.00
☐	DC, 6/28/38	1.00	1.50	2.50
☐	1st Staehle cachet	50.00		
☐ 837	3c Northwest Territory, 7/15/38, Marietta, OH (180,170)	10.00	12.00	15.00
☐	DC, 7/16/38	1.00	1.50	2.50
☐ 838	3c Iowa Territory, 8/24/38, Des Moines, IA (209,860)	10.00	12.00	15.00
☐	DC, 8/25/38	1.00	1.50	2.50
☐	1st G.S. Purcell cachet	30.00		

SCOTT NUMBER	DESCRIPTION	SINGLE	PAIR	LINE PAIR

Perf. 10 Vertically   1939 Presidential Coils

		SINGLE	PAIR	LINE PAIR
☐ 839	1c George Washington, strip of 3, 1/20/39, DC		5.00	10.00
☐ 840	1 1/2c Martha Washington, pair, 1/20/39, DC		5.00	10.00
☐ 841	2c John Adams, pair, 1/20/39, DC		5.00	10.00
☐ 842	3c Thomas Jefferson, 1/20/39, DC	5.00	7.00	10.00
☐ 843	4c James Madison, 1/20/39, DC	5.00	7.00	10.00
☐ 844	4 1/2c White House, 1/20/39, DC	5.00	7.00	10.00
☐ 845	5c James Monroe, 1/20/39, DC	5.00	7.00	10.00
☐ 846	6c John Q. Adams, 1/20/39, DC	7.00	8.00	12.50
☐ 847	10c John Tyler, 1/20/39, DC	9.00	12.50	15.00
☐	Scott 839-847 set of 9 on one cover, 1/20/39	50.00	75.00	125.00

Perf. 10 Horizontally

☐ 848	1c George Washington, strip of 3, 1/27/39, DC		5.00	10.00
☐ 849	1 1/2c Martha Washington, pair, 1/27/39, DC		5.00	10.00
☐ 850	2c John Adams, pair, 1/27/39, DC		5.00	10.00
☐ 851	3c Thomas Jefferson, 1/27/39, DC	6.00	8.00	12.50
☐	Scott 848-851 set of 4 on one cover	30.00	40.00	60.00

1939

☐	852	3c Golden Gate International Exposition, 2/18/39, San Francisco, CA (352,165)	10.00	11.00	15.00
☐	853	3c New York World's Fair, 4/1/39, New York, NY (585,565)	10.00	11.00	15.00
☐		1st Artcraft cachet	200.00	250.00	350.00
☐		1st Artcraft cachet, Unofficial city	600.00		
☐	854	3c Washington Inauguration, 4/30/39, New York, NY (395,644)	10.00	11.00	15.00
☐	855	3c Baseball Centennial, 6/12/39, Cooperstown, NY (398,199)	40.00	50.00	65.00
☐		1st Leatherstocking Stamp Club cachet	45.00		
☐	856	3c Panama Canal, 8/15/39, USS Charleston, Canal Zone (230,974)	10.00	11.00	15.00
☐	857	3c Printing Tercentenary, 9/25/39, New York, NY (295,270)	8.00	9.00	10.00
☐		1st Ross Engraving Co. cachet	35.00		
☐		1st George Newmann cachet	35.00		
☐	858	3c 50th Anniversary of Statehood 11/2/39, Bismarck, ND, (142,106)	7.00	8.00	10.00
☐		Pierre, SD, 11/2/39 (150,429)	7.00	8.00	10.00
☐		Helena, MT, 11/8/39 (130,273)	7.00	8.00	10.00
☐		Olympia, WA, 11/11/39 (150,429)	7.00	8.00	10.00

1940 Famous Americans

☐	859	1c Washington Irving, strip of 3, 1/29/40, Tarrytown, NY (170,969)	3.00	3.50	4.00
☐	860	2c James Fenimore Cooper, pair, 1/29/40, Cooperstown, NY (154,836)	3.00	3.50	4.00
☐	861	3c Ralph Waldo Emerson, 2/5/40, Boston, MA (185,148)	3.00	3.50	4.00
☐	862	5c Louisa May Alcott, 2/5/40, Concord, MA (134,325)	3.00	3.50	4.25
☐	863	10c Samuel L. Clemens, 2/13/40, Hannibal, MO (150,492)	4.00	5.00	6.50 225.00
☐	864	1c Henry W. Longfellow, strip of 3, 2/16/40, Portland, ME (160,508)	3.00	3.50	4.00
☐	865	2c John Greenleaf Whittier, pair, 2/16/40, Haverhill, MA (148,423)	3.00	3.50	4.00
☐	866	3c James Russell Lowell, 2/20/40, Cambridge, MA	3.00	3.50	4.00
☐	867	5c Walt Whitman, 2/20/40, Camden, NJ (134,185)	4.00	5.00	7.00
☐	868	10c James Whitcomb Riley, 2/24/40, Greenfield, IN (131,760)	6.00	7.00	9.00
☐	869	1c Horace Mann, strip of 3, 3/14/40, Boston, MA (186,854)	3.00	3.50	4.00
☐	870	2c Mark Hopkins, pair, 3/14/40, Williamstown, MA (140,286)	3.00	3.50	4.00
☐	871	3c Charles W. Eliot 3/28/40, Cambridge, MA (155,708)	3.00	3.50	4.00
☐	872	5c Frances E. Willard, 3/28/40, Evanston, IL (140,483)	4.00	5.00	7.00
☐	873	10c Booker T. Washington, 4/7/40, Tuskegee Institute, AL (163,507)	6.00	7.00	9.00 150.00
☐	874	1c John James Audubon, strip of 3, 4/8/40, St. Francisville, LA (144, 123)	3.00	3.50	4.00

1st Aristocrats cachet

1st Spartan cachet

895

894

896

897

898

899

900

901

1st Fleetwood cachet

903

902

904

905

906

907

908

909

910

☐ 875 2c Dr. Crawford W. Long, pair, 4/8/40, Jefferson,
GA (158,128)...3.00 3.50 4.00 150.00

☐ 876 3c Luther Burbank, 4/17/40, Santa Rosa, CA
(147,003)...3.00 3.50 4.00

☐ 877 5c Dr. Walter Reed, 4/17/40, DC (154,464) 2.50 3.50 5.00

☐ 878 10c Jane Addams, 4/26/40, Chicago, IL
(132,375)...5.00 6.00 8.00

☐ 879 1c Stephen Collins Foster, strip of 3, 5/3/40,
Bardstown, KY (183,461)...............................3.00 3.50 4.00

☐ 1st Foster Assembly of Bardstown cachet......20.00

☐ 1st Bardstown Distillery cachet.....................20.00

☐ 880 2c John Philip Sousa, pair, 5/3/40, DC (131,422) 3.00 3.50 4.00

☐ 1st Fifth Battalion Marine Corps Reserve cachet.20.00

☐ 881 3c Victor Herbert, 5/13/40, New York, NY
(168,200)...3.00 3.50 4.00

☐ 882 5c Edward A. MacDowell, 5/13/40, Peterborough,
NH (135,155)...3.00 3.50 4.00 150.00

☐ 883 10c Ethelbert Nevin, 6/10/40, Pittsburgh, PA
(121,951)...5.00 6.00 8.00

☐ 884 1c Gilbert Charles Stuart, strip of 3, 9/5/40,
Narragansett, RI (131,965)...........................3.00 3.50 4.00

☐ 885 2c James A. McNeill Whistler, pair, 9/5/40, Lowell,
MA (130,962) 3.00 3.50 4.00

☐ 886 3c Augustus Saint-Gaudens, 9/16/40, New York,
NY (138,200)...3.00 3.50 4.00 150.00

☐ 887 5c Daniel Chester French, 9/16/40, Stockbridge,
MA (124,608) 3.00 3.50 4.00

☐ 888 10c Frederic Remington, 9/30/40, Canton, NY
(116,219)...5.00 6.00 8.00

☐ 889 1c Eli Whitney, strip of 3, 10/7/40, Savannah,
GA (140,868)...3.00 3.50 4.00

☐ 890 2c Samuel F.B. Morse, pair, 10/7/40, New York,
NY (135,388)...3.00 3.50 4.00 150.00

☐ 891 3c Cyrus Hall McCormick, 10/14/40, Lexington,
VA (137,415) 3.00 3.50 4.00

☐ 1st International Harvester cachet................20.00

☐ 892 5c Elias Howe, 10/14/40, Spencer, MA (126,334) 5.00 6.00 8.00 150.00

☐ 893 10c Alexander Graham Bell, 10/28/40, Boston, MA
(125,372)...7.50 8.50 10.00

☐ 859-893 Set of 35 covers, matched cachets ....125. 175. 250.

☐ 859-893 Set on 1 cover, 10/28/40................................175.

1940

☐ 894 3c Pony Express, 4/3/40, St. Joseph, MO (194,589)....8.00 9.00 11.00

☐ Sacramento, CA (160,849)................................8.00 9.00 11.00

☐ 1st Aristocrats cachet 25.00

☐ 895 3c Pan American Union, 4/14/40, DC (182,401).........6.00 8.00 10.00

☐ 896 3c Idaho Statehood, 7/3/40, Boise, ID (156,429) 6.00 8.00 10.00

☐ 1st Papercraft Corp. cachet 30.00

☐ 1st Scenic Craft cachet 30.00

☐ 897 3c Wyoming Statehood, 7/10/40, Cheyenne, WY
(156,709)...6.00 8.00 10.00

☐ 1st Spartan cachet...30.00

1st Smartcraft cachet

1st Pent Arts cachet

916

921

922

923

924

925

926

927

928

929

930

1st Bi-Color Craft cachet

1st Fluegel Cover cachet

934

937

☐ 898 **3c Coronado Expedition,** 9/7/40, Albuquerque, NM
(161,012)..6.00 8.00 10.00
☐   1st Albuquerque Philatelic Society cachet......20.00
☐ 899 **1c Defense, strip of 3,** 10/16/40, DC...........................6.00 8.00 10.00
☐ 900 **2c Defense, pair,** 10/16/40, DC 6.00 8.00 10.00
☐ 901 **3c Defense,** 10/16/40, DC...6.00 8.00 10.00
☐   Scott 899-901 on one cover (450,083)...........10.00 12.00 15.00
☐ 902 **3c Thirteenth Amendment,** 10/20/40, World's Fair,
NY (156,146)...8.00 9.00 10.00 150.00

1941

☐ 903 **3c Vermont Statehood,** 3/4/41, Montpelier, VT
(182,423)..8.00 9.00 10.00
☐   1st Dorothy Knapp cachet ....1500.
☐   1st Fleetwood cachet 90.00

1942

☐ 904 **3c Kentucky Statehood,** 6/1/42, Frankfort, KY
(155,730)..5.00 6.00 9.00
☐   1st Signed Fleetwood cachet 75.00
☐ 905 **3c "Win the War,"** 7/4/42, DC (191,168).....................5.00 6.00 8.00
☐ 906 **5c Chinese Commemorative,** 7/7/42, Denver, CO
(168,746)...10.00 12.00 14.00

1943

☐ 907 **2c Allied Nations, pair,** 1/14/43, DC (178,865)............5.00 5.25 7.00
☐ 908 **1c Four Freedoms, strip of 3,** 2/12/43, DC (193,800)..4.00 5.25 7.00

1943-44 Overrun Countries

☐ 909 **5c Poland,** 6/22/43, Chicago, IL (88, 170)...................5.00 6.00 15.00 110.00
☐   Washington, DC (136,002) 4.00 5.00 15.00
☐   1st Smartcraft cachet.....................................20.00
☐   1st Pent Arts cachet......................................30.00
☐   1st Polonus Philatelic Society cachet.............25.00
☐ 910 **5c Czechoslovakia,** 7/12/43, DC (145,112) 4.00 5.00 15.00
☐ 911 **5c Norway,** 7/27/43, DC (130,054)............................4.00 5.00 15.00
☐ 912 **5c Luxemboarg,** 8/10/43, DC (166,367) 4.00 5.00 15.00
☐ 913 **5c Netherlands,** 8/24/43, DC (148,763) 4.00 5.00 15.00
☐ 914 **5c Belgium,** 9/14/43, DC (154,220)............................4.00 5.00 15.00
☐ 915 **5c France,** 9/28/43, DC (163,478)..............................4.00 5.00 15.00
☐ 916 **5c Greece,** 10/12/43, DC (166,553)............................4.00 5.00 15.00
☐ 917 **5c Yugoslavia,** 10/26/43, DC (161,835).......................4.00 5.00 15.00
☐ 918 **5c Albania,** 11/9/43, DC (162,275)..............................4.00 5.00 15.00
☐ 919 **5c Austria,** 11/23/43, DC (172,285) 4.00 5.00 15.00
☐ 920 **5c Denmark,** 12/7/43, DC (173,784)...........................4.00 5.00 15.00
☐   Scott 909-920 on one cover 65.00
☐ 921 **5c Korea,** 11/2/44, DC (192,860) 5.00 6.00 11.00
☐   Scott 909-921 on one cover 85.00

935

936

938

939

940

941

942

1st Artmaster cachet

1st WCO cachet

943

944

946

945

947

948

949

950

951

**Values for various cachet makers can be determined
by using the Cachet Calculator which begins on page 52A.**

1st Fulton cachet

1st C. W. George cachet

953

1st Jackson cachet

952

954

955

956

957

958

959

960

961

962

963

964

965

966

**Values for various cachet makers can be determined
by using the Cachet Calculator which begins on page 52A.**

1944

			SINGLE	BLOCK	PLATE BLOCK	CERM PROG
☐	922	3c Transcontinental Railroad, 5/10/44, Ogden, UT (151,324)	8.00	8.50	9.00	
☐		Omaha, NE (171,000)	8.00	8.50	9.00	
☐		San Francisco,CA (125,000)	8.00	8.50	9.00	
☐	923	3c Steamship, 5/22/44, Kings Point, NY (152,324)	8.00	8.50	9.00	
☐		Savannah, GA (181,472)	8.00	8.50	9.00	
☐	924	3c Telegraph, 5/24/44, DC (141,907)	8.00	8.50	9.00	
☐		Baltimore, MD (136,480)	8.00	8.50	9.00	
☐	925	3c Philippines, 9/27/44 (214,865), DC	8.00	8.50	9.00	
☐		1st Hobby Life cachet	35.00			
☐	926	3c Motion Picture, 10/31/44, Los Angeles, Hollywood Sta., CA (190,660)	8.00	8.50	9.00	
☐		New York, NY (176,473)	8.00	8.50	9.00	

1945

			SINGLE	BLOCK	PLATE BLOCK	CERM PROG
☐	927	3c Florida Statehood, 3/3/45, Tallahassee, FL (228,435)	8.00	8.50	9.00	
☐	928	5c United Nations Conference, 4/25/45, San Francisco, CA (417,450)	8.00	9.00	15.00	
☐	929	3c Iwo Jima (Marines), 7/11/45, DC (391,650)	15.00	16.00	18.00	
☐		1st Nu-Art cachet	30.00			

1945-46

			SINGLE	BLOCK	PLATE BLOCK	CERM PROG
☐	930	1c Franklin D. Roosevelt, strip of 3, 7/26/45, Hyde Park, NY (390,219)	3.00	3.50	5.50	
☐		1st Bi-Color Croft cachet	25.00			
☐	931	2c Franklin D. Roosevelt pair, 8/24/45, Warm Springs, GA (426,142)	3.00	3.50	5.50	
☐	932	3c Franklin D. Roosevelt, 6/27/45, DC (391,650)	3.00	3.50	5.50	
☐		1st Fluegel Covers cachet	75.00			
☐	933	5c Franklin D. Roosevelt, 1/30/46, DC (466,766)	3.00	3.50	5.00	
☐		Scott 930-933 on one cover	8.00			
☐	934	3c Army, 9/28/45, DC (392,300)	8.00	9.00	15.00	
☐		1st R. Lee Southworth cachet	40.00			
☐	935	3c Navy, 10/27/45, Annapolis, MD (460,352)	8.00	9.00	15.00	
☐	936	3c Coast Guard, 11/10/45, New York, NY (405,280)	7.00	8.00	9.00	110.00
☐	937	3c Alfred E. Smith, 11/26/45, New York, NY (424,950)	3.00	3.50	6.00	100.00
☐	938	3c Texas Statehood, 12/29/45, Austin, TX (397,860)	5.00	6.00	8.00	

1946

			SINGLE	BLOCK	PLATE BLOCK	CERM PROG
☐	939	3c Merchant Marine, 2/26/46, DC (432,141)	7.00	8.00	9.00	
☐		Scott 929, 934-936, 939 on one cover, 2/26/46.	30.00			
☐	940	3c Veterans of World War II, 5/9/46, DC (492,786)	7.00	8.00	9.00	
☐		1st Artmaster cachet	20.00			
☐		1st WCO cachet	30.00			
☐		Scott 929, 934-936, 939-940 on one cover,	35.00			
☐	941	3c Tennessee Statehood, 6/1/46, Nashville, TN (463,512)	3.00	3.25	3.50	
☐	942	3c Iowa Statehood, 8/3/46, Iowa City, IA (517,505)	3.00	3.25	3.50	90.00
☐		1st Iowa City Stamp Club cachet	25.00			

☐ 943	3c **Smithsonian Institution**, 8/10/46, DC (402,448) .3.00		3.25	3.50	
☐	1st Z-Special cachet...30.00				
☐ 944	3c **Kearny Expedition**, 10/16/46, Santa Fe, NM				
	(384,300)..3.00		3.25	3.50	90.00

1947

☐ 945	3c **Thomas A. Edison**, 2/11/47, Milan, OH				
	(632,473)..4.00		4.25	5.00	75.00
☐	1st Dorn's Wines cachet.......................................20.00				
☐ 946	3c **Joseph Pulitzer**, 4/10/47, New York, NY				
	(580,870)..2.00		2.50	3.50	85.00
☐ 947	3c **Postage Stamp Centenary**, 5/17/47, New York,				
	NY (712,873)..2.00		2.50	3.50	
☐	1st Fulton cachet 30.00				
☐ 948	5c & 10c **CIPEX**, souvenir sheet, 5/19/47, New				
	York, NY (502,175) 5.00				
☐ 949	3c **Doctors**, 6/9/47, Atlantic City, NJ (508,016) 8.00		9.00	15.00	
☐ 950	3c **Utah**, 7/24/47, Salt Lake City, UT (456,416) 3.00		3.50	4.00	75.00
☐ 951	3c **U.S. Frigate Constitution**, 10/21/47, Boston,				
	MA (683,416) 4.00		5.00	6.00	85.00
☐	1st C.W. George cachet 70.00				
☐	1st Sun Craft cachet 25.00				
☐ 952	3c **Everglades National Park**, 12/5/47, Florida				
	City, FL.. 3.00		3.25	3.50	75.00
☐	1st Artist Craft cachet...20.00				
☐	1st Miami Philatelic Society cachet 20.00				

1948

☐ 953	3c **George Washington Carver**, 1/5/48, Tuskegee				
	Institute, AL (402,179)..3.00		3.25	3.50	80.00
☐	1st Ira Bennett cachet 60.00				
☐	1st Jackson cachet...40.00				
☐ 954	3c **California Gold Centennial**, 1/24/48, Coloma,				
	CA (526,154) 3.00		3.25	3.50	
☐ 955	3c **Mississippi Territory**, 4/7/48, Natchez, MS				
	(434,804)..3.00		3.25	3.50	
☐ 956	3c **Four Chaplains**, 5/28/48, DC (459,070) 3.00		3.25	3.50	
☐ 957	3c **Wisconsin Statehood**, 5/29/48, Madison, WI				
	(470,280)..3.00		3.25	3.50	70.00
☐	1st Halpert cachet..20.00				
☐	1st Pearson cachet...20.00				
☐ 958	5c **Swedish Pioneers**, 6/4/48, Chicago, IL (364,318) 3.00		3.25	3.50	65.00
☐	1st American Institute of Swedish Arts,				
	Literature & Science cachet...........................20.00				
☐ 959	3c **Progress of Women**, 7/19/48, Seneca Falls, NY				
	(401,923)..3.00		3.25	3.50	
☐ 960	3c **William Allen White**, 7/31/48, Emporia, KS				
	(385,648)..3.00		3.25	3.50	
☐ 961	3c **U.S.-Canada Friendship**, 8/2/48, Niagara				
	Falls, NY (406,467) 3.00		3.25	3.50	70.00
☐ 962	3c **Francis Scott Key**, 8/9/48, Frederick,MD, (505,930)3.00		3.25	3.50	50.00
☐ 963	3c **Salute to Youth**, 8/11/48, DC (347,070)...............3.00		3.25	3.50	
☐ 964	3c **Oregon Territory**, 8/14/48, Oregon City, OR				
	(365,898)..3.00		3.25	3.50	65.00

		SINGLE	BLOCK	PLATE BLOCK	CERM PROG
☐ 965	3c Harlan Fiske Stone, 8/25/48, Chesterfield, NH (362,170)............3.00		3.25	3.50	
☐ 966	3c Palomar Mountain Observatory, 8/30/48, Palomar Mountain,CA (401,365) 3.00		3.25	3.50	75.00
☐ 967	3c Clara Barton, 9/7/48, Oxford, MA (362,000)...... 3.00		3.25	3.50	50.00
☐ 968	3c Poultry Industry, 9/9/48, New Haven, CT (475,000)............3.00		3.25	3.50	60.00
☐ 969	3c Gold Star Mothers, 9/21/48, DC (386,064)..........3.00		3.25	3.50	
☐ 970	3c Fort Kearny, 9/22/48, Minden, NE (429,633) 3.00		3.25	3.50	45.00
☐ 971	3c Volunteer Firemen, 10/4/48, Dover, DE (399,630) (2 types)* 8.00		9.00	12.00	70.00*
☐	1st Mack (Mack Trucks) cachet 25.00				
☐ 972	3c Indian Centennial, 10/15/48, Muskogee, OK (459,528)............3.00		3.25	3.50	
☐ 973	3c Rough Riders, 10/27/48, Prescott, AZ (399,198).3.00		3.25	3.50	
☐ 974	3c Juliette Low, 10/29/48, Savannah, GA (476,573) 3.00		3.25	3.50	
☐ 975	3c Will Rogers, 11/4/48, Claremore, OK (450,350) ..3.00		3.25	3.50	
☐	1st Kolor Kover cachet 125.00				
☐ 976	3c Fort Bliss, 11/5/48, El Paso, TX (421,000) 3.00		3.25	3.50	75.00
☐	1st El Paso Stamp Club cachet 20.00				
☐ 977	3c Moina Michael, 11/9/48, Athens, GA (374,090)...3.00		3.25	3.50	
☐ 978	3c Gettysburg Address, 11/19/48, Gettysburg, PA (511,990)............3.00		3.25	3.50	65.00
☐ 979	3c American Turners, 11/20/48, Cincinnati, OH (434,090)............3.00		3.25	3.50	60.00
☐	1st AmericanTurners cachet,11/21/48,Wash.DC15.00				
☐ 980	3c Joel Chandler Harris, 12/9/48, Eatonton, GA (426,199) 3.00		3.25	3.50	

1949

		SINGLE	BLOCK	PLATE BLOCK	CERM PROG
☐ 981	3c Minnesota Territory, 3/3/49, St. Paul, MN (458,750)............2.00		2.25	3.00	50.00
☐ 982	3c Washington and Lee University, 4/12/49, Lexington, VA (447,910) 2.00		2.25	3.00	50.00
☐ 983	3c Puerto Rico Election, 4/27/49, San Juan, PR (390,416)............2.00		2.25	3.00	
☐ 984	3c Annapolis Tercentenary, 5/23/49, Annapolis, MD (441,802)............2.00		2.25	3.00	50.00
☐ 985	3c G.A.R., 8/29/49, Indianapolis, IN (471,696) 2.00		2.25	3.00	50.00
☐ 986	3c Edgar Allan Poe, 10/7/49, Richmond, VA (371,020)............2.00		2.25	3.00	55.00

1950

		SINGLE	BLOCK	PLATE BLOCK	CERM PROG
☐ 987	3c Bankers, 1/3/50, Saratoga Springs, NY (388,622)..2.00		2.25	3.00	50.00
☐ 988	3c Samuel Gompers, 1/27/50, DC (332,023) 2.00		2.25	3.00	
☐ 989	3c National Capital Sesquicentennial (Freedom), 4/20/50, DC (371,743) 2.00		2.25	2.75	
☐ 990	3c National Capital Sesquicentennial (Executive), 6/12/50, DC (376,789)............2.00		2.25	2.75	55.00
☐ 991	3c National Capital Sesquicentennial (Judicial), 8/2/50, DC (324,007)............2.00		2.25	2.75	
☐ 992	3c National Capital Sesquicentennial (Legislative), 11/22/50, DC (352,215)............2.00		2.25	2.75	
☐	989-992 on one cover 6.00				

967

968

969

970

971

972

973

974

975

976

977

978

979

980

981

982

983

984

985

986

987

988

989

SCOTT NUMBER	DESCRIPTION	SINGLE	BLOCK	PLATE BLOCK	CERM PROG
☐ 993	3c Railroad Engineers, 4/29/50, Jackson, TN				
	(420,830)........................6.00		7.00	8.00	55.00
☐ 994	3c Kansas City Centenary, 6/3/50, Kansas City, MO				
	(405,390)........................2.00		2.25	2.75	40.00
☐ 995	3c Boy Scouts, 6/30/50, Valley Forge, PA (622,972).5.00		6.00	8.00	45.00
☐	1st Boy Scouts of America cachet................25.00				
☐ 996	3c Indiana Territory, 7/4/50, Vincennes, IN				
	(359,643)........................2.00		2.25	2.75	40.00
☐ 997	3c California Statehood, 9/9/50, Sacramento, CA				
	(391,919)........................2.00		2.25	2.75	

1951

SCOTT NUMBER	DESCRIPTION	SINGLE	BLOCK	PLATE BLOCK	CERM PROG
☐ 998	3c United Confederate Veterans, 5/30/51,				
	Norfolk, VA (374,235) 2.00		2.25	2.75	4(
☐	1st Dietz Printing Co. cachet 30.00				
☐ 999	3c Nevada Centennial, 7/14/51, Genoa, NV				
	(336,890) (2 types)* 2.00		2.25		2.75 30.00*
☐ 1000	3c Landing of Cadillac, 7/24/51, Detroit, MI				
	(323,094)........................2.00		2.25	2.75	35.00
☐ 1001	3c Colorado Statehood, 8/1/51, Minturn, CO				
	(311,568) 2.00		2.25	2.75	30.00
☐ 1002	3c American Chemical Society, 9/4/51, New York,				
	NY (436,419)........................2.00		2.25	2.75	30.00
☐ 1003	3c Battle of Brooklyn, 12/10/51, Brooklyn, NY				
	(420,000)........................2.00		2.25	2.75	35.00
☐	1st Velvatone cachet 100.00				

1952

SCOTT NUMBER	DESCRIPTION	SINGLE	BLOCK	PLATE BLOCK	CERM PROG
☐ 1004	3c Betsy Ross, 1/2/52, Philadelphia, PA (314,312)...2.00		2.25	2.75	30.00
☐	1st Knoble/Bogert cachet................75.00				
☐	1st Steelcraft cachet 30.00				
☐ 1005	3c 4-H Clubs, 1/15/52, Springfield, OH (383,290) ...2.00		2.25	2.75	20.00
☐ 1006	3c B. & O. Railroad, 2/28/52, Baltimore, MD				
	(441,600)........................4.00		4.25	4.50	35.00
☐	1st M.W. Beck cachet........................20.00				
☐	1st T. Raquere cachet........................20.00				
☐ 1007	3c American Automobile Association, 3/4/52,				
	Chicago, IL (520, 123)........................2.00		2.25	2.75	30.00
☐	1st American Automobile Association cachet 15.00				
☐ 1008	3c NATO, 4/4/52, DC (313,518)................2.00		2.25	2.75	
☐ 1009	3c Grand Coulee Dam, 5/15/52, Grand Coulee,				
	WA (341,680)........................2.00		2.25	2.75	30.00
☐ 1010	3c Lafayette, 6/13/52, Georgetown, SC (349,102)....2.00		2.25	2.75	30.00
☐ 1011	3c Mt. Rushmore Memorial, 8/11/52, Keystone,				
	SD (337,027) 2.00		2.25	2.75	30.00
☐ 1012	3c Engineering Centennial, 9/6/52, Chicago, IL				
	(318,483) 2.00		2.25	2.75	30.00
☐ 1013	3c Service Women, 9/11/52, DC (308,062)...............2.00		2.25	2.75	
☐ 1014	3c Gutenberg Bible, 9/30/52, DC (387,078)..............2.00		2.25	2.75	45.00
☐ 1015	3c Newspaper Boys, 10/4/52, Philadelphia, PA				
	(626,000) (2 types)* 2.00		2.25		2.75 30.00*
☐ 1016	3c Red Cross, 11/21/52, New York, NY (439,252) ...4.00		5.00	8.00	25.00

990

991

992

993

994

995

996

997

998

999

1000

1001

1002

1003

1004

Values for various cachet makers can be determined by using the Cachet Calculator which begins on page 52A.

61

1st Velvatone cachet

1005

1006

1007

1008

1009

1010

1012

1011

1013

1014

1015

1016

1017

HOW TO USE THIS BOOK
The number in the first column is its Scott number or identifying number. Following that is the denomination of the stamp, description, date of issue, and the value.

1953

☐ 1017	3c **National Guard,** 2/23/53, DC (387,618)...............2.00	2.25	2.75	30.00
☐ 1018	3c **Ohio Sesquicentennial,** 3/2/53, Chillicothe, OH			
	(407,983)...2.00	2.25	2.75	25.00
☐	1st Boerger cachet..25.00			
☐ 1019	3c **Washington Territory,** 3/2/53, Olympia, WA			
	(344,047)...2.00	2.25	2.75	40.00
☐	1st Tacoma Stamp Club cachet.....................20.00			
	1st Washington Territorial Centennial			
☐	Commission cachet 15.00			
☐ 1020	3c **Louisiana Purchase,** 4/30/53, St. Louis, MO			
	(425,600)...2.00	2.25	2.75	30.00
☐ 1021	5c **Opening of Japan Centennial,** 7/14/53, DC			
	(320,541)...2.00	2.25	2.75	30.00
☐	1st Overseas Mailers cachet 70.00			
☐ 1022	3c **American Bar Association,** 8/24/53, Boston,			
	MA (410,036)...5.00	6.00	8.00	25.00
☐ 1023	3c **Sagamore Hill,** 9/14/53, Oyster Bay, NY			
	(379,750)...2.00	2.25	2.75	30.00
☐ 1024	3c **Future Farmers,** 10/13/53, Kansas City, MO			
	(424,193)...2.00	2.25	2.75	25.00
☐ 1025	3c **Trucking Industry,** 10/27/53, Los Angeles, CA			
	(875,021)...2.00	2.25	2.75	25.00
☐ 1026	3c **General Patton,** 11/11/53, Fort Knox, KY			
	(342,000)...2.00	2.25	2.75	100.00
☐	1st World Wars Tank Corps Assoc. cachet 15.00			
☐ 1027	3c **New York City,** 11/20/53, New York, NY			
	(387,914)...2.00	2.25	2.75	25.00
☐ 1028	3c **Gadsden Purchase,** 12/30/53, Tucson, AZ			
	(363,250)...2.00	2.25	2.75	25.00

1954

☐ 1029	3c **Columbia University,** 1/4/54, New York, NY			
	(550,745)...2.00	2.25	2.75	35.00

1954-68 Liberty Issue

☐ 1030	1/2c **Benjamin Franklin,** block of 6, 10/20/55, DC			
	(223,122)...	1.00	1.25	30.00
☐ 1031	1c **George Washington,** strip of 3, 8/26/54,			
	Chicago, IL (272,581)...................................1.00	1.00	1.50	30.00
☐ 1031A	1 1/4c **Palace of the Governors,** strip of 3,			
	6/17/60, Santa Fe, NM 1.00	1.00	1.50	15.00
☐	1031A and 1054A on one cover 1.50			
	Total for Scott 1031A and 1054A is 501,848.			
☐ 1032	1 1/2c **Mount Vernon,** pair, 2/22/56, Mount			
	Vernon, VA (270,109)...................................1.00	1.25	1.50	40.00
☐ 1033	2c **Thomas Jefferson,** pair, 9/15/54, San			
	Francisco, CA (307,300) 1.00	1.25	1.50	30.00
☐ 1034	2 1/2c **Bunker Hill Monument,** pair, 6/17/59,			
	Boston, MA (315,060) 1.00	1.25	1.50	20.00
☐ 1035	3c **Statue of Liberty,** 6/24/54, Albany, NY (340,001)1.00	1.25	1.50	
	(2 types)*...			35.00*
☐ 1035a	**Statue of Liberty,** booklet pane of 6, 6/30/54, DC			
	(131,839)..5.00			
☐ 1035b	**Statue of Liberty,** tagged, 7/6/66, DC....................30.00			

1st Boerger cachet

1st Overseas Mailers cachet

1018

1019

1020

1021

1022

1023

1024

1025

1026

1027

1028

1029

1031, 1054

1033, 1055

1036, 1058

1060

**Values for various cachet makers can be determined
by using the Cachet Calculator which begins on page 52A.**

☐ 1036	4c Abraham Lincoln, 11/19/54, New York, NY			
	(374,064) (2 types)* 1.00	1.25	1.50	35.00*
☐ 1036a	Abraham Lincoln, booklet pane of 6, 7/31/58,			
	Wheeling, WV (135,825) 4.00			
☐ 1036b	Abraham Lincoln, tagged, DC (500)....................100.00			
☐ 1037	4 1/2c The Hermitage, 3/16/59, Hermitage, TN			
	(320,000)...1.00	1.25	1.50	35.00
☐ 1038	5c James Monroe, 12/2/54, Fredericksburg, VA			
	(255,650)...1.00	1.25	1.50	25.00
☐ 1039	6c Theodore Roosevelt 11/18/55, New York, NY			
	(257,551) (3 types)* 1.00	1.25	1.50	25.00*
☐ 1040	7c Woodrow Wilson, 1/10/56, Staunton, VA			
	(200,111) (2 types)* 1.00	1.25	1.50	20.00*
☐ 1041	8c Statue of Liberty, (flat plate),4/9/54, DC (340,077)1.00	1.25	1.50	20.00
☐ 1041B	8c Statue of Liberty (rotary), 4/9/54, DC 1.00	1.25	1.50	
☐ 1042	8c Statue of Liberty, (Giori press), 3/22/58,			
	Cleveland, OH, (223,899) (4 types)*..................1.00	1.25	2.00	15.00*
	1st Cascade cachet...35.00			
☐ 1042A	8c John J. Pershing, 11/17/61, New York, NY			
	(321,031)...1.00	1.25	2.00	15.00
☐ 1043	9c The Alamo, 6/14/56, San Antonio, TX			
	(207,086)...1.50	2.00	3.00	50.00
☐ 1044	10c Independence Hall, 7/4/56, Philadelphia, PA			
	(220,930)...1.00	1.25	2.00	25.00
☐ 1044b	Independence Hall, tagged, 7/6/66, DC................30.00			
☐ 1044A	11c Statue of Liberty, 6/15/61, DC (238,905)...........1.00	1.25	2.00	22.00
☐ 1044c	Statue of Liberty, tagged, 1/11/67, DC 30.00			
☐ 1045	12c Benjamin Harrison, 6/6/59, Oxford, OH			
	(225,869)...1.00	1.25	2.00	25.00
☐ 1045a	Benjamin Harrison, tagged, 5/6/68.....................30.00			
☐ 1046	15c John Jay, 12/12/58, DC (205,680).....................1.00	1.50	2.00	
☐ 1046a	John Jay, tagged, 7/6/66, DC 35.00			
☐ 1047	20c Monticello, 4/13/56, Charlottesville, VA			
	(147,860) (2 types)* 1.20	1.75	2.50	25.00*
☐ 1048	25c Paul Revere, 4/18/58, Boston, MA (196,530)			
	(2 types)*..1.30	2.00	2.50	40.00*
☐ 1049	30c Robert E. Lee, 9/21/55, Norfolk, VA			
	(120, 166) (2 types)* 1.50	2.25	2.75	35.00*
☐ 1050	40c John Marshall, 9/24/55, Richmond, VA			
	(113,972)...2.00	2.50	3.00	55.00
☐ 1051	50c Susan B. Anthony, 8/25/55, Louisville, KY			
	(110,220)...6.00	10.00	12.50	45.00
☐ 1052	$1 Patrick Henry, 10/7/55, Joplin, MO (80,191) ...10.00	15.00	25.00	70.00
☐ 1053	$5 Alexander Hamilton, 3/19/56, Paterson, NJ			
	(34,272)...50.00	90.00	125.00	100.00

| SCOTT | | | LINE | CERM |
| NUMBER | DESCRIPTION | SINGLE | PAIR | PAIR PROG |

1954-73 Liberty Coils

☐ 1054	1c George Washington, strip of 3, 10/8/54,			
	Baltimore, MD (196,318) (2 types)*.......................	1.00	1.50	25.00*
☐ 1054A	1 1/4c Palace of the Governors, strip of 3,			
	6/17/60, Santa Fe, NM	1.00	1.75	15.00
☐ 1055	2c Thomas Jefferson, 10/22/54, St. Louis, MO			
	(162,050)...	1.00	1.50	45.00

1st Cascade cachet

1061

1062

1063

1065

1066

1064

1067

1068

1069

1070

1071

1072

1073

1074

1076

1080

1077

1078

1082

66

SCOTT NUMBER	DESCRIPTION	SINGLE	PAIR	LINE PAIR	CERM PROG
☐ 1055a	Thomas Jefferson, tagged, pair, 5/6/68, DC............		20.00		
☐ 1056	2 1/2c Bunker Hill, 9/9/59, Los Angeles, CA				
	(198,680)		2.00	3.00	35.00
☐ 1057	3c Statue of Liberty, 7/20/54, DC (137,139)............1.00		1.00	1.75	
☐ 1058	4c Abraham Lincoln, 7/31/58, Mandan, ND				
	(184,079)..1.00		1.00	1.75	
☐ 1059	4 1/2c The Hermitage, 5/1/59, Denver, CO				
	(202,454)..1.75		2.00	3.00	
☐ 1059A	25c Paul Revere, 2/25/65, Wheaton, MD				
	(184,954)..1.75		2.00	3.00	
☐ 1059b	Paul Revere, tagged, 4/3/73, New York, NY...........30.00				

SCOTT NUMBER	DESCRIPTION	SINGLE	BLOCK	PLATE BLOCK	CERM PROG

1954

SCOTT NUMBER	DESCRIPTION	SINGLE	BLOCK	PLATE BLOCK	CERM PROG
☐ 1060	3c Nebraska Territory, 5/7/54, Nebraska City,				
	(401,015)..1.75		1.85	2.00	25.00
☐ 1061	3e Kansas Territory, 5/31/54, Fort Leavenworth,				
	KS (349,145) 1.75		1.85	2.00	25.00
☐ 1062	3c George Eastman, 7/12/54, Rochester, NY				
	(630,448)..1.75		1.85	2.00	30.00
☐ 1063	3c Lewis & Clark Expedition, 7/28/54, Sioux City,				
	IA (371,557) 1.75		1.85	2.00	25.00

1955

SCOTT NUMBER	DESCRIPTION	SINGLE	BLOCK	PLATE BLOCK	CERM PROG
☐ 1064	3c Pennsylvania Academy of Fine Arts, 1/15/55				
	Philadelphia, PA (307,040) 1.75		1.85	2.00	20.00
☐ 1065	3c Land Grant Colleges, 2/12/55, East Lansing,				
	(419,241)..1.75		1.85	2.00	15.00
☐ 1066	8c Rotary International, 2/23/55, Chicago, IL				
	(350,625)..1.75		2.00	3.00	50.00
☐ 1067	3c Armed Forces Reserve, 5/21/55, DC (300,436)...2.00		2.25	3.00	20.00
☐ 1068	3c New Hampshire, 6/21/55, Franconia, NH				
	(330,630)..1.00		1.10	1.50	18.00
☐	1st Texture Craft cachet 35.00				
☐ 1069	3c Soo Locks, 6/28/55, Sault Sainte Marie, MI				
	(316,616)..1.75		1.85	2.00	55.00
☐ 1070	3c Atoms for Peace, 7/28/55, DC (351,940)............1.75		1.85	2.00	
☐ 1071	3c Fort Ticonderoga, 9/18/55, Fort Ticonderoga,				
	NY (342,946)..1.75		1.85	2.00	20.00
☐ 1072	3c Andrew Mellon, 12/20/55, DC (278,897)............1.75		1.85	2.00	18.00

1956

SCOTT NUMBER	DESCRIPTION	SINGLE	BLOCK	PLATE BLOCK	CERM PROG
☐ 1073	3c Benjamin Franklin, 1/17/56, Philadelphia, PA				
	(351,260)..1.75		1.85	2.00	30.00
☐	Poor Richard Station.....................................1.75		1.85	2.00	
☐ 1074	3c Booker T. Washington, 4/5/56, Booker T.				
	Washington Birthplace, VA (272,659)...............1.75		1.85	2.00	35.00
☐ 1075	3c & 8c FIPEX, Souvenir Sheet, 4/28/56,				
	New York, NY (429,327) 5.00				35.00
☐ 1076	3c FIPEX, 4/30/56, New York, NY, (526,090)...........1.75		1.85	2.00	35.00
☐ 1077	3c Wildlife Conservation (Turkey), 5/5/56, Fond				
	du Lac, WI (292,121) 1.75		1.85	2.00	25.00

SCOTT NUMBER	DESCRIPTION	SINGLE	PLATE BLOCK	CERM BLOCK	PROG
☐ 1078	3c Wildlife Conservation (Antelope), 6/22/56, Gunnison, CO (294,731)	1.75	1.85	2.00	25.00
☐ 1079	3c Wildlife Conservation (Salmon), 11/9/56, Seattle, WA (346,800)	1.75	1.85	2.00	25.00
☐ 1080	3c Pure Food and Drug Laws, 6/27/56, DC (411,761)	1.75	1.85	2.00	18.00
☐ 1081	3c Wheatland, 8/5/56, Lancaster, PA (340,142)	1.75	1.85	2.00	18.00
☐ 1082	3c Labor Day, 9/3/56, Camden, NJ (338,450)	1.75	1.85	2.00	25.00
☐ 1083	3c Nassau Hall, 9/22/56, Princeton, NJ (350,756)	1.75	1.85	2.00	22.00
☐ 1084	3c Devils Tower, 9/24/56, Devils Tower, WY (285,090)	1.75	1.85	2.00	30.00
☐ 1085	3c Children, 12/15/56, DC (305,125)	1.75	1.85	2.00	22.00

1957

☐ 1086	3c Alexander Hamilton, 1/11/57, New York, NY (305,117)	1.75	1.85	2.00	40.00
☐ 1087	3c Polio, 1/15/57, DC (307,630)	2.00	2.25	2.75	20.00
☐ 1088	3c Coast & Geodetic Survey, 2/11/57, Seattle, WA (309,931)	1.75	1.85	2.00	15.00
☐ 1089	3c Architects, 2/23/57, New York, NY (368,840)	1.75	1.85	2.00	15.00
☐ 1090	3c Steel Industry, 5/22/57, New York, NY (473,284)	1.75	1.85	2.00	30.00
☐ 1091	3c International Naval Review, 6/10/57, U.S.S. Saratoga, Norfolk, VA (365,933) (2 types)*	1.75	1.85	2.00	15.00*
☐ 1092	3c Oklahoma Statehood, 6/14/57, Oklahoma City, OK (327,172)	1.75	1.85	2.00	18.00
☐ 1093	3c School Teachers, 7/1/57, Philadelphia, PA (375,986)	1.75	1.85	2.00	30.00
☐	"Philadelpia" error cancel	8.00	10.00		
☐ 1094	4c Flag, 7/4/57, DC (523,879)	1.75	1.85	2.00	
☐ 1095	3c Shipbuilding, 8/15/57, Bath, ME (347,432)	1.75	1.85	2.00	10.00
☐ 1096	8c Ramon Magsaysay, 8/31/57, DC (334,558)	1.75	1.85	2.00	20.00
☐ 1097	3c Lafayette Bicentenary, 9/6/57, Easton, PA (260,421) (3 types)*	1.75	1.85	2.00	25.00*
	Fayetteville, NC (230,000)	1.75	1.85	2.00	
	Louisville, KY (207,856)	1.75	1.85	2.00	
☐ 1098	3c Wildlife Conservation (Whooping Cranes), 11/22/57, New York, NY (342,970) (2 types)*	1.75	1.85	2.00	20.00*
	New Orleans, LA (154,327)	1.75	1.85	2.00	
	Corpus Christi, TX (280,990)	1.75	1.85	2.00	
☐ 1099	3c Religious Freedom, 12/27/57, Flushing NY (357,770)	1.75	1.85	2.00	12.00

1958

☐ 1100	3c Gardening-Horticulture, 3/15/58, Ithaca, NY (451,292)	1.75	1.85	2.00	25.00
☐ 1104	3c Brussels Fair, 4/17/58, Detroit, MI (428,073)	1.75	1.85	2.00	22.00
☐ 1105	3c James Monroe, 4/28/58, Montross, VA (326,988)	1.75	1.85	2.00	20.00
☐ 1106	3c Minnesota Statehood, 5/11/58, Saint Paul, MN (475,522)	1.75	1.85	2.00	25.00
☐ 1107	3c International Geophysical Year, 5/31/58, Chicago, IL (397,000)	1.75	1.85	2.00	18.00
☐ 1108	3c Gunston Hall, 6/12/58, Lorton, VA (349,801)	1.75	1.85	2.00	
☐ 1109	3c Mackinac Bridge, 6/25/58, Mackinac Bridge, MI (445,605), no cancel	1.75	1.85	2.00	45.00

SCOTT NUMBER	DESCRIPTION	SINGLE	BLOCK	PLATE BLOCK	CERM PROG
☐ 1110	4c Simon Bolivar, 7/24/58, DC........................1.75		1.85	2.00	
☐ 1111	8c Simon Bolivar, 7/24/58, DC........................1.75		1.85	2.00	
☐	Scott 1110-1111 on one cover 2.00				50.00
	Total for Scott 1110-1111 is 708,777.				
☐ 1112	4c Atlantic Cable, 8/15/58, New York, NY (365,072)1.75		1.85	2.00	25.00

1958-59

☐ 1113	1c Lincoln Sesquicentennial, 2/12/59, Hodgenville,				
	KY (379,862)..		1.00	1.50	20.00
☐ 1114	3c Lincoln Sesquicentennial, pair, 2/27/59, New				
	York, NY (437,737) 1.75		1.85	2.00	20.00
☐ 1115	4c Lincoln-Douglas Debates, 8/27/58, Freeport, IL				
	(373,063)...1.75		1.85	2.00	20.00
☐	1st Western Cachets cachet...........................25.00				
☐ 1116	4c Lincoln Sesquicentennial, 5/30/59, DC				
	(894,887)..1.75		1.85	2.00	20.00
☐	Scott 1113-16 on one cover 5.00				

1958

☐ 1117	4c Lajos Kossnth, 9/19/58, DC 1.75		1.85	2.00	
☐ 1118	8c Lajos Kossuth, 9/19/58, DC 1.75		1.85	2.00	
☐	Scott 1117-1118 on one cover 2.00				45.00
	Total for Scott 1117 and 1118 is 722,188.				
☐ 1119	4c Freedom of Press, 9/22/58, Columbia, MO				
	(411,752) (2 types)* 1.75		1.85	2.00	25.00*
☐ 1120	4c Overland Mail, 10/10/58, San Francisco, CA				
	(352,760)..1.75		1.85	2.00	40.00
☐ 1121	4c Noah Webster, 10/16/58, West Hartford, CT				
	(364,608)..1.75		1.85	2.00	30.00
☐ 1122	4c Forest Conservation, 10/27/58, Tucson, AZ				
	(405,959)..1.75		1.85	2.00	30.00
☐ 1123	4c Fort Duquesne, 11/25/58, Pittsburgh, PA				
	(421,764)..1.75		1.85	2.00	60.00

1959

☐ 1124	4c Oregon Statehood, 2/14/59, Astoria, OR				
	(452,764) (2 types)* 1.75		1.85	2.00	20.00*
☐ 1125	4c Jose de San Martin, 2/25/ 59, DC.................1.75		1.85	2.00	
☐ 1126	8c Jose de San Martin, 2/25/59, DC.................1.75		1.85	2.00	
☐	Scott 1125-1126 on one cover 2.00				30.00
	Total for Scott 1125 and 1126 is 910,208.				
☐ 1127	4c NATO, 4/1/59, DC (361,040)......................1.75		1.85	2.00	20.00
☐	1st Gold Craft cachet..............................35.00				
☐ 1128	4c Arctic Explorations, 4/6/59, Cresson, PA				
	(397,770)..1.75		1.85	2.00	25.00
☐ 1129	8c World Peace through World Trade, 4/20/59,				
	DC (503,618)...1.75		1.85	2.00	
☐ 1130	4c Silver Centennial, 6/8/59, Virginia City, NV				
	(337,233)..1.75		1.85	2.00	50.00
☐ 1131	4c St. Lawrence Seaway, 6/26/59, Massena, NY				
	(543,211)..1.75		1.85	2.00	38.00
☐ 1132	4c Flag (49 stars), 7/4/59, Auburn, NY (523,773)....1.75		1.85	2.00	40.00
☐ 1133	4c Soil Conservation, 8/26/59, Rapid City, SD				
	(400,613) (2 types)* 1.75		1.85	2.00	25.00*

1079

1081

1083

1084

1085

1086

1087

1088

1089

1090

1091

1092

1096

1093

1094

1095

1097

1098

1099

1100

Values for various cachet makers can be determined by using the Cachet Calculator which begins on page 52A.

SCOTT NUMBER	DESCRIPTION	SINGLE	BLOCK	PLATE BLOCK	CERM PROG
☐ 1134	4c Petroleum Industry, 8/27/59, Titusville, PA				
	(801,859)..1.75		1.85	2.00	25.00
☐	1st Col. Drake Philatelic Society cachet..........15.00				
☐ 1135	4c Dental Health, 9/14/59, New York, NY				
	(649,813)..5.00		5.25	5.50	25.00
☐ 1136	4c Ernst Reuter, 9/29/59 DC.....................1.75		1.85	2.00	
☐ 1137	8c Ernst Reuter, 9/29/59 DC.....................1.75		1.85	2.00	
☐	Scott 1136-1137 on one cover..........................2.00				20.00
	Total for Scott 1136 and 1137 is 1,207,933.				
☐ 1138	4c Dr. Ephraim McDowell, 12/3/59, Danville, KY				
	(344,603)..1.75		1.85	2.00	35.00

1960-61

☐ 1139	4c American Credo, George Washington, 1/20/60,				
	Mount Vernon, VA (438,335)...............1.00		1.15	2.00	20.00
☐ 1140	4c American Credo, Benjamin Franklin, 3/31/60,				
	Philadelphia, PA (497,913) 1.00		1.15	2.00	12.00
☐ 1141	4c American Credo, Thomas Jefferson, 5/18/60,				
	Charlottesville, VA (454,903) 1.00		1.15	2.00	15.00
☐ 1142	4c American Credo, Francis Scott Key, 9/14/60,				
	Baltimore, MD (501,129) (4 types)*.......1.00		1.15	2.00	15.00*
☐ 1143	4c American Credo, Abraham Lincoln, 11/19/60,				
	New York, NY (467,780) (3 types)*.......1.00		1.15	2.00	15.00*
☐	1st Ritz cachet 20.00				
☐	1st National Urban League cachet 20.00				
☐	1st Springfield, (IL) Philatelic Society cachet .15.00				
☐ 1144	4c American Credo, Patrick Henry, 1/11/61,				
	Richmond, VA (415,252) (3 types)*.......1.00		1.15	2.00	15.00*

1960

☐ 1145	4c Boy Scouts, 2/8/60, DC (1,419,955) 4.00		4.25	4.75	85.00
☐ 1146	4c Olympic Winter Games, 2/18/60, Olympic				
	Valley, CA (516,456).............................1.00		1.10	1.50	
☐ 1147	4c Thomas G. Masaryk, 3/7/60, DC.........1.00		1.10	1.50	
☐ 1148	8c Thomas G. Masaryk, 3/7/60, DC.........1.00		1.25	1.50	
☐	Scott 1147-1148 on one cover..................2.00				15.00
	Total for Scott 1147 and 1148 is 1,710,726.				
☐ 1149	4c World Refugee Year, 4/7/60, DC (413,298)..........1.00		1.10	1.50	20.00
☐ 1150	4c Water Conservation, 4/18/60, DC				
	(648,988)..1.00		1.10	1.50	25.00
☐ 1151	4c SEATO, 5/31/60, DC (514,926)...........1.10		1.00	1.50	20.00
☐ 1152	4c American Woman, 6/2/60, DC (830,385)............1.00		1.10	1.50	50.00
☐ 1153	4c 50-Star Flag, 7/4/60, Honolulu, HI (820,900)......1.00		1.10	1.50	20.00
☐ 1154	4c Pony Express Centennial, 7/19/60,				
	Sacramento, CA (520,223)......................1.00		1.10	1.50	35.00
☐ 1155	4c Employ the Handicapped, 8/28/60, New York,				
	NY (439,638)...1.00		1.10	1.50	15.00
☐ 1156	4c World Forestry Congress, 8/29/60, Seattle, WA				
	(350,848)..1.00		1.10	1.50	35.00
☐ 1157	4c Mexican Independence, 9/16/60, Los Angeles,				
	CA (360,297) 1.00		1.10	1.50	40.00
☐	Dual US and Mexico stamp with US cancel............25.00				
☐	Dual US and Mexico with Mexican cancel............200.00				
☐ 1158	4c U.S.-Japan Treaty, 9/28/60, DC (545,150)...........1.00		1.10	1.50	20.00
☐ 1159	4c Ignacy Jan Paderewski, 10/8/60, DC 1.00		1.00	1.50	

1104
1105
1106
1107
1108
1110-11
1109
1112
1115
1113
1114
1st Western Cachets cachet
1116
1117-18

Values for various cachet makers can be determined by using the Cachet Calculator which begins on page 52A.

☐ 1160	8c Ignacy Jan Paderewski, 10/8/60, DC 1.00	1.25	1.50	
☐	Scott 1159-1160 on one cover 2.00			15.00
	Total for Scott 1159 and 1160 is 1,057,438.			
☐ 1161	4c Robert A. Taft 10/10/60, Cincinnati, OH (312,116) .1.00	1.10	1.50	25.00
☐ 1162	4c Wheels of Freedom, 10/15/60, Detroit, MI			
	(380,551)..1.00	1.10	1.50	18.00
☐ 1163	4c Boys' Clubs of America, 10/18/60, New York,			
	NY (435,009)..1.00	1.10	1.50	20.00
☐ 1164	4c Automated Post Office, 10/20/60, Providence,			
	RI (458,237)..1.00	1.10	1.50	12.00
☐ 1165	4c Gustaf Emil Mannerheim, 10/26/60, DC.............1.00	1.10	1.50	
☐ 1166	8c Gustaf Emil Mannerheim, 10/26/60, DC.............1.00	1.25	1.50	
☐	Scott 1165-1166 on one cover 2.00			15.00
	Total for Scott 1165 and 1166 is 1,168, 770.			
☐ 1167	4c Camp Fire Girls, 11/1/60, New York, NY			
	(324,944)..1.00	1.10	1.50	45.00
☐ 1168	4c Giuseppe Garibaldi, 11/2/60, DC........................1.10	1.10	1.50	
☐ 1169	8c Giuseppe Garibaldi, 11/2/60, DC........................1.00	1.25	1.50	
☐	Scott 1168-1169 on one cover 2.00			15.00
	Total for Scott 1168 and 1169 is 1,001,490.			
☐ 1170	4c Walter F. George, 11/5/60, Vienna, GA			
	(278,890)..1.00	1.10	1.50	12.00
☐ 1171	4c Andrew Carnegie, 11/25/60, New York, NY			
	(318,180)..1.00	1.10	1.50	25.00
☐ 1172	4c John Foster Dulles, 12/6/60, DC (400,055) 1.00	1.10	1.50	15.00
☐ 1173	4c Echo I, 12/15/60, DC (583,747)........................3.00	3.50	4.00	25.00

1961

☐ 1174	4c Mahatma Gandhi, 1/26/61, DC............................1.00	1.10	1.50	
☐ 1175	8c Mahatma Gandhi, 1/26/61, DC............................1.00	1.25	1.50	
☐	Scott 1174-1175 on one cover 2.00			15.00
	Total for Scott 1174 and 1175 is 1,013,315.			
☐ 1176	4c Range Conservation, 2/2/61, Salt Lake City, UT			
	(357,101)..1.00	1.10	1.50	30.00
☐ 1177	4c Horace Greeley, 2/3/61, Chappaqua, NY			
	(359,205)..1.00	1.10	1.50	20.00

1961-65 Civil War Centennial

☐ 1178	4c Fort Sumter, 4/12/61, Charleston, SC (602,599).3.00	3.25	4.00	25.00
☐ 1179	4c Battle of Shiloh, 4/7/62, Shiloh, TN (526,062) ...3.00	3.25	4.00	20.00
☐ 1180	5c Battle of Gettysburg, 7/1/63, Gettysburg, PA			
	(600,205)..3.00	3.25	4.00	20.00
☐ 1181	5c Battle of Wilderness, 5/5/64, Fredericksburg,			
	VA (450,904) 3.00	3.25	4.00	20.00
☐ 1182	5c Appomattox, 4/9/65, Appomattox, VA			
	(653,121) (3 types)* 3.00	3.25	4.00	20.00*
☐ 1178-82	Civil War on one 4/9/65 ....10.00			

1961

☐ 1183	4c Kansas Statehood, 5/10/61, Council Grove, KS			
	(480,561)..1.00	1.10	1.50	15.00
☐ 1184	4c George W. Norris, 7/11/61, DC (482,875)............1.00	1.10	1.50	15.00
☐ 1185	4c Naval Aviation, 8/20/61, San Diego, CA			
	(416,391)..1.00	1.50	2.50	30.00
☐ 1186	4c Workmen's Compensation, 9/4/61, Milwaukee,			
	WI (410,236) (2 types)*......................................1.00	1.10	1.50	15.00*

FREEDOM OF THE PRESS
U.S.POSTAGE 4¢

1119

CONSERVATION
FOREST
U.S. POSTAGE 4¢

1122

OVERLAND MAIL 1858
U.S. POSTAGE 4¢

1120

UNITED STATES POSTAGE 4¢

1121

CHAMPION OF LIBERTY
UNITED STATES POSTAGE 4¢

1125-26

FORT DUQUESNE 1759
U.S. POSTAGE 4¢

1123

OREGON STATEHOOD 1859 1959
U.S. POSTAGE 4 CENTS

1124

UNITED FOR FREEDOM
NATO
1949-1959
UNITED STATES POSTAGE

1127

ARCTIC EXPLORATIONS 1909
1959
U.S.POSTAGE 4¢

1128

WORLD PEACE THROUGH WORLD TRADE
8¢ U.S. POSTAGE

1129

SILVER CENTENNIAL 1859-1959
UNITED STATES POSTAGE 4¢

1130

ST. LAWRENCE SEAWAY
UNITED STATES 4¢

1131

JULY 4, 1959 4¢
UNITED STATES POSTAGE

1132

U.S. POSTAGE 1859-1959
PETROLEUM INDUSTRY 4¢

1134

SOIL CONSERVATION
U.S. POSTAGE 4¢

1133

AMERICAN DENTAL ASSOCIATION 1859-1959
Dental Health
UNITED STATES POSTAGE 4¢

1135

CHAMPION OF LIBERTY
UNITED STATES POSTAGE 4¢

1136-37

UNITED STATES POSTAGE 4¢

1138

4¢ UNITED STATES
Give me LIBERTY or give me DEATH

1139-44

BOY SCOUTS OF AMERICA
1910 - 1960
U.S. POSTAGE 4¢

1145

VIII OLYMPIC WINTER GAMES
4¢ UNITED STATES POSTAGE

1146

CHAMPION OF LIBERTY
UNITED STATES POSTAGE 4¢

1147-48

1st Ritz cachet

SEATO
UNITY PEACE PROGRESS
U.S. POSTAGE 4¢

1151

74

SCOTT NUMBER	DESCRIPTION	SINGLE	BLOCK	PLATE BLOCK	CERM PROG
☐ 1187	4c Frederic Remington, 10/4/61, DC (723,443)	1.00	1.10	1.50	15.00
☐ 1188	4c Republic of China, 10/10/61, DC (463,900)	1.00	1.10	1.50	18.00
☐ 1189	4c Naismith-Basketball, 11/6/61, Springfield, MA				
	(479,917)	8.00	9.00	10.00	18.00
☐ 1190	4c Nursing, 12/28/61, DC (964,005) (2 types)*	14.00	15.00	20.00	15.00*
☐	1st American Hospital Supply Corp. cachet	20.00			

1962

☐ 1191	4c New Mexico Statehood, 1/6/62, Santa Fe, NM				
	(365,330)	1.00	1.10	1.50	15.00
☐	1st Glory cachet	25.00			
☐ 1192	4c Arizona Statehood, 2/14/62, Phoenix, AZ				
	(508,216)	1.00	1.10	1.50	15.00
☐	1st Vivid cachet	25.00			
☐	1st Tucson Chamber of Commerce cachet	15.00			
☐ 1193	4c Project Mercury, 2/20/62, Cape Canaveral, FL				
	(3,000,000)	3.00	4.00	6.00	
☐	Any other city	5.00	6.00	7.00	
☐	1st Marg cachet	25.00			
☐ 1194	4c Malaria Eradication, 3/30/62, DC (554, 175)	1.00	1.10	1.50	15.00
☐ 1195	4c Charles Evans Hughes, 4/11/62, DC (554,424)	1.00	1.10	1.50	15.00
☐ 1196	4c Seattle World's Fair, 4/25/62, Seattle, WA				
	(771,856)	1.00	1.10	1.50	15.00
☐	1st Top of the Needle, Inc. cachet	10.00			
☐	1st Boeing Employee's Stamp Club cachet	12.00			
☐ 1197	4c Louisiana Statehood, 4/30/62, New Orleans, LA				
	(436,681)	1.00	1.10	1.50	18.00
☐ 1198	4c Homestead Act, 5/20/62, Beatrice, NE (487,450)	1.00	1.10	1.50	15.00
☐ 1199	4c Girl Scout Jubilee, 7/24/62, Burlington, VT				
	(634,347)	3.50	3.75	4.00	22.00
☐ 1200	4c Brien McMahon, 7/28/62, Norwalk, CT				
	(384,419) (2 types)*	1.00	1.10	1.50	18.00*
☐ 1201	4c Apprenticeship, 8/31/62, DC, 1,003,548)	1.00	1.10	1.50	15.00
☐ 1202	4c Sam Rayburn, 9/16/62, Bonham, TX (401,042)	1.00	1.10	1.50	15.00
☐ 1203	4c Dag Hammarskjold, 10/23/62, New York, NY				
	(500,683)	1.00	1.10	1.50	18.00
☐	1st Dag Hammarskjold Foundation cachet	15.00			
☐	Inverted yellow, 10/26/62, Vanderveer Sta.,				
☐	Brooklyn, NY earliest known use	2,000.			
☐ 1204	4c Hanmarskjold Special Printing, yellow				
	inverted, 11/16/62, DC (c. 75,000)	6.00	7.50	10.00	
☐ 1205	4c Christmas, 11/1/62, Pittsburgh, PA (491,312)	1.10	1.50		20.00
☐ 1206	4c Higher Education, 11/14/62, DC (627,347)	1.00	1.10	1.50	15.00
☐ 1207	4c Winslow Homer, 12/15/62, Gloucester, MA				
	(498,866)	1.00	1.10	1.50	18.00

1963-66

☐ 1208	5c Flag, 1/9/63, DC (696,185)	1.00	1.10	1.50	12.00
☐ 1208a	Flag, tagged, 8/25/66, DC	25.00			

1962-66

☐ 1209	1c Andrew Jackson, 3/22/63, block of 5 or 6, New				
	York, NY (392,363)		1.00	1.50	15.00
☐ 1209a	Andrew Jackson, block of 5 or 6, tagged, 7/6/66, DC	25.00			

1149

1150

1152

1154

1153

1155

1156

1157

1158

1159-60

1161

1162

1164

1163

1167

1165-66

1168-69

1170

1171

1172

1173

1174-75

1176

1177

1178-82

SCOTT NUMBER	DESCRIPTION	SINGLE	BLOCK	PLATE BLOCK	CERM PROG
☐ 1213	5c George Washington, 11/23/62, New York, NY (360,531)........1.00				15.00
☐ 1213a	George Washington, booklet pane of 5, 11/23/62, New York, NY (111,452)........4.00				
☐ 1213b	George Washington, tagged, 10/28/63, Dayton, OH & DC........25.00				
☐ 1213c	George Washington, booklet pane of 5, tagged, 10/28/63, Dayton, OH........100.00				
☐	DC (750)........115.00				

SCOTT NUMBER	DESCRIPTION	SINGLE	PAIR	LINE PAIR	CERM PROG
☐ 1225	1c Andrew Jackson, coil, pair & strip of 3, 5/31/63, Chicago, IL (238,952)........		1.00	1.00	15.00
☐ 1225a	Andrew Jackson, coil, pair & strip of 3, tagged, 7/6/66, DC		5.00		
☐ 1229	5c George Washington, coil, 11/23/62, New York, NY (184,627)........1.00		1.00	1.00	
☐ 1229a	George Washington, coil, tagged, 10/28/63, Dayton, OH & DC		30.00		
☐	Scott 1213b, 1213c, 1229a on one cover, Dayton, OH 70.00				

SCOTT NUMBER	DESCRIPTION	SINGLE	BLOCK	PLATE BLOCK	CERM PROG

1963

SCOTT NUMBER	DESCRIPTION	SINGLE	BLOCK	PLATE BLOCK	CERM PROG
☐ 1230	5c Carolina Charter, 4/6/63, Edenton, NC (426,200) (2 types)*........1.00	1.00	1.10	1.50	15.00*
☐ 1231	5c Food for Peace, 6/4/63, DC........1.00	1.00	1.10	1.50	15.00
☐ 1232	5c West Virginia Statehood, 6/20/63, Wheeling, WV (413,389)........1.00	1.00	1.10	1.50	20.00
☐ 1233	5c Emancipation Proclamation, 8/16/63, Chicago, IL (494,886) 1.00	1.00	1.10	1.50	15.00
☐ 1234	5c Alliance for Progress, 8/17/63, DC (528,095) 1.00	1.00	1.10	1.50	15.00
☐ 1235	5c Cordell Hull, 10/5/63, Carthage, TN (391,631) ..1.00	1.00	1.10	1.50	15.00
☐ 1236	5c Eleanor Roosevelt, 10/11/63, DC (860,155) 1.00	1.00	1.10	1.50	15.00
☐ 1237	5c Science, 10/14/63, DC (504,503)........1.00	1.00	1.10	1.50	18.00
☐ 1238	5c City Mail Delivery, 10/26/63, DC (544,806) 1.00	1.00	1.10	1.50	22.00
☐ 1239	5c Red Cross Centenary, 10/29/63, DC (557,678)....1.00	1.00	1.10	1.50	15.00
☐ 1240	5c Christmas, 11/1/63, Santa Claus, IN (458,619) ..1.00	1.00	1.10	1.50	20.00
	1st Lily Spandorf cachet 20.00				
☐ 1240a	Christmas, tagged, 11/2/63, DC (500)........60.00				
☐ 1241	5c John James Audubon, 12/7/63, Henderson, KY (518,855)........1.00	1.00	1.10	1.50	15.00

1964

SCOTT NUMBER	DESCRIPTION	SINGLE	BLOCK	PLATE BLOCK	CERM PROG
☐ 1242	5c Sam Houston, 1/10/64, Houston, TX (487,986)...1.00	1.00	1.10	1.50	20.00
☐	Mr. Zip Imprint 10.00	10.00	15.00		
	Scott 1242 was the first stamp to have Mr. Zip imprints.				
☐ 1243	5c Charles M. Russell, 3/19/64, Great Falls, MT (658,745)........1.00	1.00	1.10	1.50	40.00

1183

1184

1185

1186

1187

1188

1189

1190

1191

1192

1193

1194

1195

1196

1197

1198

1st Glory cachet

1st Marg cachet

HOW TO USE THIS BOOK

The number in the first column is its Scott number or identifying number. Following that is the denomination of the stamp, description, date of issue, and the value.

1199 1200 1201

1202 1203 1204 1205

1206 1207 1209, 1225

1231 1208 1213, 1229 1230

1232 1233 1234

1235 1236 1237 1238

1239 1240

Values for various cachet makers can be determined by using the Cachet Calculator which begins on page 52A.

		SINGLE	BLOCK	PLATE BLOCK	CERM PROG
☐ 1244	5c N.Y. World's Fair, 4/22/64, World's Fair, NY				
	(1,656,346) (2 types)*........................1.00		1.10		1.50 18.00*
☐	1st Sarzin Metallic cachet.........................30.00				
☐	On Scott U546 ....5.00				
☐ 1245	5c John Muir, 4/29/64, Martinez, CA (446,925) 1.00		1.10		1.50 15.00
☐ 1246	5c Kennedy Memorial, 5/29/64, Boston, MA				
	(2,003,096)..2.50		3.50	5.00	18.00
☐	Any city 2.50		3.50	5.00	
☐	1st Cover Craft cachet.................................40.00				
☐ 1247	5c New Jersey Tercentenary, 6/15/64, Elizabeth,				
	NJ (526,879)...1.00		1.00		1.50 15.00
☐ 1248	5c Nevada Statehood, 7/22/64, Carson City, NV				
	(584,973)...1.00		1.00		1.50 15.00
☐ 1249	5c Register & Vote, 8/1/64, DC (533,439) 1.00		1.00		1.50 15.00
☐ 1250	5c Shakespeare, 8/14/64, Stratford, CT (524,053) ..1.00		1.00		1.50 50.00
☐ 1251	5c Drs. Mayo, 9/11/64, Rochester, MN (674,846) 5.00		5.50	8.00	25.00
☐ 1252	5c American Music, 10/15/64, New York, NY				
	(466,107) (2 types)*...............................1.00		1.10		1.50 15.00*
☐ 1253	5c Homemakers, 10/26/64, Honolulu, HI				
	(435,392)...1.00		1.10		1.50 15.00
☐ 1254	5c Holly, 11/9/64, Bethlehem, PA......................1.00				
☐ 1254a	Holly, tagged, 11/10/64, Dayton, OH.................20.00				
☐ 1255	5c Mistletoe, 11/9/64, Bethlehem, PA....................1.00				
☐ 1255a	Mistletoe, tagged, 11/10/64, Dayton, OH...............20.00				
☐ 1256	5c Poinsettia, 11/9/64, Bethlehem, PA 1.00				
☐ 1256a	Poinsettia, tagged, 11/10/64, Dayton, OH.............20.00				
☐ 1257	5c Sprig of Conifer, 11/9/64, Bethlehem, PA...........1.00				
☐ 1257a	Sprig of Conifer, 11/10/64, Dayton, OH 20.00				
☐ 1257b	Christmas, se-tenant (794,900)		3.00	4.00	80.00
☐ 1257b	Christmas, tagged, se-tenant............................		80.00		
☐ 1254-1257	5c Christmas, ...				80.00
☐ 1258	5c Verrazano-Narrows Bridge, 11/21/64, Staten				
	Island, NY (619,780).................................1.00		1.10		1.50 15.00
☐ 1259	5c Fine Arts, 12/2/64, DC (558,046) 1.00		1.10		1.50 20.00
☐ 1260	5c Amateur Radio, 12/15/64, Anchorage, AK 1.00		1.10		1.50 28.00

1965

		SINGLE	BLOCK	PLATE BLOCK	CERM PROG
☐ 1261	5c Battle of New Orleans, 1/8/65, New Orleans, LA				
	(466,029) (4 types)*................................1.00		1.10		1.50 25.00*
☐ 1262	5c Physical Fitness-Sokol, 2/15/65, DC (864,848) ..1.00		1.10		1.50 10.00
☐ 1263	5c Crusade Against Cancer, 4/1/65, DC (744,485)...1.00		1.10		1.50 20.00
☐ 1264	5c Churchill Memorial, 5/13/65, Fulton, MO				
	(733,580)...1.00		1.10		1.50 12.00
☐ 1265	5c Magna Carta, 6/15/65, Jamestown, VA				
	(479,065)...1.00		1.10		1.50 40.00
☐ 1266	5c International Cooperation Year, 6/26/65, San				
	Francisco, CA (402,925)................................1.00		1.10		1.50 35.00
☐ 1267	5c Salvation Army, 7/2/65, New York, NY (634,228)1.00		1.10		1.50 15.00
☐ 1268	5c Dante Alighieri, 7/17/65, San Francisco, CA				
	(424,893)...1.00		1.10		1.50 15.00
☐ 1269	5c Herbert Hoover, 8/10/65, West Branch, IA				
	(698,182)...1.00		1.10		1.50 15.00
☐ 1270	5c Robert Fulton, 8/19/65, Clermont, NY (550,330) ..1.00		1.10		1.50 15.00
☐ 1271	5c Settlement of Florida, 8/28/65, St. Augustine,				
	FL (465,000)...1.00		1.10		1.50 15.00

1245

1st Cover Craft cachet

1241

1242

1243

1244

1246

1248

1247

1249

1250

1251

1254-57

1252

1253

1258

1259

1261

1260

HOW TO USE THIS BOOK

The number in the first column is its Scott number or identifying number. Following that is the denomination of the stamp, description, date of issue, and the value.

☐	Scott 1271 with Spain stamp 100.00				
☐	Scott 1271 with Spain stamp dual cancel.............300.00				
☐ 1272	5c Traffic Safety, 9/3/65, Baltimore, MD				
	(527,075)..1.00	1.10		1.50	15.00
☐ 1273	5c John Singleton Copley, 9/17/65, DC (613,484) ...1.00	1.10		1.50	15.00
☐ 1274	11c International Telecommunication Union,				
	10/6/65, DC (332,818).......................................1.00	1.10		1.50	20.00
☐ 1275	5c Adlai E. Stevenson, 10/23/65, Bloomington, IL				
	(755,656)..1.00	1.10		1.50	15.00
☐ 1276	5c Christmas, 11/2/65, Silver Bell, AZ (705,039)				
	(2 types)*...1.00	1.10		1.50	25.00*
☐ 1276a	Christmas, tagged, 11/15/65, DC (300c).................55.00				

1965-68 Prominent Americans

☐ 1278	1c Thomas Jefferson, block of 5 or 6, 1/12/68,				
	Jeffersonville, IN...	1.00		1.00	25.00
☐ 1278a	Thomas Jefferson, booklet pane of 8, 1/12/68,				
	Jeffersonville, IN...2.50				25.00
☐	Dull gum, 3/1/71, DC...100.00				
	Total for Scott 1278, 1278a and 1299 is 655,680.				
☐ 1278b	Thomas Jefferson, booklet pane of 4 plus 2 labels,				
	5/10/71, DC..15.00				
☐ 1279	1 1/4c Albert Gallatin, 1/30/67, Gallatin, MO				
	(439,010)..	1.00		1.00	20.00
☐ 1280	2c Frank Lloyd Wright, strip of 3, 6/8/66, Spring				
	Green, WI (460,427)..1.00				18.00
☐ 1280a	Frank Lloyd Wright, booklet pane of 5 plus label,				
	1/8/68, Buffalo, NY (147,244).............................4.00				20.00
☐ 1280c	Frank Lloyd Wright, booklet pane of 6, 5/7/71,				
	Spokane, WA...15.00				50.00
☐	Dull gum, 10/31/75, Cleveland, OH..............100.00				
☐ 1281	3c Francis Parkman, 9/16/67, Boston, MA				
	(518,355)..	1.10		1.50	15.00
☐ 1282	4c Abraham Lincoln, 11/19/65, New York, NY				
	(445,629) (2 types)	1.10		1.50	15.00
☐ 1282a	Abraham Lincoln, tagged, 12/1/65, Dayton, OH 40.00				
☐	DC...45.00				
☐ 1283	5c George Washington, 2/22/66, DC (525,372)........1.00	1.10		1.50	50.00
	1st B'nai B'rith Philatelic Service cachet 20.00				
☐ 1283a	George Washington, tagged, 2/23/66, Dayton,				
	OH (c. 200) 100.00				
☐	DC...30.00				
☐ 1283B	5c George Washington, Redrawn, 11/17/67,				
	New York, NY (328,983) (2 types)* 1.00	1.10		1.50	15.00*
☐ 1284	6c Franklin D. Roosevelt, 1/29/66, Hyde Park, NY				
	(448,631)..1.00	1.10		1.50	15.00
☐ 1284a	Franklin D. Roosevelt, tagged, 12/29/66, DC 30.00				
☐ 1284b	Franklin D. Roosevelt, booklet pane of 8,				
	12/28/67, DC...3.00				
	Total for Scott 1284b and 1298 is 312,330.				
☐ 1284c	Franklin D. Roosevelt, booklet pane of 5, 1/9/68,				
	DC...125.00				
☐ 1285	8c Albert Einstein, 3/14/66, Princeton, NJ				
	(366,803)..1.50	2.00		2.75	20.00

1267   1262   1263   1264   1268

1265   1266

1269   1270   1272   1271

1273   1274   1276

1278, 1299   1287   1275

HOW TO USE THIS BOOK

The number in the first column is its Scott number or identifying number. Following that is the denomination of the stamp, description, date of issue, and the value.

SCOTT NUMBER	DESCRIPTION	SINGLE	BLOCK	PLATE BLOCK	CERM PROG
☐ 1285a	Albert Einstein, tagged, 7/6/66, DC......................30.00				
☐ 1286	10c Andrew Jackson, 3/15/67, Hermitage, TN				
	(255,945)...1.00	1.25	1.50	20.00	
☐ 1286A	12c Henry Ford, 7/30/68, Greenfield Village,				
	MI (342,850)...1.00	1.25	1.50	22.00	
☐ 1287	13c John F. Kennedy, 5/29/67, Brookline, MA				
	(391,195)...1.50	2.00	2.75	28.00	
☐ 1288	15c Oliver Wendell Holmes, 3/8/68, DC (322,970). .1.00	1.25	1.50	28.00	
☐ 1288B	15c Oliver Wendell Holmes, Redrawn, booklet				
	single, 6/14/78, Boston, MA (387, 119)..........1.00	1.25	1.50		
☐ 1288c	Oliver Wendell Holmes, booklet pane of 8................3.00				
☐ 1289	20c George C. Marshall, 10/24/67, Lexington, VA				
	(221,206)...1.00	1.25	1.50	25.00	
☐ 1289a	George C. Marshall, tagged, 4/3/73, New York, NY 25.00				
☐ 1290	25c Frederick Douglass, 2/14/67, DC (213,730) ...1.25	1.25	1.75	32.00	
☐ 1290a	Frederick Douglass, tagged, 4/3/73, New York, NY 30.00				
☐ 1291	30c John Dewey, 10/21/68, Burlington, VT				
	(162,790)...1.25	2.00	3.00	35.00	
☐ 1291a	John Dewey, tagged, 4/3/73, New York, NY 30.00				
☐ 1292	40c Thomas Paine, 1/29/68, Philadelphia, PA				
	(157,947)...1.60	2.50	4.00	40.00	
☐ 1292a	Thomas Paine, tagged, 4/3/73, New York, NY 30.00				
☐ 1293	50c Lucy Stone, 8/13/68, Dorchester, MA				
	(140,410)...3.25	4.00	7.50	45.00	
☐ 1293a	Lucy Stone, tagged, 4/3/73, New York, NY.............30.00				
☐ 1294	$1 Eugene O'Neill, 10/16/67, New London, CT				
	(103,102) (2 types)*...7.50	10.00	15.00	50.00*	
☐ 1294a	Eugene O'Neill, tagged, 4/3/73, New York, NY.......40.00				
☐ 1295	$5 John Bassett Moore, 12/3/66, Smyrna, DE				
	(41,130)..40.00	55.00	95.00	75.00	
☐ 1295a	John Bassett Moore, tagged, 4/3/73, New York, NY 100.00				
	Scott 1295 &1295a on one cover 225.00				
	Total for 1059b, 1289a, 1290a, 1291a, 1292a,				
	1293a, 1294a, 1295a is 17,533.				

SCOTT NUMBER	DESCRIPTION	SINGLE	PAIR	LINE PAIR	CERM PROG

1966-68 Prominent Americans Coils
Perf. 10 Horizontally

☐ 1297	3c Francis Parkman, 11/4/75, Pendleton, OR				
	(166,798)...		1.00	1.50	15.00
☐ 1298	6c Franklin D. Roosevelt, 12/28/67, DC..................1.00	1.10	1.50		

Perf. 10 Vertically

☐ 1299	1c Thomas Jefferson, pair & strip of 3, 1/12/68,				
	Jeffersonville, IN		1.00	1.50	25.00
☐ 1303	4c Abraham Lincoln, pair, 5/28/66, Springfield, IL				
	(322,563)...		1.00	1.50	25.00
	1st A Hartford Cover cachet 20.00				
☐ 1304	5c George Washington, 9/8/66, Cincinnati, OH				
	(245,400)...1.00	1.00	1.50	15.00	
☐ 1304C	5c George Washington, Redrawn, strip of 4,				
	3/31/81, earliest known use, DC 25.00				
☐ 1305	6c Franklin D. Roosevelt, 2/28/68, DC (317,199).....1.00	1.10	1.50		

1306

1307

1308

1309

1310-11

1312

1313

1314

1315

1316

1318

1317

SCOTT NUMBER	DESCRIPTION	SINGLE	PAIR	LINE PAIR	CERM PROG
☐ 1305E	15c Oliver Wendell Holmes 6/14/78, Boston, MA				
	(387,119)..1.00		1.25	1.50	
☐	Scott 1288c, 1305E on one cover 6.50				
☐ 1305C	$1 Eugene O'Neill 1/12/73, Hempstead, NY				
	(121,217)..5.00		7.00	9.00	50.00

SCOTT NUMBER	DESCRIPTION	SINGLE	PLATE BLOCK	CERM BLOCK PROG

1966

☐ 1306	5c Migratory Bird Treaty, 3/16/66, Pittsburgh, PA				
	(555,485)..1.00		1.10	1.50	18.00
☐ 1307	5c Humane Treatment of Animals, 4/9/66, New				
	York, NY (524,420) (2 types)* 1.00		1.10		1.50 12.00*
☐ 1308	5c Indiana Statehood, 4/16/66, Corydon, IN				
	(575,557)..1.00		1.10	1.50	15.00
☐ 1309	5c American Circus, 5/2/66, Delavan, WI				
	(754,076) (2 types)*...2.50		3.00		4.50 22.00*
	1st Cliff's Covers cachet 20.00				
☐ 1310	5c SIPEX, 5/21/66, DC (637,802) 1.00		1.10	1.50	20.00
☐ 1311	5c SIPEX, Souvenir Sheet, 5/23/66, DC (700,882). ...1.00				25.00
☐ 1312	5c Bill of Rights, 7/1/66, Miami Beach, FL				
	(562,920)..1.00		1.10	1.50	25.00
☐ 1313	5c Polish Millennium, 7/30/66, DC (712,603)............1.00		1.10	1.50	
☐ 1313	5c Polish Millennium. 7/30/66 DC..................................				15.00
☐ 1314	5c National Park Service, 8/25/66, Yellowstone				
	National Park, WY (528,170) (2 types)*.............1.00		1.10	1.50	15.00
☐ 1314a	National Park Service, tagged, 8/26/66, DC...........30.00				
☐ 1315	5c Marine Corps Reserve, 8/29/66, DC (585,923)....1.00		1.10	1.50	18.00
☐ 1315a	Marine Corps Reserve, tagged, 8/29/66, DC 30.00				
☐ 1316	5c General Federation of Women's Clubs, 9/12/66,				
	New York, NY (383,334) (2 types)* 1.00		1.10		1.50 20.00*
☐ 1316a	General Federation of Women's Clubs, tagged,				
	9/13/66, DC..30.00				
☐ 1317	5c Johnny Appleseed, 9/24/66, Leominster, MA				
	(794,610)..1.00		1.10	1.50	20.00
☐ 1317a	Johnny Appleseed, tagged, 9/26/66, DC.................30.00				
☐ 1318	5c Beautification of America, 10/5/66, DC				
	(564,440)..1.00		1.10	1.50	25.00
☐ 1318a	Beautification of America, tagged, 10/5/66, DC 30.00				
☐ 1319	5c Great River Road, 10/21/66, Baton Rouge, LA				
	(330,933)..1.00		1.10	1.50	20.00
☐ 1319a	Great River Road, tagged, 10/22/66, DC 30.00				
☐ 1320	5c Savings Bonds-Servicemen, 10/26/66, Sioux				
	City, IA (444,421) 1.00		1.10	1.50	15.00
	1st Border Croft cachet...................................25.00				
☐ 1320a	Savings Bonds-Servicemen, tagged, 10/27/66, DC 30.00				
☐ 1321	5c Christmas, 11/1/66, Christmas, MI (537,650)......1.00		1.10	1.50	25.00
☐ 1321a	Christmas, tagged, 11/2/66, DC 30.00				
☐ 1322	5c Mary Cassatt, 11/17/66, DC (593,389).................1.00		1.10	1.50	22.00
☐ 1322a	Mary Cassatt, tagged, 11/17/66, DC 30.00				

1967

☐ 1323	5c National Grange, 4/17/67, DC (603,460) 1.00		1.10	1.50	25.00

1319

1320

1321

1322

1323

1324

1325

1326

1327

1328

1330

1329

1331-32

**Values for various cachet makers can be determined
by using the Cachet Calculator which begins on page 52A.**

☐ 1324	5c Canada Centenary, 5/25/67, Montreal, Quebec				
	(711,795)..1.00	1.10		1.50	18.00
☐ 1325	5c Erie Canal, 7/4/67, Rome, NY (784,611)............1.00	1.10		1.50	18.00
☐ 1326	5c "Peace"-Lions, 7/5/67, Chicago, IL (393, 197) 1.00	1.10		1.50	15.00
☐ 1327	5c Henry David Thoreau, 7/12/67, Concord, MA				
	(696,789)..1.00	1.10		1.50	15.00
☐ 1328	5c Nebraska Statehood, 7/29/67, Lincoln, NE				
	(1,146,957)..1.00	1.10		1.50	15.00
☐ 1329	5c Voice of America, 8/1/67, DC (445,190) 1.00	1.10		1.50	20.00
☐ 1330	5c Davy Crockett, 8/17/67, San Antonio, TX				
	(462,291)..1.00	1.10		1.50	18.00
☐ 1331	5c Space-walking astronaut, 9/29/67, Kennedy				
	Space Center, FL.......................................4.00				
☐ 1331a	Space Accomplishments, se-tenant pair, FL				
	(667,267)..10.00	12.50		15.00	20.00
☐ 1332	5c Gemini 4 capsule, 9/29/67, Kennedy Space				
	Center, FL..4.00				
☐ 1333	5c Urban Planning, 10/2/67, DC (389,009) 1.00	1.10		1.50	20.00
☐ 1334	5c Finland Independence, 10/6/67, Finland, MN				
	(408,532)..1.00	1.10		1.50	18.00
☐ 1335	5c Thomas Eakins, 11/2/67, DC (648,054)..............1.00	1.10		1.50	18.00
☐ 1336	5c Christmas, 11/6/67, Bethlehem, GA (462,118) 1.00	1.10		1.50	20.00
☐ 1337	5c Mississippi Statehood, 12/11/67, Natchez, MS				
	(379,612)..1.00	1.10		1.50	18.00

1968-69

☐ 1338	6c Flag, Giori Press, 1/24/68, DC (412,120)..............1.00	1.10		1.50	15.00
☐ 1338A	6c Flag, coil, 5/30/69, Chicago, IL (248,434) 1.00pr	l.10		lp1.50	15.00
☐ 1338D	6c Flag, 8/7/70, Huck Press, DC (356,280).				
	"Plate Block" value is for block of 4 with plate				
	numbers..1.00	1.10		1.50	
☐ 1338F	8c Flag, 5/10/71, DC. "Plate Block" value is for				
	block of 4 with plate numbers.........................1.00	1.10		1.50	
☐ 1338G	8c Flag, coil, 5/10/71, DC..1.00pr	1.00		lp1.50	
	Total for Scott 1338F-1338G is 235,543.				

1968

☐ 1339	6c Illinois Statehood, 2/12/68, Shawneetown, IL				
	(761,640)..1.00	1.10		1.50	18.00
☐ 1340	6c Hemis Fair '68, 3/30/68, San Antonio, TX				
	(469,909)..1.00	1.10		1.50	18.00
☐ 1341	$1 Airlift, 4/4/68, Seattle, WA (105,088) 8.00	9.50		15.00	70.00
☐ 1342	6c Youth-Elks, 5/1/68, Chicago, IL (354,711)...........1.00	1.10		1.50	15.00
☐ 1343	6c Law and Order, 5/17/68, DC (407,081)...............1.00	1.10		1.50	20.00
☐ 1344	6c Register and Vote, 6/27/68, DC (355,685)...........1.00	1.10		1.50	20.00
☐ 1345	6c Ft. Moultrie, 7/4/68, Pittsburgh, PA 3.00				
☐ 1346	6c Ft. McHenry, 7/4/68, Pittsburgh, PA 3.00				
☐ 1347	6c Washington's Cruisers, 7/4/68, Pittsburgh, PA .3.00				
☐ 1348	6c Bennington, 7/4/68, Pittsburgh, PA 3.00				
☐ 1349	6c Rhode Island, 7/4/68, Pittsburgh, PA 3.00				
☐ 1350	6c First Stars & Stripes, 7/4/68, Pittsburgh, PA 3.00				
☐ 1351	6c Bunker Hill, 7/4/68, Pittsburgh, PA 3.00				
☐ 1352	6c Grand Union, 7/4/68, Pittsburgh, PA 3.00				
☐ 1353	6c Philadelphia Light Horse, 7/4/68, Pittsburgh, PA 3.00				
☐ 1354	6c First Navy Jack, 7/4/68, Pittsburgh, PA..............3.00				

1333

1334

1335

1336

1337

1338

1339

1340

1341

1342

1343

1344

1345-54

1356

1355

Values for various cachet makers can be determined by using the Cachet Calculator which begins on page 52A.

☐ 1354a	Se-tenant strip Historic Flags (2 types)* 12.00				20.00
	Total for Scott 1345-1354 is 2,924,962.				
☐ 1355	6c Walt Disney, 9/11/68, Marceline, MO				
	(499,505) (2 types)*.......................................15.00	16.00		20.00	45.00*
☐ 1356	6c Father Marquette, 9/20/68, Sault Sainte Marie				
	MI (379,710)..1.00	1.10		1.50	15.00
☐ 1357	6c Daniel Boone, 9/26/68, Frankfort, KY				
	(333,440)..1.00	1.10		1.50	15.00
☐ 1358	6c Arkansas River Navigation, 10/1/68, Little				
	Rock, AR (358,025) 1.00	1.10		1.50	50.00
☐ 1359	6c Leif Erikson, 10/9/68, Seattle, WA (376,565) 1.00	1.10		1.50	30.00
☐ 1360	6c Cherokee Strip, 10/15/68, Ponca, OK (339,330)..1.00	1.10		1.50	18.00
☐ 1361	6c John Trumbull, 10/18/68, New Haven, CT				
	(378,285)..1.00	1.10		1.50	20.00
☐ 1362	6c Waterfowl Conservation, 10/24/68, Cleveland,				
	OH (349,719)..1.00	1.10		1.50	25.00
☐	1st Ducks Unlimited, Inc. cachet 30.00				
☐ 1363	6c Christmas, tagged, 11/1/68, DC (739,055).				
	"Plate Block" value is for block of 4 with plate				
	numbers 1.00	1.10		1.50	25.00
☐ 1363a	6c Christmas, untagged, 11/2/68, DC 15.00				
☐ 1364	6c American Indian, 11/4/68, DC (415,964)............1.00	1.10		1.50	20.00

1969

☐ 1365	6c Capitol, Azaleas & Tulips, 1/16/69, DC 1.00				
☐ 1366	6c Washington Monument & Daffodils, 1/16/69,DC.1.00				
☐ 1367	6c Poppies & Lupines along Highway, 1/16/69, DC 1.00				
☐ 1368	6c Blooming Crabapples, 1/16/69, DC 1.00				
☐ 1368a	Se-tenant blocks, Beautification of America				
	(1,094,184)	4.00	5.00		25.00
☐ 1369	6c American Legion, 3/15/59, DC (632,035) 1.00	1.25	2.00		15.00
☐ 1370	6c Grandma Moses, 5/1/69, DC (367,880)............1.00	1.25	2.00		20.00
☐ 1371	6c Apollo 8, 5/5/69, Houston, TX (908,634) 4.00	6.00	9.00		25.00
☐ 1372	6c W.C. Handy, 5/17/69, Memphis, TN (398,216). 1.00	1.25	2.00		16.00
☐ 1373	6c California Settlement, 7/16/69, San Diego, CA				
	(530,210)..1.00	1.25	1.25		25.00
☐ 1374	6c John Wesley Powell, 8/1/69, Page, AZ (434,433) 1.00	1.25	2.00		18.00
☐ 1375	6c Alabama Statehood, 8/2/69, Huntsville, AL				
	(485,801) (2 types)*...1.00	1.25		2.00	18.00*
☐ 1376	6c Douglas Fir, 8/23/69, Seattle, WA 1.50				
☐ 1377	6c Lady's-slipper, 8/23/69, Seattle, WA 1.50				
☐ 1378	6c Ocotillo, 8/23/69, Seattle, WA 1.50				
☐ 1379	6c Franklinia, 8/23/69, Seattle, WA..........................1.50				
☐ 1379a	Se-tenant, (737,935) Botanical Congress	5.00	6.00		30.00
☐ 1380	6c Dartmouth College Case, 9/22/69, Hanover,				
	NH (416,327)..1.00	1.00		1.50	10.00
☐ 1381	6c Professional Baseball, 9/24/69, Cincinnati, OH				
	(414,942)..15.00	16.00		18.00	70.00
☐ 1382	6c Intercollegiate Football, 9/26/69, New				
	Brunswick, NJ (414,860).................................7.00	8.00		10.00	50.00
☐ 1383	6c Dwight D. Eisenhower, 10/14/69, Abilene, KS				
	(1,009,560)..1.00	1.10		1.50	15.00
☐ 1384	6c Christmas, 11/3/69, Christmas, FL (555,550).				
	"Plate Block" value is for block of 4 with plate				
	number. 1.00	1.10		1.50	25.00

1357

1358

1360

leif erikson

1359

John Trumbull

1361

1362

CHRISTMAS 6c

UNITED STATES

1363

1364

PLANT for more BEAUTIFUL CITIES

1365-68

The American Legion
50 years
Veterans as Citizens

1369

Grandma Moses
6c U.S. Postage

1370

1371

CALIFORNIA
1769-1969
United States 6 cents

1373

JOHN WESLEY POWELL

1374

ALABAMA
1819-1969
UNITED STATES

1375

DANIEL WEBSTER
The Dartmouth College Case
1819

1380

W.C. HANDY
father of the Blues

1372

6c

1376-79

1869-1969
UNITED STATES
PROFESSIONAL BASEBALL

1381

FOOTBALL
1869 - 1969
U.S. 6c

1382

**Values for various cachet makers can be determined
by using the Cachet Calculator which begins on page 52A.**

☐ 1384a **Christmas,** Precancel, New Haven, Memphis, Baltimore, Atlanta 11/4/69 (250) 100.00

☐ 1385 6c **Hope for Crippled,** 11/20/69, Columbus, OH (342,676) .... 2.00 | 2.25 | | 2.50 | 15.00

☐ 1386 6c **William M. Harnett,** 12/3/69, Boston, MA (408,860) .... 1.00 | 1.10 | | 1.50 | 18.00

1970

☐ 1387 6c **American Bald Eagle,** 5/6/70, New York, NY (2 types)* 1.50

☐ 1388 6c **African Elephant Herd,** 5/6/70, New York, NY (2 types)* 1.50

☐ 1389 6c **Tlingit Chief,** Ceremonial Canoe, 5/6/70, New York, NY (2 types)* 1.50

☐ 1390 6c **Brontosaurus, Stegosaurus & Allosaurus** 5/6/70, New York, NY 1.50

☐ 1390a **Se-tenant,** Natural History, (834,260)(2 types)* .... 4.00 | | 5.00 | 20.00*

☐ 1391 6c **Maine Statehood,** 7/9/90, Portland, ME (472,165) .... 1.00 | 1.10 | | 1.50 | 20.00

☐ 1392 6c **Wildlife Conservation,** 7/20/70, Custer, SD (309,418) .... 1.00 | 1.25 | | 2.00 | 20.00

1970-74

☐ 1393 6c **Dwight D. Eisenhower,** 8/6/70, DC .... 1.00 | 1.10 | | 1.50 | 15.00

☐ 1393a **Dwight D. Eisenhower,** booklet pane of 8, 8/6/70, DC 3.00

☐ 1393a **Dwight D. Eisenhower,** booklet pane of 8, dull gum, 3/1/71, DC 75.00

☐ 1393b **Dwight D. Eisenhower,** booklet pane of 5 plus labels, 8/6/70, DC 1.50

☐ Scott 1393a, 1393b (two different slogans in label) 3 panes on one FDC, 8/6/70, DC 11.50
Total for Scott 1393-1393b, 1401 is 823,540.

☐ 1393D 7c **Benjamin Franklin,** 10/20/72, Philadelphia, PA (309,276) .... 1.00 | 1.10 | | 1.50 | 18.00

☐ 1394 8c **Dwight D. Eisenhower,** 5/10/71, DC .... 1.00 | 1.10 | | 1.50 |

☐ 1395 8c **Dwight D. Eisenhower,** 5/10/71, DC .... 1.00 | 1.10 | | 1.50 |

☐ 1395a **Dwight D. Eisenhower,** booklet pane of 8, 5/10/71, DC 3.00

☐ 1395b **Dwight D. Eisenhower,** booklet pane of 6, 5/10/71, DC 3.00

☐ Scott 1395a, 1395b on one cover, 5/10/72, DC .5.00
Total for Scott 1394-1395b, 1402 is 813,947.

☐ 1395c **Dwight D. Eisenhower,** booklet pane of 4 plus labels, 1/28/72, Casa Grande, AZ .... 2.25 | | | | 32.00

☐ 1395d **Dwight D. Eisenhower,** booklet pane of 7 plus label, 1/28/72, Casa Grande, AZ ...... 2.00 | | | | 50.00

☐ Scott 1395c, 1395d on one cover 3.00

☐ 1396 8c **USPS Emblem,** 7/1/71, DC .... 1.00 | 1.10 | | 1.50 | 25.00

☐ Unofficial city .... —
Washington, D. C post office had "First Day of Issue" postmark, but Scott 1396 was available at every post office on 7/1/71. More than 18,000 different cities are known with first day postmarks out of 39,521 possible. Values of the individual covers range from $1.

☐ 1397 14c **Fiorello H. LaGuardia,** 4/24/72, New York, NY (180,114) .... 1.00 | 1.25 | | 1.75 | 18.00

☐ 1398 16c **Ernie Pyle,** 5/7/71, DC (444,410) .... 1.00 | 1.25 | | 1.50 | 10.00

U.S. 6¢ POSTAGE

DWIGHT D. EISENHOWER
1383

Christmas
6¢ UNITED STATES
1384

HOPE
FOR THE CRIPPLED
U.S. 6 CENTS
1385

SIX CENTS
UNITED STATES POSTAGE
AMERICAN PAINTING
WILLIAM M. HARNETT
1386

U.S 6¢
AMERICAN BALD EAGLE
1387-90

MAINE STATEHOOD
1820 1970 U.S. SIX CENTS
1391

EISENHOWER·USA
1393

EISENHOWER USA
1394, 1395, 1402

UNITED STATES POSTAGE
6¢
1392

UNITED STATES POSTAGE
U.S. MAIL
6 cents
1396

ELIZABETH BLACKWELL FIRST WOMAN PHYSICIAN
U.S. POSTAGE 18¢
1399

AMADEO P. GIANNINI
U.S.A. 21¢
1400

EDGAR LEE MASTERS
AMERICAN POET
UNITED STATES 6¢
1405

WOMAN SUFFRAGE
50ᵀᴴ ANNIVERSARY
6¢
1406

SOUTH CAROLINA
1670 1970
6¢
1407

Stone Mountain Memorial
UNITED STATES 6 CENTS
1408

GREAT NORTHWEST
1820 FORT SNELLING 1970
US 6¢
1409

SAVE OUR WATER
UNITED STATES · SIX CENTS
1410-13

Christmas
6¢ U.S.
1415-18

Christmas 6¢
1414

UNITED STATES POSTAGE 6 CENTS
UN
United Nations 25ᵗʰ Anniversary
1419

U.S. POSTAGE 6 CENTS
1420

☐ 1399 18c Elizabeth Blackwell, 1/23/74, Geneva, NY
(217,938) (2 types)*..1.00 1.50   2.50 10.00*

☐ 1400 21c Amadeo Giannini, 6/27/73, San Mateo, CA
(282,520)..1.00 1.50   2.50 12.00

1970-71 Coils

☐ 1401 6c Dwight D. Eisenhower, 8/6/70, DC 1.00pr 1.25   lp2.00
☐ 1402 8c Dwight D. Eisenhower, 5/10/71, DC 1.00pr 1.25   lp2.00

1970

☐ 1405 6c Edgar Lee Masters, 8/22/70, Petersburg, IL
(372,804)..1.00 1.10   1.50 22.00
☐ 1405 6c Edgar Lee Masters, 2nd Day. 8/23/70, Garnett, KS ...   38.00
☐ 1406 6c Woman Suffrage, 8/26/70, Adams, MA
(508,142)..1.00 1.10   1.50 25.00
☐ 1407 6c South Carolina, 9/12/70, Charleston, SC
(533,000)..1.00 1.10   1.50 20.00
☐ 1408 6c Stone Mountain Memorial, 9/19/70, Stone
Mountain, GA (558,546)....................................1.00 1.10   1.50 10.00
☐ 1409 6c Fort Shelling, 10/17/70, Fort Snelling, MN
(497,611)..1.00 1.10   1.50 12.00
☐ 1410 6c Globe & Wheat, 10/28/70, San Clemente, CA......1.25
☐ 1411 6c Globe & City, 10/28/70, San Clemente, CA 1.25
☐ 1412 6c Globe & Bluegill, 10/28/70, San Clemente, CA ...1.25
☐ 1413 6c Globe & Seagull, 10/28/70, San Clemente, CA 1.25
☐ 1413a Se-tenant, Anti-Pollution, (1,033,147). "Plate Block"
value is for block of 4 with plate numbers 4.00   5.00 30.00
☐ 1414 6c Christmas, 11/5/70, DC. "Plate Block" value
is for block of 4 with plate numbers.................1.40 1.75   3.00
☐ 1414a Christmas, precanceled, 11/5/70, DC 10.00
☐ 1414 & 1414a 11/5/70 on one cover.................................15.00
☐ 1415 6c Tin & Cast-iron Locomotive, 11/5/70, DC...........1.40
☐ 1415a Tin & Cast-iron Locomotive, precanceled 2.50
☐ 1416 6c Toy Horse on Wheels, 11/5/70, DC.....................1.40
☐ 1416a Toy Horse on Wheels, precanceled 2.50
☐ 1417 6c Mechanical Tricycle, 11/5/70, DC.......................1.40
☐ 1417a Mechanical Tricycle, precanceled............................2.50
☐ 1418 6c Doll Carriage, 11/5/70, DC.................................1.40
☐ 1418a Doll Carriage, precanceled.....................................2.50
☐ 1418b Se-tenant, "Plate Block" value is for block of 4
with plate numbers... 3.50   5.00 22.00
☐ 1418c Se-tenant, precanceled.. 6.00
☐   Scott 1414a-1418a set of 5 on one cover 35.00   55.00
       Total for Scott 1414-1418 or 1414a-1418a is 2,014,450.
☐ 1419 6c United Nations, 11/20/70, New York, NY
(474,070)..1.00 1.10   1.50 12.00
☐ 1420 6c Landing of the Pilgrims, 11/21/70, Plymouth,
MA (629,850)...1.00 1.10   1.50 15.00
☐ 1421 6c Disabled Veterans, 11/24/70, Cincinnati, OH,
or Montgomery, AL 1.00 1.10   1.50 15.00
☐ 1422 6c U.S. Servicemen, 11/24/70, Cincinnati, OH, or
Montgomery, AL...1.00 1.10   1.50 12.00
☐   Scott 1421-1422 on one cover 1.75 1.85   2.00
       476,610 covers were postmarked in Cincinnati; 336,417 in Montgomery.

50 years of service
6c
UNITED STATES
1421

HONORING U.S.SERVICEMEN
PRISONERS OF WAR
MISSING AND KILLED IN ACTION
6c UNITED STATES
1422

UNITED STATES
AMERICA'S WOOL
1423

DOUGLAS MacARTHUR
6c US
1424

giving BLOOD saves lives
6
1425

1st Bazaar cachet

1st Colorano Silk cachet

Missouri 1821-1971 United States
1426

WILDLIFE CONSERVATION
8c
UNITED STATES
CALIFORNIA CONDOR
1427-30

John Sloan
American Artist
1871-1951
United States
8 cents
1433

8
U.S.
ANTARCTIC TREATY
1961-1971
1431

UNITED STATES IN SPACE ... A DECADE OF ACHIEVEMENT
1434-35

U.S.POSTAGE 8c
AMERICAN REVOLUTION BICENTENNIAL
1776-1976
1432

Emily Dickinson
U.S. 8
1436

SAN JUAN, PUERTO RICO
8c
1437

Prevent drug abuse
United States Postage 8c
1438

CARE
1946-1971
u.s.8c
1439

HISTORIC PRESERVATION
U.S.8c
1440-43

Christmas
8c US
National Gallery of Art
1444

8c
1445

8c
SIDNEY LANIER
American Poet
1446

Peace Corps
8c
United States
1447

96

1971

		SINGLE	BLOCK	PLATE BLOCK	CERM PROG
☐ 1423	6c American Wool Industry, 1/19/71, Las Vegas, NV (379,911)..1.00		1.10	1.50	18.00
☐	1st Bazaar cachet 25.00				
☐	1st Colorono Silk cachet................................250.00				
☐ 1424	6c Gen. Douglas MacArthur, 1/26/71, Norfolk, VA (720,035)...1.00		1.10	1.50	15.00
☐ 1425	6c Blood Donor, 3/12/71, New York, NY (644,497)..1.00		1.10	1.50	18.00
☐ 1426	8c Missouri Sesquicentennial, 5/8/71, Independence, MO (551,000). "Plate Block" value is for block of 4 with plate numbers.......1.00		1.25	1.50	18.00
☐ 1427	8c Trout, 6/12/71, Avery Island, LA.....................1.25				
☐ 1428	8c Alligator, 6/12/71, Avery Island, LA.....................1.25				
☐ 1429	8c Polar Bear & Cubs, 6/12/71, Avery Island, LA 1.25				
☐ 1430	8c California Condor, 6/12/71, Avery Island, LA 1.25				
☐ 1430a	Se-tenant (679,483)...		3.00	5.00	25.00
☐ 1431	8c Antarctic Treaty, 6/23/71, DC (419,200) 1.00		1.25	1.50	12.00
☐ 1432	8c American Revolution Bicentennial, 7/4/71, DC (434,930)...1.00		1.25	1.50	
☐	1st Medallion cachet 25.00				
☐ 1433	8c John Sloan, 8/2/71, Lock Haven, PA (482,265)....1.00		1.25	1.50	12.00
☐ 1434a	8c Space Achievement Decade, se-tenant pair, 8/2/71, Kennedy Space Center, FL (1,403,644).2.50		3.25	4.00	
☐	Houston, TX (811,560), pair 2.50		3.25	4.00	
☐	Huntsville, AL (524,000), pair (3 papers)*...........3.00		4.00	5.00	35.00*
☐	1st Manned Space Flight Covers cachet 15.00				
☐	1st Swanson cachet...15.00				
☐ 1436	8c Emily Dickinson, 8/28/71, Amherst, MA (498,180)..1.00		1.25	1.50	12.00
☐ 1437	8c San Juan, 9/12/71, San Juan, PR (501,688) 1.00		1.25	1.50	18.00
☐ 1438	8c Prevent Drug Abuse, 10/4/71, Dallas, TX (425,330). "Plate Block" value is for block of 4 with plate numbers..1.00		1.25	1.50	15.00
☐ 1439	8c CARE, 10/27/71, New York, NY (402,121). "Plate Block" value is for block of 4 with plate numbers 1.00		1.25	1.50	18.00
☐ 1440	8c Decatur House, 10/29/71, DC 1.25				
☐ 1441	8c Whaling Ship Charles W. Morgan, 10/29/71, DC..1.25				
☐ 1442	8c Cable Car, 10/29/71, DC......................................1.25				
☐ 1443	8c San Xavier del Bac Mission, 10/29/71, DC..........1.25				
☐ 1443a	Se-tenant, (783,242)...		3.00	4.00	75.00
☐ 1444	8c Christmas, 11/10/71, DC (348,038).....................1.00		1.25	1.50	10.00
☐ 1445	8c Christmas, 11/10/71, DC (580,062).....................1.00		1.25	1.50	10.00
☐	Scott 1444-1445 on one cover 1.75				

1972

		SINGLE	BLOCK	PLATE BLOCK	CERM PROG
☐ 1446	8c Sidney Lanier, 2/3/72, Macon, GA (394,800).......1.00		1.25	1.50	12.00
☐ 1447	8c Peace Corps, 2/11/72, DC (453,660), "Plate Block" value is for block of 4 with plate numbers.......1.00		1.25	1.50	12.00

1453

1448-51

1452

1455

1454

COLONIAL AMERICAN CRAFTSMEN

UNITED STATES POSTAGE 8 CENTS

1456-59

1460-62

P.T.A.
1897
1972
Parent Teacher Association
8¢
U.S.

1463

1464-67

100th Anniversary of Mail Order

1468

1469

Tom Sawyer

United States 8¢

1470

Christmas

1471

1472

Stamp Collecting U.S. 8¢

1474

1st Coulson cachet

PHARMACY

UNITED STATES POSTAGE

1473

1484-87

1475

1476-79

THE BOSTON TEA PARTY 8¢ U.S.

BICENTENNIAL ERA

1480-83

98

National Parks Centennial

☐ 1451a 2c Cape Hatteras National Seashore, se-tenant,
      4/5/72, Hatteras, NC (505,697) 1.25   2.00

☐ 1448-1451 2c National Parks Centennial. 4/5/72. Hatteras, NC
      (without insert) 15.00

☐ 1452 6c Wolf Trap Farm, 6/26/72, Vienna, VA (403,396) .1.00 1.25 1.50 35.00

☐ 1453 8c Old Faithful, 3/1/72, Yellowstone National
      Park, WY 1.00 1.25 1.50 25.00

☐   DC (847,500) 1.00 1.25 1.50

☐ 1454 15c Mt. McKinley, 7/28/72, Mt. McKinley
      National Park, AK (491,456)............................1.00 1.25 2.00 45.00

☐ 1455 8c Family Planning, 3/18/72, New York, NY
      (691,385) 1.00 1.25 1.50 15.00

☐ 1456 8c Glass Blower, 7/4/72, Williamsburg, VA 1.00
☐ 1457 8c Silversmith, 7/4/72, Williamsburg, VA..................1.00
☐ 1458 8c Wigmaker, 7/4/72, Williamsburg, VA...................1.00
☐ 1459 8c Hatter, 7/4/72, Williamsburg, VA 1.00
☐ 1459a Se-tenant, Colonial American Craftsmen(1,914,976)...... 2.50 3.50 15.00
☐ 1460 6c Olympics, 8/17/72, DC. "Plate Block" value is
      for block of 4 with plate numbers 1.00 1.25 1.50

☐ 1461 8c Winter Olympics, 8/17/72, DC. "Plate Block"
      value is for block of 4 with plate numbers 1.00 1.25 1.50

☐ 1462 15c Olympics, 8/17/72, DC. "Plate Block" value is
      for block of 4 with plate numbers 1.00 1.50 2.00
      Scott 1460-1462 and C85 on one cover............2.00
      Total for Scott 1460-1462 and C85 is 971,536.

☐ 1460-1462, C85 6c-15c Olympic Games, (2 types)* 10.00*
☐ 1463 8c Parent Teacher Association, 9/15/72, San
      Francisco, CA (523,454)...................................1.00 1.25 1.50 10.00

☐ 1464 8c Fur Seals, 9/20/72 Warm Springs, OR 1.50
☐ 1465 8c Cardinal, 9/20/72 Warm Springs, OR...................1.50
☐ 1466 8c Brown Pelican, 9/20/72 Warm Springs, OR.........1.50
☐ 1467 8c Bighorn Sheep, 9/20/72 Warm Springs, OR 1.50
☐ 1467a Se-tenant, (733,778)... 3.00 5.00 12.00
☐ 1468 8c Mall Order, 9/27/72, Chicago, IL (759,666).
      "Plate Block" value is for block of 4 with plate
      numbers..1.00 1.25 2.00 30.00

☐ 1469 8c Osteopathic Medicine, 10/9/72, Miami, FL
      (607, 160). "Plate Block" value is for block of 4
      with plate numbers..1.00 1.25 2.00 10.00

☐ 1470 8c Tom Sawyer, 10/13/72, Hannibal, MO (459,013).1.00 1.25 2.00 20.00
      1st Coulson cachet 15.00

☐ 1471-1472 8c Christmas, 11/9/72, DC, either stamp 1.00 1.25 2.00 12.00
      Scott 1471-1472 on one cover
      (718,821 total for both)....................................2.00

☐ 1473 8c Pharmacy, 11/10/72, Cincinnati, OH (804,320). 10.00 11.00 15.00 10.00
☐ 1474 8c Stamp Collecting, 11/17/72, New York, NY
      (434,680)..1.50 1.75 2.00 12.00

1973

☐ 1475 8c Love, 1/26/73, Philadelphia, PA (422,294).
      "Plate Block" value is for block of 4 with plate
      numbers..1.00 1.25 1.50 12.00

Progress in Electronics

1500-02

Copernicus
1473 - 1973

8¢ U.S

1488

U.S. POSTAL SERVICE 8¢

1489-98

Harry S. Truman

U.S Postage 8 cents

1499

Lyndon B. Johnson
United States
8 cents

1503

RURAL AMERICA

10¢

1504-06

Christmas

Raphael
National Gallery
of Art

8¢ U.S

1507

U.S. 8¢

CHRISTMAS

1508

UNITED 10 STATES

1509, 1519

We hold these Truths...

UNITED STATES 10¢

1510, 1520

V.F.W.
75th Anniversary
VETERANS of SPANISH
AMERICAN and OTHER
FOREIGN WARS ★ U.S

10¢

1525

·10·
Robert Frost
AMERICAN POET

1526

IT ALL DEPENDS ON
ZIP
CODE

1511

6·3¢

U.S. Postage

1518

HORSE RACING

U.S. postage 10 cents

1528

US 10¢

Skylab

1529

EXPO 74 - US 10¢
PRESERVE THE ENVIRONMENT

1527

Letters
mingle souls
Donne   Raphael

10cU.S

1530-37

1538-41

FIRST KENTUCKY
SETTLEMENT
FORT HARROD
1774   1974

1542

CONSERVATION

UNITED
STATES

1547

100

Communications in Colonial Times

☐ 1476	8c Pamphleteer, 2/16/73, Portland, OR (431,784) ...1.00	1.25	1.50	12.00
☐ 1477	8c Broadside, 4/13/73, Atlantic City, NJ (423,437) ..1.00	1.25	1.50	12.00
☐ 1478	8c Postrider, 6/22/73, Rochester, NY (586,850)........1.00	1.25	1.50	12.00
☐ 1479	8c Drummer, 9/28/73, New Orleans, LA (522,427)..1.00	1.25	1.50	12.00
☐ 1480	8c British merchantman, 7/4/73, Boston, MA 1.00			
☐ 1481	8c British three-master, 7/4/73, Boston, MA 1.00			
☐ 1482	8c Boats & ship's hulk 7/4/73, Boston, MA 1.00			
☐ 1483	8c Boat & dock, 7/4/73, Boston, MA 1.00			
☐ 1483a	Se-tenant, Boston Tea Party, (897,870)..........................	3.00	4.00	25.00

American Arts

☐ 1484	8c George Gershwin, 2/28/73, Beverly Hills, CA (448,814). "Plate Block" value is for block of 4 with plate numbers.....................................1.00	1.25	1.50	45.00
☐ 1485	8c Robinson Jeffers, 8/13/73, Carmel, CA (394,261). "Plate Block" value is for block of 4 with plate numbers.....................................1.00	1.25	1.50	12.00
☐ 1486	8c Henry O. Tanner, 9/10/73, Pittsburgh, PA (424,065). "Plate Block" value is for block of 4 with plate numbers.....................................1.00	1.25	1.50	12.00
☐ 1487	8c Willa Cather, 9/20/73, Red Cloud, NE (435,784). "Plate Block" value is for block of 4 with plate numbers.....................................1.00	1.25	2.00	8.00
☐ 1488	8c Nicolaus Copernicus, 4/23/73, DC (734,190).......1.00	1.25	1.50	10.00
☐ 1489	8c Stamp Counter, 4/30/73, any city 1.00			
☐ 1490	8c Mail Collection, 4/30/73, any city 1.00			
☐ 1491	8c Letter Facing on Conveyor Belt, 4/30/73, any city1.00			
☐ 1492	8c Parcel Post Sorting, 4/30/73, any city 1.00			
☐ 1493	8c Mail Canceling, 4/30/73, any city 1.00			
☐ 1494	8c Manual Letter Routing, 4/30/73, any city 1.00			
☐ 1495	8c Electronic Letter Routing, 4/30/73, any city.......1.00			
☐ 1496	8c Loading Mail on Truck, 4/30/73, any city 1.00			
☐ 1497	8c Mailman, 4/30/73, any city 1.00			
☐ 1498	8c Rural Mail Delivery, 4/30/73, any city.................1.00			
	Any block of 4/block of 4 with plate number..........	1.25	2.00	
	Strip of 10 on one cover.......................................7.00			
☐ 1498a	Postal Service Employees (4 cities)................................			15.00
☐ 1499	8c Harry S. Truman, 5/8/73, Independence, MO (938,636)...1.00	1.25	1.50	15.00
☐ 1500	6c Electronics, 7/10/73, New York, NY 1.00	1.25	1.50	
☐ 1501	8c Electronics, 7/10/73, New York, NY 1.00	1.25	1.50	
☐ 1502	15c Electronics, 7/10/73, New York, NY 1.00	1.25	1.75	
	Scott 1500-1502 and C86 on one cover..................	3.00	5.00	30.00
	Total for Scott 1500-1502 and C86 is 1,197,700.			
☐ 1503	8c Lyndon B. Johnson, 8/27/73, Austin, TX (701,490)...1.00	1.25	1.50	15.00

1973-74 Rural America

☐ 1504	8c Angus Cattle, 10/5/73, St. Joseph, MO (521,427)...1.00	1.25	1.50	15.00
☐ 1505	10c Chautauqua, 8/6/74, Chautauqua, NY (411,105) (2 types)*...1.00	1.25	1.50	15.00*
☐ 1506	10c Wheat, 8/16/74, Hillsboro, KS (468,280) 1.00	1.25	1.50	15.00

1543-46

1548

Retarded Children
Can Be Helped

1549

15 51

1552

1550

1553

1555

1556

1554

1557

1558

US Bicentennial 10c
1564

Sybil Ludington
1559-62

US Bicentennial IOcents
1563

1565-68

APOLLO SOYUZ 1975

APOLLO SOYUZ SPACE TEST PROJECT

1569-70

1st Gothic Covers cachet

1571

1973

☐ 1507	8c Christmas, 11/7/73, DC	1.00	1.25	1.50	
☐ 1508	8c Christmas, 11/7/73, DC	1.00	1.25	1.50	
	Scott 1507-1508 on one cover				
	(807,468 total for both)		1.75		15.00

1973-74

☐ 1509	10c Crossed Flags, 12/8/73, San Francisco, CA.				
	"Plate Block" value is for block of 4 with plate				
	numbers	1.00	1.25	1.50	18.00
	Total for Scott 1509 and 1519 is 341,528.				
☐ 1510	10c Jefferson Memorial, 12/14/73, DC	1.00	1.25	1.50	
☐ 1510b	Jefferson Memorial, booklet pane of 5 plus labels,				
	12/14/73, DC	2.25			
☐ 1510c	Jefferson Memorial, booklet pane of 8, 12/14/73, DC	2.50			
☐ 1510d	Jefferson Memorial, booklet pane of 6, 8/5/74,				
	Oakland, CA	5.00			25.00
	Total for Scott 1510, 1510b, 1510c, and 1520 is 686,300.				
☐ 1511	10c Zip Code, 1/4/74, DC (335,220). "Plate Block"				
	value is for block of 4 with plate numbers	1.00	1.00	1.50	
☐ 1518	6.3c Liberty Bell, coil, 10/1/74, DC (221,141) (2 types)*	pr1.00	lp1.50	10.00*	
☐ 1519	10c Crossed Flags, coil, 12/8/73, DC	1.00	pr1.00	lp1.50	60.00
☐ 1520	10c Jefferson Memorial, coil, 12/14/73, DC	1.00	pr1.25	lp1.50	

1974

☐ 1525	10c Veterans of Foreign Wars, 3/11/74, DC				
	(543,598)	1.00	1.25	1.50	15.00
☐ 1526	10c Robert Frost, 3/26/74, Derry, NH (500,425)	1.00	1.25	1.50	12.00
☐ 1527	10c EXPO '74, 4/18/74, Spokane, WA (565,548).				
	"Plate Block" value is for block of 4 with plate				
	numbers	1.00	1.25	1.50	15.00
☐ 1528	10c Horse Racing, 5/4/74, Louisville, KY				
	(623,983)	2.00	2.50	3.50	22.00
☐	1st Henry Koehler cachet	15.00			
☐ 1529	10c Skylab, 5/14/74, Houston, TX (972,326)	2.00	2.50	3.50	20.00
☐ 1530	10c Michelangelo, 6/6/74, DC	1.00			20.00
☐ 1531	10c Five Feminine Virtues, 6/6/74, DC	1.00			20.00
☐ 1532	10c Old Scraps, 6/6/74, DC	1.00			20.00
☐ 1533	10c The Lovely Reader, 6/6/74, DC	1.00			20.00
☐ 1534	10c Lady Writing Letter, 6/6/74, DC	1.00			20.00
☐ 1535	10c Inkwell & Quill, 6/6/74, DC	1.00			20.00
☐ 1536	10c Mrs. John Douglas, 6/6/74, DC	1.00			20.00
☐ 1537	10c Don Antonio Noriega, 6/6/74, DC	1.00			20.00
	Any block of 4/block of 4 with plate numbers		1.75	2.00	
	Strip of 8 on one cover	4.00			
	Total for Scott 1530-1537 is 1,374,765.				
☐ 1538	10c Petrified Wood, 6/13/74, Lincoln, NE	1.00			22.00
☐ 1539	10c Tourmaline, 6/13/74, Lincoln, NE	1.00			22.00
☐ 1540	10c Anethyst 6/13/74, Lincoln, NE	1.00			22.00
☐ 1541	10c Rhodochrosite, 6/13/74, Lincoln, NE	1.00			22.00
☐ 1541a	Se-tenant (865,368)		2.50	4.00	
☐ 1542	10c Kentucky Settlement, 6/15/74, Harrodsburg,				
	KY (478,239)	1.00	1.25	1.50	10.00

1572-75

1576

1579-80

1577-78

1584

1592, 1617

1593

1596

1599, 1619

1608

1622, 1625

HOW TO USE THIS BOOK
The number in the first column is its Scott number or identifying number. Following that is the denomination of the stamp, description, date of issue, and the value.

SCOTT NUMBER	DESCRIPTION	SINGLE	PLATE BLOCK	CERM PROG

☐ 1543 10c Carpenter's Hall, 7/4/74, Philadelphia, PA 1.00

☐ 1544 10c "We ask but for peace," 7/4/74,
Philadelphia, PA...1.00

☐ 1545 10c "Deriving their just powers," 7/4/74,
Philadelphia, PA...1.00

☐ 1546 10c Independence Hall, 7/4/74, Philadelphia, PA 1.00

☐ 1546a Se-tenant First Continental Congress (2,124,957) 2.75 3.50 22.00

☐ 1547 10c Energy Conservation, 9/23/74, Detroit, MI
(587,210) (2 types)*...1.00 1.25 1.50 10.00*

☐ 1548 10c Legend of Sleepy Hollow, 10/10/74, North
Tarrytown, NY (514,836) 1.00 1.25 1.50 20.00

☐ 1549 10c Retarded Children, 10/12/74, Arlington, TX
(412,882)...1.00 1.25 1.50 20.00

☐ 1550 10c Christmas, 10/23/74, New York, NY. "Plate Block"
value is for block of 4 with plate numbers. 1.00 1.25 1.50

☐ 1551 10c Christmas, 10/23/74, New York, NY. "Plate Block"
value is for block of 4 with plate numbers. 1.00 1.25 1.50

☐ Scott 1550-1551 on one 1.75 25.00

☐ 1552 10c Christmas, self-adhesive, 11/15/74, New York,
NY (477,410). 1.00

☐ 1st Glen cachet..20.00

☐ 1550-1552 Christmas 1552 was added to the 1550-1551 program 85.00

1975 American Arts

☐ 1553 10c Benjamin West, 2/10/75, Swarthmore, PA
(465,017). "Plate Block" value is for block of 4
with plate numbers..1.00 1.25 1.50 20.00

☐ 1554 10c Paul Laurence Dunbar, 5/1/75, Dayton, OH
(397,347). "Plate Block" value is for block of 4
with plate numbers..1.00 1.25 1.50 12.00

☐ 1555 10c D.W. Griffith, 5/27/75, Beverly Hills, CA
(424,167)..1.00 1.25 1.50 12.00

☐ 1556 10c Pioneer-Jupiter, 2/28/75, Mountain View, CA
(594,896)..2.00 2.50 4.00 20.00

☐ 1557 10c Mariner 10, 4/4/75, Pasadena, CA (563,636).....2.00 2.50 4.00 20.00

☐ 1558 10c Collective Bargaining, 3/13/75, DC (412,329).
"Plate Block" value is for block of 4 with
plate numbers..1.00 1.25 1.50 15.00

☐ 1559 8c Sybil Ludington, 3/25/75, Carmel, NY
(394,550). "Plate Block" value is for block of 4
with plate numbers..1.00 1.25 1.50 12.00

☐ 1560 10c Salem Poor, 3/25/75, Cambridge, MA
(415,565). "Plate Block" value is for block of 4
with plate numbers..1.00 1.25 1.50 15.00

☐ 1561 10c Haym Salomon, 3/25/75, Chicago, IL
(447,630). "Plate Block" value is for block of 4
with plate numbers..1.00 1.25 1.50 18.00

☐ 1562 18c Peter Francisco, 3/25/75, Greensboro, NC
(415,000). "Plate Block" value is for block of 4
with plate numbers..1.00 1.25 1.50 15.00

☐ Scott 1559-1562 set on one cover, any city 5.00

☐ 1563 10c Lexington-Concord Battle, 4/19/75, Lexington,
MA, or Concord, MA (975,020). "Plate Block"
value is for block of 4 with plate numbers 1.00 1.25 1.50 15.00

☐ Dual cancel...2.00

☐ **1564** 10c **Battle of Bunker Hill**, 6/17/75, Charlestown, MA, (557,130). "Plate Block" value is for block of 4 with plate numbers (2 types)*........................1.00   1.25   1.50 15.00*

☐ **1565** 10c **Soldier with Flintlock Musket**, 7/4/75, DC........1.00

☐ **1566** 10c **Sailor with Grappling Hook**, 7/4/75, DC...........1.00

☐ **1567** 10c **Marine with Musket**, 7/4/75, DC........................1.00

☐ **1568** 10c **Militiaman**, 7/4/75, DC......................................1.00

☐ **1568a** **Se-tenant**, Military uniforms(1,134, 831). "Plate Block" value is for block of 4 with plate numbers 2.50   3.50 18.00

☐ **1569** 10c **Apollo**, Soyuz before link-up, 7/15/75, Kennedy Space Center, FL 3.00

☐ **1569a** **Se-tenant**, (1,427,046)................................4.00   5.00   6.00

☐ **1570** 10c **Apollo**, Soyuz after link-up, 7/15/75, Kennedy Space Center, FL 3.00

☐ Scott 1569-1570 with Russian stamps, dual cancel400.00

☐ **1571** 10c **International Women's Year**, 8/26/75, Seneca Falls, NY (476,769). "Plate Block" value is for block of 4 plate numbers 1.00   1.25   1.50 18.00

☐ 1st Gothic Covers cachet..................................20.00

☐ **1572** 10c **Stagecoach & Trailer Truck**, 9/3/75, Philadelphia, PA 1.00

☐ **1573** 10c **Locomotives**, 9/3/75, Philadelphia, PA..............1.00

☐ **1574** 10c **Early Mail Plane**, Jet, 9/3/75, Philadelphia, PA. 1.00

☐ **1575** 10c **Satellite, Dishes**, 9/3/75, Philadelphia, PA.........1.00

☐ **1575a** **Se-tenant**, Postal Service Bicentennial(969,999), "Plate Block" value is for block of 4 with plate numbers...   1.25   1.50 18.00

☐ **1576** 10c **World Peace through Law**, 9/29/75, DC (386,736) 1.00   1.25   1.50

☐ **1577** 10c **"Banking,"** coins, 10/6/75, New York, NY..........1.00

☐ **1577a** **Se-tenant**, Banking & Commerce (555,580) "Plate Block" value is for block of 4 with plate numbers 1.10   1.00   1.50 12.00

☐ **1578** 10c **"Commerce,"** coins, 10/6/75, New York, NY......1.00

☐ **1579** 10c **Christmas**, 10/14/75, DC, "Plate Block" value is for block of 4 with plate numbers 1.00   1.25   1.50

☐ **1580** 10c **Christmas**, 10/14/75, DC, "Plate Block" value is for block of 4 with plate numbers 1.00   1.25   1.50

☐ Scott 1579-1580 on one cover (730,079) 2.00

☐ (2 types)* 20.00

1975-81 Americana Issue

☐ **1581** 1c **Inkwell & Quill**, multiple for First Class rate, 12/8/77, St. Louis, MO 1.00   1.25

☐ **1582** 2c **Speaker's Stand**, multiple for First Class rate, 12/8/77, St. Louis, MO 1.00   1.25

☐ **1584** 3c **Early Ballot Box**, multiple for First Class rate, 12/8/77, St. Louis, MO 1.00   1.25

☐ **1585** 4c **Books, Bookmark & Eyeglasses**, multiple for First Class rate, 12/8/77, St. Louis, MO...................   1.00   1.25

☐ **1581-1585** 1c-4c American Series 12.00
     Total for Scott 1581-1585 is 530,033.

☐ **1590** 9c **Dome of the Capitol**, booklet single plus postage for First Class rate, 3/11/77, New York, NY....10.00

☐ **1591** 9c **Dome of the Capitol**, perf. 11 x 10 1/2, multiple for First Class rate, 11/24/75, DC (190,117) 1.00   1.25   1.50

cover binders

Padded, durable, 3-ring binder will hold up to 100 covers. Features the "D" ring mechanism on the right hand side of album so you don't have to worry about creasing or wrinkling covers when opening or closing binder.

Item	Description	Retail
CBRD	Cover Binder - Red	$7.95
CBBL	Cover Binder - Blue	$7.95
CBGY	Cover Binder - Gray	$7.95
CBBK	Cover Binder - Black	$7.95

Cover pages sold separately.

T2	Cover Pages Black (25 per pckg)	$4.95
CBBL	Cover Pages Clear (25 per pckg)	$4.95

The cover binders and pages are available from your favorite stamp dealer or direct from:

SCOTT

P.O. Box 828 Sidney OH 45365-0828

to order call 1-800-572-6885

				PLATE	CERM
☐ 1592	10c **Contemplation of Justice,** multiple for First Class rate, 11/17/77, New York, NY (359,050)..1.00		1.25	1.75	10.00
☐ 1593	11c **Early American Printing Press,** multiple for First Class rate, 11/13/75, Philadelphia, PA (217,755)..................1.00		1.25	1.75	12.00
☐ 1594	12c **Torch,** multiple for First Class rate, 4/8/81, Dallas, TX..................1.00		1.25	1.75	12.00
	Total for Scott 1594 and 1816 is 280,930.				
☐ 1595	13c **Liberty Bell,** booklet single, 10/31/75, Cleveland, OH..................1.00				
☐ 1595a	**Liberty Bell,** booklet pane of 6, 10/31/75, Cleveland, OH..................2.00				
☐ 1595b	**Liberty Bell,** booklet pane of 7 + label, 10/31/75, Cleveland, OH..................2.75				
☐ 1595c	**Liberty Bell,** booklet pane of 8, 10/31/75, Cleveland, OH..................2.50				
☐ 1595a-1595c	**Liberty Bell,** booklet panes..................				20.00
	Total for Scott 1595a-1595c is 256, 734.				
☐ 1595d	**Liberty Bell,** booklet pane of 5 + label, 4/2/76, Liberty, MO (92,223) 2.25				15.00
☐ 1596	13c **Eagle & Shield,** 12/1/75, Juneau, AK (418,272). "Plate Block" value is for block of 4 with plate numbers..................1.00		1.25	1.75	12.00
☐ 1597	15c **Ft. McHenry Flag,** 6/30/78, Baltimore, MD. "Plate Block" value is for block of 4 with plate numbers.......1.00		1.25	1.75	12.00
☐ 1598	15c **Ft. McHenry Flag,** booklet single, 6/30/78, Baltimore, MD..................1.00				
☐ 1598a	**Ft. McHenry Flag** booklet pane of 8..................2.50				50.00
	Total for Scott 1597-1598 and 1618C is 315,359.				
☐ 1599	16c **Head,** Statue of Liberty, 3/31/78, New York, NY 1.00		1.25	1.75	
	Total for Scott 1599 and 1619 is 376,338.				
☐ 1603	24c **Old North Church,** 11/14/75, Boston, MA (208,973) 1.00		1.25	1.75	12.00
☐ 1604	28c **Ft. Nisqually,** 8/11/78, Tacoma, WA (159,639)...1.25		1.75	3.00	10.00
☐ 1605	29c **Sandy Hook Lighthouse,** 4/14/78, Atlantic City, NJ (193,476)..................1.25		1.50	2.50	12.00
☐ 1606	30c **Morris Township School No. 2,** 8/27/79, Devils Lake, ND (186,882)..................1.25		1.50	2.50	15.00
☐ 1608	50c **Iron "Betty" Lamp,** 9/11/79, San Juan, PR (159,540) 1.50		2.00	3.00	22.00
☐ 1610	$1 **Rush Lamp & Candle Holder,** 7/2/79, San Francisco, CA (255,575)..................3.00		4.50	7.50	
☐ 1611	$2 **Kerosene Table Lamp,** 11/16/78, New York, NY (173,596)..................7.00		8.50	10.00	18.00
☐ 1612	$5 **Railroad Lantern,** 8/23/79, Boston, MA (129,192) 15.00		20.00	25.00	30.00

1975-79 Americana Coils

				LINE	CERM
☐ 1613	3.1c **Guitar,** 10/25/79, Shreveport, LA (230,403)............	1.00	1.50		
☐ 1614	7.7c **Saxhorns,** 11/20/76, New York, NY (285,298)	1.00	1.50	12.00	
☐ 1615	7.9c **Drum,** 4/23/76, Miami, FL (193,270)	1.00	1.50	12.00	
☐ 1615C	8.4c **Piano,** 7/13/78, Interlochen, MI (200,392)..............	1.00	1.50	35.00	
☐ 1616	9c **Dome of the Capitol,** 3/5/76, Milwaukee, WI (128,171)..................	1.00	1.50	15.00	

SCOTT NUMBER	DESCRIPTION	SINGLE	PAIR	LINE PAIR	CERM PROG
☐ 1617	10c **Contemplation of Justice**, 11/4/77, Tampa, FL				
	(184,954)..		1.00	1.50	12.00
☐	1st Bill Ressl cachet 15.00				
☐	1st Sandra's Cachets cachet...........................15.00				
☐ 1618	13c **Liberty Bell**, 11/25/75, Allentown, PA (320,387) .1.00		1.10	1.50	12.00
☐ 1618C	15c **Ft. McHenry Flag**, 6/30/78, Baltimore, MD........1.00		1.00	1.10	50.00
☐ 1619	16c **Statue of Liberty Head**, 3/31/78, New York, NY 1.00		1.10	1.50	

SCOTT NUMBER	DESCRIPTION	SINGLE	PLATE BLOCK	CERM BLOCK PROG

1975-77

☐ 1622	13c **Flag over Independence Hall**, 11/15/75,			
	Philadelphia, PA, "Plate Block" value is for block			
	of 4 with plate numbers....................................1.00	1.25	1.75	12.00
☐ 1623	13c **Flag over Capitol**, booklet single, perf.			
	11x10 1/2, 3/11/77, New York, NY.....................1.00			
☐ 1623a	**Flag over Capitol**, booklet pane of 7 + 1 Scott			
	1590, 3/11/77, New York, NY.........................30.00			
☐1623b	**Flag over Capitol**, booklet single, perf. 10,			
	3/11/77, New York, NY...................................1.50			
☐ 1623c	**Flag over Capitol**, booklet pane of 7 + 1 Scott			
	1590a, 3/11/77, New York, NY 15.00			20.00
☐	1623c-1623d **Flag over Capitol**, booklet pane of 8 with			
	perf. 10 1/2x11 stamps added.			60.00
	Total for all versions of Scott 1623 is 242.208.			
☐	Scott 1622 & 1625 on one cover.......................5.00			

SCOTT NUMBER	DESCRIPTION	SINGLE	PAIR	LINE PAIR	CERM PROG
☐ 1625	13c **Flag over Independence Hall**, coil, 11/15/75,				
	Philadelphia, PA..		1.00	1.50	50.00
	Total for Scott 1622 and 1625 is 362,959.				

SCOTT NUMBER	DESCRIPTION	SINGLE	PLATE BLOCK	CERM BLOCK PROG

1976

☐ 1629	13c **Drummer boy**, 1/1/76, Pasadena, CA.................1.75			
☐ 1630	13c **Old Drummer**, 1/1/76, Pasadena, CA 1.75			
☐ 1631	13c **Fifer**, 1/1/76, Pasadena, CA 1.75			
☐ 1631a	**Se-tenant**, (1,013,067). "Block"value is for block of 6. "Plate			
	Block" value is for block of 6 with plate numbers...	2.00	2.25	
☐	1st Postmasters of America cachet.................30.00			
☐ 1632	13c **Interphil '76**, 1/17/76, Philadelphia, PA (519,902)1.00	1.25	1.75	15.00
☐ 1633	13c **Delaware**, 2/23/76, DC 1.25			
☐ 1634	13c **Pennsylvania**, 2/23/76, DC 1.25			
☐ 1635	13c **New Jersey**, 2/23/76, DC 1.25			
☐ 1636	13c **Georgia**, 2/23/76, DC.......................................1.25			
☐ 1637	13c **Connecticut**, 2/23/76, DC 1.25			
☐ 1638	13c **Massachusetts**, 2/23/76, DC..............................1.25			
☐ 1639	13c **Maryland**, 2/23/76, DC.....................................1.25			
☐ 1640	13c **South Carolina**, 2/23/76, DC.............................1.25			
☐ 1641	13c **New Hampshire**, 2/23/76, DC 1.25			
☐ 1642	13c **Virginia**, 2/23/76, DC.......................................1.25			
☐ 1643	13c **New York**, 2/23/76, DC....................................1.25			
☐ 1644	13c **North Carolina**, 2/23/76, DC 1.25			
☐ 1645	13c **Rhode Island**, 2/23/76, DC................................1.25			

1623

1629-31

1st Postmasters of America cachet

1632

1633-82

1683

1686

1684

1685

JULY 4, 1776
1691-94

1687

1688

1689

1st Metropolitan FDC Society cachet

1690

Values for various cachet makers can be determined by using the Cachet Calculator which begins on page 52A.

☐ 1646	13c Vermont, 2/23/76, DC..............................1.25				
☐ 1647	13c Kentucky, 2/23/76, DC.............................1.25				
☐ 1648	13c Tennessee, 2/23/76, DC...........................1.25				
☐ 1649	13c Ohio, 2/23/76, DC...................................1.25				
☐ 1650	13c Louisiana, 2/23/76, DC............................1.25				
☐ 1651	13c Indiana, 2/23/76, DC...............................1.25				
☐ 1652	13c Mississippi, 2/23/76, DC.........................1.25				
☐ 1653	13c Illinois, 2/23/76, DC................................1.25				
☐ 1654	13c Alabama, 2/23/76, DC.............................1.25				
☐ 1655	13c Maine, 2/23/76, DC.................................1.25				
☐ 1656	13c Missouri, 2/23/76, DC.............................1.25				
☐ 1657	13c Arkansas, 2/23/76, DC............................1.25				
☐ 1658	13c Michigan, 2/23/76, DC............................1.25				
☐ 1659	13c Florida, 2/23/76, DC...............................1.25				
☐ 1660	13c Texas, 2/23/76, DC..................................1.25				
☐ 1661	13c Iowa, 2/23/76, DC...................................1.25				
☐ 1662	13c Wisconsin, 2/23/76, DC...........................1.25				
☐ 1663	13c California, 2/23/76, DC............................1.25				
☐ 1664	13c Minnesota, 2/23/76, DC...........................1.25				
☐ 1665	13c Oregon, 2/23/76, DC................................1.25				
☐ 1666	13c Kansas, 2/23/76, DC.................................1.25				
☐ 1667	13c West Virginia, 2/23/76, DC......................1.25				
☐ 1668	13c Nevada, 2/23/76, DC................................1.25				
☐ 1669	13c Nebraska, 2/23/76, DC.............................1.25				
☐ 1670	13c Colorado, 2/23/76, DC.............................1.25				
☐ 1671	13c North Dakota, 2/23/76, DC.......................1.25				
☐ 1672	13c South Dakota, 2/23/76, DC.......................1.25				
☐ 1673	13c Montana, 2/23/76, DC..............................1.25				
☐ 1674	13c Washington, 2/23/76, DC..........................1.25				
☐ 1675	13c Idaho, 2/23/76, DC...................................1.25				
☐ 1676	13c Wyoming, 2/23/76, DC..............................1.25				
☐ 1677	13c Utah, 2/23/76, DC....................................1.25				
☐ 1678	13c Oklahoma, 2/23/76, DC............................1.25				
☐ 1679	13c New Mexico, 2/23/76, DC.........................1.25				
☐ 1680	13c Arizona, 2/23/76, DC...............................1.25				
☐ 1681	13c Alaska, 2/23/76, DC.................................1.25				
☐ 1682	13c Hawaii, 2/23/76, DC.................................1.25				
	Complete set of 50..75.00				
☐ 1682a	Se-tenant, State Flags complete pane on one				
	(4 cities)..				60.00
☐	Canceled at state capitals, each.....................2.00				
☐	Canceled at state capitals, complete set of 50......100.00				
☐	2/23/76, dual cancels (State & DC).......................150.00				
	Total for Scott 1633-1682 is 3,514,070.				
☐ 1683	13c Telephone Centenary, 3/10/76, Boston, MA				
	(662,515)..1.00	1.25	1.50	15.00	
☐ 1684	13c Commercial Aviation, 3/19/76, Chicago, IL				
	(631,555). "Plate Block" value is for block of 4				
	with plate numbers.......................................1.00	1.25	1.50	15.00	
☐	1st hfb cachet..15.00				
☐ 1685	13c Chemistry, 4/6/76, New York, NY (557,600).				
	"Plate Block" value is for block of 4 with				
	plate numbers...1.00	1.25	1.50	15.00	
☐ 1686	13c Surrender of Cornwallis, souvenir sheet,				
	5/29/76, Philadelphia, PA..................................6.00				

1695-98

1699

1700

1701

1702

1st Carrollton cachet

1704

US Bicentennial 13¢

1705

1st Doris Gold cachet

1710

1706-09

1st GAMM cachet

1st Spectrum cachet

HOW TO USE THIS BOOK
The number in the first column is its Scott number or identifying number. Following that is the denomination of the stamp, description, date of issue, and the value.

☐ 1687	18c **Declaration of Independence,** souvenir sheet, 5/29/76, Philadelphia, PA 7.50				
☐ 1688	24c **Washington Crossing the Delaware,** souvenir sheet, 5/29/76, Philadelphia, PA........................9.00				
☐ 1689	31c **Washington at Valley Forge,** souvenir sheet, 5/29/76, Philadelphia, PA 10.00				
	Scott 1686a-1689e, any single from sheets 1.00				
	Total for Scott 1686-1689 is 879,890.				
☐ 1686-1689	13c-31c Bicentennial Souvenir Sheets (any single stamp)(2 types)*.....................................				25.00*
☐ 1690	13c **Benjamin Franklin,** 6/1/76, Philadelphia, PA ...1.00		1.25	1.50	15.00
	In Combo with Canadian issue, dual cancels....1.75				
	1st Metropolitan FDC Society cachet 15.00				
☐ 1691	13c **Declaration of Independence,** 7/4/76, Philadelphia, PA...1.00				
☐ 1692	13c **Declaration of Independence,** 7/4/76, Philadelphia, PA...1.00				
☐ 1693	13c **Declaration of Independence,** 7/4/76, Philadelphia, PA...1.00				
☐ 1694	13c **Declaration of Independence,** 7/4/76, Philadelphia, PA...1.00				
☐ 1694a	Se-tenant, "Plate Block" value is for block of 8 with plate numbers...		2.00	2.50	40.00
	Total for Scott 1691-1694 is 2,093,880.				
☐ 1695	13c **Diving,** 7/16/76, Lake Placid, NY.......................1.00				
☐ 1696	13c **Skiing,** 7/16/76, Lake Placid, NY.......................1.00				
☐ 1697	13c **Running,** 7/16/76, Lake Placid, NY 1.00				
☐ 1698	13c **Skating,** 7/16/76, Lake Placid, NY.....................1.00				
☐ 1698a	Se-tenant, Olympic Games, (1,140,189). "Plate Block" value is for block of 4 with plate numbers		2.00	2.50	22.00
☐ 1699	13c **Clara Maass,** 8/18/76, Belleville, NJ (646,506). "Plate Block" value is for block of 4 with plate numbers......................................2.00		2.25	2.75	15.00
☐ 1700	13c **Adolph S. Ochs,** 9/18/76, New York, NY (582,580) 1.00		1.25	1.50	
☐ 1701	13c **Christmas (Nativity),** 10/27/76, Boston, MA. "Plate Block" value is for block of 4 with plate numbers 1.00		1.25	1.50	
☐ 1702	13c **Christmas ("Winter Pastime"),** 10/27/76, Boston, MA. "Plate Block" value is for block of 4 with plate numbers..1.00		1.25	1.50	
	Scott 1701-1702 set on one cover.....................1.75				
☐ 1703	13c **Christmas ("Winter Pastime"),** 10/27/76, Boston, MA. "Plate Block" value is for block of 4 with plate numbers..1.00		1.25		
☐ 1701-1702	**Christmas** (Copley & Currier)				20.00
☐ 1701-1703	**Christmas** (Copley & Currier), Photogravure				45.00
	Total for Scott 1701-1703 is 330,450.				

1977

☐ 1704	13c **Washington at Princeton,** 1/3/77, Princeton, NJ (695,335). "Plate Block" value is for block of 4 with plate numbers..1.00		1.25	1.50	18.00
	1st Carrollton cachet.......................................20.00				
☐ 1705	13c **Sound Recording,** 3/23/77, DC (632,216) 1.00		1.25	1.50	18.00
	1st Weddle cachet 100.00				

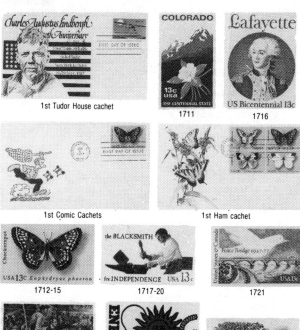

1st Tudor House cachet

1711

COLORADO
13c USA
THE CENTENNIAL STATE

Lafayette
US Bicentennial 13c

1716

1st Comic Cachets

1st Ham cachet

Checkerspot
USA 13C *Euphydryas phaeton*

1712-15

the BLACKSMITH
for INDEPENDENCE USA 13c

1717-20

United States of Canada Peace Bridge 1927-77
USA13c

1721

Herkimer at Oriskany 1777 by Yohn
US Bicentennial 13 cents

1722

ENERGY
DEVELOPMENT USA 13c

1723-24

First Civil Settlement-Alta California 1777
USA 13c

1725

HOW TO USE THIS BOOK

The number in the first column is its Scott number or identifying number. Following that is the denomination of the stamp, description, date of issue, and the value.

114

		SINGLE	BLOCK	PLATE BLOCK	CERM PROG
☐ 1706	13c **Zia Pot**, 4/13/77, Santa Fe, NM..........................1.00				
☐ 1707	13c **San Ildefonso Pot**, 4/13/77, Santa Fe, NM.........1.00				
☐ 1708	13c **Hopi Pot**, 4/13/77, Santa Fe, NM 1.00				
☐ 1709	13c **Acoma Pot**, 4/13/77, Santa Fe, NM....................1.00				
☐ 1709a	**Se-tenant,** Pueblo Pottery (1,194,554). "Plate Block"				
	value is for block of 4 with plate numbers..............		2.00	3.00	12.00
☐	1st Jack Davis Covers cachet..........................30.00				
☐	"Sante Fe" error in cancel 10.00	12.00			
☐ 1710	13c **Lindbergh Flight**, 5/20/77, Roosevelt Field				
	Sta., NY (3,985,989). "Plate Block" value is for				
	block of 4 with plate numbers 3.00		3.25	3.50	25.00
☐	1st Doris Gold cachet 50.00				
☐	1st GAMM cachet..50.00				
☐	1st Spectrum cachet.......................................25.00				
☐	1st Tudor House cachet 20.00				
☐	1st Global Cachets..20.00				
☐	1st Z-Silk cachet...20.00				
☐ 1711	13c **Colorado Statehood**, 5/21/77, Denver, CO				
	(510, 880). "Plate Block" value is for block of 4				
	with plate numbers..1.00		1.25	1.50	12.00
☐ 1712	13c **Swallowtail**, 6/6/77, Indianapolis, IN.................1.00				
☐ 1713	13c **Checkerspot**, 6/6/77, Indianapolis, IN...............1.00				
☐ 1714	13c **Dogface**, 6/6/77, Indianapolis, IN.....................1.00				
☐ 1715	13c **Orange-tip**, 6/6/77, Indianapolis, IN 1.00				
☐ 1715a	**Se-tenant,** Butterflies(1,218,278). "Plate Block"				
	value is for block of 4 with plate numbers..............		2.00	3.00	18.00
☐	1st Comic cachet 20.00				
☐	1st Ham cachet 450.00				
☐ 1716	13c **Lafayette**, 6/13/77, Charleston, SC (514,506) 1.00		1.25	1.50	15.00
☐ 1717	13c **Seamstress**, 7/4/77, Cincinnati, OH....................1.00				
☐ 1718	13c **Blacksmith**, 7/4/77, Cincinnati, OH....................1.00				
☐ 1719	13c **Wheelwright**, 7/4/77, Cincinnati, OH 1.00				
☐ 1720	13c **Leatherworker**, 7/4/77, Cincinnati, OH..............1.00				
☐ 1720a	**Se-tenant,** Skilled Hands for Independence				
	(1,263,568). "Plate Block" value is for				
	block of 4 with plate numbers 1.75		2.50		18.00
☐ 1721	13c **Peace Bridge**, 8/4/77, Buffalo, NY (512,995).....1.00		1.25	1.50	15.00
☐	**U.S. and Canadian** stamps on one cover,				
	U.S. cancel...2.00				
☐	Dual U.S. and Canadian cancels 3.00				
☐ 1722	13c **Battle of Oriskany**, 8/6/77, Herkimer, NY				
	(605,906). "Plate Block" value is for block of 4				
	with plate numbers..1.00		1.25	1.50	22.00
☐ 1723	13c **Energy Conservation**, 10/20/77, DC 1.00				
☐ 1723a	**Se-tenant,** "Plate Block" value is for block of 4				
	with plate numbers..1.25		1.25	1.50	
☐ 1724	13c **Energy Development**, 10/20/77, DC 1.00				
	Total for Scott 1723-1724 is 410,299.				
☐ 1725	13c **Alta California**, 9/9/77, San Jose, CA				
	(709,457)..1.00		1.25	1.50	10.00
☐ 1726	13c **Articles of Confederation**, 9/30/77, York, PA				
	(605,455)..1.00		1.25	1.50	16.00
☐ 1727	13c **Talking Pictures**, 10/6/77, Hollywood, CA				
	(570,195)..2.00		2.25	3.00	25.00

1726

1727

US Bicentennial 13 cents
1728

1729

1730

1734

1731

1732

1st Calhoun Collector's Society Gold Foil Cachet

1733

1735

1st Rob Cuscaden cachet

1st Western Silk Cachets

HOW TO USE THIS BOOK

The number in the first column is its Scott number or identifying number. Following that is the denomination of the stamp, description, date of issue, and the value.

☐ 1728   **13c Surrender at Saratoga,** 10/7/77, Schuylerville, NY (557,529). "Plate Block" value is for block of 4 with plate numbers.................1.00   1.25   1.50 15.00

☐ 1729   **13c Christmas (Valley Forge),** 10/21/77, Valley Forge, PA (583,139). "Plate Block" value is for block of 4 with plate numbers 1.00   1.25   1.50 25.00

☐   1st HJS cachet.....................................15.00

☐ 1730   **13c Christmas (mailbox),** 10/21/77, Omaha, NE (675,786). "Plate Block" value is for block of 4 with plate numbers.............................1.00   1.25   1.50 20.00

☐   Scott 1729-1730 on one cover 3.00

☐   Scott 1729-1730 on one cover with dual cancels .4.00

1978

☐ 1731   **13c Carl Sandburg,** 1/6/78, Galesburg, IL (493,826)...1.00   1.25   1.50 15.00

☐   1st Calhoun Collector's Society Gold Foil Cachet 25.00

☐   1st Rob Cuscaden cachet 15.00

☐   1st Western Silk cachet....................35.00

☐   1st Nova cachet..................................15.00

☐   1st Susan Richardson cachet 15.00

☐ 1732   **13c Captain Cook,** 1/20/78, Honolulu, HI, or Anchorage, AK 1.00   1.25   1.50

☐ 1732a   **Se-tenant,** Captain Cook 1.75   1.85   2.00

☐ 1733   **13c Resolution & Discovery,** 1/20/78, Honolulu, HI, or Anchorage, AK..................................1.00   1.25   1.50 18.00

☐   Scott 1732-1733 on one cover with dual cancel .2.00

☐   1st K.M.C. Venture cachet..............70.00

          Total for Scott 1732-33 is 1,496,659.

☐ 1734   **13c Indian Head Penny,** 1/11/78, Kansas City, MO (512,426) (2 types)*..................................1.00   1.25   2.00 15.00*

1978-80 Regular Issues

☐ 1735   **(15c) "A" & Eagle,** non-denominated, 5/22/78, Memphis, TN....................................1.00   1.25   1.50

☐   1st G. Peltin cachet 30.00

☐ 1736   **(15c) "A" & Eagle,** non-denominated, booklet single, 5/22/78, Memphis, TN...........1.00   1.25   1.50

☐ 1736a   **"A" & Eagle,** booklet pane of 8 ....2.50

☐ 1737   **15c Roses,** booklet single, 7/11/78, Shreveport, LA, (445,003) 1.00

☐ 1737a   **Roses,** booklet pane of 8 ....2.50   20.00

☐ 1738   **15c Windmills,** 2/7/80, Lubbock, TX, booklet single...1.00

☐ 1739   **15c Windmills,** 2/7/80, Lubbock, TX, booklet single...1.00

☐ 1740   **15c Windmills,** 2/7/80, Lubbock, TX, booklet single...1.00

☐ 1741   **15c Windmills,** 2/7/80, Lubbock, TX, booklet single...1.00

☐ 1742   **15c Windmills,** 2/7/80, Lubbock, TX, booklet single...1.00

☐ 1742a   **Booklet pane of 10**....................................3.50   48.00

          Total for Scott 1738-1742 is 708,411.

☐ 1743   **(15c) "A" & Eagle,** coil, 5/22/78, Memphis, TX........1.00 pr l.00 lp l.50

☐   1st Kribbs Kover cachet...................40.00

          Total for Scott 1735, 1736 and 1743 is 689,049.

SCOTT NUMBER	DESCRIPTION	SINGLE	PLATE BLOCK	BLOCK	CERM PROG
☐ 1744	13c Harriet Tubman, 2/1/78, DC (493,495) "Plate Block" value is for block of 4 with plate numbers. 1.00		1.25	2.00	25.00
☐ 1745	13c Quilt design, 3/8/78, Charleston, WV.................1.00				
☐ 1746	13c Quilt design, 3/8/78, Charleston, WV.................1.00				
☐ 1747	13c Quilt design, 3/8/78, Charleston, WV.................1.00				
☐ 1748	13c Quilt design, 3/8/78, Charleston, WV.................1.00				
☐ 1748a	Se-tenant, American Quilts (1,081,827), "Plate Block" value is for block of 4 with numbers		2.00	3.00	20.00
☐	1st F. Collins cachet.......................................500.00				
☐ 1749	13c Ballet, 4/26/78, New York, NY 1.00				
☐ 1750	13c Theatre Dance, 4/26/78, New York, NY.............1.00				
☐ 1751	13c Folk Dance, 4/26/78, New York, NY...................1.00				
☐ 1752	13c Modern Dance, 4/26/78, New York, NY.............1.00				
☐ 1752a	Se-tenant, American Dance (1,626,493) "Plate Block" value is for block of 4 with plate numbers		1.75	2.50	10.00
☐	1st Andrews cachet..30.00				
☐	1st Annable cachet...15.00				
☐	1st Great Picture Covers cachet......................20.00				
☐ 1753	13c French Alliance, 5/4/78, York, PA (705,240) 1.00		1.25	1.50	12.00
☐ 1754	13c Early Cancer Detection, 5/18/78, DC (535,584)..1.00		1.25	1.50	25.00
☐ 1755	13c Jimmie Rodgers, 5/24/78, Meridian, MS (599,287). "Plate Block" value is for block of 4 with plate numbers...1.00		1.25	1.50	22.00
☐ 1756	15c George M. Cohan, 7/3/78, Providence, RI (740,750). "Plate Block" value is for block of 4 with plate numbers...1.00		1.25	1.50	18.00
☐	1st Richard S. Byron cachet............................15.00				
☐ 1757	13c CAPEX Souvenir Sheet, 6/10/78, Toronto, Ontario (1,994,067)..3.50				
☐ 1757a	13c Cardinal 1.00				
☐ 1757b	13c Mallard 1.00				
☐ 1757c	13c Canada Goose 1.00				
☐ 1757d	13c Blue Jay 1.00				
☐ 1757e	13c Moose...1.00				
☐ 1757f	13c Chipmunk...1.00				
☐ 1757g	13c Red Fox 1.00				
☐ 1757h	13c Raccoon...1.00				
☐ 1758	15c Photography, 6/26/78, Las Vegas, NV (684,987). "Plate Block" value is for block of 4 with plate numbers...1.50		1.75	2.00	15.00
☐ 1759	15c Viking Missions to Mars, 7/20/78, Hampton, VA (805,051)..2.00		2.50	3.00	25.00
☐	1st Softones cachet 20.00				
☐ 1760	15c Great gray Owl, 8/26/78, Fairbanks, AK..........1.00				
☐ 1761	15c Saw-whet Owl, 8/26/78, Fairbanks, AK............1.00				
☐ 1762	15c Barred Owl, 8/26/78, Fairbanks, AK 1.00				
☐ 1763	15c Great Horned Owl, 8/26/78, Fairbanks, AK 1.00				
☐ 1763a	Se-tenant, American Owls, (1,690,474)............................		2.00	2.50	18.00
☐ 1764	15c Giant Sequoia, 10/9/78, Hot Springs National Park, AR..1.00				
☐ 1765	15c White Pine, 10/9/78, Hot Springs National Park, AR..1.00				

1st F. Collins Cachet

1744

1749-52

1st Andrews Cachet cachet

1753

1754

1755

1756

Photography USA 15c
1758

Viking missions to Mars
1759

1st Softones cachet

1764-67

1760-63

**Values for various cachet makers can be determined
by using the Cachet Calculator which begins on page 52A.**

SCOTT NUMBER	DESCRIPTION	SINGLE	PLATE BLOCK	CERM BLOCK	PROG
☐ 1766	15c White Oak, 10/9/78, Hot Springs National Park, AR 1.00				
☐ 1767	15c Gray Birch, 10/9/78, Hot Springs National Park, AR 1.00				
☐ 1767a	Se-tenant, American Trees (1,139,100)		2.00	2.50	18.00
☐ 1768	15c Christmas (Madonna), 10/18/78, DC (553,064)...1.00		1.25	1.50	32.00
☐ 1769	15c Christmas (Hobby Horse), 10/18/78, Holly, MI (603,008). "Plate Block" value is for block of 4 with plate numbers (2 types)*...................1.00		1.25	1.50	22.00*
☐	Scott 1768-1769 on one cover 3.00				
☐	Scott 1768-1769 dual cancels 4.00				

1979

SCOTT NUMBER	DESCRIPTION	SINGLE	PLATE BLOCK	CERM BLOCK	PROG
☐ 1770	15c Robert F. Kennedy, 1/12/79, DC (624,582) 2.00		2.50	3.50	30.00
☐	1st Bittings cachet..20.00				
☐	1st DRC cachet 50.00				
☐ 1771	15c Martin Luther King, Jr. 1/13/79, Atlanta, GA (726, 149). "Plate Block" value is for block of 4 with plate numbers 1.00		1.25	1.50	30.00
☐ 1772	15c International Year of the Child, 2/15/79, Philadelphia, PA (716,782).........................1.00		1.25	1.50	10.00
☐ 1773	15c John Steinbeck, 2/27/79, Salinas, CA (709,073)..1.00		1.25	1.50	15.00
☐ 1774	15c Albert Einstein, 3/4/79, Princeton, NJ (641,423)..1.50		2.00	3.00	18.00
☐ 1775	15c Coffeepot, 4/19/79, Lancaster, PA.....................1.00				
☐ 1776	15c Tea Caddy, 4/19/79, Lancaster, PA....................1.00				
☐ 1777	15c Sugar Bowl, 4/19/79, Lancaster, PA...................1.00				
☐ 1778	15c Coffeepot, 4/19/79, Lancaster, PA.....................1.00				
☐ 1778a	Se-tenant, Pennsylvania Toleware(1,581,963). "Plate Block" value is for block of 4 with plate numbers...		2.00	2.50	12.00
☐ 1779	15c Virginia Rotunda, 6/4/79, Kansas City, MO 1.00				
☐ 1780	15c Baltimore Cathedral, 6/4/79, Kansas City,MO ...1.00				
☐ 1781	15c Boston State House, 6/4/79, Kansas City, MO. ..1.00				
☐ 1782	15c Philadelphia Exchange, 6/4/79, Kansas City,MO...1.00				
☐ 1782a	Se-tenant, American Architecture, (1,219,258)		2.00	2.50	20.00
☐ 1783	15c Persistent Trillium, 6/7/79, Milwaukee, WI 1.00				
☐ 1784	15c Hawaiian Wild Broadbean, 6/7/79, Milwaukee, WI 1.00				
☐ 1785	15c Contra Costa Wallflower, 6/7/79, Milwaukee, WI 1.00				
☐ 1786	15c Antioch Dunes Evening Primrose, 6/7/79, Milwaukee, WI 1.00				
☐ 1786a	Se-tenant, Endangered Flora(1,436,268). "Plate Block" value is for block of 4 with plate numbers		2.00	2.50	15.00
☐ 1787	15c Seeing Eye Dogs, 6/15/79, Morristown, NJ (588,826). "Plate Block" value is for block of 4 with plate numbers 1.00		1.25	1.50	28.00
☐ 1788	15c Special Olympics, 8/9/79, Brockport, NY (651,344). "Plate Block" value is for block of 4 with plate numbers 1.00		1.25	1.50	18.00
☐ 1789	15c John Paul Jones, 9/23/79, Annapolis, MD, perf. 11x12. "Plate Block" value is for block of 4 with plate numbers 1.00		1.25	1.50	15.00

1770

1768

1769

1772

1771

1773

1st Bittings cachet

1774

1775-8

1st DRC cachet

1779-82

1783-6

1787

1788

1789

1790

1795-8

1799

1800

1802

**Values for various cachet makers can be determined
by using the Cachet Calculator which begins on page 52A.**

☐ 1789a	**John Paul Jones**, perf. 11. "Plate Block" value is for block of 4 with plate numbers....................1.00		1.25	1.50	
☐	1st D. Cunningham cachet 8.00				
	Total for Scott 1789 and 1789a is 587,018.				
☐ 1790	**10¢ Olympic Games**, 9/5/79, Olympia, WA (305, 122). "Plate Block" value is for block of 4 with plate numbers...1.00		1.50	2.00	15.00
☐ 1791	**15¢ Running**, 9/28/79, Los Angeles, CA....................1.00				
☐ 1792	**15¢ Swimming**, 9/28/79, Los Angeles, CA 1.00				
☐ 1793	**15¢ Rowing**, 9/28/79, Los Angeles, CA 1.00				
☐ 1794	**15¢ Equestrian**, 9/28/79, Los Angeles, CA...............1.00				
☐ 1794a	**Se-tenant**, Olympic Games(1,561,366). "Plate Block" value is for block of 4 with plate numbers		2.00	2.50	15.00
☐ 1795	**15¢ Speed Skating**, 2/1/80, Lake Placid, NY...........1.00				
☐ 1796	**15¢ Downhill Skiing**, 2/1/80, Lake Placid, NY..........1.00				
☐ 1797	**15¢ Ski Jump**, 2/1/80, Lake Placid, NY....................1.00				
☐ 1798	**15¢ Hockey**, 2/1/80, Lake Placid, NY 1.00				
☐ 1798a	**Se-tenant**, Winter Olympic Games (1,166,302). "Plate Block" value is for block of 4 with plate numbers...		2.00	2.50	
☐ 1795-1798	**15¢** Winter Olympic Games				15.00
☐ 1799	**15¢ Christmas (Madonna & Child)**, 10/18/79, DC (686,990). "Plate Block" value is for block of 4 with plate numbers...1.00		1.25	1.50	12.00
☐ 1800	**15¢ Christmas (Santa Claus)**, 10/18/79, North Pole, AK (511,829). "Plate Block" value is for block of 4 with plate numbers 1.00		1.25	2.00	15.00
☐	Scott 1799-1800 on one cover 2.00				
☐	Scott 1799-1800 on one cover, dual cancels.....3.00				
☐ 1801	**15¢ Will Rogers**, 11/4/79, Claremore, OK (1,643,151). "Plate Block" value is for block of 4 with plate numbers (2 types)*............................1.00		1.25	1.50	23.00*
☐	1st Jemm Covers cachet.................................25.00				
☐ 1802	**15¢ Vietnam Veterans**, 11/11/79, DC (445,934). "Plate Block" value is for block of 4 with plate numbers 2.50		3.00	4.00	25.00
☐	1st Brennan cachet 15.00				
☐ 1803	**15¢ W.C. Fields**, 1/29/80, Beverly Hills, CA (633,303). "Plate Block" value is for block of 4 with plate numbers 1.25		1.50	2.50	25.00
☐	1st Gill Craft cachet 30.00				
☐	1st Kover Kids cachet 20.00				
☐ 1804	**15¢ Benjamin Banneker**, 2/15/80, Annapolis, MD (647,126). "Plate Block" value is for block of 4 with plate numbers 1.00		1.25	1.50	25.00
☐	1st Queensbury cachet....................................20.00				
☐ 1805	**15¢ "Letters Preserve Memories,"** 2/25/80, DC.......1.00				
☐ 1806	**15¢ "P.S. Write Soon,"** 2/25/80, DC 1.00				
☐ 1807	**15¢ "Letters Lift Spirits,"** 2/25/80, DC.....................1.00				
☐ 1808	**15¢ "P.S. Write Soon,"** 2/25/80, DC 1.00				
☐ 1809	**15¢ "Letters Shape Opinions,"** 2/25/80, DC.............1.00				
☐ 1810	**15¢ "P.S. Write Soon,"** 2/25/80, DC 1.00				
☐ 1810a	**Se-tenant**, National Letter Writing Week, (1,083,360) on one 2.50				12.00

Note: Marginal markings require 12 stamps, plate blocks 36.

1801   1803   1804   1805-10   1811

1st Brennan cachet   1st Gill Craft cachet

1818-20   1821   1823   1824   1825

1822

1st American Postal Arts Society Cachet (Post/Art)   1st D.J. Graf Cachet

HOW TO USE THIS BOOK
The number in the first column is its Scott number or
identifying number. Following that is the denomination
of the stamp, description, date of issue, and the value.

1980-81 Americana Coils

☐ 1811	1c Inkwell & Quill, 3/6/80, New York, NY (262,921).......	1.00	1.25	
☐ 1813	3.5c Weaver Violins, 6/23/80, Williamsburg, PA	1.00	1.25	
	Total for Scott 1813 and U590 is 716,988.			
☐ 1816	12c Torch, 4/8/81, Dallas, TX	1.00	1.25	
	Total for Scott 1594 and 1816 is 280,930.			

☐ 1818	(18c) "B" & Eagle, 3/15/81, San Francisco, CA........1.00	1.25	1.65		
☐ 1819	(18c) "B" & Eagle, booklet single, 3/15/81, San Francisco, CA 1.00				
☐ 1819a	"B" & Eagle, booklet pane of 8 ....3.00				
☐ 1820	(18c) "B" & Eagle coil, 3/15/81, San Francisco, CA 1.00	1.25	1.65		
	Total for Scott 1818-1820, U592 and UX88 is 511,688.				

1980

		SINGLE	BLOCK	PLATE BLOCK	CERM PROG
☐ 1821	15c Frances Perkins, 4/10/80, DC (678,966)............1.00	1.25	1.50	10.00	
	1st Samuel Gompers Stamp Club cachet 12.00				
☐ 1822	15c Dolley Madison, 5/20/80, DC (331,048) 1.00	1.25	1.50	10.00	
	1st American Postal Arts Society cachet (Post/Art) 30.00				
☐	1st D.J. Graf cachet..25.00				
☐ 1823	15c Emily Bissell, 5/31/80, Wilmington, DE (649,509)...1.00	1.25	2.00	8.00	
☐ 1824	15c Helen Keller, 6/27/80, Tuscumbia, AL (713,061)...1.00	1.25	1.65	18.00	
☐ 1825	15c Veterans Administration, 7/21/80, DC (634,101)...1.00	1.25	1.50	10.00	
☐ 1826	15c Bernardo de Galvez, 7/23/80, New Orleans, LA (658,061)...1.00	1.25	1.50	10.00	
☐ 1827	15c Brain Coral, Beaugregory Fish, 8/26/80, Charlotte Amalie, VI...1.00				
☐ 1828	15c Elkhorn Coral, Porkfish, 8/26/80, Charlotte Amalie, VI 1.00				
☐ 1829	15c Chalice Coral, Moorish Idol 8/26/80, Charlotte Amalie, VI...1.00				
☐ 1830	15c Finger Coral, Sabertooth Blenny, 8/26/80, Charlotte Amalie, VI...1.00				
☐ 1830a	Se-tenant, Coral Reefs (1,195,126) "Plate Block" value is for block of 4 with plate numbers	2.00	2.50	28.00	
☐ 1831	15c Organized Labor, 9/1/80, DC (759,973). "Plate Block" value is for block of 4 with plate numbers. 1.00	1.25	1.50		

1826 1827-30 1831 1832 1833

1834-7 1838-41 1842 1843

1845 1860 1866 1874 1875

**Values for various cachet makers can be determined
by using the Cachet Calculator which begins on page 52A.**

126

		SINGLE	PLATE BLOCK	PLATE BLOCK	CERM PROG
☐ 1832	15c Edith Wharton, 9/5/80, New Haven, CT (633,917)..1.00		1.25	1.50	12.00
☐ 1833	15c American Education, 9/12/80, DC (672,592). "Plate Block" value is for block of 4 with plate numbers...1.00		1.25	1.50	10.00
☐ 1834	15c Bella Bella Tribe, 9/25/80, Spokane, WA 1.00				
☐ 1835	15c Chilkat Tlingit Tribe, 9/25/80, Spokane, WA 1.00				
☐ 1836	15c Tlingit Tribe, 9/25/80, Spokane, WA 1.00				
☐ 1837	15c Bella Coola Tribe, 9/25/80, Spokane, WA..........1.00				
☐ 1837a	Se-tenant, Pacific Northwest Indian Masks, (2,195,136) "Plate Block" value is for block of 4 with plate numbers...		2.00	2.50	20.00
☐ 1838	15c Smithsonian, 10/9/80, New York, NY 1.00				
☐ 1839	15c Trinity Church, 10/9/80, New York, NY............1.00				
☐ 1840	15c Penn Academy, 10/9/80, New York, NY............1.00				
☐ 1841	15c Lyndhurst, 10/9/80, New York, NY...................1.00				
☐ 1841a	Se-tenant American Architecture, (2,164,721)		2.00	2.50	10.00
☐ 1842	15c Christmas (Madonna & Child), 10/31/80, DC (718,614). "Plate Block" value is for block of 4 with plate numbers...1.00		1.25	1.50	14.00
☐ 1843	15c Christmas (Wreath & Toys), 10/31/80, Christmas, MI (755,108). "Plate Block" value is for block of 4 with plate numbers....................1.00		1.25	1.50	20.00
☐	Scott 1842-1843 on one cover 3.00				
☐	Scott 1842-1843 on one cover, dual cancels.....4.00				

1980-85 Great Americans

		SINGLE	PLATE BLOCK	PLATE BLOCK	CERM PROG
☐ 1844	1c Dorothea Dix, 9/23/83, Hampden, ME (164,140)	1.00	1.00		8.00
☐ 1845	2c Igor Stravinsky, 11/18/82, New York, NY (501,719)..	1.00	1.00		6.00
☐	1st Phil-Mart cachet...15.00				
☐ 1846	3c Henry Clay, 7/13/83, DC (204,320)	1.00	1.00		8.00
☐ 1847	4c Carl Schurz, 6/3/83, Watertown, WI (165,010)	1.00	1.00		8.00
☐ 1848	5c Pearl Buck, 6/23/83, Hillsboro, WV (231,852)............	1.00	1.00		15.00
☐ 1849	6c Walter Lippmann, 9/19/85, Minneapolis, MN (371,990)...1.00	1.00	1.50		8.00
☐ 1850	7c Abraham Baldwin, 1/25/85, Athens, GA (402,285)..1.00	1.25	1.50		8.00
☐	1st RTI cachet 20.00				
☐ 1851	8c Henry Knox, 7/25/85, Thomaston, ME (315,937)..1.00	1.25	1.50		8.00
☐ 1852	9c Sylvanus Thayer, 6/7/85, Braintree, MA (345,649)..1.00	1.25	1.50		8.00
☐ 1853	10c Richard Russell, 5/31/84, Winder, GA (183,581)..1.00	1.25	1.65		8.00
☐ 1854	11c Alden Partridge, 2/12/85, Northfield, VT (442,311)..1.00	1.25	1.65		8.00
☐ 1855	13c Crazy Horse, 1/15/82, Crazy Horse, SD 1.00	1.25	1.65		28.00
☐ 1856	14c Sinclair Lewis, 3/21/85, Sauk Centre, MN (308,612)..1.00	1.25	1.65		8.00
☐ 1857	17c Rachel Carson, 5/28/81, Springdale, PA (273,686)..1.00	1.25	1.75		16.00
☐ 1858	18c George Mason, 5/7/81, Gunston Hall, VA (461,937)..1.00	1.25	1.75		8.00

Rose USA 18c

1876-9

1880-9
1949

1894

Mail Wagon 1880s
USA 9.3c

1903

Fire Pumper
1860s
USA 20c

1908

Exploring
the Moon
USA 18c

1912-9

The Gift of Self
USA
18c
American Red Cross

1910

SAVINGS AND LOANS
SAV
USA 18c

1911

Professional
Management
USA 18c

1920

1st Double A Cachet

Save Wetland Habitats
USA
18c

1921-4

USA 18c

Disabled doesn't mean Unable

1925

Alcoholism
You can beat it!
USA 18c

1927

1926

Babe Zaharias
USA
18c

1932

Bobby Jones
USA
18c

1933

Architecture USA 18c

1928-31

FREDERIC REMINGTON
American
Sculptor
18c
USA

1934

USA 18c
James Nelson White House Architect

1935-36

18¢ USA

1937-38

**Values for various cachet makers can be determined
by using the Cachet Calculator which begins on page 52A.**

SCOTT NUMBER	DESCRIPTION	SINGLE	BLOCK	PLATE BLOCK	CERM PROG
☐ 1859	19c Sequoyah, 12/27/80, Tahlequah, OK (241,325).1.00		1.25	1.75	14.00
☐ 1860	20c Ralph Bunche, 1/12/82, New York, NY.............1.00		1.25	1.75	12.00
☐ 1861	20c Thomas Gallaudet, 6/10/83, West Hartford,				
	CT (261,336) 1.00		1.25	1.75	12.00
☐ 1862	20c Harry S Truman, 1/26/84, DC (267,631) 1.00		1.25	1.75	8.00
☐	1st Caricature cachet....................................25.00				
☐ 1863	22c John J. Audubon, 4/23/85, New York, NY				
	(516,249)..1.00		1.35	2.00	6.00
☐ 1864	30c Frank Laubach, 9/2/84, Benton, PA (118,974)				
	(2 types)*..1.25		1.35	2.00	8.00*
☐ 1865	35c Charles Drew, 6/3/81, DC (383,882) 1.25		2.00	3.00	16.00
☐ 1866	37c Robert Millikan, 1/26/82, Pasadena, CA 1.25		2.00	3.00	10.00
☐ 1867	39c Grenville Clark, 3/20/85, Hanover, NH				
	(297,797) 1.25		2.00	3.00	10.00
☐ 1868	40c Lillian Gilbreth, 2/24/84, Montclair, NJ				
	(110,588) 1.25		2.00	3.00	10.00
☐ 1869	50c Chester W. Nimitz, 2/22/85, Fredericksburg,				
	TX (376,166) 2.00		3.00	3.50	15.00
☐	1st Gulf Coast FDC Group cachet...................15.00				

1981

SCOTT NUMBER	DESCRIPTION	SINGLE	BLOCK	PLATE BLOCK	CERM PROG
☐ 1874	15c Everett Dirksen, 1/4/81, Pekin, IL (665,755).....1.00		1.25	1.50	18.00
☐ 1875	15c Whitney Moore Young, Jr., 1/30/81, New				
	York, NY (963,870)..1.00		1.25	1.50	12.00
☐ 1876	18c Rose, 4/23/81, Ft. Valley, GA............................1.00				
☐ 1877	18c Camellia, 4/23/81, Ft. Valley, GA 1.00				
☐ 1878	18c Dahlia, 4/23/81, Ft. Valley, GA.........................1.00				
☐ 1879	18c Lily, 4/23/81, Ft. Valley, GA..............................1.00				
☐ 1879a	Se-tenant Flowers, (1,966,599)............................		2.50	3.00	18.00
☐ 1880	18c Bighorn, 5/14/81, Boise, ID................................1.00				
☐ 1881	18c Puma, 5/14/81, Boise, ID....................................1.00				
☐ 1882	18c Harbor seal, 5/14/81, Boise, ID 1.00				
☐ 1883	18c Bison, 5/14/81, Boise, ID....................................1.00				
☐ 1884	18c Brown bear, 5/14/81, Boise, ID..........................1.00				
☐ 1885	18c Polar bear, 5/14/81, Boise, ID............................1.00				
☐ 1886	18c Elk, 5/14/81, Boise, ID...1.00				
☐ 1887	18c Moose, 5/14/81, Boise, ID...................................1.00				
☐ 1888	18c White-tailed deer, 5/14/81, Boise, ID 1.00				
☐ 1889	18c Pronghorn, 5/14/81, Boise, ID 1.00				
☐ 1889a	Booklet pane of 10 (1,641,749)................................5.00				18.00
☐ 1890	18c Flag and Anthem, 4/24/81, Portland,ME.				
	"Plate Block" value is for block of 4 with				
	plate numbers 1.00		1.25	1.50	
☐ 1891	18c Flag and Anthem, coil, 4/24/81, Portland, ME..1.00		pr1.25		
☐ 1892	6c Field of Stars, booklet single, 4/24/81,				
	Portland, ME 1.00				
☐ 1893	18c Flag and Anthem, booklet single, 4/24/81,				
	Portland, ME 1.00				
☐ 1893a	Flag and Anthem, booklet pane of 8				
	(6 Scott 1893 + 2 Scott 1892) 2.50				20.00
	Total for all versions Scott 1890-1893 is 691,526.				
☐ 1894	20c Flag over Supreme Court, 12/17/81, DC.				
	"Plate Block" value is for block of 4 with plate				
	numbers 1.00		1.25	1.50	
☐ 1895	20c Flag over Supreme Court, coil, 12/17/81, DC ...1.00		pr1.25		

SCOTT NUMBER	DESCRIPTION	SINGLE	BLOCK	PLATE BLOCK	CERM PROG
☐ 1896	20c Flag over Supreme Court, booklet single, 12/17/81, DC......1.00		1.25	1.50	
☐ 1896a	Flag over Surpeme Court, booklet pane of 6......6.00				
☐	Scott 1894, 1895, 1896a on one cover 7.00				
☐ 1896b	Flag over Supreme Court, booklet pane of 10, 6/1/82 ......10.00				10.00

SCOTT NUMBER	DESCRIPTION	SINGLE	PAIR	LINE PAIR	CERM PROG

1981-84 Transportation Coils

SCOTT NUMBER	DESCRIPTION	SINGLE	PAIR	LINE PAIR	CERM PROG
☐ 1897	1c Omnibus, 8/19/83, Arlington, VA (109,436)...............		1.00	12.50	12.00
☐ 1897A	2c Locomotive, 5/20/82, Chicago, IL (290,020)		1.00	12.50	15.00
☐ 1898	3c Handcar, 3/25/83, Rochester, NY (77,900)................		1.00	12.50	15.00
☐ 1898A	4c Stagecoach, 8/19/82, Milwaukee, WI (152,940)		1.00	10.00	15.00
☐ 1899	5c Motorcycle, 10/10/83, San Francisco, CA (188,240)................		1.00	12.50	22.00
☐ 1900	5.2c Sleigh, 3/21/83, Memphis, TN (141,979)		1.00	25.00	
☐	Combination with Scott U604		1.00	25.00	
☐ 1900a	Sleigh, untagged (Bureau precanceled), 3/21/83......	200.00	800.00		
☐ 1901	5.9c Bicycle, 2/17/82, Wheeling, WV (814,419)...............		1.00	20.00	
☐ 1901a	Bicycle, untagged (Bureau precanceled), 2/17/82	300.00	*2,000*		
☐ 1902	7.4c Baby Buggy, 4/7/84, San Diego, CA (187,797).........	1.00			
☐ 1902a	Baby Buggy, untagged (Bureau precanceled), 4/7/84 ......500.00				
☐ 1903	9.3c Mail Wagon, 12/15/81, Shreveport, LA (199,645)................		1.00	20.00	
☐ 1903a	Mail Wagon, untagged (Bureau precanceled), 12/15/81 ......500.00			*2,000*	
☐ 1904	10.9c Hansom Cab, 3/26/82, Chattanooga, TN................		1.00	25.00	20.00
☐ 1904a	Hansom Cab, untagged (Bureau precanceled), 3/26/82 ......500.00			*2,000*	
☐ 1905	11c Railroad Caboose, 2/3/84, Chicago, IL (172,753)......1.00		1.00		
☐ 1906	17c Electric Auto, 6/25/81, Greenfield Village, MI (239,458)......1.00		1.25	17.50	
☐	1st Four Flags Cover Group cachet 12.00				
☐ 1907	18c Surrey, 5/18/81, Notch, MO (207,801) 1.00		1.25	30.00	18.00
☐ 1908	20c Fire Pumper, 12/10/81, Alexandria, VA (304,668)......1.00		1.25	30.00	

SCOTT NUMBER	DESCRIPTION	SINGLE	BLOCK	PLATE BLOCK	CERM PROG

1983

SCOTT NUMBER	DESCRIPTION	SINGLE	BLOCK	PLATE BLOCK	CERM PROG
☐ 1909	$9.35 Eagle and Moon, 8/12/83, booklet single, Kennedy Space Center, FL (77,858)......70.00				
☐	Flown on Space Shuttle, (not FDC) 30.00				
☐ 1909a	Eagle and Moon, booklet pane of 3......175.00				

1981

SCOTT NUMBER	DESCRIPTION	SINGLE	BLOCK	PLATE BLOCK	CERM PROG
☐ 1910	18c American Red Cross, 5/1/81, DC (874,972)......1.00		1.25	1.50	10.00
☐ 1911	18c Savings Loans Sesquicentennial, 5/8/81, Chicago, IL. (740,910)......1.00		1.25	1.50	10.00
☐ 1912	18c Moon Walk, 5/21/81, Kennedy Space Center, FL 1.00				

☐ 1913	18c **Columbia Launch**, 5/21/81, Kennedy Space Center, FL............1.00				
☐ 1914	18c **Columbia Releasing Satellite**, 5/21/81, Kennedy Space Center, FL 1.00				
☐ 1915	18c **Skylab**, 5/21/81, Kennedy Space Center, FL 1.00				
☐ 1916	18c **Pioneer II**, 5/21/81, Kennedy Space Center, FL.1.00				
☐ 1917	18c **Columbia & Booster**, 5/21/81, Kennedy Space Center, FL............1.00				
☐ 1918	18c **Columbia in Orbit**, 5/21/81, Kennedy Space Center, FL............ 1.00				
☐ 1919	18c **Space Telescope**, 5/21/81, Kennedy Space Center, FL............1.00				
☐ 1919a	Se-tenant, Space Achievement, (7,027,549)..................	1.25	4.00	22.00	
☐ 1920	18c **Professional Management**, 6/18/81, Philadelphia, PA (713,096)............1.00	1.00	1.50	8.00	
☐	1st Garik Covers cachet 30.00				
☐ 1921	18c **Great Blue Heron**, 6/26/81, Reno, NV 1.00				
☐ 1922	18c **Badger**, 6/26/81, Reno, NV..................1.00				
☐ 1923	18c **Grizzly Bear**, 6/26/81, Reno, NV 1.00				
☐ 1924	18c **Ruffed Grouse**, 6/26/81, Reno, NV....................1.00				
☐ 1924a	Se-tenant, Preservation of Wildlife Habitats (2,327,609).....................	2.50	3.00	10.00	
☐	1st Double A cachet 20.00				
☐ 1925	18c **International Year of the Disabled**, 6/29/81, Milford, MI (714,244).......................1.00	1.25	1.50	8.00	
☐ 1926	18c **Edna St. Vincent Millay**, 7/10/81, Austerlitz, NY (725,978)......................1.00	1.25	1.50	10.00	
☐ 1927	18c **Alcoholism**, 8/19/81, DC. "Plate Block" value is for block of 4 with plate numbers.................1.00	1.25	1.50	8.00	
☐	1st Uncovers cachet 25.00				
☐ 1928	18c **New York University Library**, 8/28/81, New York, NY.......................1.00				
☐ 1929	18c **Biltmore House**, 8/28/81, New York, NY 1.00				
☐ 1930	18c **Palace of the Arts**, 8/28/81, New York, NY 1.00				
☐ 1931	18c **National Farmer's Bank**, 8/28/81, New York, NY.1.00				
☐ 1931a	Se-tenant, American Architecture, (1,998,208)..............	2.50	3.00	8.00	
☐ 1932	18c **Mildred Didrikson Zaharias**, 9/22/81,.................... Pinehurst, NC......................5.00	5.50	6.00		
☐ 1933	18c **Robert Tyre Jones**, 9/22/81, Pinehurst, NC........8.00	8.50	9.00		
☐	Scott 1932-1933 on one cover 9.00			15.00	
	Total for Scott 1932-1933 is 1,231,543.				
☐ 1934	18c **Frederic Remington**, 10/9/81, Oklahoma City, OK (1,367,009).....................1.00	1.25	1.50	12.00	
☐ 1935	18c **James Hoban**, 10/13/81, DC 1.00	1.25	1.50		
☐ 1936	20c **James Hoban**, 10/13/81, DC 1.00	1.25	1.50		
☐	Scott 1935-1936 on one cover 3.00			30.00	
☐	Scott 1935-1936 on one cover with Irish Hoban stamp.....................9.00				
	Total for Scott 1935-1936 is 635,012.				
☐ 1937	18c **Battle of Yorktown**, 10/16/81, Yorktown, VA ...1.00				
☐ 1938	18c **Battle of Virginia Capes**, 10/16/81, Yorktown,VA.1.00				
☐ 1938a	Se-tenant, Battles of Yorktown & Virginia Capes............	1.50	2.00	12.00	
	Total for Scott 1937-1938 is 1,098,278.				

1st Court of Honor cachet

1st Pugh Cachet

1st M.J. Philatelics cachet

1939

John Hanson
President Continental Congress
USA 20c
1941

Franklin D. Roosevelt
1950

Domestic Mail
C US Postage
1946-48

George Washington
1952

South Carolina
USA 20c
1953-2002

Season's Greetings
USA
1981
1940

LOVE
USA 20c
1951

1982 USA THE NETHERLANDS
2003

**Values for various cachet makers can be determined
by using the Cachet Calculator which begins on page 52A.**

SCOTT NUMBER	DESCRIPTION	SINGLE	PLATE BLOCK	CERM BLOCK	PROG
☐ 1939	(20c) Christmas (Botticelli), 10/28/81, Chicago, IL				
	(481,395)..1.00	1.25	1.50	12.00
☐	1st Court of Honor cachet............................15.00			
☐ 1940	(20c) Christmas (Bear & Sleigh), 10/28/81,				
	Christmas Valley, OR (517,989)........................1.00	1.25	1.50	18.00
☐	Scott 1939-1940 on one cover, one cancel 2.00	3.00	4.00	
☐	Scott 1939-1940 on one cover, dual cancels.....3.00	4.00		
☐ 1941	20c John Hanson, 11/5/81, Frederick, MD				
	(605,616)...1.00	1.25	1.50	10.00
☐ 1942	20c Barrel Cactus, 12/11/81, Tucson, AZ.................1.00			
☐ 1943	20c Agave, 12/11/81, Tucson, AZ...........................1.00			
☐ 1944	20c Beavertail Cactus, 12/11/81, Tucson, AZ 1.00			
☐ 1945	20c Saguaro, 12/11/81, Tucson, AZ..........................1.00			
☐ 1945a	Se-tenant, Desert Plants, (1,770,187) (2 types)*	2.50	3.00	18.00*
☐	1st Pugh cachet..75.00			
☐ 1946	(20c) "C" and Eagle, 10/11/81, Memphis, TN..........1.00	1.25	1.50	
☐ 1947	(20c) "C" and Eagle, coil, 10/11/81, Memphis, TN ..1.00 pr1.25	lp1.50		
☐ 1948	(20c) "C" and Eagle, booklet single, 10/11/81,				
	Memphis, TN...1.00			
☐ 1948a	"C" and Eagle, booklet pane of 10............................3.50			
	Total for Scott 1946-1948, U594 and UX92 is 304,404.			

1982

SCOTT NUMBER	DESCRIPTION	SINGLE	PLATE BLOCK	CERM BLOCK	PROG
☐ 1949	20c Bighorn Sheep, booklet single, 1/8/82,				
	Bighorn, MT...1.00			
☐	1st New Direxions cachet 15.00			
☐ 1949a	Bighorn Sheep, booklet pane of 10...........................6.00			18.00
☐ 1950	20c Franklin D. Roosevelt, 1/30/82, Hyde Park, NY 1.00	1.25	1.50	12.00
☐	1st Aurora Covers cachet................................15.00			
☐ 1951	20c Love, 2/1/82, Boston, MA (325,727)...................1.00	1.25	1.50	10.00
☐	1st Chaczyk Cachets & Covers cachet.............30.00			
☐ 1952	20c George Washington, 2/22/82, Mount Vernon,				
	VA...1.00	1.25	1.50	10.00
☐	1st M.J. Philatelic cachet 15.00			
☐	1st Ricale cachet 15.00			
☐ 1953	20c Alabama, 4/14/82, DC......................................1.25			
☐ 1954	20c Alaska, 4/14/82, DC 1.25			
☐ 1955	20c Arizona, 4/14/82, DC..1.25			
☐ 1956	20c Arkansas, 4/14/82, DC 1.25			
☐ 1957	20c California, 4/14/82, DC 1.25			
☐ 1958	20c Colorado, 4/14/82, DC......................................1.25			
☐ 1959	20c Connecticut, 4/14/82, DC 1.25			
☐ 1960	20c Delaware, 4/14/82, DC......................................1.25			
☐ 1961	20c Florida, 4/14/82, DC...1.25			
☐ 1962	20c Georgia, 4/14/82, DC..1.25			
☐ 1963	20c Hawaii, 4/14/82, DC...1.25			
☐ 1964	20c Idaho, 4/14/82, DC 1.25			
☐ 1965	20c Illinois, 4/14/82, DC 1.25			
☐ 1966	20c Indiana, 4/14/82, DC..1.25			
☐ 1967	20c Iowa, 4/14/82, DC..1.25			
☐ 1968	20c Kansas, 4/14/82, DC...1.25			
☐ 1969	20c Kentucky, 4/14/82, DC......................................1.25			
☐ 1970	20c Louisiana, 4/14/82, DC.....................................1.25			
☐ 1971	20c Maine, 4/14/82, DC..1.25			
☐ 1972	20c Maryland, 4/14/82, DC......................................1.25			

☐ 1973	20c Massachusetts, 4/14/82, DC..................1.25			
☐ 1974	20c Michigan, 4/14/82, DC..........................1.25			
☐ 1975	20c Minnesota, 4/14/82, DC.........................1.25			
☐ 1976	20c Mississippi, 4/14/82, DC.......................1.25			
☐ 1977	20c Missouri, 4/14/82, DC...........................1.25			
☐ 1978	20c Montana, 4/14/82, DC............................1.25			
☐ 1979	20c Nebraska, 4/14/82, DC...........................1.25			
☐ 1980	20c Nevada, 4/14/82, DC 1.25			
☐ 1981	20c New Hampshire, 4/14/82, DC 1.25			
☐ 1982	20c New Jersey, 4/14/82, DC........................1.25			
☐ 1983	20c New Mexico, 4/14/82, DC.......................1.25			
☐ 1984	20c New York, 4/14/82, DC...........................1.25			
☐ 1985	20c North Carolina, 4/14/82, DC 1.25			
☐ 1986	20c North Dakota, 4/14/82, DC.....................1.25			
☐ 1987	20c Ohio, 4/14/82, DC..................................1.25			
☐ 1988	20c Oklahoma, 4/14/82, DC..........................1.25			
☐ 1989	20c Oregon, 4/14/82, DC..............................1.25			
☐ 1990	20c Pennsylvania, 4/14/82, DC.....................1.25			
☐ 1991	20c Rhode Island, 4/14/82, DC.....................1.25			
☐ 1992	20c South Carolina, 4/14/82, DC 1.25			
☐ 1993	20c South Dakota, 4/14/82, DC.....................1.25			
☐ 1994	20c Tennessee, 4/14/82, DC..........................1.25			
☐ 1995	20c Texas, 4/14/82, DC.................................1.25			
☐ 1996	20c Utah, 4/14/82, DC..................................1.25			
☐ 1997	20c Vermont, 4/14/82, DC.............................1.25			
☐ 1998	20c Virginia, 4/14/82, DC............................1.25			
☐ 1999	20c Washington, 4/14/82, DC 1.25			
☐ 2000	20c West Virginia, 4/14/82, DC 1.25			
☐ 2001	20c Wisconsin, 4/14/82, DC..........................1.25			
☐ 2002	20c Wyoming, 4/14/82, DC 1.25			
☐	Complete set of 50 ....75.00			
☐	Cancels of state capitals, any single 1.75			
☐	Complete set of 50 state capitals 90.00			
☐ 2002a	Complete pane State Birds & Flowers (4 cities).............			30.00
☐ 2003	20c U.S.-Netherlands, 4/20/82, DC. "Plate Block"			
	value is for block of 4 with plate numbers.......1.00	1.25	1.50	22.00
☐	Combination with Netherlands stamp 7.50			
☐ 2004	20c Library of Congress, 4/21/82, DC......................1.00	1.25	1.50	8.00
☐ 2005	20c Consumer Education, coil, 4/27/82, DC.............1.00 pr1.25 lp25.00			8.00
☐ 2006	20c Solar Energy, 4/29/82, Knoxville, TN 1.00			
☐ 2007	20c Synthetic Fuels, 4/29/82, Knoxville, TN 1.00			
☐ 2008	20c Breeder Reactor, 4/29/82, Knoxville, TN...........1.00			
☐ 2009	20c Fossil Fuels, 4/29/82, Knoxville, TN 1.00			
☐ 2009a	Se-tenant Knoxville World's Fair..............................	2.50	3.00	10.00
☐ 2010	20c Horatio Alger, 4/30/82, Willow Grove, PA 1.00	1.25	1.50	12.00
☐ 2011	20c Aging Together, 5/21/82, Sun City, AZ			
	(510,677)...1.00	1.25	1.50	10.00
☐ 2012	20c The Barrymores, 6/8/82, New York, NY............1.00	1.25	1.50	6.00
☐ 2013	20c Dr. Mary E. Walker, 6/10/82, Oswego, NY 1.00	1.25	1.50	10.00
☐ 2014	20c International Peace Gardens, 6/30/82,			
	Dunseith, ND..1.00	1.25	1.50	10.00
☐ 2015	20c America's Libraries, 7/13/82, Philadelphia, PA.1.00	1.25	1.50	8.00
☐	1st WSC cachet 15.00			
☐ 2016	20c Jackie Robinson, 8/2/82, Cooperstown, NY.......8.00	9.00	10.00	35.00
☐	1st Armadillo Covers cachet 15.00			

135

2004

2005

2006-9

2010

2011

2014

2012

2013

2017

2018

2015

2019-22

2023

2016

HOW TO USE THIS BOOK
The number in the first column is its Scott number or identifying number. Following that is the denomination of the stamp, description, date of issue, and the value.

SCOTT NUMBER	DESCRIPTION	SINGLE	BLOCK	PLATE BLOCK	CERM PROG
☐ 2017	20c Touro Synagogue, 8/22/82, Newport, RI (517,264). "Plate Block" value is for block of 4 with plate numbers....................................1.00	1.00	1.25	1.65	10.00
☐ 2018	20c Wolf Trap Farm Park, 9/1/82, Vienna, VA (764,361)...1.00	1.00	1.25	1.50	8.00
☐ 2019	20c Fallingwater, 9/30/82, DC....................................1.00	1.00			
☐ 2020	20c Illinois Institute of Technology, 9/30/82, DC.....1.00	1.00			
☐ 2021	20c Gropius House, 9/30/82, DC.................................1.00	1.00			
☐ 2022	20c Dulles Airport, 9/30/82, DC 1.00	1.00			
☐ 2022a	Se-tenant, American Architecture, (1,552,567)		2.50	3.00	8.00
☐ 2023	20c St. Francis of Assisi, 10/7/82, San Francisco, CA (530,275) 1.00	1.00	1.25	1.50	18.00
☐ 2024	20c Ponce de Leon, 10/12/82, San Juan, PR (530,275). "Plate Block" value is for block of 4 with plate numbers...1.00	1.00	1.25	1.50	10.00
☐ 2025	13c Christmas (Kitten & Puppy), 11/3/82, Danvers, MA (239,219) 1.00	1.00	1.25	1.50	20.00
☐ 2026	20c Christmas (Madonna & Child), 10/28/82, DC (462,982). "Plate Block" value is for block of 4 with plate numbers...1.00	1.00	1.25	1.50	10.00
☐ 2027	20c Children & Sleds, 10/28/82, Snow, OK 1.00	1.00			
☐ 2028	20c Children & Snowman, 10/28/82, Snow, OK.......1.00	1.00			
☐ 2029	20c Children Playing, 10/28/82, Snow, OK..............1.00	1.00			
☐ 2030	20c Children Decorating Tree, 10/28/82, Snow, OK.1.00	1.00			
☐ 2030a	Se-tenant, Christmas (Children) (676,950)....................		2.50	3.00	18.00
☐	Scott 2026-2030, either city...............................1.50	1.50			
☐	Scott 2026-3030 dual cancels...........................2.50	2.50			

1983

SCOTT NUMBER	DESCRIPTION	SINGLE	BLOCK	PLATE BLOCK	CERM PROG
☐ 2031	20c Science & Industry, 1/19/83, Chicago, IL (526,693)..1.00	1.00	1.25	1.50	10.00
☐ 2032	20c Intrepid, Albuquerque, NM, & DC.....................1.00	1.00			
☐ 2033	20c Balloons Ascending, Albuquerque, NM, & DC. .1.00	1.00			
☐ 2034	20c Balloons Ascending, Albuquerque, NM, & DC. .1.00	1.00			
☐ 2035	20c Explorer II, Albuquerque, NM, & DC.................1.00	1.00			
☐ 2035a	Se-tenant, Balloons, (989,305)		2.50	3.00	18.00
☐ 2036	20c U.S.-Sweden, 3/24/83, Philadelphia, PA (526,373)..1.00	1.00	1.25	1.50	14.00
☐	1st Panda cachet...25.00	25.00			
☐	Combination cover with Swedish issue.............6.00	6.00			
☐ 2037	20c Civilian Conservation Corps, 4/5/83, Luray, VA (483,824) 1.00	1.00	1.25	1.50	8.00
☐ 2038	20c Joseph Priestley, 4/13/83, Northumberland, PA (673,266)..1.00	1.00	1.25	1.50	8.00
☐ 2039	20c Voluntarism, 4/20/83, DC (574,708). "Plate Block" value is for block of 4 with plate numbers.......1.00	1.00	1.25	1.50	8.00
☐ 2040	20c U.S.-Germany, 4/29/83, Germantown, PA (611,109)..1.00	1.00	1.25	1.50	15.00
☐	Combination cover with German issue.............6.00	6.00			
☐ 2041	20c Brooklyn Bridge, 5/17/83, Brooklyn, NY (815,085)..1.00	1.00	1.25	1.50	6.00
☐ 2042	20c T.V.A., 5/18/83, Knoxville, TN (837,588). "Plate Block" value is for block of 4 with plate numbers...1.00	1.00	1.25	1.50	8.00

Christmas USA 20c
Tiepolo National Gallery of Art
2026

Ponce de León USA 20c
2024

USA 13c
2025

Science & Industry
USA 20c
2031

KOREA
USA
2032-5

Season's Greetings USA 20c
2027-30

20
USA
2036

1933-1983
Civilian Conservation Corps USA 20c
2037

Volunteer
lend a hand
USA 20c
2039

Joseph Priestley
USA 20c
2038

Concord 1683 USA 20c
Geman
Immigration
Tricentennial
2040

Brooklyn Bridge
1883-1983
USA 20c
2041

Tennessee
Valley
Authority
USA 20c
2042

Physical Fitness
USA
20c
2043

Scott Joplin
Black Heritage USA 20c
2044

Babe Ruth
USA
20c
2046

Hawthorne
USA 20c
2047

HOW TO USE THIS BOOK
The number in the first column is its Scott number or
identifying number. Following that is the denomination
of the stamp, description, date of issue, and the value.

Scott Number	Description	Single	Block	Plate Block	Cerm Prog
☐ 2043	20c **Physical Fitness**, 5/14/83, Houston, TX (501,336). "Plate Block" value is for block of 4 with plate numbers 1.00	1.25	1.50	10.00
☐ 2044	20c **Scott Joplin**, 6/9/83, Sedalia, MO (472,667) 1.00	1.25	1.50	32.00
☐ 2045	20c **Medal of Honor**, 6/7/83, DC (1,623,995) 1.00	1.25	1.50	14.00
☐ 2046	20c **Babe Ruth**, 7/6/83, Chicago, IL (1,277,907) (2 types)* 6.00	6.50	8.00	40.00*
☐	1st Eastern Covers, Inc., cachet...... ....15.00			
☐	1st Dome cachet.............................25.00			
☐ 2047	20c **Nathaniel Hawthorne**, 7/8/83, Salem, MA (442,793)..1.00	1.25	1.50	10.00
☐ 2048	13c **Discus**, 7/28/83, South Bend, IN 1.00			
☐ 2049	13c **High Jump**, 7/28/83, South Bend, IN.................1.00			
☐ 2050	13c **Archery**, 7/28/83, South Bend, IN 1.00			
☐ 2051	13c **Boxing**, 7/28/83, South Bend, IN......................1.00			
☐ 2051a	**Se-tenant**, 1984 Los Angeles Olympics, (909,332)..........	2.50	3.00	12.00
☐ 2052	20c **Signing of Treaty of Paris**, 9/2/83, DC (651,208)..1.00	1.25	1.50	10.00
☐	1st TF cachet 30.00			
☐	Combo with French stamp............................10.00			
☐ 2053	20c **Civil Service**, 9/9/83, DC (422,206) 1.00	1.25	1.50	8.00
☐ 2054	20c **Metropolitan Opera**, 9/14/83, New York, NY (807,609)..1.00	1.25	1.50	6.00
☐	1st Desert Sun cachet 15.00			
☐ 2055	20c **Charles Steinmetz**, 9/21/83, DC.......................1.00			
☐ 2056	20c **Edwin Armstrong**, 9/21/83, DC 1.00			
☐ 2057	20c **Nikola Tesla**, 9/21/83, DC 1.00			
☐ 2058	20c **Philo T. Farnsworth**, 9/21/83, DC....................1.00			
☐ 2058a	**Se-tenant**, American Inventors, (1,006,516).................	2.50	3.00	8.00
☐ 2059	20c **First American streetcar**, 10/8/83, Kennebunkport, ME........................1.00			
☐ 2060	20c **Electric Streetcar**, 10/8/83, Kennebunkport, ME1.00			
☐ 2061	20c **"Bobtail" Horsecar**, 10/8/83, Kennebunkport, ME..1.00			
☐ 2062	20c **St. Charles Streetcar**, 10/8/83, Kennebunkport, ME..1.00			
☐ 2062a	**Se-tenant**, Streetcars, (1,116,909)	2.50	3.00	12.00
☐ 2063	20c **Christmas (Madonna & Child)**, 10/28/83, DC (361,874)..1.00	1.25	1.50	10.00
☐ 2064	20c **Christmas (Santa Claus)**, 10/28/83, Santa Claus, IN (388,749). "Plate Block" value is for block of 4 with plate numbers 1.00	1.25	1.50	10.00
☐ 2065	20c **Martin Luther**, 11/11/83, DC (463,777) 1.50	2.00	2.50	10.00

1984

Scott Number	Description	Single	Block	Plate Block	Cerm Prog
☐ 2066	20c **Alaska Statehood**, 1/3/84, Fairbanks, AK (816,591)..1.00	1.25	1.50	8.00
☐ 2067	20c **Ice Dancing**, 1/6/84, Lake Placid, NY 1.00			
☐ 2068	20c **Alpine Skiing**, 1/6/84, Lake Placid, NY.............1.00			
☐ 2069	20c **Nordic Skiing**, 1/6/84, Lake Placid, NY.............1.00			
☐ 2070	20c **Hockey**, 1/6/84, Lake Placid, NY 1.00			
☐ 2070a	**Se-tenant**, Winter Olympic Games, (1,245,807)..............	2.50	3.00	12.00
☐ 2071	20c **Federal Deposit Insurance Corporation**, 1/12/84, DC (536,329) 1.00	1.25	1.50	8.00

Medal of Honor
USA 20c
2045

2048-2051

Treaty of Paris 1783
US Bicentennial 20 cents
2052

CIVIL SERVICE
1883
1983
USA 20c
2053

METROPOLITAN OPERA
1883 1983 USA 20c
2054

20c Charles Steinmetz
2055-2058

USA 20c
First American streetcar, New York City 1832
2059-2062

Season's Greetings USA 20c
2064

Christmas USA 20c
Raphael, 15th cent. National Gallery
2063

Martin Luther
1483-1983 USA 20c
2065

USA 20c
1959-1984 Alaska Statehood
2066

Olympics 84 USA 20c
2067-2070

FEDERAL DEPOSIT INSURANCE CORPORATION
2071

LOVE LOVE LOVE LOVE LOVE USA 20c
2072

Carter G. Woodson
Black Heritage USA 20c
2073

SOIL AND WATER CONSERVATION
USA 20c
2074

ACT OF 1934
USA 20c
2075

NATIONAL ARCHIVES
USA
2081

**Values for various cachet makers can be determined
by using the Cachet Calculator which begins on page 52A.**

		SINGLE	BLOCK	PLATE BLOCK	CERM PROG
☐ 2072	20c Love, 1/31/84, DC (327,727). "Plate Block" value is for block of 4 with plate numbers.......1.00		1.25	1.50	8.00
☐ 2073	20c Carter Woodson, 2/1/84, DC (387,583)..............1.00		1.25	1.50	10.00
☐ 2074	20c Soil & Water Conservation, 2/6/84, Denver, CO (426,101) 1.00		1.25	1.50	8.00
☐ 2075	20c Credit Union Act, 2/10/84, Salem, MA (523,583)...1.00		1.25	1.50	8.00
☐ 2076	20c Wild Pink Orchid, 3/5/84, Miami, FL.................1.00				
☐ 2077	20c Yellow Lady's Slipper Orchid, 3/5/84, Miami, FL1.00				
☐ 2078	20c Spreading Pogonia Orchid, 3/5/84, Miami, FL..1.00				
☐ 2079	20c Pacific Calypso Orchid, 3/5/84, Miami, FL........1.00				
☐ 2079a	Sc-tenant, Orchids, (1,063,237)	2.50		3.00	14.00
☐ 2080	20c Hawaii Statehood, 3/12/84, Honolulu, HI (546,930)...1.00		1.25	1.50	8.00
☐ 2081	20c National Archives, 4/16/84, DC (414,415).........1.00		1.25	1.50	8.00
☐ 2082	20c Diving, 5/4/84, Los Angeles, CA.......................1.00				
☐ 2083	20c Long Jump, 5/4/84, Los Angeles, CA 1.00				
☐ 2084	20c Wrestling, 5/4/84, Los Angeles, CA...................1.00				
☐ 2085	20c Kayak, 5/4/84, Los Angeles, CA 1.00				
☐ 2085a	Se-tenant, 1984 Los Angeles Olympics (1,172,313).2.50		3.00		12.00
☐ 2086	20c New Orleans World Exposition, 5/11/84, New Orleans, LA (467,408)..................................1.00		1.25	1.50	8.00
☐ 2087	20c Health Research, 5/17/84, New York, NY (845,007)..1.00		1.25	1.50	6.00
☐ 2088	20c Douglas Fairbanks, 5/23/84, Denver, CO (547, 134). "Plate Block" value is for block of 4 with plate numbers..................................1.00		1.25	1.50	8.00
☐ 2089	20c Jim Thorpe, 5/24/84, Shawnee, OK (568,544)...6.00		7.00	9.00	25.00
☐	(2nd Day), 5/25/84, Yale, OK				35.00
☐ 2090	20c John McCormack, 6/6/84, Boston, MA (464,117)...1.00		1.25	1.50	10.00
☐	Scott 2090 with Ireland stamp, dual cancel...........15.00				
☐ 2091	20c St. Lawrence Seaway, 6/26/84, Massena, NY (550,173)...1.00		1.25	1.50	10.00
☐ 2092	20c Waterfowl Preservation Act, 7/2/84, Des Moines, IA (549,388)..1.00		1.25	1.50	12.00
☐	1st George Van Natta cachet 40.00				
☐ 2093	20c Roanoke Voyages, 7/13/84, Manteo, NC (443,725)...1.00		1.25	1.50	25.00
☐ 2094	20c Herman Melville, 8/1/84, New Bedford, MA (379,293)...1.00		1.25	1.50	12.00
☐ 2095	20c Horace A. Moses, 8/6/84, Bloomington, IN (459,386). "Plate Block" value is for block of 4 with plate numbers..................................1.00		1.25	1.50	8.00
☐ 2096	20c Smokey the Bear, 8/13/84, Capitan, NM (506,833)...2.00		3.00	4.00	15.00
☐	1st Long Island Cover Society cachet 15.00				
☐ 2097	20c Roberto Clemente, 8/17/84, Carolina, PR (547,387)...15.00	16.00	17.00	35.00	
☐ 2098	20c Beagle & Boston Terrier, 9/7/84, New York, NY1.00				
☐ 2099	20c Chesapeake Bay Retriever & Cocker Spaniel, 9/7/84, New York, NY 1.00				
☐ 2100	20c Alaskan Malamute & Collie, 9/7/84, New York, NY 1.00				
☐ 2101	20c Black & Tan Coonhound & American Foxhound, 9/7/84, New York, NY..1.00				

Hawaii Statehood 1959-1984
USA 20c
2080

2076-2079

Wildpush Arcticus bulbus
USA 20c

Olumpas 84
USA 20c
2082-2085

Louisiana
World
Exposition
USA 20c
Fresh water as a source of Life
2086

Health Research USA 20c
2087

USA 20c
2091

Preserving Wetlands
1934
1984
USA 20c
2092

DOUGLAS
FAIRBANKS
Performing Arts USA 20c
2088

Jim Thorpe
C
USA 20c
2089

JOHN McCORMACK
Performing Arts USA 20c
2090

Roanoke Voyages
North
Carolina
1584
USA 20c
2093

Herman Melville
USA 20c
2094

Horace Moses
USA 20c
2095

SMOKEY
USA 20c
2096

Roberto
Clemente
P
USA 20c
2097

**Values for various cachet makers can be determined
by using the Cachet Calculator which begins on page 52A.**

SCOTT NUMBER	DESCRIPTION	SINGLE	BLOCK	PLATE BLOCK	CERM PROG
☐ 2101a	Se-tenant, Dogs, (1,157,373)		2.50	3.00	10.00
☐	1st Heartland FDC cachet	20.00			
☐ 2102	20c Crime Prevention, 9/26/84, DC (427,564)	1.00	1.25	1.50	8.00
☐ 2103	20c Hispanic Americans, 10/31/84, DC (416,796)	1.00	1.25	1.50	10.00
☐ 2104	20c Family Unity, 10/1/84, Shaker Heights, OH (400,659). "Plate Block" value is for block of 4 with plate numbers	1.00	1.25	1.50	8.00
☐ 2105	20c Eleanor Roosevelt, 10/11/84, Hyde Park, NY (479,919)	1.00	1.25	1.50	8.00
☐ 2106	20c Nation of Readers, 10/16/84, DC (437,559)	1.00	1.25	1.50	8.00
☐ 2107	20c Christmas (Madonna), 10/30/84, DC (386,385)	1.00	1.25	1.50	10.00
☐ 2108	20c Christmas (Santa Claus), 10/30/84, Jamaica, NY (430,843)	1.00	1.25	1.50	10.00
☐ 2109	20c Vietnam Veterans' Memorial, 11/10/84, DC (434,489)	1.00	1.25	1.50	18.00

1985

SCOTT NUMBER	DESCRIPTION	SINGLE	BLOCK	PLATE BLOCK	CERM PROG
☐ 2110	22c Jerome Kern, 1/23/85, New York, NY (503,855)	1.00	1.25	1.50	6.00
☐ 2111	(22c) "D" & Eagle, 2/1/85, Los Angeles, CA	1.00	1.25	1.50	
☐ 2112	(22c) "D" & Eagle, coil, 2/1/85, Los Angeles, CA	1.00	pr1.25		
☐ 2113	(22c) "D" & Eagle, booklet single, 2/1/85, Los Angeles, CA	1.00			
☐ 2113a	"D" & Eagle, booklet pane of 10	7.50			
	Total for Scott 2111-2113a is 513,027.				
☐ 2114	22c Flag over Capitol Dome, 3/29/85, DC	1.00	1.25	1.50	
☐ 2115	22c Flag over Capitol Dome, coil, 3/29/85 DC	1.00	pr1.25		
☐ 2114-2115	Flag, sheet and coil				10.00
	Total for Scott 2114-2115 is 268,161.				
☐ 2115b	22c Flag over Capitol Dome, pre-phosphored, coil, 5/23/87, Secaucus, NJ	1.00	pr5.00		8.00
☐ 2116	22c Flag over Capitol Dome, booklet single, 3/29/85, Waubeka, WI (234,318)	1.00			
☐ 2116a	Flag over Capitol Dome, booklet pane of 5	3.50			
☐ 2117	22c Frilled Dogwinkle, 4/4/85, Boston, MA	1.00			
☐ 2118	22c Reticulated Helmet, 4/4/85, Boston, MA	1.00			
☐ 2119	22c New England Neptune, 4/4/85, Boston, MA	1.00			
☐ 2120	22c Calico Scallop, 4/4/85, Boston, MA	1.00			
☐ 2121	22c Lightning Whelk, 4/4/85, Boston, MA	1.00			
☐ 2121a	Booklet pane of 10	7.50			15.00
	Total for Nos. 2117-2121 is 426,290.				
☐ 2122	$10.75 Eagle & Half Moon, 4/29/85, San Francisco, CA (93,154)	60.00			
☐ 2122a	Eagle & Half Moon, booklet pane of 3	150.00			
☐ 2122b	Reissue, bk sgl, 6/19/89	200.00			
☐ 2122b	Reissue, booklet pane of 3	700.00			

HOW TO USE THIS BOOK

The number in the first column is its Scott number or identifying number. Following that is the denomination of the stamp, description, date of issue, and the value.

USA 20c

2098-01

TAKE A BITE OUT OF CRIME

2102

Hispanic Americans
A Proud Heritage USA 20
2103

2104

Eleanor Roosevelt
USA 20c
2105

A Nation of Readers
USA 20c
2106

Christmas USA 20c
Fra Filippo Lippi, National Gallery
2107

USA 20c
Season's Greetings
2108

Domestic Mail
D US Postage
2111

JEROME KERN
Performing Arts USA
2110

Vietnam Veterans Memorial USA 20c
2109

USA 22
New England Neptune
2117-21

USA 22
2114

Tricycle 1880s
6 USA
2126

USA $10.75
2122

Mary McLeod Bethune
Black Heritage USA 22
2137

Iceboat 1880s
USA 14
2134

Mallard Decoy
Folk Art USA 22
2138-41

Winter Special Olympics
22 USA
2142

22 USA
Rural Electrification Administration
2144

**Values for various cachet makers can be determined
by using the Cachet Calculator which begins on page 52A.**

144

SCOTT NUMBER	DESCRIPTION	SINGLE	PAIR	LINE PAIR	CERM PROG

1985-88 Transportation Coils

☐ 2123	3.4c School Bus, 6/8/85, Arlington, VA (131,480) ....—		1.00	12.50	12.00
☐ 2123a	School Bus, untagged (Bureau precanceled), 6/8/85, Arlington, VA, earliest known use ....—		—	—	
☐ 2124	4.9c Buckboard, 6/21/85, Reno, NV............................—		1.00	13.50	
☐ 2124a	Buckboard, untagged (Bureau precanceled), 6/21/85, DC, earliest known use ....—		—	—	
☐ 2125	5.5c Star Route Truck, 11/1/86, Ft. Worth, TX (136,021) ....—		1.00		20.00
☐ 2125a	Star Route Truck, untagged (Bureau precanceled), 11/1/86, DC ....—		5.00		
☐ 2126	6c Tricycle, untagged (Bureau precanceled), 5/6/85, Childs, MD (151,494) ....—		1.00		12.00
☐ 2127	7.1c Tractor, 2/6/87, Sarasota, FL (167,555) ....—		1.00		12.00
☐ 2127a	Tractor, untagged (Bureau precancel "Nonprofit Org." in black), 2/6/87, Sarasota, FL...............................		5.00		8.00
☐ 2127a	Tractor, untagged (Bureau precancel "Nonprofit 5-Digit Zip+4" in black), 5/26/89, Rosemont, IL		1.00		
☐ 2128	8.3c Ambulance, 6/21/85, Reno, NV ....—		1.00	10.00	
☐ 2128a	Ambulance, untagged (Bureau precanceled), 6/21/85, DC, earliest known use ....—		—	—	
☐ 2129	8.5c Tow Truck, 1/24/87, Tucson, AZ (224,285) ....—		1.00		12.00
☐ 2129a	Tow Truck, untagged (Bureau precanceled), 1/24/87, DC ....—		5.00		
☐ 2130	10.1c Oil Wagon, 4/18/85, Oil Center, NM....................—		1.00		12.00
☐ 2130a	Oil Wagon, untagged (black Bureau precancel), 4/18/85, DC, earliest known use..........................—		—		
☐ 2130a	Oil Wagon, untagged (red Bureau precancel), 6/27/88, DC ....—		1.00		
☐ 2131	11c Stutz Super Bearcat, 6/11/85, Baton Rouge, LA (135,037)...—		1.00	15.00	12.00
☐ 2132	12c Stanley Steamer, 4/2/85, Kingfield, ME, (173,998) ....—		1.00	12.50	
☐ 2132a	Stanley Steamer, untagged (Bureau precanceled), 4/2/85, DC ....—		—	—	
☐ 2133	12.5c Pushcart, 4/18/85, Oil Center, NM....................—		1.25		
	Total for Scott 2130 and 2133 is 319,953.				
☐ 2133a	Pushcart, untagged (Bureau precanceled), 4/18/85, DC ....—		—		
☐ 2134	14c Ice Boat, 3/23/85, Rochester, NY (324,710)...........—		1.25	15.00	12.00
	1st C.L. cachets 15.00				
☐ 2135	17c Dog Sled, 8/20/86, Anchorage, AK (112,009)........—		1.25		12.00
☐ 2136	25c Bread Wagon, 11/22/86, Virginia Beach, VA (151,950)..1.25		1.25		12.00

Uncacheted covers sell for about 10% of catalogue value.

2143

2146

F.A. Bartholdi, Statue of Liberty Sculptor

2147

Veterans Korea

2152

Social Security Act 1935 1985 USA 22

2153

AMERIPEX86
International Stamp Show, Chicago
May 22 to June 1, 1986

2145

2149

2150

Veterans World War I

2154

Morgan

2155-58

22
USA

Public
Education

2159

YMCA Youth Camping

2160-63

Help End Hunger

2164

CHRISTMAS

USA 22

2165

Season's Greetings

2166

**Values for various cachet makers can be determined
by using the Cachet Calculator which begins on page 52A.**

1985-86

		SINGLE	BLOCK	PLATE BLOCK	CERM PROG
☐ 2137	22c Mary McLeod Bethune, 3/5/85, DC (413,244)...1.00		1.25	1.50	8.00
☐ 2138	22c Broadbill Decoy, 3/22/85, Shelburne, VT 1.00				
☐ 2139	22c Mallard Decoy, 3/22/85, Shelburne, VT............1.00				
☐ 2140	22c Canvasback Decoy, 3/22/85, Shelburne, VT......1.00				
☐ 2141	22c Redhead Decoy, 3/22/85, Shelburne, VT 1.00				
☐ 2141a	Se-tenant, Duck Decoys, (923,249)		2.75	3.50	14.00
☐ 2142	22c Winter Special Olympics, 3/25/85, Park City,				
	UT (253,074)..1.00		1.25	1.50	10.00
☐ 2143	22c Love, 4/17/85, Hollywood, CA (283,072)............1.00		1.25	1.50	10.00
☐ 2144	22c Rural Electrificafion Administration, 5/11/85,				
	Madison, SD (472,895). "Plate Block" value is				
	for block of 4 with plate numbers (2 types)*....1.00		1.25	1.50	10.00*
☐ 2145	22c Ameripex '86, 5/25/85, Rosemont, IL (457,038)1.00		1.25	1.50	10.00
☐ 2146	22c Abigail Adams, 6/14/85, Quincy, MA (491,026).1.00		1.25	1.50	10.00
☐ 2147	22c Frederic Auguste Bartholdi, 7/18/85,				
	New York, NY (594,896) 1.00		1.25	1.50	12.00

SCOTT NUMBER	DESCRIPTION	SINGLE	PAIR	CERM PROG
☐ 2149	18c George Washington & Monument, 11/6/85, ...			
	(376,238)..	1.25		12.00
☐ 2149a	George Washington & Monument, untagged			
	(Bureau precanceled), 11/6/85		5.00	
☐ 2150	21.1c Envelopes, 10/22/85, DC (119,941)........................	1.25		12.00
☐ 2150a	Envelopes, untagged (Bureau precanceled),			
	10/22/85, DC..		5.00	

SCOTT NUMBER	DESCRIPTION	SINGLE	PLATE BLOCK BLOCK	CERM PROG
☐ 2152	22c Korean War Veterans, 7/26/85, DC (391,754)...1.00		1.25 1.50	12.00
☐ 2153	22c Social Security Act, 8/14/85, Baltimore, MD			
	(265,143)..1.00		1.25 1.50	15.00
☐ 2154	22c World War I Veterans, 8/26/85, Milwaukee,WI.1.00		1.25 1.50	10.00
☐ 2155	22c Quarter Horse, 9/25/85, Lexington, KY.............1.25			
☐ 2156	22c Morgan, 9/25/85, Lexington, KY........................1.25			
☐ 2157	22c Saddlebred, 9/25/85, Lexington, KY.................1.25			
☐ 2158	22c Appaloosa, 9/25/85, Lexington, KY 1.25			
☐ 2158a	Se-tenant, Horses. (1,135,368)...................................		5.00 6.00	14.00
☐ 2159	22c Public Education in America, 10/1/85,			
	Boston, MA (356,030) 1.00		1.25 1.50	6.00
☐ 2160	22c YMCA Youth Camping, 10/7/85, Chicago, IL.....1.00			
☐ 2161	22c Boy Scouts, 10/7/85, Chicago, IL 1.00			
☐ 2162	22c Big Brothers/Big Sisters, 10/7/85, Chicago, IL.1.00			
☐ 2163	22c Camp Fire, Inc., 10/7/85, Chicago, IL..............1.00			
☐ 2163a	Se-tenant, International Youth Year, (1,202,541)		2.50 3.00	8.00
☐ 2164	22c Help End Hunger, 10/15/85, DC (299,485)........1.00		1.25 1.50	8.00
☐ 2165	22c Christmas (Madonna & Child), 10/30/85,			
	Detroit, MI...1.00		1.25 1.50	10.00
☐ 2166	22c Christmas (Poinsettia), 10/30/85, Nazareth,			
	MI (524,929) 1.00		1.25 1.50	10.00

Arkansas Statehood
USA 22
2167

Margaret Mitchell
USA 1
2168

Paul Dudley White MD
USA 3
2170

Father Flanagan USA
4
2171

Hugo L. Black
5 USA
2172

14 USA
Julia Ward Howe
2177

USA 17
2179

USA 25
Jack London
2183

John Harvard
USA 56
2191

Bernard Revel
USA $1
2194

Bryan $2
William Jennings USA
2195

STAMP COLLECTING
USA 22
2198-2201

LOVE
USA 22
2202

Sojourner Truth
22
Black Heritage USA
2203

USA 22
San Jacinto 1836
Republic of Texas
2204

22 USA
Muskellunge
2205-09

Public Hospitals USA 22
2210

USA 22
Elisha Kent Kane
2220-23

USA 22
George Washington
2216a

John Tyler
USA 22
2217a

Duke Ellington
22 USA
2211

Liberty
1886-1986
USA 22
2224

USA 22
Rutherford B. Hayes 1877-1881
2218a

Warren G. Harding 1921-1923
USA 22
2219a

1986

☐ 2167   22c **Arkansas Statehood**, 1/3/86, Little Rock, AR

      (364,729)..1.00   1.25   1.50   8.00

☐   1st LMG cachets.......................................30.00

1986-94 Great Americans

☐ 2168   1c **Margaret Mitchell**, 9/17/86, Atlanta, GA

      (316,764)..1.00   1.25   1.50   8.00

☐ 2169   2c **Mary Lyon**, 2/28/87, S. Hadley, MA (349,831) 1.00   1.25   1.50 12.00

☐ 2170   3c **Dr. Paul Dudley White**, 9/15/86, Washington,DC 1.00   1.25   1.50   8.00

☐ 2171   5c **Father Flanagan**, 7/14/86, Boys Town, NE

      (367,883)..1.00   1.25   1.50   8.00

☐ 2172   5c **Hugo Black**, 2/27/86, DC (303,012) 1.00   1.25   1.50   8.00

      1st Key Kachets cachet...................................20.00

☐ 2173   5c **Luiz Munoz Marin**, 2/18/90, San Juan, PR..........1.00   1.25   1.00   6.00

☐ 2175   10c **Red Cloud**, 8/15/87, Red Cloud, NE (300,472)...1.00   1.25   1.50 10.00

☐ 2176   14c **Julia Ward Howe**, 2/12/87, Boston, MA

      (454,829)..1.00   1.25   1.50   8.00

☐ 2177   15c **Buffalo Bill Cody**, 6/6/88, Cody, WY

      (356,395)..1.00   1.25   1.50 18.00

☐ 2178   17c **Belva Ann Lockwood**, 6/18/86, Middleport, NY

      (249,215)..1.00   1.25   1.65   6.00

☐ 2179   20c **Virginia Apgar**, 10/24/94, Dallas. TX 1.00   1.25   1.65   6.00

☐ 2180   21c **Chester Carlson**, 10/21/88, Rochester, NY

      (288,073)..1.00   1.25   1.65 20.00

☐ 2181   23c **Mary Cassatt**, 11/4/88, Philadelphia, PA

      (322,537)..1.00   1.25   1.65 10.00

☐ 2182   25c **Jack London**, 1/11/86, Glen Ellen, CA

      (358,686)..1.25   1.25   1.65   8.00

☐ 2182a **Jack London**, booklet pane of 10, 5/3/88,

      San Francisco, CA..6.00

☐ 2183   28c **Sitting Bull**, 9/14/89, Rapid City, SD

      (126,777)..1.25   1.50   1.75   6.00

☐ 2184   29c **Earl Warren**, 3/9/92, DC (175,517)....................1.25   6.00

☐ 2185   29c **Thomas Jefferson**, 4/13/93

      Charlottesville, VA 1.25   8.00

☐ 2186   35c **Dennis Chavez**, 4/3/91, Albuquerque, NM

      (285,570)... 1.25   8.00

☐ 2187   40c **Claire Chennault**, 9/6/90, Monroe, LA

      (186,761)..1.50   6.00

☐ 2188   45c **Harvey Cushing**, 6/17/88, Cleveland, OH

      (135,140)..1.25   10.00

☐ 2189   52c **Hubert Humphrey**, 6/3/91,

      Minneapolis, MN (93,391)...............................1.35   10.00

☐ 2190   56c **John Harvard**, 9/3/86, Boston, MA.................1.25   2.50   3.00 10.00

☐ 2191   65c **Hap Arnold**, 11/5/88, Gladwyne, PA (129,829)..1.50   3.00   3.50 10.00

☐ 2192   75c **Wendell Wilkie**, 2/18/92, Bloomington, IN

      47,086)...1.50   3.00   3.50

☐ 2193 $1 **Dr. Bernard Revel**, 9/23/86, New York, NY.........2.00   4.50   5.00   8.00

☐ 2194 $1 **Johns Hopkins**, 6/7/89, Baltimore, MD

      (159,049)..3.00   4.50   6.00 15.00

☐ 2195 $2 **William Jennings Bryan**, 3/19/86, Salem, IL

      (123,430)..5.00 10.00 15.00 15.00

☐ 2196 $5 **Bret Harte**, 8/25/87, Twain Harte, CA

      (111,431)...20.00 25.00 30.00 25.00

☐ 2197　25c Jack London, booklet single, 5/3/88,
　　　　　San Francisco, CA..1.25
☐ 2197a Jack London, booklet pane of 6 ....4.00
　　　　　Total for Scott 2183a, 2197, and 2197a is 94,655.

1986

☐ 2198　22c Handstamped Cover, Memorabilia, 1/23/86
　　　　　State College, PA...1.00
☐ 2199　22c Boy & Stamp Collection, 1/23/86
　　　　　State College, PA...1.00
☐ 2200　22c Scott U.S. 836, Sweden 268 & 271, 1/23/86
　　　　　State College, PA...1.00
☐ 2201　22c Scott U.S. 2216, 1/23/86 State College, PA........1.00
☐ 2201a Booklet pane of 4 ....5.00　　　　　　　　　12.00
☐ 2201b Booklet pane of 4, black omitted on 2198, 2201...350.00
　　　　　Total for Scott 2198-2201 is 675,924.
☐ 2202　22c Love, 1/30/86, New York, NY ....1.00　1.25　1.50　12.00
　　　　　1st Cat-Chet cachet..20.00
☐ 2203　22c Sojourner Truth, 2/4/86, New Paltz, NY
　　　　　(342,985)...1.00　1.25　1.50　6.00
☐ 2204　22c Republic of Texas, 3/2/86, San Antonio, TX
　　　　　(380,450)...1.00　1.25　1.50　10.00
☐ 2205　22c Muskellunge, 3/21/86, Seattle, WA...................1.00
☐ 2206　22c Atlantic Cod, 3/21/86, Seattle, WA...................1.00
☐ 2207　22c Largemouth Bass, 3/21/86, Seattle, WA............1.00
☐ 2208　22c Bluefin Tuna, 3/21/86, Seattle, WA 1.00
☐ 2209　22c Catfish, 3/21/86, Seattle, WA 1.00
☐ 2209a Booklet pane of 5 (2 types)*................................2.50　　　　　　　　　12.00*
☐　　　　1st Ohio Cachetmakers Association cachet 15.00
　　　　　Total for Scott 2205-2209 is 988,184.
☐ 2210　22c Public Hospitals, 4/11/86, New York, NY
　　　　　(403,665)...1.00　1.25　1.50　6.00
☐ 2211　22c Duke Ellington, 4/29/86, New York, NY
　　　　　(397,894)...1.00　1.25　1.50　8.00
☐ 2216　Sheet of 9, 5/22/86, Chicago, IL...............................4.00　　　　　　　　　15.00
☐ 2216a 22c George Washington 1.00
☐ 2216b 22c John Adams 1.00
☐ 2216c 22c Thomas Jefferson 1.00
☐ 2216d 22c James Madison 1.00
☐ 2216e 22c James Monroe 1.00
☐ 2216f 22c John Quincy Adams 1.00
☐ 2216g 22c Andrew Jackson 1.00
☐ 2216h 22c Martin Van Buren 1.00
☐ 2216I 22c William H. Harrison 1.00
☐ 2217　Sheet of 9, 5/22/86, Chicago, IL...............................5.00
☐ 2217a 22c John Tyler 1.00
☐ 2217b 22c James Knox Polk...1.00
☐ 2217c 22c Zachary Taylor 1.00
☐ 2217d 22c Millard Fillmore 1.00
☐ 2217e 22c Franklin Pierce..1.00
☐ 2217f 22c James Buchanan..1.00
☐ 2217g 22c Abraham Lincoln...1.00
☐ 2217h 22c Andrew Johnson 1.00
☐ 2217i 22c Ulysses S. Grant 1.00

			PLATE	CERM
☐ 2218	Sheet of 9, 5/22/86, Chicago, IL............25.00			
☐ 2218a	22c Rutherford B. Hayes 1.00			
☐ 2218b	22c James A. Garfield 1.00			
☐ 2218c	22c Chester A. Arthur...............................1.00			
☐ 2218d	22c Grover Cleveland 1.00			
☐ 2218e	22c Benjamin Harrison.............................1.00			
☐ 2218f	22c William McKinley 1.00			
☐ 2218g	22c Theodore Roosevelt 1.00			
☐ 2218h	22c William H. Taft 1.00			
☐ 2218i	22c Woodrow Wilson..................................1.00			
☐ 2219	Sheet of 9, 5/22/86, Chicago, IL............5.00			
☐ 2219a	22c Warren G. Harding..............................1.00			
☐ 2219b	22c Calvin Coolidge...................................1.00			
☐ 2219c	22c Herbert Hoover 1.00			
☐ 2219d	22c Franklin Delano Roosevelt 1.00			
☐ 2219e	22c White House 1.00			
☐ 2219f	22c Harry S. Truman 1.00			
☐ 2219g	22c Dwight D. Eisenhower 1.00			
☐ 2219h	22c John F. Kennedy..................................1.00			
☐ 2219i	22c Lyndon B. Johnson 1.00			
	Total for Scott 2216-2219 and 2216a-2219i is 9,009,599.			
☐ 2220	22c Elisha Kent Kane, 5/28/86, North Pole, AK 1.00			
☐ 2221	22c Adolphus W. Greely, 5/28/86, North Pole, AK ...1.00			
☐ 2222	22c Vilhjalmur Stefansson, 5/28/86, North Pole,AK1.00			
☐ 2223	22c Robert E. Peary & Matthew Henson, 5/28/86,			
	North Pole, AK 1.00			
☐ 2223a	Se-tenant, Polar Exploreres, (760,999)...........................	2.50	3.00	8.00
☐ 2224	22c Statue of Liberty, 7/4/86, New York, NY			
	(1,540,308)...2.00	2.50	3.50	30.00

1986-87 Transportation Coils

		SINGLE	PAIR	CERM PROG
☐ 2225	1c Omnibus, re-engraved, 11/26,86, DC (57,845)........—	1.00		
☐ 2226	2c Locomotive, re-engraved, 3/6/87,			
	Milwaukee, WI (169,484) ...._	1.00		12.00
☐ 2228	4c Stagecoach, re-engraved, 8/15/86, DC, earliest			
	known use.. 150.00			
☐ 2231	8.3c Ambulance, re-engraved, 8/24/86, DC, earliest			
	known use.. 150.00			

1986

		SINGLE	PLATE BLOCK	CERM PROG
☐ 2235	22c Navajo Art, 9/4/86, Window Rock, AZ..............1.00			
☐ 2236	22c Navajo Art, 9/4/86, Window Rock, AZ..............1.00			
☐ 2237	22c Navajo Art, 9/4/86, Window Rock, AZ..............1.00			
☐ 2238	22c Navajo Art, 9/4/86, Window Rock, AZ..............1.00			
☐ 2238a	Se-tenant, Navajo Art, (1,102,520)	2.50	3.00	10.00
☐ 2239	22c T.S. Eliot, 9/26/86, St. Louis, MO (304,764).......1.00	1.25	1.50	8.00
☐ 2240	22c Highlander Figure, 10/1/86, DC 1.00			
☐ 2241	22c Ship Figurehead, 10/1/86, DC 1.00			
☐ 2242	22c Nautical Figure, 10/1/86, DC.............................1.00			
☐ 2243	22c Cigar-store Figure, 10/1/86, DC 1.00			
☐ 2243a	Se-tenant, Woodcarved Figurines, (629,399)................	2.50	3.00	12.00

2235-38 2239 2240-43 2246

2244 2245 2247 2248

2249 2250 2251 2253 2255

2259 2264

2267-74 2275 2276

2286-2335 2336 2337 2338

152

SCOTT NUMBER	DESCRIPTION	SINGLE	PLATE BLOCK	BLOCK	CERM PROG
☐ 2244	22c Christmas (Madonna & Child), 10/24/86, DC (467,999)	1.00	1.25	1.50	12.00
☐ 2245	22c Christmas (Winter Village), 10/24/86 Snow Hill, MD (504,851)	1.00	1.25	1.50	12.00

1987

SCOTT NUMBER	DESCRIPTION	SINGLE	PLATE BLOCK	BLOCK	CERM PROG
☐ 2246	22c Michigan Statehood, 1/26/87, Lansing, MI (379,117)	1.00	1.25	1.50	8.00
☐ 2247	22c Pan American Games, 1/29/87, Indianapolis, IN (344,731)	1.00	1.25	1.50	8.00
☐ 2248	22c Love, 1/30/87, San Francisco, CA (333,329)	1.00	1.25	1.50	8.00
☐ 2249	22c Jean Baptiste Pointe du Sable, 2/20/87, Chicago, IL (313,054)	1.00	1.25	1.50	10.00
☐ 2250	22c Enrico Caruso, 2/27/87, New York, NY (389,834)	1.00	1.25	1.50	6.00
☐ 2251	22c Girl Scouts, 3/12/87, DC (556,391)	1.00	1.25	1.50	10.00

SCOTT NUMBER	DESCRIPTION	SINGLE	PAIR	CERM PROG

1987-88 Transportation Coils

SCOTT NUMBER	DESCRIPTION	SINGLE	PAIR	CERM PROG
☐ 2252	3c Conestoga Wagon, 2/29/88, Conestoga, PA (155,203)	—	1.00	12.00
☐	1st Gil Lewis cachet		15.00	
☐ 2253	5c Milk Wagon, 9/25/87, Indianapolis, IN	—	1.00	12.00
☐ 2254	5.3c Elevator, 9/16/88, New York, NY (142,705)	—	1.00	10.00
☐ 2255	7.6c Carreta, 8/30/88, San Jose, CA (140,024)	—	1.00	12.00
☐ 2256	8.4c Wheel Chair, 8/12/88, Tucson, AZ (136,337)	—	1.00	12.00
☐ 2257	10c Canal Boat, 4/11/87, Buffalo, NY (171,952)	—	1.00	10.00
☐ 2258	13c Patrol Wagon, 10/29/88, Anaheim, CA (132,928)	—	1.25	10.00
☐ 2259	13.2c Coal Car, 7/19/88, Pittsburgh, PA (123,965)	—	1.25	12.00
☐ 2260	15c Tugboat, 7/12/88, Long Beach, CA (134,926)	—	1.25	12.00
☐	1st One Fifty-Five Co. cachet		20.00	
☐ 2261	16.7c Popcorn Wagon, 7/7/88, Chicago, IL (117,908)	—	1.25	14.00
☐ 2262	17.5c Racing Car, 9/25/87, Indianapolis, IN	—	1.25	
☐ 2262a	Racing Car, untagged (Bureau precanceled)	—	5.00	
☐ 2263	20c Cable Car, 10/28/88, San Francisco, CA (150,068)	—	1.25	12.00
☐ 2264	20.5c Fire Engine, 9/28/88, San Angelo, TX (123,043)	—	1.25	12.00
☐ 2265	21c Railroad Mail Car, 8/16/88, Santa Fe, NM (124,430)		1.25	12.00
☐ 2266	24.1c Tandem Bicycle, 10/26/88, Redmond, WA (136,593)	—	1.25	12.00

SCOTT NUMBER	DESCRIPTION	SINGLE	PLATE BLOCK	BLOCK	CERM PROG

1987

SCOTT NUMBER	DESCRIPTION	SINGLE
☐ 2267	22c "Congratulations," 4/20/87, Atlanta, GA	1.75
☐ 2268	22c "Get Well," 4/20/87, Atlanta, GA	1.75
☐ 2269	22c "Thank You," 4/20/87, Atlanta, GA	1.75
☐ 2270	22c "Love You, Dad," 4/20/87, Atlanta, GA	1.75
☐ 2271	22c "Best Wishes," 4/20/87, Atlanta, GA	1.75
☐ 2272	22c "Happy Birthday," 4/20/87, Atlanta, GA	1.75
☐ 2273	22c "Love You, Mother," 4/20/87, Atlanta, GA	1.75

		SINGLE	BLOCK	PLATE BLOCK	CERM PROG
☐ 2274	22c "Keep In Touch," 4/20/87, Atlanta, GA	1.75			
☐ 2274a	Booklet pane of 10	7.00			15.00
	Total for Scott 2267-2274 is 1,588, 129.				
☐ 2275	22c United Way Centenary, 4/28/87, DC				
	(556,391) (2 types)*	1.00	1.25	2.00	8.00*
☐ 2276	22c Flag & Fireworks, booklet single, 5/9/87,				
	Denver, CO (398,855) (2 types)*	1.00	1.25	2.00	8.00*
☐ 2276a	Flag & Fireworks, booklet pane of 20	12.00			
☐ 2277	(25c) "E" & Earth, 3/22/88, DC	1.25	1.25	2.00	
☐ 2278	25c Flag and Clouds, 5/6/88, Boxborough, MA				
	(131,265)	1.25	1.25	2.00	10.00
☐ 2279	(25c) "E" and Earth, coil, 3/22/88, DC	1.25			
☐ 2280	25c Flag Over Yosemite, coil, 5/20/88,				
	Yosemite, CA (144,339)	1.25			10.00
☐ 2281	25c Honeybee, coil, 9/2/88, Omaha, NE				
	(122,853)	1.25			12.00
☐	1st Ralph J. Pohl cachet	15.00			
☐ 2282	(25c) "E" & Earth, booklet single, 3/22/88, DC	1.25			
☐ 2282a	"E" & Earth, booklet pane of 10	6.00			
	Total for Scott 2277, 2279 and 2282 is 363,639.				
☐ 2283	25c Pheasant, booklet single, 4/29/88, Rapid				
	City, SD (167,053)	1.25			
☐ 2283a	Pheasant, booklet pane of 10	6.00			15.00
☐ 2284	25c Owl, booklet single, 5/28/88, Arlington, VA.	1.25			
☐ 2285	25c Grosbeak, booklet single, 5/28/88,				
	Arlington, VA	1.25			
☐ 2285b	Booklet pane of 10	6.00			10.00
	Total for Scott 2284-2285 is 272,359.				
☐ 2285A	25c Flag and Clouds, booklet single, 7/5/88, DC				
	(117,303)	1.25			
☐ 2285c	Flag and Clouds, booklet pane of 6	4.00			
☐ 2286	22c Barn Swallow, 6/13/87, Toronto, ONT	1.00			
☐ 2287	22c Monarch Butterfly, 6/13/87, Toronto, ONT	1.00			
☐ 2288	22c Bighorn Sheep, 6/13/87, Toronto, ONT	1.00			
☐ 2289	22c Broad-tailed Hummingbird, 6/13/87,				
	Toronto, ONT	1.00			
☐ 2290	22c Cottontail, 6/13/87, Toronto, ONT	1.00			
☐ 2291	22c Osprey, 6/13/87, Toronto, ONT	1.00			
☐ 2292	22c Mountain Lion, 6/13/87, Toronto, ONT	1.00			
☐ 2293	22c Luna Moth, 6/13/87, Toronto, ONT	1.00			
☐ 2294	22c Mule Deer, 6/13/87, Toronto, ONT	1.00			
☐ 2295	22c Gray Squirrel, 6/13/87, Toronto, ONT	1.00			
☐ 2296	22c Armadillo, 6/13/87, Toronto, ONT	1.00			
☐ 2297	22c Eastern Chipmunk, 6/13/87, Toronto, ONT	1.00			
☐ 2298	22c Moose, 6/13/87, Toronto, ONT	1.00			
☐ 2299	22c Black Bear, 6/13/87, Toronto, ONT	1.00			
☐ 2300	22c Tiger Swallowtail, 6/13/87, Toronto, ONT	1.00			
☐ 2301	22c Bobwhite, 6/13/87, Toronto, ONT	1.00			
☐ 2302	22c Ringtail, 6/13/87, Toronto, ONT	1.00			
☐ 2303	22c Red-winged Blackbird, 6/13/87, Toronto, ONT	1.00			
☐ 2304	22c American Lobster, 6/13/87, Toronto, ONT	1.00			
☐ 2305	22c Black-tailed Jack Rabbit, 6/13/87, Toronto, ONT	1.00			
☐ 2306	22c Scarlet Tanager, 6/13/87, Toronto, ONT	1.00			
☐ 2307	22c Woodchuck, 6/13/87, Toronto, ONT	1.00			

☐ 2308	22c Roseate Spoonbill, 6/13/87, Toronto ONT	1.00
☐ 2309	22c Bald Eagle, 6/13/87, Toronto, ONT	1.00
☐ 2310	22c Alaskan Brown Bear, 6/13/87, Toronto, ONT	1.00
☐ 2311	22c Iiwi, 6/13/87, Toronto, ONT	1.00
☐ 2312	22c Badger, 6/13/87, Toronto, ONT	1.00
☐ 2313	22c Pronghorn, 6/13/87, Toronto, ONT	1.00
☐ 2314	22c River Otter, 6/13/87, Toronto, ONT	1.00
☐ 2315	22c Ladybug, 6/13/87, Toronto, ONT	1.00
☐ 2316	22c Beaver, 6/13/87, Toronto, ONT	1.00
☐ 2317	22c White-tailed Deer, 6/13/87, Toronto, ONT	1.00
☐ 2318	22c Blue Jay, 6/13/87, Toronto, ONT	1.00
☐ 2319	22c Pika, 6/13/87, Toronto, ONT	1.00
☐ 2320	22c Bison, 6/13/87, Toronto, ONT	1.00
☐ 2321	22c Snowy Egret, 6/13/87, Toronto, ONT	1.00
☐ 2322	22c Gray Wolf, 6/13/87, Toronto, ONT	1.00
☐ 2323	22c Mountain Goat, 6/13/87, Toronto, ONT	1.00
☐ 2324	22c Deer Mouse, 6/13/87, Toronto, ONT	1.00
☐ 2325	22c Black-tailed Prairie Dog, 6/13/87, Toronto, ONT	1.00
☐ 2326	22c Box Turtle, 6/13/87, Toronto, ONT	1.00
☐ 2327	22c Wolverine, 6/13/87, Toronto, ONT	1.00
☐ 2328	22c American Elk, 6/13/87, Toronto, ONT	1.00
☐ 2329	22c California Sea Lion, 6/13/87, Toronto, ONT	1.00
☐ 2330	22c Mockingbird, 6/13/87, Toronto, ONT	1.00
☐ 2331	22c Raccoon, 6/13/87, Toronto, ONT	1.00
☐ 2332	22c Bobcat, 6/13/87, Toronto, ONT	1.00
☐ 2333	22c Black-footed Ferret, 6/13/87, Toronto, ONT.	1.00
☐ 2334	22c Canada Goose, 6/13/87, Toronto, ONT	1.00
☐ 2335	22c Red Fox, 6/13/87, Toronto, ONT	1.00
☐	1st Bennett Cachetoon cachet	30.00
☐	Complete Set	75.00
☐ 2335a	Pane of 50	30.00			35.00

1987-90 Ratification of the Constitution

☐ 2336	22c Delaware, 7/4/87, Dover, DE (505,770)	1.75	2.00	2.50	12.00
☐ 2337	22c Pennsylvania, 8/26/87, Harrisburg, PA				
	(367,184)	1.75	2.00	2.50	12.00
☐ 2338	22c New Jersey, 9/11/87, Trenton, NJ (432,899)	1.75	2.00	2.50	12.00
☐ 2339	22c Georgia, 1/6/88, Atlanta, GA (467,804)	1.75	2.00	2.50	12.00
	1st 7-1-71 Chapter 50 cachet	15.00			
☐ 2340	22c Connecticut, 1/9/88, Hartford, CT (379,706)	1.75	2.00	2.50	12.00
☐ 2341	22c Massachusetts, 2/6/88, Boston, MA (412,616)	1.75	2.00	2.50	12.00
☐ 2342	22c Maryland, 2/15/88, Annapolis, MD (376,403)	1.75	2.00	2.50	12.00
☐ 2343	25c South Carolina, 5/23/88, Columbia, SC (322,938)	1.75	2.00	2.50	12.00
☐ 2344	25c New Hampshire, 6/21/88, Concord, NH				
	(374,402) (2 types)*	1.75	2.00	2.50	12.00*
☐ 2345	25c Virginia, 6/25/88, Williamsburg, VA (474,079)	1.75	2.00	2.50	12.00
☐ 2346	25c New York, 7/26/88, Albany, NY (385,793)	1.75	2.00	2.50	12.00
☐ 2347	25c North Carolina, 8/22/89, Fayetteville, NC				
	(392,953)	1.75	2.00	2.50	10.00
☐ 2348	25c Rhode Island, 5/29/90, Pawtucket, RI				
	(305,566) (2 types)*	1.75	2.00	2.50	14.00*

1987

☐ 2349	22c U.S.-Morocco Diplomatic Relations,				
	7/17/87, DC (372,814)	1.00	1.25	1.50	10.00
☐	1st Anagram cachet	20.00			

22 USA
January 2, 1788
Georgia
2339

22 USA
January 9, 1788
Connecticut
2340

22 USA
Feb 6, 1788
Massachusetts
2341

April 28, 1788 USA
Maryland 22
2342

Friendship
with Morocco
1787-1987
USA 22
2349

William Faulkner
USA 22
2350

Lacemaking USA 22
2351-54

U.S. Constitution
1787-1987 22 USA
2360

CPA
22 USA
2361

The Bicentennial
of the Constitution of
the United States
of America
1787-1987   USA 22
2355-59

Stourbridge Lion
1829   USA 22
2362-66

CHRISTMAS
22 USA
Moroni, National Gallery
2367

USA 22 GREETINGS
2368

22 USA
2369

Happy Bicentennial
Australia!
1788
1988   USA 22
2370

James Weldon
Johnson
22
2371

USA 22
Siamese Cat, Exotic Shorthair Cat
2372-75

22 USA
KNUTE ROCKNE
2376

156

☐ 2350	22c **William Faulkner**, 8/3/87, Oxford, MS				
	(480,024)..1.00		1.25	1.50	8.00
☐ 2351	22c **Lacemaking**, 8/14/87 Ypsilanti, MI...................1.00				
☐ 2352	22c **Lacemaking**, 8/14/87 Ypsilanti, MI...................1.00				
☐ 2353	22c **Lacemaking**, 8/14/87 Ypsilanti, MI...................1.00				
☐ 2354	22c **Lacemaking**, 8/14/87 Ypsilanti, MI...................1.00				
☐ 2354a	Se-tenant, Lacemaking		2.75	3.50	8.00
☐ 2355	22c **"The Bicentennial,"** 8/28/87, DC.......................1.50				
☐ 2356	22c **"We the People,"** 8/28/87, DC............................1.50				
☐ 2357	22c **"Establish Justice,"** 8/28/87, DC 1.50				
☐ 2358	22c **"And Secure,"** 8/28/87, DC................................1.50				
☐ 2359	22c **"Do Ordain,"** 8/28/87, DC 1.50				
☐ 2359a	**Booklet pane of 5**, Constitution Bicentennial...........9.00				10.00
	Total for Scott 2355-2359 is (1,008,799).				
☐ 2360	22c **Signing of the Constitution**, 9/17/87,				
	Philadelphia, PA (719,975) 1.00		1.25	1.50	
☐	1st Alexia cachet 25.00				
☐	1st Olde Well cachet 35.00				
☐ 2361	22c **Certified Public Accounting**, 9/21/87,				
	New York, NY (362,099) 10.00		11.00	15.00	30.00
☐ 2362	22c **Stourbridge Lion**, 10/1/87, Baltimore, MD........1.00				
☐ 2363	22c **Best Friend of Charleston**, 10/1/87,				
	Baltimore, MD...1.00				
☐ 2364	22c **John Bull**, 10/1/87, Baltimore, MD 1.00				
☐ 2365	22c **Brother Jonathan**, 10/1/87, Baltimore, MD 1.00				
☐ 2366	22c **Gowan & Marx**, 10/1/87, Baltimore, MD...........1.00				
☐ 2366a	**Booklet pane of 5**, Locomotives 3.00				15.00
	Total for Scott 2362-2366 is 976,694.				
☐ 2367	22c **Christmas (Madonna & Child)**, 10/23/87,				
	DC (320,406)..1.00		1.25	1.50	8.00
☐ 2368	22c **Christmas (Ornaments)**, 10/23/87,				
	Anaheim, CA (375,858)....................................1.00		1.25	1.50	16.00

1988

☐ 2369	22c **1988 Winter Olympics**, 1/10/88, Anchorage, AK				
	(395, 198)..1.00		1.25	1.50	10.00
☐ 2370	22c **Australia Bicentennial**, 1/26/88, DC				
	(523,465)...1.00		1.25	1.50	10.00
☐ 2371	22c **James Weldon Johnson**, 2/2/88, Nashville, TN				
	(465,282)...1.00		1.25	1.50	10.00
☐ 2372	22c **Siamese & Exotic Shorthair**, 2/5/88,				
	New York, NY...2.50				
☐ 2373	22c **Abyssinian & Himalayan**, 2/5/88, New York, NY2.50				
☐ 2374	22c **Maine Coon & Burmese**, 2/5/88, New York, NY2.50				
☐ 2375	22c **American Shorthair & Persian**, 2/5/88,				
	New York, NY...2.50				
☐ 2375a	Se-tenant Cats, (872,734)...		6.00	8.00	12.00
☐ 2376	22c **Knute Rockne**, 3/9/88, Notre Dame, IN				
	(404,311)..4.00		4.50	5.00	15.00
☐ 2377	25c **Francis Ouimet**, 6/13/88, Brookline, MA				
	(383,168)..4.00		4.50	5.00	10.00
☐ 2378	25c **Love**, 7/4/88, Pasadena, CA (399,038).........1.25		1.50	1.75	
☐ 2379	45c **Love**, 8/8/88, Shreveport, LA (121,808)........1.25		2.00	2.50	10.00
☐ 2380	25c **Summer Olympics**, 8/19/88, Colorado Springs, CO				
	(402,616)...1.25		1.50	1.75	10.00

2377

2390-93

2379

2378

2380

2386-89

2394

2395-98

2399

2400

		SINGLE	BLOCK	PLATE BLOCK	CERM PROG
☐ 2381	25c 1928 Locomobile, 8/25/88, Detroit, MI.............1.25				
☐ 2382	25c 1929 Pierce-Arrow, 8/25/88, Detroit, MI...........1.25				
☐ 2383	25c 1931 Cord, 8/25/88, Detroit, MI.......................1.25				
☐ 2384	25c 1932 Packard, 8/25/88, Detroit, MI...................1.25				
☐ 2385	25c 1935 Duesenberg, 8/25/88, Detroit, MI.............1.25				
☐ 2385a	Booklet pane of 5...3.00				12.00
	Total for Scott 2381-2385 is 875,801.				
☐ 2386	25c Nathaniel Palmer, 9/14/88, DC........................1.25				
☐ 2387	25c Lt. Charles Wilkes, 9/14/88, DC.......................1.25				
☐ 2388	25c Richard E. Byrd, 9/14/88, DC..........................1.25				
☐ 2389	25c Lincoln Ellsworth, 9/14/88, DC........................1.25				
☐ 2389a	Se-tenant, Antarctic Explorers, (720,537)	3.00		3.50	10.00
☐ 2390	25c Deer, 10/1/88, Sandusky, OH............................1.50				
☐ 2391	25c Horse, 10/1/88, Sandusky, OH 1.50				
☐ 2392	25c Camel, 10/1/88, Sandusky, OH..........................1.50				
☐ 2393	25c Goat, 10/1/88, Sandusky, OH 1.50				
☐ 2393a	Se-tenant, Carousel Animals, (856,380)...................	3.50		4.00	30.00
☐ 2394	$8.75 Eagle in Flight, 10/6/88, Terre Haute, IN				
	(66,558)...30.00	40.00	50.00	25.00	
☐	Sheet of 20 ....350.00				
☐ 2395	25c "Happy Birthday," 10/22/88,				
	King of Prussia, PA 1.25				
☐ 2396	25c "Best Wishes," 10/22/88, King of Prussia, PA ...1.25				
☐ 2396a	Booklet pane of 6 (3 No. 2395 +3 No. 2396) 4.00				18.00
☐ 2397	25c "Thinking of You," 10/22/88, King of				
	Prussia, PA...1.25				
☐ 2398	25c "Love You," 10/22/88, King of Prussia, PA 1.25				
☐ 2398a	Booklet pane of 6 (3 No. 2397 + 3 No. 2398) 4.00				
	Total for Scott 2395-2398 is 126, 767.				
☐ 2399	25c Christmas (Madonna), 10/20/88, DC (247,291).1.25	1.50		1.75	10.00
☐ 2400	25c Christmas (Sleigh & Village), 10/20/88,				
	Berlin, NH (412,213)..1.25	1.50		1.75	10.00

1989

		SINGLE	BLOCK	PLATE BLOCK	CERM PROG
☐ 2401	25c Montana Statehood, 1/15/89, Helena, MT				
	(353,319)...1.25	1.50		1.75	8.00
☐	1st Steve Wilson cachet 30.00				
☐ 2402	25c A. Philip Randolph, 2/3/89, New York, NY				
	(363,174)..1.25	1.50		1.75	6.00
☐ 2403	25c North Dakota Statehood, 2/21/89, Bismarck, ND				
	(306,003)..1.25	1.50		1.75	6.00
☐ 2404	25c Washington Statehood, 2/22/89, Olympia,WA				
	(445,174)...1.25	1.50		1.75	6.00
☐ 2405	25c Experiment, 3/3/89, New Orleans, LA...............1.25				
☐ 2406	25c Phoenix, 3/3/89, New Orleans, LA....................1.25				
☐ 2407	25c New Orleans, 3/3/89, New Orleans, LA 1.25				
☐ 2408	25c Washington, 3/3/89, New Orleans, LA...............1.25				
☐ 2409	25c Walk in the Water, 3/3/89, New Orleans,LA...1.25				
☐ 2409a	Booklet pane of 5...4.00				10.00
	Total for Scott 2405-2409 is 981,674.				
☐ 2410	25c World Stamp Expo '89, 3/16/89, New York,NY				
	(296,310)...1.25	1.50		1.75	6.00
☐ 2411	25c Arturo Toscanini, 3/25/89, New York, NY				
	(309,441)...1.25	1.50		1.75	6.00

2401

Black Heritage USA

2402, 2442, 2567,
2617, 2746

North Dakota 1889
2403

2410

2404

Experiment 1788-1790
2405-2409

2411

2412-2415

South Dakota 1889
2416

Lou Gehrig
2417

Hemingway
2418

Letter Carriers We Deliver
2420

$2.40
2419

Bill of Rights
2421

2422-2425

2426, 2512

WORLD STAMP EXPO '89

The classic 1869 U.S.
Abraham Lincoln stamp
is reborn in these four
larger versions now
maintaining World
Stamp Expo '89, held in
Washington, D.C. during
the 20th Universal
Postal Congress of the
UPU. These stamps
show the issued colors
and those of the actual
proof color.

2433

CHRISTMAS

Carracci, National Gallery
2427, 2514
2578, 2710

Greetings USA 25

2428-2429,
2515-2516,
2579-2585,
2711-2719

USA 25
2431

1989-90

			SINGLE	BLOCK	PLATE BLOCK	CERM PROG
☐ 2412	25c House of Representatives, 4/4/89, DC (327,755)	1.25	1.50	1.75	6.00
☐ 2413	25c Senate, 4/6/89, DC (341,288)	1.25	1.50	1.75	100.00
☐ 2414	25c Executive Branch, 4/30/89, Mount Vernon, VA (387,644)	1.25	1.50	1.75	6.00
☐ 2415	25c Supreme Court, 2/2/90, DC	1.25	1.50	1.75	6.00

1989

			SINGLE	BLOCK	PLATE BLOCK	CERM PROG
☐ 2416	25c South Dakota Statehood, 5/3/89, Pierre, SD (348,370)	1.25	1.50	1.75	6.00
☐ 2417	25c Lou Gehrig, 6/10/89, Cooperstown, NY (694,227)	6.00	7.00	9.00	15.00
☐	1st Edken cachet	25.00			
☐ 2418	25c Ernest Hemingway, 7/17/89, Key West, FL (345,436)	1.25	1.50	1.75	8.00
☐ 2419	$2.40 Moon Landing, 7/20/89, DC (208,982)	7.00	12.00	17.50	8.00
	(with NASA program)				60.00
☐ 2420	25c Letter Carriers, 8/30/89, Milwaukee, WI (372,241)	1.25	1.50	1.75	6.00
☐ 2421	25c Bill of Rights, 9/25/89, Philadelphia, PA (900,384)	1.25	1.50	1.75	6.00
☐ 2422	25c Tyrannosaurus Rex, 10/1/89, Orlando, FL	1.25			
☐ 2423	25c Pteranodon, 10/1/89, Orlando, FL	1.25			
☐ 2424	25c Stegosaurus, 10/1/89, Orlando, FL	1.25			
☐ 2425	25c Brontosaurus, 10/1/89, Orlando, FL	1.25			
☐ 2425a	Se-tenant, Dinosaurs, (871,634)		3.00	3.50	20.00
☐ 2426	25c America, 10/12/89, San Juan, PR (215,285)	1.25	1.50	1.75	
☐ 2427	25c Christmas (Madonna & Child), 10/19/89,DC (395,321)	1.25	1.50	1.75	
☐ 2427a	Booklet pane of 10	6.00			8.00
☐ 2427, 2427a	Traditional Christmas, sheet stamp & booklet pane (10/19/89), DC				8.00
☐ 2428	25c Christmas (Sleigh), 10/19/89, Westport, CT	1.25	1.50	1.75	
☐ 2428, 2429a	Contemporary Christmas sheet stamp & booklet pane (10/19/89), Westport, CT				8.00
☐ 2429	25c Christmas (Sleigh), booklet single, 10/19/89, Westport, CT	1.25			
☐ 2429a	Booklet pane of 10	6.00			
	Total for Scott 2428-2429a was 345,931.				
☐ 2431	25c Eagle & Shield, self-adhesive, booklet single, 11/10/89, Virginia Beach, VA	1.25			6.00
☐ 2433	90c World Stamp Expo, souvenir sheet of 4, 11/17/89, DC	15.00			20.00
☐ 2434	25c Stagecoach, 11/19/89, DC	1.25			
☐ 2435	25c Paddlewheel Steamer, 11/19/89, DC	1.25			
☐ 2436	25c Biplane, 11/19/89, DC	1.25			
☐ 2437	25c Depot-hack type Automobile, 11/19/89, DC	1.25			
☐ 2437a	Se-tenant, Traditional Mail Delivery, (916,389)		3.00	3.50	10.00
☐ 2438	25c Traditional Mail Delivery, souvenir sheet of 4, 11/27/89, DC (241,634)	2.00			10.00

1990

			SINGLE	BLOCK	PLATE BLOCK	CERM PROG
☐ 2439	25c Idaho Statehood, 1/6/90, Boise, ID (252,493)	1.25	1.50	1.75	18.00
☐ 2440	25c Love, 1/18/90, Romance, AR	1.25	1.50	1.75	

		SINGLE	PLATE BLOCK	BLOCK	CERM PROG
☐ 2441	25c Love, booklet single, 1/18/90, Romance, ID.......1.25				
☐ 2441a	Love, booklet pane of 10 ....7.00				
	Total for Scott 2440-2441a was 257, 788.				
☐ 2440-2441a	Love, sheet stamp & booklet pane, Romance, AR...				6.00
☐ 2442	25c Ida B. Wells, 2/1/90, Chicago, IL (229,226) 1.25		1.50	1.75	6.00
☐ 2443	25c Beach Umbrella, booklet single, 2/3/90,				
	Sarasota, FL..1.50				
☐ 2443a	Beach Umbrella, booklet pane of 10 (72,286) 8.00				6.00
☐ 2444	25c Wyoming Statehood, 2/23/90, Cheyenne, WY				
	(317,654)..1.25		1.50	1.75	6.00
☐ 2445	25c The Wizard of Oz, 3/23/90, Hollywood, CA.......3.00				
☐ 2446	25c Gone with the Wind, 3/23/90, Hollywood,CA....3.00				
☐ 2447	25c Beau Geste, 3/23/90, Hollywood, CA 1.25				
☐ 2448	25c Stagecoach, 3/23/90, Hollywood, CA 1.25				
☐ 2448a	Se-tenant (863,079)		7.00	9.00	14.00
☐ 2449	25c Marianne Moore, 4/18/90, Brooklyn, NY				
	(390,535)..1.25		1.50	1.75	6.00

1990-95 Transportation Coil

		SINGLE	PLATE BLOCK	BLOCK	CERM PROG
☐ 2451	4c Steam Carriage, 1/25/91, Tucson, AZ (100,393).....— pr 1.00				
☐ 2452	5c Circus Wagon, 8/31/90, Syracuse, NY (71,806).......— pr 1.00				8.00
☐ 2452B	5c Circus Wagon, photogravure, 12/8/92				
	Cincinnati, OH ....— pr 1.25				
☐ 2452D	5c Circus Wagon, photogravure, with cent sign,				
	5/20/95, Kansas City, MO (20,835) ....— pr 1.25				
☐ 2453	5c Canoe, engraved, 5/25/91, Secaucus, NJ				
	(108,634)..— pr 1.25				10.00
☐ 2454	5c Canoe, photogravure, 12/22/91,				
	Secaucus, NJ...— pr 1.25				
☐ 2457	10c Tractor Trailer, 5/25/91, Secaucus, NJ				
	(84,717)..— pr 1.25				10.00
☐ 2458	10c Tractor Trailer, photogravure, 5/25/94 (15,431) ..— pr 1.25				
☐ 2463	20c Cog Railway, 6/9/95, Dallas, TX (28,883)..............— pr 1.25				
☐ 2464	23c Lunch Wagon, 4/12/91, Columbus, OH				
	(115,830)..— pr 1.25				
☐ 2466	32c Ferry Boat, 6/2/95, McLean, VA 1.25				
☐ 2468	$1 Seaplane, 4/20/90, Phoenix, AZ ....3.00 pr 4.00				10.00

1990

		SINGLE	PLATE BLOCK	BLOCK	CERM PROG
☐ 2470	25c Admiralty Head, WA, 4/26/90, DC....................1.50				
☐ 2471	25c Cape Hatteras, NC, 4/26/90, DC........................1.50				
☐ 2472	25c West Quoddy Head, ME, 4/26/90, DC...............1.50				
☐ 2473	25c American Shoals, FL, 4/26/90, DC 1.50				
☐ 2474	25c Sandy Hook, NJ, 4/26/90, DC............................1.50				8.00
☐ 2474a	Booklet pane of 5 (805, 133) 4.00				10.00
☐ 2475	25c Flag, plastic self-adhesive, 5/18/90, Seattle, WA				
	(97,567)..1.25				6.00

1991-95 Flora & Fauna

		SINGLE	PLATE BLOCK	BLOCK	CERM PROG
☐ 2476	1c Kestrel, 6/22/91, Aurora, CO (77,781) ....—		1.25		12.00
☐ 2477	1c Kestrel with cent sign, 5/10/95, Aurora, CO				
	(21,767) ....—		1.25		
☐ 2478	3c Eastern Bluebird, 6/22/91, Aurora, CO (76,149) ....—		1.25		
☐ 2479	19c Fawn, 3/11/91, DC (100,212) 1.25				
☐ 2480	30c Cardinal, 6/22/91, Aurora, CO (101,290)..........1.25				
☐ 2481	45c Pumpkinseed Sunfish, 12/2/92, DC (38,696).....1.75				6.00

REST EASY!

You've got the best first day covers money
can buy when you choose COLORANO!
For over a quarter century,
the choice of knowledgeable collectors.

Your FDC's aren't COLORANO?
Better send for a free sample now, and in the
meantime reach for the sleeping pills!

COLORANO

7 HIGH ST - SUITE 300 - HUNTINGTON, NY 11743
1-800-533-2262
Visit Our Website: www.colorano.com

163

2434-2438

IDAHO

USA 25 1890

2439

L O V E
USA 25

2440-2441,
2535-2536, 2618

Wyoming USA 25

2444

USA 15

2543

The WIZARD OF Oz

USA 25

2445-2448

Marianne Moore

25 USA

American Poet 1887-1972

2449

25 USA

2475, 2522

$2 USA

2476

29 USA

2481-2494

25

2501-2505

OLYMPIAN ☍

USA 25

2470-2474   2496-2500

Dwight David Eisenhower

USA 25

2513

Federated States of Micronesia

USA 25

2506-2507

1990

USA 25 Killer Whale

2508-2511

F Flower
USA

2517-2520
2524-2527

This U.S. stamp, along with 25¢ of additional U.S. postage, is equivalent to the 'F' stamp rate

2521

29 USA

2523, 2523A

19 USA

2529

USA 19

2530

USA 29

2528

USA 29

2531

50 USA

Switzerland Founded 1291

2532

Vermont

USA 29

2533

SCOTT NUMBER	DESCRIPTION	SINGLE	PLATE BLOCK	CERM BLOCK	PROG
☐ 2482	$2 Bobcat, 6/1/90, Arlington, VA (49,660)..............7.00		11.00	15.00	10.00
☐ 2483	20c Blue Jay, booklet single, 6/15/95,				
	Kansas City, MO (16,847) ....—		1.25		
☐ 2483a	Booklet pane of 10..4.00				
☐ 2484	29c Wood Duck, black denomination, 4/12/91,				
	Columbus, OH 1.25				
☐ 2484a	Booklet pane of 10..5.00				
☐ 2485	29c Wood Duck, red denomination, 4/12/91,				
	Columbus, OH 1.25				
☐ 2485a	Booklet pane of 10..5.00				
	First day cancel was applied to 205,305 covers				
	bearing one or more of Nos. 2484-2485				
	2484a-2485a.				
☐ 2486	29c African Violet, 10/8/93, Beaumont, TX (40,167)1.25				
☐ 2486a	Booklet pane of 10..5.00				
☐ 2487	32c Peach, bklt single, 7/8/95, Reno, NV.................1.25				
☐ 2488	32c Pear, bklt single, 7/8/95, Reno, NV..................1.25				
☐ 2488a	Booklet pane of 10, 5 each #2487-2488..................7.50				
☐ 2488b	Pair 2487-2488 ....1.50				
☐ 2489	29c Red Squirrel, 6/25/93, Milwaukee, WI (48,546)1.25				6.00
☐ 2490	29c Red Rose, 8/19/93, Houston, TX (37,916)..........1.25				
☐ 2491	29c Pine Cone, 11/5/93, Kansas City, MO (110,929).1.25				
☐ 2492	29c Pink Rose, 6/2/95, McLean, VA...........................1.25				
	First Day cancel was applied to 59,100 covers bearing				
	one or more of Nos. 2466, 2492				
☐ 2493	32c Peach, serpentine, die cut, 7/8/95, Reno, NV 1.25				
☐ 2494	32c Pear, serpentine die cut, 7/8/95, Reno,NV.........1.25				
☐ 2495	32c Peach, serpentine die cut, vert., 7/8/95,				
	Reno, NV..1.25				
☐ 2495A	32c Pear, serpentine die cut vert., 7/8/95, Reno, NV1.25				
	First Day cancels was applied to 71,086 covers bearing				
	Nos. 2487-2488, 2488a, 2493-2495A				

1990

☐ 2496	25c Jesse Owens, 7/6/90, Minneapolis, MN..............1.25				8.00
☐ 2497	25c Ray Ewry, 7/6/90, Minneapolis, MN...................1.25				
☐ 2498	25c Hazel Wightman, 7/6/90, Minneapolis, MN.......1.25				
☐ 2499	25c Eddie Eagan, 7/6/90, Minneapolis, MN..............1.25				
☐ 2500	25c Helene Madison, 7/6/90, Minneapolis, MN.........1.25				
☐ 2500a	Strip of 5, Olympians, (1,143,404) 3.00		5.00	6.00	10.00
☐ 2501	25c Assiniboin, 8/17/90, Cody, WY 1.25				
☐ 2502	25c Cheyenne, 8/17/90, Cody, WY 1.25				
☐ 2503	25c Comanche, 8/17/90, Cody, WY 1.25				
☐ 2504	25c Flathead, 8/17/90, Cody, WY...............................1.25				
☐ 2505	25c Shoshone, 8/17/90, Cody, WY 1.25				
☐ 2505a	Booklet pane of 10, 2 each, #2501-2505 (979,580).6.00				6.00
☐ 2506	25c Federated States of Micronesia, 9/28/90, DC				
	(3 types)*...1.25				8.00*
☐ 2507	25c Republic of the Marshall Islands, 9/28/90,DC...1.25				
☐ 2507a	Se-tenant Pair, Nos. 2506-2507 ....2.50		3.00		
	Total for Scott 2506-2507a was 343,816.				
☐	Scott 2506-2507 with Micronesia and Marshall Islands stamps				
	dual cancel...15.00				
☐ 2508	25c Killer Whales, 10/3/90, Baltimore, MD..............1.25				10.00
☐ 2509	25c Northern Sea Lions, 10/3/90, Baltimore, MD....1.25				

		SINGLE	BLOCK	PLATE BLOCK	CERM PROG
☐ 2510	25c **Sea Otter**, 10/3/90, Baltimore, MD....................1.25				
☐ 2511	25c **Common Dolphin**, 10/3/90, Baltimore, MD........1.25				
☐ 2511a	**Se-tenant**, Sea Creatures, (706,047)				
	Baltimore, MD, Grand Rapids, MI...........................	4.00	4.50		10.00
☐ 2512	25c **Grand Canyon**, 10/12/90, Grand Canyon, AZ				
	(164,190)...1.25		1.50	1.75	16.00
☐ 2513	25c **Dwight D. Eisenhower**, 10/13/90, Abilene, KS				
	(487,988)..1.25		1.50	1.75	8.00
☐ 2514	25c **Christmas (Madonna & Child)**, 10/18/90,				
	DC (378,383) 1.25		1.50	1.75	8.00
	Error program (2514 only)				12.00
☐ 2515	25c **Christmas (Tree)**, sheet stamp, 10/18/90,				
	Evergreen, CO..1.25		1.50	1.75	8.00
	Error program (2515 only)				12.00
☐ 2516	25c **Christmas (Tree)**, booklet single, 10/18/90,				
	Evergreen, CO..1.25				
☐ 2516a	**Booklet pane of 10**...6.00				
	Total for Scott 2515-2516a was 230,586.				

1991-92

		SINGLE	BLOCK	PLATE BLOCK	CERM PROG
☐ 2517	(29c) **Flower**, non-denominated sheet stamp,				
	1/22/91, DC...1.25		1.50	1.75	
☐ 2518	(29c) **Flower**, non-denominated coil stamp,				
	1/22/91, DC...1.25				
☐ 2519	(29c) **Flower**, non-denominated booklet single				
	(printed by BEP), 1/22/91, DC...........................1.25				
☐ 2519a	**Booklet pane of 10**...6.00				
☐ 2520	(29c) **Flower**, non-denominated booklet single				
	(printed by KCS), 1/22/91, DC...........................1.25				
☐ 2520a	**Booklet pane of 10**...6.00				
☐ 2521	(4c) **Make-up rate**, non-denominated, text only,				
	1/22/91, DC...1.25		1.50	1.75	
☐ 2522	(29c) **Flag**, non-denominated ATM single,				
	self-adhesive, 1/22/91, DC...............................1.25				
☐ 2523	29c **Flag over Mt. Rushmore**, engraved, 1/29/91,				
	Mt. Rushmore, SD (233,793)............................1.25		1.50		6.00
☐ 2523A	29c **Flag over Mt. Rushmore**, photogravure, 7/4/91,				
	Mt. Rushmore, SD (80,662)..............................1.25		1.50		
☐ 2524	29c **Flower**, 4/5/91 Rochester, NY (132,233)............1.25		1.50	1.75	12.00
☐ 2525	29c **Flower**, roulette 10 coil, 4/5/91, Rochester, NY				
	(144,750)...1.25		1.50		
☐ 2526	29c **Flower**, perf. 10 coil, 3/3/92, Rochester, NY				
	(35,877)..1.25		1.50		
☐ 2527	29c **Flower**, bklt. single, 5/5/91, Rochester, NY 1.25		1.50		
☐ 2524, 2527	**Flower**, sheet & booklet, 4/5/91				12.00
☐ 2527a	**Booklet pane of 10** 6.00				
	First day cancel was applied to 16,975 covers				
	bearing one or more of Nos. 2527-2527a.				
☐ 2528	29c **Flag and Olympic Rings**, bklt. single, 4/21/91,				
	Atlanta, GA..1.25				10.00
☐ 2528	29c **Flag and Olympic Rings**, (not 1st day) 4/22/91				
	Austin, TX				15.00
	Ceremony Programs (not 1st day), 4/22/91,				
	Bismarck, ND (set of 7)				
☐ 2528a	**Booklet pane of 10** 5.00				

SCOTT NUMBER	DESCRIPTION	SINGLE	BLOCK	PLATE BLOCK	CERM PROG
☐ 2529	19c **Fishing Boat,** two loops 8/8/91, DC (82,698).........—		1.25		
☐ 2529C	19c **Fishing Boat,** one loop, 6/25/94, Arlington, VA				
	(14,538) ....—		1.25		
☐ 2530	19c **Balloon,** 5/17/91, Denver, CO 1.25				
☐ 2530, C129, UC63, UC63a, 19c Balloon, 40c William Piper,					
	45c Eagle aerograms, 5/17/91, Denver CO				12.00
☐ 2530a	**Booklet pane of 10**..6.00				
	First day cancel was applied to 96,351 covers				
	bearing one or more of Nos. 2530-2530a.				
☐ 2531	29c **Flags on Parade,** 5/30/91, Waterloo, NY				
	(104,046)...1.25		1.50	1.75	6.00
☐ 2531A	29c **Liberty Torch,** 6/25/91 New York, NY (68,456).1.25				

1991-93

SCOTT NUMBER	DESCRIPTION	SINGLE	BLOCK	PLATE BLOCK	CERM PROG
☐ 2532	50c **Switzerland,** 2/22/91, DC (316,047)...................1.35		1.75	2.50	6.00
☐	Scott 2532 with Switzerland stamp, dual cancel......15.00				
☐ 2533	29c **Vermont,** 3/1/91, Bennington, VT (308,105)......1.25		1.50	1.75	6.00
☐ 2534	29c **Savings Bonds,** DC 4/30/91 (341,955) 1.25		1.50	1.75	6.00
☐ 2535	29c **Love,** 5/9/91, Honolulu, HI (336,132).................1.25		1.50	1.75	
☐ 2536	29c **Love,** bklt. single, 5/9/91, Honolulu, HI..............1.25				
☐ 2536a	**Booklet pane of 10**..5.00				
	First day cancel was applied to 43,336 covers				
	bearing one or more of Nos. 2536-2536a.				
☐ 2537	52c **Love,** 5/9/91, Honolulu, HI (90,438)...................1.35		1.75	2.00	
☐ 2535, 2537, U621 29c Love stamps & envelope..........................					6.00
☐ 2538	29c **William Saroyan,** 5/22/91, Fresno, CA (334,373)1.25		1.50	1.75	6.00
☐	Scott 2538 with Russian stamp, dual cancel 15.00				
☐ 2539	$1 **USPS & Olympic Rings,** 9/29/91, Orlando, FL				
	(69,241)...3.00		6.00	7.50	6.00
☐ 2540	$2.90 **Eagle & Olympic Rings,** 7/7/91, San Diego, CA				
	(79,555)...10.00		40.00	50.00	15.00
☐ 2541	$9.95 **Eagle & Olympic Rings,** 6/16/91,				
	Sacramento, CA (68,657)......................25.00		85.00	100.00	25.00
☐ 2542	$14 **Eagle,** 8/31/91, Hunt Valley, MD (54,727)........30.00		125.00	150.00	
☐ 2543	$2.90 **Futuristic Space Shuttle,** 6/3/93, Kennedy				
	Space Center, FL 8.00		40.00	50.00	15.00
☐ 2544	$3 **Challenger Shuttle,** 6/22/95, Anaheim, CA........8.00		15.00	17.00	14.00
☐ 2544A	$10.75 **Endeavour Shuttle,** Express Mail, 8/14/95,				
	Irvine, CA...25.00		45.00	50.00	22.00
☐ 2549a	29c **Fishing Flies** booklet pane of 5, 5/31/91,				
	Cuddebackville, NY (1,045,726).......................3.00				12.00
☐ 2545-2549, any single..1.25					
☐ 2550	29c **Cole Porter,** 6/8/91, Peru, IN (304,363) 1.25		1.50	1.75	6.00
☐ 2551	29c **Desert Storm/ Desert Shield,** 7/2/91, DC 2.00		2.50	3.00	10.00
☐ 2552	29c **Desert Storm/ Desert Shield,** bklt. single,				
	7/2/91, DC (cerm. prog. includes No. 2551)......2.00				50.00
☐ 2552a	**Booklet pane of 5** 4.00				8.00
	First day cancel was applied to 860,455 covers				
	bearing one or more of Nos. 2551-2552, 2552a.				
☐ 2557a	29c **Summer Olympics,** 7/12/91, Los Angeles, CA				
	(886,984)...3.00				8.00
☐ 2553-2557, any single 1.25					
☐ 2558	29c **Numismatics,** 8/13/91, Chicago, IL (288,519)....1.25		1.50	1.75	6.00

2534

2537

2559, 2697, 2765

Royal Wulff

2545-2549

2540-2542

2539

2543

Cole Porter

2550

2551-2552

2558

2560

2561

2562-2566

2568-2577

2594, 2594B

2595-2597

2607

2608-2608B

2609

2619

2616

2620-2629

☐ 2559	29c World War II Souvenir Sheet of 10, 9/3/91,				
	Phoenix, AZ (1,832,967) 10.00				12.00
☐ 2559a-2559j, any single.....................................1.25					
☐ 2560	29c Basketball, 8/28/91, Springfield, MA (295,471).2.00		2.50	3.50	12.00
☐ 2561	29c District of Columbia, 9/7, DC (299,989) (2 types)*1.25		1.50	1.75	12.00*
☐ 2566a	29c Comedians booklet pane of 10, 8/29/91,				
	Hollywood, CA.................................5.00				8.00
☐ 2562-2566, any single..1.25					
	First day cancel was applied to 954,293 covers				
	bearing one or more of Nos. 2562-2566a.				
☐ 2567	29c Jan Matzeliger, 9/15/91, Lynn, MA (289,034) ...1.25		1.50	1.75	8.00
☐ 2577a	29c Space Exploration booklet pane of 10, 10/1/91,				
	Pasadena, CA 5.00				10.00
☐ 2568-2577, any single..1.25					
	First day cancel was applied to 1,465,111 covers				
	bearing one or more of Nos. 2568-2577a.				
☐ 2578	(29c) Christmas (religious), 10/17/91, Houston, TX 1.25		1.50	1.75	6.00
☐ 2579	(29c) Christmas (secular), 10/17/91, Santa, ID				
	(169,750)..1.25		1.50	1.75	
☐ 2579, 2980-2985 29c Contemporary Christmas					6.00
☐ 2581b	(29c) Christmas booklet pane of 4, 10/17/91,				
	Santa, ID 2.50				
☐ 2580-2581, any single..1.25					
☐ 2582	(29c) Christmas, bklt. single, 10/17/91, Santa, ID....1.25				
☐ 2582a Booklet pane of 4..2.50					
☐ 2583	(29c) Christmas, bklt. single, 10/17/91, Santa, ID....1.25				
☐ 2583a Booklet pane of 4..2.50					
☐ 2584	(29c) Christmas, bklt. single, 10/17/91, Santa, ID....1.25				
☐ 2584a Booklet pane of 4..2.50					
☐ 2585	(29c) Christmas, bklt. single, 10/17/91, Santa, ID....1.25				
☐ 2585a Booklet pane of 4..2.50					
☐ 2587	32c Polk, 11/2/95, Columbia, TN 2.00		2.25	2.50	8.00
☐ 2590	$1 Surrender at Saratoga, 5/5/94, New York, NY ...3.00		4.50	5.00	8.00
☐ 2592	$5 Washington & Jackson, 8/19/94, Pittsburgh, PA.14.00		24.00	30.00	12.00
☐ 2593	29c Pledge of Allegiance, black denomination,				
	9/8/92, Rome, NY 1.25				6.00
☐ 2593a Booklet pane of 10...5.00					
	First day cancel was applied to 61,464 covers				
	bearing one or more of Nos. 2594-2594a.				
☐ 2595	29c Eagle & Shield, brown denomination, 9/25/92,				
	Dayton, OH.....................................1.25				
☐ 2596	29c Eagle & Shield, green denomination, 9/25/92,				
	Dayton, OH.....................................1.25				
☐ 2597	29c Eagle & Shield, red denomination, 9/25/92,				
	Dayton, OH.....................................1.25				
	First day cancel was applied to 65,822 covers				
	bearing one or more of Nos. 2595-2597.				
☐ 2595-2597 Eagle & Shield					10.00
☐ 2598	29c Eagle ATM, 2/5/94, Sarasota, FL (67,300).........1.25				6.00
☐ 2599	29c Statue of Liberty, 6/24/94, Haines City, FL(39,810)1.25				6.00
☐ 2602	(10c) Eagle & Shield, Bulk Rate USA, 11/13/91,				
	Kansas City, MO 1.25		1.50		
☐ 2603	(10c) Eagle & Shield, USA Bulk Rate, 5/29/93,				
	Secaucus, NJ 1.25		1.50		

☐	2604	(10c) Eagle & Shield, gold eagle, 5/29/93, Secaucus, NJ 1.25	1.50		
☐	2605	23c Flag, 9/27/91, DC.............................1.25	1.50		10.00
☐	2606	23c Reflected Flag, 7/21/92, Kansas City, MO (35,673)..........................1.25	1.50		
☐	2607	23c Reflected Flag, 7mm "23" 10/9/92, Kansas City, MO 1.25	1.50		
☐	2608	23c Reflected Flag, 8 1/2mm "First Class" 5/14/93, Denver, CO 1.25	1.50		
☐	2609	29c Flag and White House, 4/23/92 , DC (56,505)...1.25	1.50		

1992

☐	2615a	29c Winter Olympics, strip of 5, 1/11/92, Orlando, FL (1,062,048)........................3.00			
☐		2611-2615, any single 1.25			
☐	2616	29c World Columbian Stamp Expo, 1/24/92, Rosemont, IL (309,729)...........................1.25	1.50	1.75	10.00
☐		1st Info cachet 25.00			
☐	2617	29c W.E.B. Du Bois, 1/31/92, Atlanta, GA (196,219)1.25	1.50	1.75	18.00
☐	2618	29c Love, 2/6/92, Loveland, CO (218,043) 1.25	1.50	1.75	10.00
☐	2619	29c Olympic Baseball, 4/3/92, Atlanta, GA (105,996)4.00	5.00	7.00	
☐	2623a	29c Voyages of Columbus, block of 4, 4/24/92, Christiansted, VI (509,170) 2.75			
☐		2620-2623, any single 1.25			8.00
☐		Scott 2620-2623 with Italy stamps, dual cancel...300.00			
☐	2624	First Sighting of Land Souvenir Sheet of 3, 5/22/92, Chicago, IL 5.00			
☐	2624a	1c 1.25			
☐	2624b	4c 1.25			
☐	2624c	$1 ....3.00			
☐	2625	Claiming a New World Souvenir Sheet of 3, Chicago, IL 12.00			
☐	2625a	2c 1.25			
☐	2625b	3c 1.25			
☐	2625c	$4 ....10.00			
☐	2626	Seeking Royal Support Souvenir Sheet of 3, 5/22/92, Chicago, IL 4.00			
☐	2626a	5c 1.25			
☐	2626b	30c 1.25			
☐	2626c	50c 2.00			
☐	2627	Royal Favor Restored Souvenir Sheet of 3, 5/22/92, Chicago, IL 12.00			
☐	2627a	6c 1.25			
☐	2627b	8c 1.25			
☐	2627c	$3 ....8.00			
☐	2628	Reporting Discoveries Souvenir Sheet of 3, 5/22/92, Chicago, IL 15.00			
☐	2628a	10c 1.25			
☐	2628b	15c 1.25			
☐	2628c	$2 ....6.00			
☐	2629	$5 Christopher Columbus Souvenir Sheet, 5/22/92, Chicago, IL 15.00			
☐		2624-2629 Columbian Souvenir Sheets			60.00

First day cancel was applied to 211,142 covers bearing one or more of Nos. 2624-2629.

2630

2631

2635

2636

2637

2642

2647

2698

2699

2700

2704

2705

2710

2711

2720

2721

2741

2746

2747

	Description	SINGLE	BLOCK	PLATE BLOCK	CERM PROG
☐ 2630	29c New York Stock Exchange, 5/17/92, New York, NY (261,897)......1.25		1.50	1.75	6.00
☐ 2634a	29c Space Accomplishments, block of 4, 5/29/92, Chicago, IL......2.75				6.00
☐ 2631-2634, any single......1.25					
	First day cancel was applied to 277,853 covers bearing one or more of Nos. 2631-2634a.				
☐ 2635	29c Alaska Highway, 5/30/92, Fairbanks, AK (186,791)......1.25		1.50	1.75	6.00
☐ 2636	29c Kentucky, 6/1/92, Danville, KY (251,153)......1.25		1.50	1.75	6.00
☐ 2641a	29c Summer Olympics, strip of 5, 6/11/92, Baltimore, MD (713,942)......3.00				
☐ 2637-2641, any single......1.25					
☐ 2646a	29c Hummingbirds booklet pane of 5, 6/15/92, DC...4.00				22.00
☐ 2642-2646, any single......1.25					
	First day cancel was applied to 995,278 covers bearing one or more of Nos. 2642-2646a.				
☐ 2696a	29c Wildflowers, pane of 50, 7/24/92, Columbus, OH (3,693,972) (2 types)*......30.00				8.00*
☐ 2647-2696, any single......1.25					
☐ 2697	29c World War II Souvenir Sheet of 10, 8/17/92, Indianapolis, IN (1,734,880) 8.00				10.00
☐ 2697a-2697j, any single......1.25					
☐ 2698	29c Dorothy Parker, 8/22/92, West End, NJ (266,323)..1.25		1.50	1.75	6.00
☐ 2699	29c Theodore von Karman, 8/31, DC (256,986)......1.25		1.50	1.75	28.00
☐ 2703a	29c Minerals, DC 9/17/92 (681,416)......2.75				10.00
☐ 2700-2703, any single......1.25					10.00
☐ 2704	29c Juan Rodriguez Cabrillo, 9/28/92, San Diego, CA (290,720)......1.25		1.50	1.75	6.00
☐ 2709a	29c Wild Animals booklet pane of 5, 10/1/92, New Orleans, LA 3.25		8.00		6.00
☐ 2705-2709, any single......1.50					
	First day cancel was applied to 604,205 covers bearing one or more of Nos. 2705-2709a.				
☐ 2710	29c Christmas (religious), 10/22/92, DC......1.25		1.50	1.75	6.00
☐ 2710a	Booklet pane of 10......7.25				
	First day cancel was applied to 201,576 covers bearing one or more of Nos. 2710-2710a.				
☐ 2714a	29c Christmas (secular), 10/22/92, Kansas City, MO..2.75				
☐ 2711-2714, any single......1.25					
☐ 2718a	29c Christmas (secular) booklet pane of 4, 10/22/92, Kansas City, MO 2.75				6.00
☐ 2715-2718, any single......1.25					
☐ 2715-2718	29c Contemporary Christmas......ts				6.00
	First day cancel was applied to 461,937 covers bearing one or more of Nos. 2711-2714, 2715-2718 and 2718a.				
☐ 2719	29c Christmas (secular), self-adhesive, 10/28/92, New York, NY (48,873) 1.25				8.00
☐ 2720	29c Chinese New Year, 11/30/92, San Francisco, CA..1.25		1.50	1.75	6.00

1993

	Description	SINGLE	BLOCK	PLATE BLOCK	CERM PROG
☐ 2721	29c Elvis (Presley), 1/8/93, Memphis, TN, AM cancellation......2.00		2.50	4.00	14.00
☐	Any city, PM cancellation......1.25		1.50	1.75	

		SINGLE	BLOCK	PLATE BLOCK	CERM PROG
☐ 2722	29c Oklahoma!, 3/30/93, Oklahoma City, OK 1.25		1.50	1.75	25.00
☐ 2723	29c Hank Williams, 6/9/93, Nashville, TN.................1.25		1.50	1.75	
☐ 2730a	29c Rock & Roll/Rhythm & Blues Musicians, strip of 7,				
	6/16/93, Cleveland, OH or Santa Monica, CA............5.00				10.00
☐	Any other city...5.00				
☐ 2724-2730, any single 1.25					
☐	Any single, any other city.....................................1.25				
	Value for No. 2730a is also for any se-tenant				
	configuration of seven different stamps.				
☐ 2737a	29c Rock & Roll/Rhythm & Blues Musicians booklet				
	pane of 8, 6/16/93, Cleveland, OH or				
	Santa Monica, CA 5.25				
☐	Any other city...5.25				
☐ 2731-2737, any single 1.25					
☐	Any single, any other city.....................................5.25				
☐ 2737b	29c Rock & Roll/Rhythm & Blues Musicians booklet				
	pane of 4, 6/16/93, Cleveland, OH or				
	Santa Monica, CA 2.75				
☐	Any other city...2.75				
☐ 2745a	29c Space Fantasy booklet pane of 5, 1/25/93,				
	Huntsville, AL 3.25				8.00
☐ 2741-2745, any single 1.25					
☐ 2746	29c Percy Lavon Julian, 1/29/93, Chicago, IL.........1.25		1.50	1.75	6.00
☐ 2747	29c Oregon Trail, 2/12/93, Salem, OR......................1.25		1.50	1.75	6.00
	No. 2747 was also available on the first day of issue				
	in 36 cities along the route of the Oregon Trail.				
☐ 2748	29c World University Games, 2/25/93, Buffalo, NY .2.00		2.25	2.50	6.00
☐ 2749	29c Grace Kelly, 3/24/93, Beverly Hills, CA..............1.25		1.50	1.75	10.00
☐ 2753a	29c Circus, block of 4, 4/6/93, DC.............................3.50				10.00
☐ 2750-2753, any single 1.25					
☐ 2754	29c Cherokee Strip Land Run, 4/17/93, Enid, OK ...1.25		1.50	1.75	6.00
☐ 2755	29c Dean Acheson, 4/21/93, DC 1.25		1.50	1.75	6.00
☐ 2759a	29c Sporting Horses, 5/1/93, Louisville, KY.............2.75				8.00
☐ 2756-2759, any single 1.25					
☐ 2764a	29c Garden Flowers booklet pane of 5, 5/15/93,				
	Spokane, WA 3.25				6.00
☐ 2760-2764, any single 1.25					
☐ 2765	29c World War II Souvenir Sheet of 10, 5/31/93, DC .7.00				15.00
☐ 2765a-2765j, any single 1.25					
☐ 2766	29c Joe Louis, 6/22/93, Detroit, MI 1.25		1.50	1.75	8.00
☐ 2770a	29c Broadway Musicals booklet pane of 4,				
	7/14/93, New York, NY 3.25				25.00
☐ 2767-2770, any single 1.25					
☐ 2782a	29c National Postal Museum, block of 4,				
	7/30/93, DC...2.75				6.00
☐ 2779-2782, any single 1.25					
☐ 2784a	29c Deafness/Sign Language, se-tenant pair, 9/20/93,				
	Burbank CA 2.00				8.00
☐ 2783-2784, any single 1.25					6.00
☐ 2788a	29c Classic Books, block of 4, 10/23/93,				
	Louisville, KY 2.75				25.00
☐ 2785-2788, any single 1.25					
☐ 2789	29c Christmas (religious), 10/21/93, Raleigh, NC 1.25		1.50	1.75	6.00

World University Games Buffalo '93
2748

GRACE KELLY
2749

CIRCUS
2750

Cherokee Strip Land Run 1893
2754

Dean Acheson
2755

2756

Hyacinth
2760

National Postal Museum
2779

Recognizing Deafness
2783

REBECCA OF SUNNYBROOK FARM
2785

CHRISTMAS
2789

Greetings
2791

Commonwealth of the Northern Mariana Islands
2804

2805

AIDS
2806

2807

Edward R. Murrow
2812

LOVE
2813

LOVE
2814

LOVE
2815

		SINGLE	BLOCK	PLATE BLOCK	CERM PROG
☐ 2790	29c Christmas (religious), booklet single, 10/21/93, Raleigh, NC 1.25				
☐ 2790a	Booklet pane of 4 ....2.00				
☐ 2794a	29c Christmas (secular), sheet stamps, 10/23/93, New York, NY 2.75				
☐ 2791-2794, any single 1.25					
☐ 2798a	29c Christmas (secular) booklet pane of 10, 10/21/93, New York, NY.................................6.50				
☐ 2798b	29c Christmas (secular) booklet pane of 10, 10/21/93, New York, NY.................................6.50				
☐ 2795-2798, any single 1.25					
☐ 2799	29c Christmas (snowman), large self-adhesive, 10/28/93, New York, NY.................................1.25				
☐ 2799-2802	Contemporary Christmas, self-adhesive................				6.00
☐ 2800	29c Christmas (soldier), self-adhesive, 10/28/93, New York, NY..1.25				
☐ 2801	29c Christmas (jack-in-the-box), self-adhesive, 10/28/93, New York, NY.......................................1.25				
☐ 2802	29c Christmas (reindeer), self-adhesive, 10/28/93, New York, NY..1.25				
☐ 2799-2802 on one cover...2.50					6.00
☐ 2803	29c Christmas (snowman), small self-adhesive, 10/28/93, New York, NY.................................1.25				
☐ 2804	29c Mariana Islands, 11/4/93, Saipan, MP 1.25		1.50	1.75	6.00
☐ 2805	29c Columbus' Landing in Puerto Rico, 11/19/93, San Juan, PR...1.25		1.50	1.75	6.00
☐ 2806	29c AIDS Awareness, 12/1/93, New York, NY..........1.25		1.50	1.75	14.00
☐ 2806a	29c AIDS Awareness, booklet single, perf. 11 vert., 12/1/93, New York, NY..............1.25				
☐ 2806b	Booklet pane of 5 ....3.25				

1994

		SINGLE	BLOCK	PLATE BLOCK	CERM PROG
☐ 2811a	29c Winter Olympics, strip of 5, 1/6/94, Salt Lake City, UT...3.00				6.00
☐ 2807-2811, any single 1.25					
☐ 2812	29c Edward R. Murrow, 1/21/94, Pullman, WA.....1.25		1.50	1.75	6.00
☐ 2813	29c Love, self-adhesive, 1/27/94, Loveland, OH 1.25				6.00
☐ 2814	29c Love, booklet single, 2/14/94, Niagara Falls, NY1.25				6.00
☐ 2814a	Booklet pane of 10 ....6.50				
☐ 2814C	29c Love, 6/11/94, Niagara Falls, NY 1.25		1.50	1.75	
☐ 2815	52c Love, 2/14/94, Niagara Falls, NY 1.35		2.75	3.00	6.00
☐ 2816	29c Dr. Allison Davis, 2/1/94, Williamstown, MA.....1.25		1.50	1.75	6.00
☐ 2817	29c Chinese New Year, 2/5/94, Pomona, CA 1.25		1.50	1.75	12.00
☐ 2818	29c Buffalo Soldiers, 4/22/94, Dallas, TX 1.25		1.50	1.75	15.00
☐	1st Dynamite Cover 20.00				
	No. 2818 was also available on the first day of issue in forts in Kansas, Texas and Arizona.				
☐ 2828a	29c Silent Screen Stars, block of 10, 4/27/94, San Francisco, CA...7.00				10.00
☐ 2819-2828, any single 1.25					
☐ 2833a	29c Garden Flowers booklet pane of 5, 4/28/93, Cincinnati, OH..3.25				10.00
☐ 2829-2833, any single 1.25					
☐ 2834	29c World Cup Soccer, 5/26/94, New York, NY........1.25		1.50	1.75	12.00

2816

2817

2818

2819

2829

2834

2839

2841a

2842

2843

2848

2849

2854

2862

2863

2867

2871

2872

2873

2874

	2835	40c World Cup Soccer, 5/26/94, New York, NY........1.25	2.25	2.50	12.00
	2836	50c World Cup Soccer, 5/26/94, New York, NY........1.35	2.50	2.75	12.00
	2837	World Cup Soccer, Souvenir Sheet, 5/26/94,			
		New York, NY			12.00
	2838	29c World War II Souvenir Sheet of 10, 6/6/94,			
		USS Normandy 10.00			12.00
	2838a-2838j, any single...1.25				
		No. 2838 was also available on the first day of			
		issue in 13 other locations.			
	2839	29c Norman Rockwell, 7/1/94, Stockbridge, MA 1.25	1.50	1.75	10.00
	2840	50c Norman Rockwell Souvenir Sheet of 4, 7/1/94,			
		Stockbridge, MA 5.00			10.00
	2840a-2840d, any single..1.60				
	2841	29c Moon Landing Sheet of 12, 7/20/94, DC 10.00			12.00
	2841a	single stamp 1.35			
	2842	$9.95 Moon Landing, 7/20/94, DC........................25.00	85.00	100.00	
	2847a	29c Locomotives booklet pane of 5, 7/28/93,			
		Chama, NM 3.25			8.00
	2843-2847 Any single..1.25				
	2848	29c George Meany, 8/16/94, DC 1.25	1.50	1.75	6.00
	2853a	29c American Music Series, 9/1/94, New York, NY 4.00			
	2849-2853 Any single 1.25				
	2861a	29c American Music, 9/17/94, Greenville MS 6.00			10.00
	2854-2861 Any single...1.25				
	2862	29c James Thurber, 9/10/94, Columbus, OH 1.25	1.50	1.75	6.00
	2866a	29c Wonders of the Sea, 10/3/94, Honolulu, HI 3.50			10.00
	2863-2866 Any single 1.25				
	2868a	29c Cranes, 10/9/94, DC 2.00			10.00
	2867-2868 Any single 1.25				
	2869	29c Legends of the West, pane of 20,10/18/94,			
		Laramie, WY, Tucson, AZ or Lawton, OK, ...25.00			12.00
	2869a-2869t Any single...1.25				
	2869	Any other city, any single 1.25			
	2871	29c Christmas, religious, 10/20/94, DC 1.25	1.50	1.75	8.00
	2871a	Perf. 9.8 x 10.8..1.25			
	2872	Christmas (stocking), 10/20/94, Harmony, MN........1.25	1.50	1.75	
	2873	Christmas (Santa), 10/20/94, Harmony, MN 1.25			
	2874	Christmas (cardinal), 10/20/94, Harmony, MN........1.25			
	2875	$2 Bureau of Engraving & Printing, souvenir sheet			
		of 4, 11/9/94, New York, NY 20.00			25.00
		Major Double Transfer, 11/9/94 ....150.00			
	2876	29c Chinese New Year, 12/30/94, Sacramento, CA ..1.25	1.50	1.75	12.00

1994-97

	2877	(3c) Dove, bright blue, 12/13/94, DC.......................1.50			
	2878	(3c) Dove, dark blue, 12/13/94, DC........................1.50			
	2879	(20c) G, black, 12/13/94, DC..................................1.50			
	2880	(20c) G, red, 12/13/94, DC.....................................1.50			
	2881	(32c) G, black, 12/13/94, DC..................................1.50			
	2881a	Booklet pane of 10 ....6.00			
	2882	(32c) G, red, 12/13/94, DC.....................................1.50			
	2883	(32c) G, black, perf 10x9.9 booklet stamp,			
		12/13/94, DC...1.50			
	2883a	Booklet pane of 10 ....6.00			
	2884	(32c) G, black, perf 10.9 booklet stamp,			
		12/13/94, DC...1.50			

2876

2877

2879

2881

2888

2897

2902

2905

2908

2911

2919

2948

2949

2950

2951

Richard Nixon

2955

BLACK HERITAGE

2956

32 USA

2976

2980

2983

32
USA

Aster

2993

2998

☐ 2884a	Booklet pane of 10 ....6.00				
☐ 2885	(32c) G, red, booklet stamp,12/13/94, DC.................1.50				
☐ 2885a	Booklet pane of 10 ....6.00				
☐ 2886	(32c) G, gray, blue, light blue, red & black,				
	self-adhesive, 12/13/94, DC...........................1.50				
☐ 2887	(32c) G, black, blue & red, self-adhesive,				
	12/13/94, DC..1.50				
☐ 2888	(25c) G, black, coil stamp, 12/13/94, DC 1.50				
☐ 2889	(32c) G, black, coil stamp, 12/13/94, DC 1.50				
☐ 2890	(32c) G, blue, coil stamp, 12/13/94, DC...................1.50				
☐ 2891	(32c) G, red, coil stamp, perforated, 12/13/94, DC.....1.50				
☐ 2892	(32c) G, red, coil stamp, rouletted, 12/13/94, DC......1.50				
☐ 2897	32c Flag over porch, 5/19/95, Denver, CO 1.25	1.50	1.75		
☐ 2902	(5c) Butte, coil, 3/10/95 State College, PA................1.25				
☐ 2902B	(5c) Butte, self-adhesive coil, 6/15/96				
	San Antonio, TX...1.25				
☐ 2903	(5c) Mountain, purple & multi coil, 3/16/96...................			8.00	
	San Jose, CA ....— pr 1.25				
☐ 2904	(5c) Mountain, blue & multi coil, 3/16/96				
	State College, PA.....................................— pr 1.25				
☐ 2904A	(5c) Mountain, self-adhesive coil, 6/15/96,				
	San Antionio, TX...1.25				
☐ 2904B	(5c) Mountain, self-adhesive, inscription outlined,				
	1/24/97, Tuscon, AZ 1.25				
☐ 2905	(10c) Auto, coil, 3/10/95, State College, PA.............— pr 1.25				
☐ 2906	(10c) Auto, self-adhesive coil, 6/15/96,				
	San Antonio, TX...1.25				
☐ 2907	(10c) Eagle & Shield, USA Bulk Rate,				
	self-adhesive coil, 5/21/96, DC......................1.25				
☐ 2908	(15c) Auto tail fin, coil, 3/17/95, New York, NY ....— pr 1.25				
☐ 2909	(15c) Auto tail fin, dark orange yellow, coil,				
	3/17/95, New York, NY ....— pr 1.25				
☐ 2910	(15c) Auto tail fin, buff, self-adhesive coil,				
	6/15/96, San Antonio, TX...............................1.25				
☐ 2911	(25c) Juke Box, coil, 3/17/95, New York, NY ....— pr 1.25				
☐ 2912	(25c) Juke Box, coil, 3/17/95, New York, NY ....— pr 1.25				
☐ 2912A	(25c) Juke Box, self-adhesive coil, serpentine die cut,				
	11.5 vert., 6/15/96, New York, NY 1.25				
☐ 2912B	(25c) Juke Box, self-adhesive coil, serpentine die cut				
	9.8 vert., 1/24/97, Tuscon, AZ 1.25				
☐ 2913	32c Flag over porch, coil, 5/19/95, Denver, CO........1.25				
☐ 2914	32c Flag over porch, coil, 5/19/95, Denver, CO........1.25				
☐ 2915	32c Flag over porch, self-adhesive, serpentine die				
	cut 8.7, 4/18/95, DC.....................................1.25				
☐ 2915A	32c Flag over porch, serpentine die cut 9.8 vert.,				
	11 teeth, 5/21/96, DC 1.25				
☐ 2915B	32c Flag over porch, self adhesive, serpentine die				
	cut 11.5, 6/15/95, San Antonio, TX..................1.25				
☐ 2915C	32c Flag over porch, serpentine die cut 10.9,				
	5/21/96, DC..1.25				
☐ 2915D	32c Flag over porch, serpentine die cut 9.8 vert.,				
	9 teeth btwn cuts, 1/24/97, Tuscon, AZ 1.25				
☐ 2916	32c Flag over porch, booklet single, 5/19/95,				
	Denver, CO 1.25				
☐ 2916a	booklet pane of 10 ....7.50				

2999

3001

3003

3012

3013

3030

3059

3060

3061

3065

3066

3067

3069

3070

3072

3077

3081

3082

3083

3087

3088

SCOTT NUMBER	DESCRIPTION	SINGLE	BLOCK	PLATE BLOCK	CERM PROG
☐ 2919	32c **Flag over field**, self-adhesive, 3/17/95..............1.25				
☐ 2920	32c **Flag over porch**, self-adhesive, 4/18/95, Washington, DC..1.25				
☐ 2921	32c **Flag over porch**, booklet single, serpentine die cut 9.8 on 2 or 3 adjacent sides, 5/21/96, DC.........1.25				
☐ 2933	32c **Milton Hershey**, 7/11/95, Hershey, PA...............1.25	1.50	1.75	8.00	
☐ 2934	32c **Cal Farley**, 4/26/96, Amarillo, TX.....................1.25			8.00	
☐ 2935	32c **Henry Luce**, 4/3/98, New York...........................1.25	1.50	1.75		
☐ 2936	32c **Lila & DeWitt Wallace**, 7/16/98, Pleasantville, NY	1.25	1.50	1.75	
☐ 2938	40c **Ruth Benedict**, 7/11/95, Virginia Beach, VA......1.35	1.60	1.85		
☐ 2940	55c **Alice Hamilton**, 7/11/95, Boston, MA 1.35	1.60	1.85	8.00	
☐ 2943	78c **Alice Paul**, 8/18/95, Mount Laurel, NJ...............1.50	1.75	2.00	8.00	

1995

SCOTT NUMBER	DESCRIPTION	SINGLE	BLOCK	PLATE BLOCK	CERM PROG
☐ 2948	(32c) **Love**, 2/1/95, Valentines, VA 1.25	1.50	1.75		
☐ 2949	(32c) **Love**, self adhesive, 2/1/95, Valentines, VA ...1.25	1.50	1.75	8.00	
☐ 2950	32c **Florida Statehood**, 3/3/95, Tallahassee, FL.......1.25	1.50	1.75	10.00	
☐ 2954a	32c **Earth Day**, 4/20/95, DC		2.75		
☐ 2951-2954, block of 4, any single...1.25					
☐ 2955	32c **Richard Nixon**, 4/26/95, Yorba Linda, CA 1.25	1.50	1.75	10.00	
☐ 2956	32c **Bessie Coleman**, 4/27/95, Chicago, IL...............1.25	1.50	1.75	10.00	
☐ 2957	32c **Love**, 5/12/95, Lakeville, PA..............................1.25	1.50	1.75		
☐ 2958	55c **Love**, 5/12/95, Lakeville, PA..............................1.35				
☐ 2959	32c **Love**, booklet single, 5/12/95, Lakeville, PA.......1.25				
☐ 2959a	booklet pane of 10 ....7.50				
☐ 2960	55c **Love**, self adhesive, 5/12/95, Lakeville, PA 1.35				
☐ 2965a	32c **Recreational Sports**, 5/20/95, Jupiter, FL 3.25				
☐ 2961-2965, any single...1.50				12.00	
☐ 2966	32c **Prisoners of War & Missing in Action**, 5/29/95, DC..1.25	1.50	1.75	12.00	
☐ 2967	32c **Marilyn Monroe**, 6/1/95, Universal City, CA 1.25	1.50	1.75	12.00	
☐	Any other city..1.25	1.50	1.75	8.00	
☐ 2968	32c **Texas Statehood**, 6/16/95, Austin, TX...............1.25	1.50	1.75		
☐ 2973a	32c **Great Lakes Lighthouses**, booklet pane of 5, 6/17/96, Cheboygan, MI 4.00				
☐ 2969-2973, any single...1.25				12.00	
☐ 2974	32c **UN, 50th Anniv.**, 6/26/95, San Francisco...........1.25	1.50	1.75	10.00	
☐ 2975	32c **Civil War sheet of 20**, 6/29/95, Gettysburg, PA	13.00			10.00
☐	Any other city..13.00				
☐ 2975a-2975t, any single, Gettysburg, PA.............................1.25					
☐	Any other city..1.25				12.00	
☐ 2979a	32c **Carousel Horses**, 7/21/95, Lahaska, PA..................	3.25			
☐ 2976-2979, any single...1.25				10.00	
☐ 2980	32c **Women Suffrage**, 8/26,95, DC..........................1.25	1.50	1.75	12.00	
☐ 2981	32c **World War II sheet of 10**, 9/2/95, Honolulu, HI	6.50			
☐ 2981a-2981j, any single..1.25					
☐ 2982	32c **American Music Series**, 9/1/95, New Orleans, LA 1.25	1.50	1.75	14.00	
☐ 2992a	32c **American Music Series**, 9/16/95, Monterey, CA	6.50			18.00
☐ 2983-2992, any single..1.25					
☐ 2997a	32c **Garden Flowers booklet pane of 5**, 9/19/96, Encintas, CA....................................4.00				12.00
☐ 2993-2997, any single..1.25					
☐ 2998	60c **Eddie Rickenbacker**, 9/25/95, Columbus, OH ...1.50	1.75	2.00	8.00	
☐ 2999	32c **Republic of Palau**, 9/29/95, Agana, GU.............1.25	1.50	1.75	8.00	
☐ 3000	32c **Comic Strips Pane of 20**, 10/1/95, Boca Raton, FL..13.00				18.00

3090

3091

3096

3100

3104

3106

3107

3108

3109

3110

3111

3117

3118

3120

3121

3122

3123

3124

3125

		SINGLE	BLOCK	PLATE BLOCK	CERM PROG
☐	3000a-3000t, any single 1.25				
☐ 3001	32c US Naval Academy, 10/10/95, Annapolis, MD...1.25		1.50	1.75	8.00
☐ 3002	32c Tennessee Williams, 10/13/95, Clarksdale, MS.1.25		1.50	1.75	8.00
☐ 3003	32c Christmas Madonna, 10/19/95, DC...................1.25		1.50	1.75	8.00
☐ 3003a	Perf. 9.8x10.8...1.25		1.50	1.75	
☐ 3003b	Booklet pane of 10 ....7.25				
☐ 3007a	32c Christmas (secular) sheet, 9/30/95,				
	North Pole, NY		3.25		10.00
☐	3004-3007, any single 1.25				
☐ 3007b	Booklet pane of 10, 3 #3004, etc. 7.25				
☐ 3007c	Booklet pane of 10, 2 #3004, etc. 7.25				
☐ 3008	32c Christmas (Santa, Sled) self-adhesive bklt.,				
	9/30/95, North Pole, NY 1.25				
☐ 3009	32c Christmas (Jumping Jack) self-adhesive bklt.,				
	9/30/95, North Pole, NY 1.25				
☐ 3010	32c Christmas (Santa, Chimney) self-adhesive bklt.,				
	9/30/95, North Pole, NY 1.25				
☐ 3011	32c Christmas (Child, Tree) self-adhesive bklt.,				
	9/30/95, North Pole, NY 1.25				
☐	3008-3011 on one cover 1.25				
☐ 3012	32c Angel, 10/19/95, Christmas, FL 1.25				12.00
☐ 3013	32c Children sledding, 10/19/95, Christmas, FL......1.25				
☐ 3014	32c Christmas (Santa, Sled), self-adhveive coil,				
	9/30/95, North Pole, NY 1.25				
☐ 3015	32c Christmas (Jumping Jack), self-adhesive coil,				
	9/30/95, North Pole, NY 1.25				
☐ 3016	32c Christmas (Santa, Chimney), self-adhesive coil,				
	9/30/95, North Pole, NY 1.25				
☐ 3017	32c Christmas, (Child, Tree), self-adhesive coil,				
	9/30/95, North Pole, NY 1.25				
☐	3014-3017 on one cover 3.25				8.00
☐ 3018	32c Angel, Self adhesive coil, 10/19/95,				
	Christmas, FL...1.25				
☐ 3023a	32c Antique Automobiles, 11/3/95, New York , NY.3.25				12.00
☐	3019-3023, any single 1.25				
☐ 3024	32c Utah Statehood Cent.,1/4/96, Salt Lake City, UT1.25		1.50	1.75	8.00
☐ 3029a	32c Garden Flowers booklet pane, 1/19/96,				
	Kennett Square, PA..4.00				12.00
☐	3025-3029, any single 1.25				
☐ 3030	32c Love self-adhesive, 1/20/96, New York , NY 1.25				
☐ 3032	2c Red-headed woodpecker, 2/2/96, Sarasota, FL...1.25		1.50	1.75	10.00
☐ 3033	3c Eastern Bluebird, 4/3/96, DC 1.25		1.50	1.75	10.00
☐ 3044	1c American Kestrel, coil, 1/20/96, New York, NY..1.25		1.50	1.75	8.00
☐ 3048	20c Blue Jay, booklet stamp, self-adhesive, 8/2/96,				
	St. Louis, MO...1.25				
☐ 3049	32c Yellow Rose, booklet stamp, self-adhesive, 10/24/96,				
	Pasadena, CA (7,849)..1.25				8.00
☐ 3050	20c Ring-necked Pheasant, booklet stamp, self-adhesive,				
	7/31/98, Somerset, NJ 1.25pr				
☐ 3053	20c Blue Jay, coil stamp, self-adhesive, 8/2/96,				
	St. Louis, MO...1.25				
☐ 3055	20c Ring-necked Pheasant, coil stamp, self-adhesive,				
	7/31/98, Somerset, NJ 1.25pr				
	First day cancel was applied to 32,633 covers bearing one				
	or more of Nos. 3048-3053.				

SCOTT NUMBER	DESCRIPTION	SINGLE	PLATE BLOCK	CERM BLOCK	PROG
☐ 3058	32c Ernest E. Just, 2/1/96, DC	1.25	1.50	1.75	8.00
☐ 3059	32c Smithsonian, 150th anniv., 2/7/96, DC	1.25	1.50	1.75	14.00
☐ 3060	32c Chinese New Year, 2/8/96, San Francisco, CA	1.25	1.50	1.75	14.00
☐ 3064a	32c Pioneers of Commuication, 2/22/96, New York, NY		3.25		12.00
☐ 3061-3064, any single		1.25			
☐ 3065	32c Fulbright Scholarships, 2/28/96, Fayetteville, AR	1.25	1.50	1.75	8.00
☐ 3066	50c Jacquline Cochran, 3/9/96, Indio, CA	1.35	1.75	2.00	8.00
☐ 3067	32c Marathon, 4/11/96, Boston, MA	1.25	1.50	1.75	12.00
☐ 3068	32c Olympics, pane of 20, 5/2/96, DC	13.00			
☐ 3068a-3068t, any single		1.25	1.50	1.75	15.00
☐ 3069	32c Georgia O'Keeffe, 5/23/96, Santa Fe, NM	1.25	1.50	1.75	12.00
☐ 3070	32c Tennessee Statehood, 5/31/96, Knoxville, Memphis or Nashville, TN	1.25	1.50	1.75	14.00
☐ 3071	32c Tennessee, self-adhesive, 5/31/96, Knoxville, Memphis or Nashville, TN	1.25			
☐ 3070-3071 on one cover		1.75			
☐ 3076a	32c American Indian Dances, strip of 5, 6/7/96, Oklahoma City, OK	3.50			
☐ 3072-3076, any single		1.25			15.00
☐ 3080a	32c Prehistoric Animals, 6/8/96, Toronto, Canada		3.25		
☐ 3077-3080, any single		1.25			15.00
☐ 3081	32c Breast Cancer Awareness, 6/15/96, DC	1.25	1.50	1.75	14.00
☐ 3082	32c James Dean, 6/24/96, Burbank, CA	1.25	1.50	1.75	14.00
☐ 3086a	32c Folk Heroes, 7/11/96, Anaheim, CA	3.25			
☐ 3083-3086, any single		1.25			15.00
☐ 3087	32c Centennial Olympic Games, 7/19/96, Atlanta, GA	1.25	1.50	1.75	12.00
☐ 3088	32c Iowa Statehood, 150th Anniv., 8/1/96, Dubuque, IA	1.25	1.50	1.75	8.00
☐ 3089	32c Iowa Statehood, self-adhesive, 8/1/96, Dubuque, IA	1.25			
☐ 3088-3089 on one cover		1.75			
	First day cancel was applied to 215,181 covers bearing one or more of Nos. 3088-3089				
☐ 3090	32c Rural Free Delivery, 8/7/96, Charleston, WV (192,070)	1.25	1.50	1.75	8.00
☐ 3095a 32c Riverboats strip of 5, 8/22/96, Orlando, FL		3.50			
☐ 3091-3095, any single		1.25			14.00
	First day cancel was applied to 770,384 covers bearing one or more of Nos. 3091-3095				
☐ 3099a	32c Big Band Leaders, block of 4, 9/11/96, New York, NY		3.25		
☐ 3096-3099, any single		1.25			15.00
☐ 3103a 32c Songwriters, block of 4, 9/11/96, New York, NY		3.25			
☐ 3100-3103, any single		1.25			15.00
	First day cancel was applied to 1,235,166 covers bearing one or more of Nos. 3096-3103				
☐ 3104	23c F. Scott Fitzgerald, 9/27/96, St. Paul, MN (150,783)	1.25	1.50	1.75	
☐ 3105	32c Endangered Species, pane of 15, 10/2/96, San Jose, CA	7.50			
☐ 3105a-3105o, any single		1.25			15.00
	First day cancel was applied to 941,442 covers bearing one or more of Nos. 3105a-3105o				

		SINGLE	BLOCK	PLATE BLOCK	CERM PROG
☐ 3106	32c **Computer Technology,** 10/8/96, Aberdeen Proving Ground, MD (153,688)..1.25	1.50	1.75		8.00
☐ 3107	32c **Christmas Madonna,** 11/1/96, Richmond, VA........1.25	1.50	1.75		8.00
☐ 3111a	32c **Christmas (Secular),** 10/8/96, North Pole, AK..............	3.25			10.00
☐	3108-3111, any single..1.25				
☐ 3112	32c **Christmas Madonna,** self-adhesive, 11/1/96, Richmond, VA...1.25				10.00
	First day cancel was applied to 164,447 covers bearing one or more of Nos. 3107, 3112.				
☐ 3113	32c **Family at fireplace,** self-adhesive, 10/8/96, North Pole, AK..1.25				
☐ 3114	32c **Decorating Tree,** self-adhesive, 10/8/96, North Pole, AK..1.25				
☐ 3115	32c **Dreaming of Santa,** self-adhesive, 10/8/96, North Pole, AK..1.25				
☐ 3116	32c **Holiday shopping,** self-adhesive, 10/8/96, North Pole, AK..1.25				
☐	3113-3116 on one cover 3.25				
☐ 3117	32c **Skaters,** self-adhesive, 10/8/96, North Pole, AK..1.25				
	First day cancel was applied to 884,339 covers bearing one or more of Nos. 3108-3111, 3111a, 3113-3117.				
☐ 3118	32c **Hanukkah,** 10/22/96, DC, (179,355) 1.25				15.00
☐ 3119	50c **Cycling** souvenir sheet of 2, 11/1/96, New York, NY...2.50				14.00
☐	3119a-3119b, any single..1.50				
	First day cancel was applied to 290,091 covers bearing one or more of Nos. 3119, 3119a-3119b.				

1997

		SINGLE	BLOCK	PLATE BLOCK	CERM PROG
☐ 3120	32c **Chinese New Year,** 1/5/97, Honolulu, HI 1.25	1.50	1.75		12.00
☐ 3121	32c **Benjamin O. Davis, Sr.,** 1/28/97, DC..................1.25				8.00
☐ 3122	32c **Statue of Liberty,** serpentine die cut 11, 2/1/97, San Diego, CA 1.25				
☐ 3123	32c **Love (Swans),** 2/7/97, Los Angeles, CA..............1.25				
☐ 3124	55c **Love (Swans),** 2/7/97, Los Angeles, CA..............1.50				
☐	3123-3124 on one cover 2.00				10.00
☐ 3125	32c **Helping Children Learn,** 2/18/97, DC.................1.25				8.00
☐ 3126	32c **Merian Prints, Citron** (large size), 3/3/97, DC...1.25				
☐ 3127	32c **Merian Prints, Pineapple** (large size), 3/3/97, DC...1.25				
☐	3126-3127 on one cover 1.75				8.00
☐ 3128	32c **Merian prints, Citron** (small size), 3/3/97, DC...1.25				
☐ 3128a	Mixed die cut...1.25				
☐ 3129	32c **Merian Prints, Pineapple** (small size),3/3/97, DC1.25				
☐ 3129a	Mixed die cut...1.25				
☐	3128-3129 on one cover 1.75				
☐ 3131a	32c **Pacific 97 pair,** 3/3/97, New York, NY	2.00	2.25		
☐	3130-3131 any single...1.25				12.00
☐ 3132	(25c) **Juke Box,** self-adhesive imperf., 3/14/97, New York, NY..1.25pr				
☐ 3133	32c **Flag over porch,** self-adhesive, serpentine die cut 9.9 vert.,..1.25				
☐ 3134	32c **Thornton Wilder,** 4/17/97, Hamden, CT 1.25	1.50	1.75		8.00

3126

3127

3130

3134

3137a

3139a

3140a

3141

3152

3166

3174

3179

3181

3198

3203

3211

3221

SCOTT NUMBER	DESCRIPTION	SINGLE	PLATE BLOCK	CERM BLOCK	PROG
☐ 3135	32c Raoul Wallenberg, 4/24/97, DC	1.25	1.50	1.75	10.00
☐ 3136	32c Dinosaurs, pane of 15, 5/1/97,				
	Grand Junction, CO	7.50			
☐ 3136a-3136o, any single		1.25			14.00
☐ 3137a	32c Bugs Bunny, die cut single, 5/22/97,				
	Burbank, CA	1.25			16.00
☐ 3138c	32c Bugs Bunny, imperf pane, 5/22/97,				
	Burbank, CA	250.00			
☐ 3139	50c Franklin, pane of 12, 5/29/97,				
	San Francisco, CA				14.00
☐ 3139a	single stamp	2.00			
☐ 3140	60c Washington, pane of 12, 5/30/97,				
	San Francisco, CA				16.00
☐ 3140a	single stamp	2.50			
☐ 3141	32c Marshall Plan, 6/4/97,				
	Cambridge, MA	1.25	1.50	1.75	8.00
☐ 3146a	32¢ Legendary Football Coaches, 7/25/97,				
	Canton, OH		3.25		10.00
☐ 3143-3146, any single		1.25	1.50	1.75	
☐ 3147	32c Vince Lombardi, 8/5/97, Green Bay, WI	1.25	1.50	1.75	10.00
☐ 3148	32c Bear Bryant, 8/7/97, Tuscaloosa, AL	1.25	1.50	1.75	10.00
☐ 3149	32c Pop Warner, 8/8/97, Philadelphia, PA	1.25	1.50	1.75	10.00
☐ 3150	32c George Halas, 8/16/97, Chicago, IL	1.25	1.50	1.75	10.00
☐ 3151	32c Classic American Dolls, pane of 20, 7/28/97,				
	Anaheim, CA	13.00			18.00
☐ 3151a-3151t, any single		1.25			
☐ 3152	32c Humphrey Bogart, 7/31/97, Los Angeles, CA	1.25	1.50	1.75	12.00
☐ 3153	32c "The Stars and Stripes Forever!", 8/21/97,				
	Milwaukee, WI	1.25	1.50	1.75	10.00
☐ 3151a	32c Opera Singers, 9/10/97, New York, NY		3.25		15.00
☐ 3154-3157, any single		1.25			
☐ 3165a	32c Classical Composers and Conductors, 9/12/97,				
	Cincinnati, OH		5.25		14.00
☐ 3158-3165, any single		1.25			
☐ 3166	32c Padre Felix Varela, 9/15/97, Miami, FL	1.25	1.50	1.75	10.00
☐ 3167	32c Department of the Air Force, 9/18/97, DC	1.25	1.50	1.75	10.00
☐ 3172a	32c Movie Monsters, strip of 5, 9/30/97,				
	Universal City, CA	3.75			
☐ 3168-3172, any single		1.25			
☐ 3173	32c Supersonic Flight, self-adhesive, 10/14/97,				
	Edwards AFB, CA	1.25			10.00
☐ 3174	32c Women in the Military Service, 10/18/97, DC	1.25	1.50	1.75	10.00
☐ 3175	32c Kwanzaa, self-adhesive, 10/22/97,				
	Los Angeles, CA	1.25			14.00
☐ 3176	32c Holiday Traditional, self-adhesive, 10/27/97,				
	DC	1.25			10.00
☐ 3177	32c Holiday Contemporary, self-adhesive, 10/30/97,				
	New York, NY	1.25			12.00
☐ 3179	32c Chinese New Year, 1/5/98, Seattle, WA	1.25	1.50	1.75	12.00
☐ 3180	32c Alpine Skiing, 1/22/98, Salt Lake City, UT	1.25	1.50	1.75	12.00
☐ 3181	32c Madam C. J. Walker, self-adhesive, 1/28/98,				
☐	Indianapolis, IN	1.25			12.00
☐ 3182	32c 1900-1909, sheet of 15, 2/3/98, DC	7.50			
☐ 3182a-3182o, any single		1.25			
☐ 3183	32c 1910-1919, sheet of 15, 2/3/98, DC	7.50			

191

		SINGLE	BLOCK	PLATE BLOCK	CERM PROG
☐ 3183a-3183o, any single..1.25					
☐ 3184	32c 1920-1929, sheet of 15, 5/28/98, Chicago. IL 7.50				
☐ 3184a-3184o, any single..1.25					
☐ 3192	32c **Remember the Maine**, 2/15/98, Key West, FL...1.25		1.50	1.75	10.00
☐ 3193-3197	32c **Flowering Trees**, any single, 3/19/98,				
	New York , NY...1.25				12.00
☐ 3202a 32c **Alexander Calder** strip of 5, 3/25/98, DC 3.75					
☐ 3198-3202, any single...1.25					
☐ 3203	32c **Cinco de Mayo**, self-adhesive, 4/16/98,				
	San Antonio, TX...1.25				
☐ 3204a 32c **Sylvester & Tweety**, self-adhesive, 4/27/98.					
	New York, NY...1.25				
☐ 3205c 32c **Sylvester & Tweety**, self-adhesive, imperf. pane,					
	4/27/98, New York, NY ....-				
☐ 3206	32c **Wisconsin**, self-adhesive, 5/29/98, Madison, WI1.25				
☐ 3207	(5c) **Wetlands**, 6/5/98, McLean, VA...........................1.25				
☐ 3208	(25c) **Diner**, 6/5/98, McLean, VA ....1.25 pr				
☐ 3209	**Trans-Mississippi Centennial**, sheet of 9, 6/18/98,				
	Anaheim, CA..6.50				
☐ 3209a-3209f, 1c-10c, any single..1.25					
☐ 3209g 50c 1.50					
☐ 3209h $1 ....2.00					
☐ 3209i $2 ....4.00					
☐ 3210 $1 **Trans-Mississippi Centennial** sheet of 9, 6/18/98,					
	Anaheim, CA...15.00				
☐ 3211	32c **Berlin Airlift**, 6/26/98, Berlin, Germany...........1.25		1.50	1.75	
☐ 3215a 32c **Folk Musicians**, 6/26/98. DC...................................		3.25			
☐ 3212-3215, any single...1.25					
☐ 3219a 32c **Gospel Musicians**, 7/15/98, New Orleans, LA...........		3.25			
☐ 3216-3219, any single...1.25					
☐ 3220	32c **Spanish Settlement of Southwest**, 6/26/98,				
	Espanola, NM...1.25		1.50	1.75	
☐ 3221 32c **Stephan Vincent Benet**, 7/22/98,					
	Harpers Ferry, WV..1.25				
☐ 3225a 32c **Tropical Birds**, 7/29/98, Ponce, PR.........................		3.25			
☐ 3222-3225, any single...1.25					
☐ 3226	32c **Alfred Hitchcock**, 8/3/98, Los Angeles, CA........1.25				

☐ _____
☐ _____
☐ _____
☐ _____
☐ _____
☐ _____
☐ _____
☐ _____
☐ _____
☐ _____
☐ _____
☐ _____
☐ _____
☐ _____
☐ _____
☐ _____
☐ _____
☐ _____
☐ _____
☐ _____
☐ _____
☐ _____
☐ _____
☐ _____
☐ _____
☐ _____
☐ _____
☐ _____
☐ _____
☐ _____
☐ _____

Semi-Postal Stamp

☐ B1   (32c+8c) **Breast Cancer Awareness,** self-adhesive, 7/29/98, DC..1.25

☐ _____

☐ _____

☐ _____

☐ _____

☐ _____

☐ _____

☐ _____

☐ _____

☐ _____

☐ _____

☐ _____

☐ _____

☐ _____

☐ _____

☐ _____

☐ _____

☐ _____

☐ _____

☐ _____

☐ _____

☐ _____

☐ _____

☐ _____

☐ _____

☐ _____

☐ _____

☐ _____

☐ _____

C1-C3

C7-C9

C10

AIR POST
1918

- [ ] C1 6c Jenny, 12/10/18, DC ....20,000. —
- [ ]   Washington, DC 12/16/18 ....2,000. —
- [ ]   Philadelphia, PA 12/16/18 ....2,000. —
- [ ]   New York, NY 12/16/18 ....2,000. —
- [ ] C2 16c Jenny, 7/11/18, DC 2 known ....30,000. —
- [ ]   Washington, DC 7/15/18 ....800.00 —
- [ ]   Philadelphia, PA 7/15/18 ....800.00 —
- [ ]   New York, NY 7/15/18 ....800.00 —
- [ ] C3 24c Jenny, 5/13/18, DC ....27,500. —
- [ ]   Washington, DC 5/15/18 ....750.00 —
- [ ]   Philadelphia, PA 5/15/18 ....750.00 —
- [ ]   New York, NY 5/15/18 ....750.00 —

The earliest date listed under C1-C3 is the first day of issue. The other date is the first flight for the three different air mail rates of 1918.

1923

- [ ] C4 8c Propeller, 8/15/23, DC...............................400.00 700.00
- [ ] C5 16c Insignia, 8/17/23, DC...............................600.00 1,150.
- [ ] C6 24c Biplane, 8/21/23, DC ....750.00 2,000.

1926-27

- [ ] C7 10c Map, 2/13/26, DC........................... 80.00 150.00 — —
- [ ]   Chicago, IL...85.00 160.00 — —
- [ ]   Cleveland, OH..125.00 200.00 — —
- [ ]   Dearborn, MI...125.00 200.00 — —
- [ ]   Detroit, MI ....90.00 160.00 — —
- [ ]   Unofficial city ....150.00 — — —

FDC/first flight covers on 2/15/26 sell for 25% more than values listed.

- [ ] C8 15c Map, 9/18/26, DC...............................90.00 150.00 500.00 —
- [ ] C9 20c Map, 1/25/27, DC.............................100.00 175.00 — —
- [ ]   New York, NY ....125.00 200.00 — —
- [ ]   1st Albert E. Gorham cachet............................ 250.00 —
- [ ] C10 10c Lindbergh's Plane, 6/18/27, DC ....30.00 35.00 150.00 —
- [ ]   Detroit, MI...35.00 40.00 150.00 —
- [ ]   Little Falls, MN.......................................35.00 40.00 150.00 —
- [ ]   St. Louis, MO ....25.00 30.00 150.00 —
- [ ]   Air Mail Field, Chicago, unofficial...........150.00 — — —
- [ ]   Any other unofficial city.........................160.00 — 175.00 —
- [ ]   1st Milton Mauck cachet.................................. 300.00 —
- [ ] C10a Lindbergh's Plane, booklet pane of 3,
- [ ]   5/26/28, DC..825.00 —
- [ ]   Cleveland Mid. Phil. Sta ....800.00 —
- [ ]   Plus Scott 645, Cleveland Mid. Phil. Sta....1000. —

C11

C12, C16, C17, C19

C13, C15

C18

C20-C22

C23

C24

C25, C35

C32

C33, C37, C39, C41

C34

C38

C40

C42

C45

C46

C47

C48, C50

C49

C51, C52, C60, C61

SCOTT NUMBER	DESCRIPTION	UNCACHETED SINGLE BLOCK		CACHETED SINGLE BLOCK	
☐ C10a	**Lindbergh's Plane**, booklet single, DC............110.00			1000.	
☐	Cleveland Mid. Phil. Sta 100.00			1000.	
☐	Plus Scott 645......................................150.00			1200.	
	Unofficial city 150.00				

Lindbergh booklet pane FDC's and Scott C10a plus 645 FDC's are both known on Garfield Perry Shield Eagle and Biplane general purpose cacheted envelopes. These sell for a 10% to 20% premium over uncacheted FDCS.

1928

☐ C11	**5c Beacon**, 7/25/28, DC.............................50.00	60.00	200.00	—	
☐	With single stamp and postage due stamp 100.00	—	250.00	—	
☐	Unofficial city (pair) 175.00	—	250.00	—	
☐	Single stamp with no postage due 150.00	—	350.00	—	
☐	Predate...700.00				

1930

☐ C12	**5c Winged Globe**, 2/10/30, DC......................12.00	14.00	100.00	—	
☐ C13	**65c Zeppelin**, 4/19/30, DC...............1,200.	2,400.	2,500.	4,000.	
☐ C14	**$1.30 Zeppelin**, 4/19/30, DC ....1,000.	1,800.	2,500.	3,000.	
☐ C15	**$2.60 Zeppelin**, 4/19/30, DC ....1,000.	2,400.	2,500.	3,000.	
☐ C13-C15	complete set on one cover....................12,000.	—	—	—	
☐ C13-C15	complete set of pl# sgl on one cover......20,000.	—	—	—	

FDC's flown on Zeppelin flights sell for a premium.

1931-32

☐ C16	**5c Winged Globe**, 8/19/31, DC......................175.00	300.00	350.00	—	
☐ C17	**8c Winged Globe**, 9/26/32, DC.......................15.00	18.00	45.00	50.00	

1933

☐ C18	**50c Zeppelin**, 10/2/33, New York, NY				
	(3,500) 175.00	225.00	250.00	450.00	
☐	Akron, OH 10/4/33.........................275.00	400.00	425.00	650.00	
☐	Washington, DC, 10/5/33 ....225.00	350.00	425.00	575.00	
☐	Miami, FL, 10/6/33 ....200.00	250.00	325.00	450.00	
☐	Chicago, IL, 10/7/33........................275.00	375.00	400.00	550.00	

FDC's flown on a Zeppelin flight sell for a premium.

1934

☐ C19	**6c Winged Globe**, Baltimore, MD, 6/30/34 .....175.00	—	600.00	—	
☐	New York, NY 800.00	—	1600.	—	
☐	Brooklyn, NY ....1200.	—	1700.	—	
☐	7/1/34, DC.....................................8.00	10.00	35.00	45.00	
☐	Unofficial city 20.00	—	—	—	
☐	On Scott UC3 ....60.00				

1935

☐ C20	**25c China Clipper**, 11/22/35, San				
	Francisco, CA (15,000).......................17.50	20.00	45.00	55.00	
☐	DC (10,910)...................................20.00	22.50	50.00	60.00	

1937

☐ C21	**20c China Clipper**, 2/15/37, DC 20.00	22.50	50.00	55.00	
☐ C22	**50c China Clipper**, 2/15/37, DC 20.00	22.50	55.00	60.00	
☐	Both on one cover 37.50	40.00	125.00	165.00	

Total for Scott C21 and C22 is 40,000.

C54

C53

C55

C56

C57, C59, C62, C63

C64-C65

C67

C68

C66

C69

C70

C71

C72-C73

C74

C77

C78, C82

C84

1st Readers Digest cachet

C79, C83

SCOTT NUMBER	DESCRIPTION	UNCACHETED SINGLE	UNCACHETED BLOCK	CACHETED SINGLE	CACHETED BLOCK

1938

☐ C23	6c Eagle Holding Shield, 5/14/38, Dayton, OH (116,443) 10.00	12.00	25.00	30.00
☐	St. Petersburg, FL (95,121) 10.00	12.00	25.00	30.00
☐	DC, 5/15/38 ....3.50			

1939

☐ C24	30c Winged Globe, 5/16/39, New York, NY (63,634) 20.00	30.00	50.00	75.00

SCOTT NUMBER	DESCRIPTION	SINGLE	BLOCK	PLATE BLOCK	CERM PROG

1941-44

☐ C25	6c Plane, 6/25/41, DC (99,986) 4.00	5.00	8.00	
☐ C25a	Plane, booklet pane of 3, 3/18/43, DC (50,216) 30.00			
☐ C25a	Plane, booklet single...10.00			
☐ C26	8c Plane, 3/21/44, DC (147,484) 4.00	5.00	8.00	
☐ C27	10c Plane, 8/15/41, Atlantic City, NJ (87,712) 8.00	10.00	15.00	
☐ C28	15c Plane, 8/19/41, Baltimore, MD (74,000) 10.00	15.00	25.00	
☐ C29	20c Plane, 8/27/41, Philadelphia, PA (66,225) 12.50	17.50	25.00	
☐ C30	30c Plane, 9/25/41, Kansas City, MO (57,175)........20.00	25.00	35.00	30.00
☐ C31	50c Plane, 10/29/41, St. Louis, MO (54,580) 40.00	50.00	100.00	

1946

☐ C32	5c DC-4, 9/25/46, DC...3.00	4.00	6.00	80.00
☐	1st William W. Bayless cachet..................................15.00	—	—	
	Total for Scott C32 and UC14 is 396,639.			

1947

☐ C33	5c DC-4, 3/26/47, DC (342,634) 3.00	4.00	5.00	
☐ C34	10c Pan Am. Bldg., 8/30/47, DC (265,773)..............3.00	4.00	5.00	50.00
☐	1st Glenn L. Martin Co. cachet 20.00			
☐ C35	15c N.Y. Skyline, 8/20/47, New York, NY (230,338)...3.00	4.00	6.00	45.00
☐ C36	25c Bay Bridge, 7/30/47, San Francisco, CA (201,762)...3.00	5.75	8.50	45.00

1948

☐ C37	5c DC-4, coil, 1/15/48, DC (192,084)........................2.00pr3.50	1p4.50		
☐ C38	5c Map, 7/31/48, New York, NY (371,265) 1.75	2.75	3.75	

1949

☐ C39	6c DC-4, 1/18/49, DC (266,790) 1.50	2.50	3.50	
☐ C39a	DC-4, booklet pane of 3, 11/18/49, New York, NY 9.00			
☐ C40	6c Alexandria Bicentennial, 5/11/49, Alexandria, VA (386,717) 1.25	2.00	3.00	40.00
☐ C41	6c DC-4, coil, 8/25/49, DC (240,386)........................1.25pr2.50	1p4.00		
☐ C42	10c P.O. Bldg., 11/18/49, New Orleans, LA (270,000) 1.75	2.75	3.75	45.00
☐ C43	15c Globes & Doves, 10/7/49, Chicago, IL (246,833)...2.25	4.00	7.00	45.00
☐	1st Jack Knight Air Mail Society cachet 30.00			

SCOTT NUMBER	DESCRIPTION	SINGLE	BLOCK	PLATE BLOCK	CERM PROG
☐ C44	25c Boeing Stratocruiser, 11/30/49, Seattle, WA (220,215)	3.00	4.00	7.00	45.00
☐ C45	6c Wright Bros., 12/17/49, Kitty Hawk, NC (378,585)	3.50	5.00	8.00	50.00

1952

☐ C46	80c Diamond Head, 3/26/52, Honolulu, HI (89,864)	18.00	25.00	50.00	60.00

1953

☐ C47	6c Powered Flight, 5/29/53, Dayton, OH (359,050).	1.50	2.50	3.50	35.00

1954

☐ C48	4c Eagle, 9/3/54, Philadelphia, PA (295,720)	1.00	1.50	2.50	45.00

1957

☐ C49	6c Air Force, 8/1/57, DC (356,683)	1.75	2.75	3.75	

1958

☐ C50	5c Eagle, 7/31/58, Colorado Springs, CO, (207,954)	1.00	2.50	3.50	
☐	1st United States Air Force Academy cachet	18.00			
☐ C51	7c Blue Jet, 7/31/58, Phila. PA, (204,401)	1.00	2.50	3.50	30.00
☐ C51a	Blue Jet, booklet pane of 6, 7/31/58, San Antonio, TX (119,769)	9.50			
☐ C52	7c Blue Jet, coil, 7/31/58, Miami, FL(181,603)	1.00	pr2.00	lp3.00	25.00

1959

☐ C53	7c Alaska, 1/3/59, Juneau, AK (489,752)	1.00	1.75	2.75	20.00
☐	1st Gastineau Stamp Club cachet	15.00			
☐ C54	7c Balloon, 8/17/59, Lafayette, IN (383,556)	1.10	2.75	3.75	40.00
☐ C55	7c Hawaii, 8/21/59, Honolulu, HI (533,464)	1.00	2.50	3.50	30.00
☐ C56	10c Pan Am. Games, 8/27/59, Chicago, IL (302,206) (2 types)*	1.00	2.00	3.00	20.00*

1959- 66

☐ C57	10c Liberty Bell, 6/10/60, Miami, FL (246,509) (2 types, uncanceled)*	1.25	2.00	4.00	20.00*
☐ C58	15c Statue of Liberty, 11/20/59, New York, NY (259,412)	1.25	2.00	4.00	25.00
☐ C59	25c Lincoln, 4/22/60, San Francisco, CA (211,235)	1.75	2.75	4.75	30.00
☐ C59a	Lincoln, tagged, 12/29/66, DC (3,000)	30.00	—	—	

1960

☐ C60	7c Red Jet, 8/12/60, Arlington, VA (247,190)	1.00	1.00	2.50	20.00
☐ C60a	Red Jet, booklet pane of 6, 8/19/60, St. Louis, MO (143,363)	9.50			20.00
☐ C61	7c Red Jet, coil, 10/22/60, Atlantic City, NJ (197,995)	1.00	pr1.25	lp3.00	30.00

1961- 67

☐ C62	13c Liberty Bell, 6/28/61, New York, NY (316,166)	1.00	1.00	2.75	18.00
☐ C62a	Liberty Bell, tagged, 2/15/67, DC	30.00	—	—	
☐ C63	15c Statue of Liberty, 1/13/61, Buffalo, NY (192,976)	1.00	2.50	3.50	25.00

SCOTT NUMBER	DESCRIPTION	SINGLE	BLOCK	PLATE BLOCK	CERM PROG
☐ C63a	Statue of Liberty, tagged, 1/11/67, DC	25.00	—		—

1962-65

☐ C64	8c Capitol, 12/5/62, DC (288,355) (2 types)*	1.00	1.00		2.50 30.00*
☐ C64a	8c Capitol, tagged, 8/1/63, Dayton, OH (262,720)	2.00	2.50	4.00	
☐	1st National Cash Register Co. cachet	15.00			
☐ C64b	Capitol, booklet pane of 5 + label, 12/5/62, DC				
	(146,835)	2.00			
☐ C64c	Capitol, booklet tagged singlew/zip slogan,11/23/64	150.00			
☐ C65	8c Capitol, coil, 12/5/62, DC(220,173)	1.00pr	1.00	lp2.75	
☐ C65a	Capitol, coil, tagged, 1/14/65, New Orleans, LA	30.00	—		—

1963

☐ C66	15c Montgomery Blair, 5/3/63, Silver Spring, MD				
	(260,031)	1.10	2.50	3.50	12.00
☐ C67	6c Bald Eagle, 7/12/63, Boston, MA (268,265)	1.00	1.00	2.50	14.00
☐ C67a	Bald Eagle, tagged, 2/15/67, DC	50.00	—		—
☐ C68	8c Amelia Earhart, 7/24/63, Atchison, KS				
	(437,996)	1.75	2.25	2.75	18.00
☐	1st The Ninety-Nines, Inc., cachet	15.00			

1964

☐ C69	8c Robert H. Goddard, 10/5/64, Roswell, NM				
	(421,020)	1.75	2.25	2.75	10.00

1967

☐ C70	8c Alaska, 3/30/67, Sitka, AK (554,784)	1.00	1.00	2.50	15.00
☐	1st Sheldon Jackson College cachet	15.00			
☐ C71	20c Audubon, 4/26/67, New York, NY (227,930)				
	(2 types)*	2.00	3.50	4.50	12.00*

1968

☐ C72	10c 50-Star Runway, 1/5/68, San Francisco, CA	1.00	1.00	2.50	14.00
☐ C72b	50-Star Runway, booklet pane of 8, 1/5/68, DC	3.50			
☐ C72c	50-Star Runway, booklet pane of 5 plus				
	Mail Early Tab, 1/6/68, DC	125.00			
☐ C72c	50-Star Runway, booklet pane of 5 plus Zip Tab,				
	1/6/68, DC	125.00			
☐ C73	10c 50-Star Runway, coil 1/5/68 San Francisco, CA.	1.00 pr	1.50	lp2.50	
	Total for Scott C72- C73 is 814, 140.				
☐ C74	10c Jenny, 5/15/68, DC (521,084) (5 types)*	1.50	2.75	3.75	12.00
	1st Readers Digest cachet	20.00	—		—
☐ C75	20c "USA," 11/22/68, New York, NY (276,244)	1.10	2.75	3.75	14.00

1969

☐ C76	10c First Man on Moon, 9/9/69, DC (8,743,070)				
	(2 types)*	4.50	6.00	9.00	30.00*
☐	1st Dow-Unicover cachet	15.00			

1971-73

☐ C77	9c Delta Plane, 5/15/71, Kitty Hawk, NC (2 types)*	1.00	1.25	2.50	18.00*
	Total for Scott C77 and UXC10 is 379,442.				
☐ C78	11c Jet, 5/7/71, Spokane, WA	1.00	1.25	2.50	25.00
☐ C78a	Jet, booklet pane of 4 + 2 labels, 5/7/71, Spokane,				
	WA	1.75			45.00

C75, C81

FIRST MAN ON THE MOON

C76

C85

C86

C87

C88

C89

C90

C99

Philip Mazzei
Patriot Remembered

USAirmail
40c

C98

C100

C105-8

C101-4

USAirmail

33

Alfred V. Verville
Aviation Pioneer

C113

Lawrence and
Elmer Sperry
Aviation
Pioneers

USAirmail 39 C114

C115

Junipero
Serra   USAirmail

44 C116

C118

36 USAirmail

Igor Sikorsky

C119

202

		SINGLE	BLOCK	BLOCK	PROG
☐ C79	13c Winged Envelope, 11/16/73, New York, NY (282,550) (2 types)*............1.00	1.25		2.50	10.00
☐ C79a	Winged Envelopes, booklet pane of 5 + label, 12/27/73, Chicago, IL 1.75				30.00
☐ C80	17c Statue of Liberty, 7/13/71 Lakehurst, NJ (172,269)............1.00	1.25		2.50	20.00
☐ C81	21c "USA," 5/21/71, DC (293,140) (2 types)*............1.00	1.25		2.50	18.00*
☐ C82	11c Jet, coil, 5/7/71, Spokane, WA............1.00 pr1.25 lp2.50				35.00
	Total for Scott C78, C78a and C82 is 464, 750.				
☐ C83	13c Winged Envelope, coil 12/27/73, Chicago, IL 1.00	1.25	2.00		
	Total for Scott C79a and C83 is 204,756.				

1972

		SINGLE	BLOCK	BLOCK	PROG
☐ C84	11c City of Refuge, 5/3/72, Honaunau, HI (364,816)............1.00	1.25		2.50	35.00
☐ C85	11c Olympics, 8/17/72, DC............1.00	1.25	2.50		
	Total for Scott 1460-1462 and C85 is 971,536.				

1973

		SINGLE	BLOCK	BLOCK	PROG
☐ C86	11c Electronics, 7/10/73, New York, NY 1.00	1.25		2.50	30.00
	Total for set Scott 1500-1502 and C86 is 1,197,700.				

1974

		SINGLE	BLOCK	BLOCK	PROG
☐ C87	18c Statue of Liberty, 1/11/74, Hempstead, NY (216,902)............1.00	1.25		2.50	20.00
☐	1st James Hogg cachet 15.00				
☐ C88	26c Mt. Rushmore, 1/2/74, Rapid City, SD (210,470)............1.25	1.50	2.75		

1976

		SINGLE	BLOCK	BLOCK	PROG
☐ C89	25c Plane and Globes, 1/2/76, Honolulu, HI 1.25	1.50	2.75		
☐ C90	31c Plane, Globe and Flag, 1/2/76, Honolulu, HI 1.25	1.50	3.00		
☐	Scott C89 & C90 on one 3.00				25.00

1978

		SINGLE	BLOCK	BLOCK	PROG
☐ C91	31c Wright Bros., 9/23/78, Dayton, OH 3.00				
☐ C92	31c Wright Bros., 9/23/78, Dayton, OH 3.00				
☐ C92a	Se-tenant pair 4.00	5.00	6.00		14.00

1979

		SINGLE	BLOCK	BLOCK	PROG
☐ C93	21c Octave Chanute, 3/29/79, Chanute, KS............3.00				
☐ C94	21c Octave Chanute, 3/29/79, Chanute, KS............3.00				
☐ C94a	Se-tenant pair 4.00	5.00	6.00		14.00
	Total for Scott C93 and C94 is 459,235.				
☐ C95	25c Wiley Post, 11/20/79, Oklahoma City, OK 3.00				
☐ C96	25c Wiley Post, 11/20/79, Oklahoma City, OK 3.00				
☐ C96a	Se-tenant pair 4.00	5.00	6.00		14.00
☐ C97	31c Olympics, 11/1/79, Colorado Springs, CO 1.25	1.65	2.35		14.00

1980

		SINGLE	BLOCK	BLOCK	PROG
☐ C98	40c Philip Mazzei, 10/13/80, DC............1.75	2.75	4.00		8.00
☐ C99	28c Blanche Stuart Scott, 12/30/80, Hammondsport, NY (238,502) 1.25	1.50		2.75	15.00

SCOTT NUMBER	DESCRIPTION	SINGLE	BLOCK	PLATE BLOCK	CERM PROG
☐ C100	35c Glenn Curtiss, 12/30/80, Hammondsport, NY (208,502)	1.25	1.75	3.00	
☐	Scott C99 & C100 on one	2.50	—	—	15.00

1983

☐ C101	28c Gymnastics, 6/17/83, San Antonio, TX	1.25	—	—	
☐ C102	28c Hurdles, 6/17/83, San Antonio, TX	1.25	—	—	
☐ C103	28c Basketball, 6/17/83, San Antonio, TX	1.25	—	—	
☐ C104	28c Soccer, 6/17/83, San Antonio, TX	1.25	—	—	
☐ C104a	Se-tenant, (901,028)	—	3.75	4.50	15.00
☐ C105	40c Shot Put, 4/8/83, Los Angeles, CA	1.75	—	—	
☐ C106	40c Gymnastics, 4/8/83, Los Angeles, CA	1.75	—	—	
☐ C107	40c Swimming, 4/8/83, Los Angeles, CA	1.75	—	—	
☐ C108	40c Weight Lifting, 4/8/83, Los Angeles, CA	1.75	—	—	
☐ C108a	Se-tenant, (1,001,657)	—	5.00	6.00	18.00
☐ C109	35c Fencing, 11/4/83, Colorado Springs, CO	1.75	—	—	
☐ C110	35c Cycling, 11/4/83, Colorado Springs, CO	1.75	—	—	
☐ C111	35c Volleyball, 11/4/83, Colorado Springs, CO	1.75	—	—	
☐ C112	35c Pole Vaulting, 11/4/83, Colorado Springs, CO	1.75	—	—	
☐ C112a	Se-tenant, (897,729)	—	4.50	5.50	18.00

1985

☐ C113	33c Alfred Verville, 2/13/85, Garden City, NY	1.75	2.00	2.50	8.00
☐ C114	39c Lawrence & Elmer Sperry, 2/13/85, Garden City, NY	1.75	2.00	2.50	8.00
☐ C113-C114	33c Verville & Sperry, 2/13/85, Garden City, NY				8.00
☐ C115	44c Transpacific Air Mail, 2/15/85, San Francisco, CA (269,229)	1.75	2.00	2.50	8.00
☐ C116	44c Junipero Serra, 8/22/85, San Diego, CA (254,977)	1.75	2.00	2.50	8.00

1988

☐ C117	44c Settling of New Sweden, 3/29/88, Wilmington, DE (213,445)	1.75	2.00	2.50	14.00
☐ C118	45c Samuel P. Langley, 5/14/88, San Diego, CA	1.75	2.00	2.50	12.00
☐ C119	36c Igor Sikorsky, 6/23/88, Stratford, CT (162,986)	1.50	2.00	2.50	12.00

1989

☐ C120	45c French Revolution Bicentennial, 7/14/89, DC (309,975)	1.75	2.50	3.00	8.00
☐ C121	45c America, 10/12/89, San Juan, PR (93,569)	1.75	2.50	3.00	
☐ C122	45c Spacecraft, 11/28/89, DC	1.75	—	—	
☐ C123	45c Hover Car, 11/28/89, DC	1.75	—	—	
☐ C124	45c Moon Rover, 11/28/89, DC	1.75	—	—	
☐ C125	45c Space Shuttle, 11/28/89, DC	1.75	—	—	
☐ C125a	Se-tenant, (765,479)	—	6.00	7.00	10.00
☐ C126	45c Futuristic Mail Delivery, souvenir sheet, 11/24/89, DC (237,826)	6.00	—	—	10.00

1990

☐ C127	45c America, 10/12/90, Grand Canyon, AZ (137,068)	2.00	2.25	2.50	10.00

1991

		SINGLE	BLOCK	PLATE BLOCK	CERM PROG
☐ C128	50c Harriet Quimby, 4/27/91, Plymouth, MI	2.00	2.25	2.50	
☐ C129	40c William T. Piper, 5/17/91, Denver, CO	2.00	2.25	2.50	
☐ C130	50c Antarctic Treaty, 6/21/91, DC	2.00	2.25	2.50	6.00
☐ C131	50c Bering Land Bridge, 10/12/91, Anchorage, AK	2.00	2.25	2.50	6.00

Cachet values in this catalogue are for an average cacheted First Day Cover. Some FDC's, depending on the cachet, can sell for many times the catalogue value, while others sell for less. The Cachet Calculator lists cachetmakers, the dates they produced FDC's and a market value multiplier. The Calculator begins on page 52A.

AIRPOST SPECIAL DELIVERY

CE1-CE2

E1

E12-E13, E15-E18

E14, E19

E22-E23

E20-E21

FA1

1934

☐ CE1   **16c Great Seal,** 8/30/34, Chicago, IL (AAMS
Convention Sta.) (40,171)................................30.00 35.00 40.00
☐   DC, 8/31/34..15.00 17.50 22.50
For Scott CE1 design imperforate, see Scott 771.

1936

☐ CE2   **16c Great Seal,** 2/10/36, DC (72,981) 25.00 27.50 32.50

SPECIAL DELIVERY
1885

☐ E1   **10c Messenger,** at special delivery offices, 10/1/1885....8,500.

1888

☐ E2   **10c Messenger,** at any post office, 12/18/1888,
earliest known use ....—

1893

☐ E3   **10c Messenger,** 2/11/1893, earliest known use ....—

1894

☐ E4   **10c Messenger,** unwmkd, 11/21/1894, earliest known use ..—

1895-99

☐ E5   **10c Messenger,** wmk USPS, 10/3/1895, earliest known use.—

1903

☐ E6   **10c Bicycle,** perf. 12, dbl-line wmk, 1/22/03,
earliest known use ....—

1908

☐ E7 10c Mercury, 12/14/08, earliest known use ....—

1911

☐ E8 10c Bicycle, perf. 12, sgl-line wmk, 1/14/11,
    earliest known use ....—

1914

☐ E9 10c Bicycle, perf. 10, sgl-line wmk, 10/26/14,
    earliest known use ....—

1916

☐ E10 10c Bicycle, perf. 10, unwmk, 11/4/16, earliest known use..—

1917

☐ E11 10c Bicycle, perf. 11, unwmk, 6/12/17, earliest known use..—

1922

☐ E12 10c Motorcycle, perf. 11, 7/12/22...................................400.00

1925

☐ E13 15c Motorcycle, perf. 11, 4/11/25...................................225.00   375.00
☐ E14 20c P.O. Truck, perf. 11, 4/25/25 ....100.00   200.00

1927-41

☐ E15 10c Motorcycle, perf. 11 x 10 1/2, 11/29/27, DC 90.00   200.00
☐ E15 Motorcycle, electric eye, perf 11 x 10 1/2, 9/8/41, DC.....25.00   35.00
    Values given for Scott E15 Electric Eye are for covers
    with sheet salvage with Electric Eye markings.

1931

☐ E16 15c Motorcycle, perf. 11 x 10 1/2, 8/13/31, DC.............125.00   200.00
☐   Easton, PA, 8/6/31...2000.   —
    8/6/31 is the earliest known use of Scott E16,
    8/13/31 is the first day of sale at the Philatelic Agency.

1944

☐ E17 13c Motorcycle, 10/30/44, DC...12.50   15.00
☐ E18 17c Motorcycle, 10/30/44, DC...12.50   15.00
☐   Scott E17 & E18 on one cover ....15.00   —
    Total for Scott E17 and E18 is 158,863

1951

☐ E19 20c P.O. Truck, 11/30/51, DC (33,139)................................5.00   8.00

1954-57

☐ E20 20c Letter, 10/13/54, Boston, MA (194,043)......................3.00   5.00   45.00
☐ E21 30c Letter, 9/3/57, Indianapolis, IN (111,451)...................2.25   4.25   30.00

1969-71

☐ E22 45c Arrows, 11/21/69, New York, NY (192,391)................3.50   6.00   20.00
☐ E23 60c Arrows, 5/10/71, Phoenix, AZ (129,562).....................3.50   6.00   20.00

CERTIFIED MAIL/REGISTRATION

☐ FA1 15c Certified Mail, 6/6/55, DC (176,308) 3.25   5.00
☐ F1   10c Registry, 12/1/11, any city...12,000.

SPECIAL HANDLING

QE1-QE4   Q2   J68   J88

SCOTT NUMBER	DESCRIPTION	UNCACHETED SINGLE	BLOCK	CACHETED SINGLE
☐ QE1	10c Special Handling, 6/25/28 ....50.00		65.00	200.00
☐ QE2	15c Special Handling, 6/25/28 ....50.00		65.00	200.00
☐ QE3	20c Special Handling, 6/25/28 ....50.00		65.00	200.00
☐ QE4	25c Special Handling, 4/11/25 ....225.00		275.00	300.00
☐	Scott QE4 & E13 on one cover, 4/11/25..........1,300.			1,500.

PARCEL POST

Parcel Post Service (fourth class) began January 1, 1913, and these stamps were issued
for that service only. The 1c, 2c, 4c and 5c are known with January 1, 1913, postmarks
— the 2c undoubtedly for fourth class usage, the others possible but unproven. Beginning
July 1, these stamps could be used for any purpose, thus a few first class FDCs were prepared for some of the lower denominations. There was not an official first day city for
either date.

		4th Class (1/1/13)	1st Class (7/1/13)
☐ Q1	1c Post Office Clerk, any city ....3,500.		2,500.
	Scott Q1 known on picture postcard.		
☐ Q2	2c City Carrier, any city ....4,500.		2,500.
☐ Q3	3c Railway Postal Clerk, any city ....—		4,500.
☐ Q4	4c Rural Carrier, any city ....—		5,000.
☐ Q5	5c Mail Train, any city...4,000.		7,000.
	Scott Q4 & Q5 on wrapper......................................—		8,000.

SCOTT NUMBER	DESCRIPTION	CACHETED SINGLE	BLOCK	CERM PROG

OFFICIALS
1983-85

☐ O127	1c Great Seal, 1/12/83, DC..................................1.00		1.25	
☐ O128	4c Great Seal, 1/12/83, DC..................................1.00		1.25	
☐ O129	13c Great Seal, 1/12/83, DC.................................1.00		1.25	
☐ O129A	14c Great Seal, 5/15/85 DC.................................1.00		1.25	
☐ O130	17c Great Seal, 1/12/83, DC.................................1.00		1.25	
☐ O132	$1 Great Seal, 1/12/83, DC 3.00		6.00	
☐ O133	$5 Great Seat, 1/12/83, DC.................................15.00		20.00	
☐ O135	20c Great Seal Coil,1/12/83, DC 1.00		pr1.25	

SCOTT NUMBER	DESCRIPTION	CACHETED SINGLE BLOCK	CERM PROG
☐	Scott O127-O129, O130-O135 on one cover..........15.00		
☐	Scott O127-O129, O130-O135 on Official Postal Card		
	(Scott UZ2) or envelope (Scott UO73)....................20.00		
☐ 0136	22c Great Seal Coil, 5/15/85, DC 1.00	pr1.25	
☐ 0138	(14c) Great Seal, 2/4/85, DC 1.00	1.25	

SCOTT NUMBER	DESCRIPTION	CACHETED SINGLE PAIR	CERM PROG

1988

SCOTT NUMBER	DESCRIPTION	CACHETED SINGLE	PAIR	CERM PROG
☐ 0138A	15c Great Seal Coil, 6/11/88, Corpus Christi, TX 1.00	1.25	
☐ 0138A & 0141	....		8.00
☐ 0138B	20c Great Seal Coil, with frame line, 5/19/88, DC 1.00	1.25	
☐ 0139	(22c) Great Seal Coil, 2/4/85, DC.....................................1.00	1.25	
☐ 0140	(25c) Great Seal Coil, 3/22/88, DC...................................1.75	2.00	
☐ 0141	25c Great Seal Coil, 6/11/88, Corpus Christi, TX 1.75	2.00	

SCOTT NUMBER	DESCRIPTION	CACHETED SINGLE BLOCK	CERM PROG

1989

SCOTT NUMBER	DESCRIPTION	CACHETED SINGLE BLOCK	CERM PROG
☐ 0143	1c Great Seal, lithographed, 7/5/89, DC 1.00	1.10	

1991-95

☐ 0144	(29c) Great Seal, non-denominated, 1/22/91, DC............1.75	2.00	
☐ 0145	29c Great Seal, 5/24/91, Seattle, WA...............................1.75	2.00	
☐ 0146	4c Great Seal, 4/6/91, Oklahoma City, OK 1.75	2.00	
☐ 0146A	10c Great Seal, 10/19/93, DC..1.25	2.00	
☐ 0147	19c Great Seal, 5/24/91, Seattle, WA...............................1.75	2.00	
☐ 0148	23c Great Seal, 5/24/91, Seattle, WA...............................1.75	2.00	
☐ 0152	(32c) G, Great Seal, 12/13/94, DC....................................1.25		
☐ 0153	32c Great Seal, 5/9/95, DC..1.25		
☐ 0154	1c Great Seal, microscopic text, 5/9/95, DC 1.25	2.00	
☐ 0155	20c Great Seal, microscopic text, 5/9/95, DC 1.25	2.00	
☐ 0156	23c Great Seal, microscopic text, 5/9/95, DC 1.25	2.00	

SCOTT NUMBER	DESCRIPTION	SINGLE	CERM PROG

POSTAGE DUE
1925

☐ J68	1/2c Dull Red, 4/15/25, earliest known use....................	—	

1959

☐ J88	1/2c Red and Black, 6/19/59...75.00		
☐ J89	1c Red and Black, 6/19/59 ....75.00		
☐ J89-J101	1/2c -$5 Postage Due 6/19/59 (without due stamps).........		35.00
☐ J90	2c Red and Black, 6/19/59 ....75.00		
☐ J91	3c Red and Black, 6/19/59 ....75.00		
☐ J92	4c Red and Black, 6/19/59 ....75.00		
☐ J93	5c Red and Black, 6/19/59 ....100.00		
☐ J94	6c Red and Black, 6/19/59 ....100.00		
☐ J95	7c Red and Black, 6/19/59 ....100.00		
☐ J96	8c Red and Black, 6/19/59 ....100.00		

☐	J97	10c Red and Black, 6/19/59	100.00
☐	J98	30c Red and Black, 6/19/59	100.00
☐	J99	50c Red and Black, 6/19/59	100.00
☐	J100	$1 Red and Black, 6/19/59	100.00
☐	J101	$5 Red and Black, 6/19/59	150.00

1978-85

☐	J102	11c Red and Black, 1/2/78	5.00
☐	J103	13c Red and Black, 1/2/78	5.00
☐	J104	17c Red and Black, 6/10/85	5.00

POSTAL NOTES

☐	PN1	1c Black, 2/1/45, on complete 3 part money order form	45.00
☐	PN1-PN18	1c to 90c Black, 2/1/45 on 18 money order forms	600.00

Last day covers of this service also exist, dated 3/31/51.
These sell for $15-$20.

POSTAL SAVINGS
1941

☐	PS11	10c Red, 5/1/41, any city	175.00

REVENUES

These examples of Revenue FD's are postmarked with fiscal
rather than postal cancellations.

1898

☐	R154	1c Green, Franklin, 7/1/98	—
☐	R155	2c Washington, 7/1/98	—
☐	R166	4c Rose Battleship, 7/1/98	—

HUNTING PERMIT STAMPS

The following are not postage stamp items. They are listed here only for collectors'
interest. Ceremony Program prices are for programs without a stamp affixed.

☐	RW3	$1 Canada Geese, 7/1/36, Warren, NJ	700.00	
☐	RW43	$5 Canada Geese, 7/1/76, any city	150.00	
☐	RW46	$7.50 Green-winged Teal, 7/1/79, any city	150.00	
☐	RW47	$7.50 Mallards, 7/1/80, any city	150.00	
☐	RW48	$7.50 Ruddy Ducks, 7/1/81, any city	75.00	
☐	RW49	$7.50 Canvas Backs, 7/1/82, any city	55.00	
☐	RW50	$7.50 Pintail, 7/1/83, any city	50.00	
☐	RW51	$7.50 Wigeons, 7/1/84, any city	50.00	
☐	RW52	$7.50 Cinnamon Teal, 7/1/85, any city	45.00	
☐	RW53	$7.50 Fulvous Whistling Duck, 7/1/86, any city	45.00	
☐	RW54	$10 Redheads, 7/1/87, any city	45.00	15.00
☐	RW55	$10 Snow Goose, 7/1/88, any city	45.00	20.00
☐	RW56	$12.50 Lesser Scaup, 6/30/89, any city	45.00	25.00
☐	RW57	$12.50 Black Bellied Whistling Duck, 6/30/90, any city	45.00	35.00
☐	RW58	$15 Elders, 7/1/91, DC..	35.00	30.00
☐	RW59	$15 Spectacled Eider, 7/1/92, DC...	35.00	30.00
☐	RW60	$15 Canvasback, 7/1/93	35.00	30.00
☐	RW61	$15 Mergansers, 7/1/94	35.00	30.00
☐	RW62	$15 Mallard, 6/30/95, DC	35.00	30.00
☐	RW63	$15 Surf Scoter, 6/27/96, DC..	35.00	25.00
☐	RW64	$15 Canada Goose, 6/21/97, DC..	35.00	25.00

ENVELOPES

Sizes of U.S. Envelope FD's are as follows: Size 5 — 89x160mm,
Size 6 3/4 - 92x165mm, Size 7 - 98x225mm, Size 7 1/2 —
99x190mm, Sizes 8 and 10 — 105x240mm, Size 13 — 95x171mm.
Where a paper difference is shown, the watermark of "Standard
Quality" is similar to Watermark 28 and "Extra Quality" is similar to Watermark 29.
All FDC's prior to 1946 have normal cancels.
**** Denotes: Does not exist with either a standard FDOI cancel or with any other
cancel used specifically for that First Day. (1946 and later)**

U481, U436-9,
U529-31

U522

U523-28

U532-4,
U536, U544

U541-2

U543

U546

1861

☐ U35   3c **George Washington**, pink, 8/10/1861,
earliest known use ....—

1876

☐ U221   3c **Centennial**, green, 5/10/1876, earliest known use,
Centennial cancel, size 3, wmk 3 ....3,500.

1883

☐ U227   2c **George Washington**, 10/2/1883, size 5, wmk 6,
earliest known use 350.00

1886

☐ U293   2c **U.S. Grant**, letter sheet, 8/18/1886,
earliest known use ....—

1916-32

☐ U436a **3c George Washington**, white paper, extra quality,
6/16/32, DC, size 5, die 1, wmk 29 ....75.00   —
☐   size 8, die 1, wmk 29..25.00   75.00
☐ U436e **3c George Washington**, white paper, extra quality,
6/16/32, DC, size 5, die 7, wmk 29 ....35.00   50.00
☐   size 13, die 7, wmk 29 ....35.00   50.00

☐ U436f 3c George Washington, white paper, extra quality,
6/16/32, DC, size 5, die 9, wmk 29 ....12.00   30.00

☐   size 13, die9, wmk 29 ....15.00   30.00

☐ U437a 3c George Washington, amber paper, 7/13/32, DC, size
5, wmk 28, standard quality....................................50.00   —

☐   7/19/32, DC, size 5, wmk 29, extra quality.............35.00   —

☐ U439a 3c George Washington, blue paper, 7/13/32, DC, size 5,
wmk 28, standard quality..40.00   —

☐   size 13, wmk 28, standard quality..........................65.00   —

☐   9/9/32, DC, size 8, wmk 28, standard quality ....85.00   —

☐   3c George Washington, blue paper, 7/19/32, DC, extra
quality, size 5, wmk 29 ....40.00   —

1921

☐ U446   2c on 3c George Washington, 5/21/21,
earliest known use...—

1925

☐ U481   1 1/2c George Washington, 3/19/25, DC, size 5,
wmk 27 ....35.00   —

☐   size 8, wmk 27 ....70.00   —

☐   size 13, wmk 26 ....50.00   —

☐   size 13, wmk 26 with Scott 553 ....60.00   —

☐ U495   1 1/2c on 1c Benjamin Franklin, 6/1/25, DC size 5 ....50.00   —

☐   6/3/25, DC, size 8 ....65.00   —

☐   6/2/25, DC, size 13 ....60.00   —

☐ U515   1 1/2c on lc Benjamin Franklin, 8/1/25, Des Moines,
IA, size 5, die 1 ....50.00   —

☐ U521   1 1/2c on 1c Benjamin Franklin, 10/22/25, DC, size 5,
die 1, wmk 25 ....100.00   —

1926

☐ U522a 2c Liberty Bell, 7/27/26, Philadelphia, PA, size 5,
wmk 27** 20.00   30.00

☐   7/27/26, DC, size 5, wmk 27 ....22.50   32.50

☐   7/27/26, unofficial city, size 5, wmk 27.................35.00   45.00

1932

☐ U523   1c Mount Vernon, 1/1/32, DC, size 5, wmk 29 ....8.00   20.00

☐   size 8, wmk 29 ....10.00   20.00

☐   size 13, wmk 29 ....8.00   20.00

☐ U524   1 1/2c Mount Vernon, 1/1/32, DC, size 5,wmk 29.............8.00   20.00

☐   size 8, wmk 29 ....10.00   20.00

☐   size 13, wmk 29 ....8.00   20.00

☐ U525   2c Mount Vernon, 1/1/32, DC, size 5, wmk 29 ....8.00   20.00

☐   size 8, wmk 29 ....10.00   20.00

☐   size 13, wmk 29 ....8.00   20.00

☐ U526   3c Mount Vernon, 6/16/32, DC, size 5, wmk 29 ....15.00   20.00

☐   size 8, wmk 29 ....25.00   40.00

☐   size 13, wmk 29 ....20.00   30.00

☐ U527   4c Mount Vernon, 1/1/32, DC, size 8, wmk 29 ....15.00   25.00

☐ U528   5c Mount Vernon, 1/1/32, DC, size 5, wmk 29 ....10.00   22.00

☐   size 8, wmk 29 ....12.00   22.00

☐ U529 6c **George Washington**, white paper, 8/18/32, Los
  Angeles, CA, size 8, wmk 29 ....15.00 —
☐   8/19/32, DC, size 7, wmk 29 ....20.00 —
☐   8/19/32, DC, size 9, wmk 29 ....20.00 —
☐ U530 6c **George Washington**, amber paper, 8/18/32, Los
  Angeles, CA, size 8, wmk 29 ....15.00 —
☐   8/19/32, DC, size 7, wmk 29 ....20.00 —
☐   8/19/32, DC, size 9, wmk 29 ....20.00 —
☐   size 8, wmk 29, with Scott 723 pair ....25.00 —
☐ U531 6c **George Washington**, blue paper, 8/18/32, Los Angeles,
  size 8, wmk 29 ....15.00 —
☐   8/19/32, DC. size 7, wmk 29 ....20.00 —
☐   8/19/32. DC. size 9, wmk 29 ....20.00 —

1950

☐ U532 1c **Benjamin Franklin**, 11/16/50, New York, NY, size
  13, wmk 42 ....1.50 2.50
☐ U533a 2c **George Washington**, 11/17/50, New York, NY, size
  13, wmk 42 ....1.50 2.50
☐ U534a 3c **George Washington**, die 1, 11/18/50, New York,
  NY, size 13, wmk 42 ....1.50 2.50
☐ U534b 3c **George Washington**, die 2, 11/19/50, New York,
  NY, size 8, wmk 42** 5.00 10.00

1952

☐ U535 1 1/2c **George Washington**, 10/21/52, Dover or Kenvil,
  NJ, size 13, wmk 42, earliest known use ....— —

1958

☐ U536 4c **Benjamin Franklin**, 7/31/58, Montpelier, VT
  (163,746), size 6 3/4, wmk 46 ....1.00 1.50
☐   size 8, wmk 46** ....60.00 —
☐   size 13, wmk 46** ....60.00 —
☐   7/31/58, Wheeling, WV, size 6 3/4, wmk 46 with Scott
  1036a** ....35.00 —
☐   size 13, window** ....35.00 —
☐ U540 3c + 1c **George Washington** (U534c), 7/22/58, Kenvil,
  NJ, size 8, wmk 46, die 3, earliest known use** .....50.00 —

1960

☐ U541 1 1/4c **Benjamin Franklin**, 6/25/60, Birmingham, AL
  (211,500), size 6 3/4, wmk 46 ....1.00 1.25 25.00
☐ U542 2 1/2c **George Washington**, 5/28/60, Chicago, IL
  (196,977), size 6 3/4, wmk 46 ....1.00 1.25 30.00
☐ U543 4c **Pony Express Rider**, 7/19/60, St. Joseph, MO
  (407,160), size 6 3/4, wmk 46 ....1.00 1.25 30.00
☐   7/19/60, Sacramento, CA, with Scott 1154, size 6 3/4,
  wmk 46 ....3.50 5.00

**Values for various cachet makers can be determined
by using the Cachet Calculator which begins on page 52A.**

U547, U548,
U548A, U556

U549, U552

U550, U553

U551, U561

U554

U555, U562

U557

U563

U564

U565

U567

U569

U568

U571-75

U576

U581

U584

1962

☐ **U544** 5c **Abraham Lincoln**, 11/19/62, Springfield, IL
(163,258), size 6 3/4, wmk 48......................1.00   1.25   15.00

☐ **U546** 5c **New York World's Fair**, 4/22/64, World's Fair, NY
(466,422), size 6 3/4, wmk 48......................1.00   1.25   18.00

1965-69

☐ **U547** 1 1/4c **Liberty Bell**, 1/6/65, DC, size 6 3/4, wmk 49..........1.00   1.00

☐   1/8/65, DC, size 10, wmk 48**.................................10.00   20.00

☐   cerm. prog. includes U549...   18.00

☐ **U548** 1 4/10c **Liberty Bell**, 3/26/68, Springfield, MA
(134,832), size 6 3/4, wmk 49.....................1.00   1.00   18.00

☐   3/27/68, DC, size 10, wmk 48**................................5.00   8.00

☐ **U548A** 1 6/10c **Liberty Bell**, 6/16/69, DC, size 6 3/4,
wmk 47 (130,109)......................................1.00   1.00

☐   size 10, wmk 49**..1.25   1.75

☐ **U549** 4c **Old Ironsides**, 1/6/65, DC, size 6 3/4, wmk 49.............1.00   1.00

☐   1/8/65, DC, size 6 3/4, window, wmk 49**..............10.00   20.00

☐   size 10, wmk 49**..10.00   20.00

☐   size 10, window, wmk 49 **.....................................10.00   20.00

     Total for Scott U547 and U549 is 451,960.

☐ **U550** 5c **Eagle**, 1/5/65, Williamsburg, PA (246,496), size 6 3/4,
wmk 49...1.00   1.00   18.00

☐   1/8/65, DC, size 6 3/4, window, wmk 49**..............10.00   20.00

☐   size 10, wmk 49**..10.00   20.00

☐   size 10, window, wmk 49**......................................10.00   20.00

☐ **U550a Eagle**, tagged, 8/15/67, DC & Dayton, OH, size 6 3/4,
wmk 50**..3.50   5.00

☐   size 6 3/4, window, wmk 48......................................3.50   5.00

☐   size 10, wmk 48 ....3.50   5.00

☐   size 10, wmk 49, Dayton only 4.50   7.50

☐   size 10, window, wmk 49 ....3.50   5.00

     There were no FDOI cancels for any sizes or formats of U550a

☐ **U551** 6c **Statue of Liberty**, 1/4/68, New York, NY (184,784),
size 6 3/4, wmk 47 or 48 ....1.00   1.25   15.00

☐   1/5/68, DC, size 6 3/4, window, wmk 48 or 49** 5.00   10.00

☐   size 10, wmk 47**..5.00   10.00

☐   size 10, window, wmk 49**......................................5.00   10.00

☐   11/15/68, DC, new shiny plastic window, size 6 3/4,
window, wmk 48**..................................3.00   10.00

1968

☐ **U552** 4c + 2c **Old Ironsides**, 2/5/68, DC, size 6 3/4, wmk 50** .5.00   7.50

☐   size 6 3/4, window, wmk 48......................................5.00   7.50

☐   size 10, wmk 47..5.00   7.50

☐   size 10, window, wmk 49...5.00   7.50

☐ **U553** 5c + 1c **Eagle**, 2/5/68, DC, size 6 3/4, wmk 49 ....5.00   7.50

☐   size 10, window, wmk 49...5.00   7.50

☐ **U553a Eagle**, tagged, 2/5/68, DC, size 6 3/4, wmk 48**..............5.00   7.50

☐   size 10, wmk 47 or 49 ....5.00   7.50

☐   size 10, window, wmk 49...5.00   7.50

     There were no FDOI cancels for any sizes or formats of U552, U553, U553a

1970

☐ **U554** 6c **Moby Dick**, 3/7/70, New Bedford, MA (433,777)
size 6 3/4, wmk 47 ....1.00   1.25   12.00

1971

☐ U555 6c Youth Conference, 2/24/71, DC, (264,559), size 6 3/4,
wmk 49 ....1.00   1.00   25.00

☐ U556 1 7/10c Liberty Bell, 5/10/71, Baltimore, MD (150,767),
size 6 3/4, wmk 48A 1.00   1.00

☐   5/10/71, DC, size, 6 3/4, wmk 49** 9.00   15.00

☐   5/11/71, DC, size10, wmk 47 or 49** 7.50   12.00

☐   5/11/71, DC, size 10, wmk 48A** 3.50   6.00

☐ U557 8c Eagle, 5/6/71, Williamsburg, PA (193,000), size 6 3/4,
wink 48A 1.00   1.00   20.00

☐   size 6 3/4 window, wmk 49** ....10.00   —

☐   size 10, wmk 49** ....10.00   —

☐   size 10, window, wmk 47** ....10.00   —

☐ U561 6c + (2c) Statue of Liberty, 5/16/71, DC, size 6 3/4,
wmk 47 ....2.00   4.00

☐   size 6 3/4, wmk 48A, (25 known) 15.00   25.00

☐   size 6 3/4, wmk 49 ....2.50   4.00

☐   size 6 3/4, window, wmk 47 ....2.00   3.00

☐   size 10, wmk 48A 2.00   3.00

☐   size 10, wmk 49 ....3.50   6.00

☐   size 10, window, wmk 47 ....2.00   3.00

☐   size 10, window, wmk 49 ....3.00   5.00

☐ U562 6c + (2c) Youth Conference, 5/16/71, DC, size 6 3/4,
wmk 47 ....20.00   30.00

☐   size 6 3/4, wmk 49 ....2.50   5.00

There were no FDOI cancels for any sizes or formats of U561 and U562

☐ U563 8c Bowling, 8/21/71, Milwaukee, WI (267,029),
wmk 49 ....1.00   1.25   18.00

☐   size 10, wmk 49 ....1.00   2.00

☐ U564 8c Aging Conference, 11 / 15/71, DC (125,000),
size 6 3/4, wmk 48A 1.00   1.00   25.00

1972

☐ U565 8c International Transportation Exposition, 5/2/72, DC,
size 6 3/4, wmk 47 ....2.50   3.00   18.00

☐   size 6 3/4, wmk 49 ....1.00   1.00

1973

☐ U566 8c + 2c Eagle, 12/1/73, DC, size 6 3/4, wmk 47 or 49 ....1.50   2.50

☐   size 6 3/4, window, wmk 48A ....7.50   —

☐   size 6 3/4, window, wmk 49 ....3.00   4.50

☐   size 10, wmk 47 ....3.00   4.50

☐   size 10, window, wmk 47 ....3.00   4.50

There were no FDOI cancels for any sizes or formats of U566

☐ U567 10c Liberty Bell, 12/5/73, Philadelphia, PA (142,141),

☐   size 6 3/4, wmk 47, old knife depth 58mm 1.00   1.00   25.00

☐   size 6 3/4, wmk 47, new knife depth 51mm 1.00   1.50

☐   size 6 3/4 window, wmk 47 ....10.00

☐   size 10, wmk 47** ....10.00   —

☐   size 10, window, wmk 47** ....10.00   —

1974

☐ U568 1 8/10c Volunteer Yourself, 8/23/74, Cincinnati, OH,
size 6 3/4, wmk 47 ....1.00   1.00   12.00

		UNCACH	CACH	CERM PROG
☐	size 10, wmk 47 ....1.00		1.50	
☐ U569	**10c Tennis Centenary**, 8/31/74, Forest Hills, NY			
	(245,000), size 6 3/4, wmk 49.....................1.00		1.25	
☐	size 10, wmk 49 ....1.00		3.00	
☐	9/3/74, DC, size 6 3/4, window, wmk 49** 2.50		5.00	
☐	size 10, window, wmk 49** 2.50		5.00	
	Note: Window envelopes were sold and canceled on the first day, contrary to regulations.			

1975-76 Bicentennial Era

		UNCACH	CACH	CERM PROG
☐ U571	**10c Seafaring Tradition**, 10/13/75, Minneapolis, MN			
	(255,304), size 6 3/4.................................1.00		1.00	12.00
☐	size 10 ....1.00		1.25	
☐ U572	**13c American Homemaker**, 2/2/76, Biloxi, MS			
	(196,647), size 6 3/4.................................1.00		1.00	12.00
☐	size 10 ....1.00		1.25	
☐ U573	**13c American Farmer**, 3/15/76, New Orleans, LA			
	(214,563), size 6 3/4.................................1.00		1.00	15.00
☐	size 10 ....1.00		1.25	
☐ U574	**13c American Doctor**, 6/30/76, Dallas, TX,			
	(251,272) size 6 3/4.................................1.00		1.00	12.00
☐	size 10 ....1.00		1.25	
☐ U575	**13c American Craftsman**, 8/6/76, Lunesboro, MA,			
	(215,000) size 6 3/4.................................1.00		1.00	12.00
☐	size 10 ....1.00		1.25	

1975

		UNCACH	CACH	CERM PROG
☐ U576	**13c Liberty Tree**, 11/8/75, Memphis, TN (226,824)			
	size 6 3/4, wmk 48A.................................1.00		1.00	12.00
☐	size 10, wmk 47 ....1.00		1.25	

1976-78

		UNCACH	CACH	CERM PROG
☐ U577	**2c Star and Pinwheel**, 9/10/76, Hempstead, NY			
	(81,388), size 6 3/4, wmk 48A or 49.................1.00		1.00	10.00
☐	size 10, wmk 48A.................................1.00		1.25	
☐ U578	**2.1c (Non-Profit)**, 6/3/77, Houston, TX (120,280)			
	size 6 3/4, wmk 47.................................1.00		1.00	10.00
☐	size 10, wmk 47 ....1.00		1.25	
☐ U579	**2.7c (Non-Profit)**, 7/5/78, Raleigh, NC (92,687),			
	size 6 3/4, wmk 47.................................1.00		1.00	
☐	size 10, wmk 47 ....1.00		1.25	
☐ U580	**(15c) "A" & Eagle**, 5/22/78, Memphis, TN, size 6 3/4			
	wmk 47 ....1.00		1.50	
☐	size 6 3/4, wmk 48A.................................1.00		1.00	
☐	size 6 3/4, wmk 47 or 48A.................................1.25		2.00	
☐	size 10, wmk 47 or 49 ....1.00		1.25	
☐	size 10, window, wmk 47 or 49 ....1.25		2.00	
☐	size 6 3/4, wmk 48A with sheet, coil & booklet pane 5.00		10.00	
☐ U581	**15c Uncle Sam**, 6/3/78, Williamsburg, PA (176,000),			
	size 6 3/4, wmk 47 or 49 ....1.00		1.00	
☐	size 6 3/4, window, wmk 47.................................1.25		2.00	
☐	size 10, wmk 47 or 48A.................................1.00		1.25	
☐	size 10, window, wmk 48A or 49.................................1.25		2.00	

U587   U590   U593

U595   U598

U602

U606   U607   U608

U609

SCOTT NUMBER	DESCRIPTION	UNCACH	CACH	CERM PROG

1976

☐ U582 13c **Bicentennial**, 10/15/76, Los Angeles, CA (277,222),
    size 6 3/4, wmk 48A ....2.00 | 3.00 | 12.00
☐   size 6 3/4, wmk 49 ....1.00 | 1.00
☐   size 6 3/4, wmk 49, dark green ....— | 7.50
☐   size 10, wmk 49 ....1.00 | 1.25

1977

☐ U583 13c **Golf**, 4/7/77, Augusta, GA (252,000), size 6 3/4,
    wmk 49 ....1.00 | 7.00
☐   size 10, wmk 49 ....1.00 | 7.00
☐   4/8/77, DC, size 6 3/4, window, wmk 49** ....2.00 | 7.50
☐   size 10, window, wmk 49** ....2.00 | 7.50
☐ U584 13c **Energy Conservation**, 10/20/77, Ridley Park, PA,
    San Francisco, CA, size 6 3/4, wmk 49 ....1.00 | 1.00
☐   size 6 3/4, window, wmk 49 ....1.50 | 2.50
☐   size 10, wmk 49 ....1.00 | 1.25.
☐   size 10, window, wmk 49 ....1.50 | 2.50
☐   10/20/77, DC, with Scott 1723-1724, all sizes ....3.50 | 4.00
☐ U585 13c **Energy Development**, 10/20/77, Ridley Park, PA,
    San Francisco, CA, size 6 3/4, wmk 49 ....1.00 | 1.00
☐   size 6 3/4, window, wmk 49 ....1.50 | 2.50
☐   size 10, wmk 49 ....1.00 | 1.25
☐   size 10, window, wmk 49 ....1.50 | 2.50
☐   10/20/77, DC, with Scott 1723-1724, all sizes ....3.50 | 4.00
Total for Scott U584 and U585 is 353,515.

1978

☐ U586 15c **on 16c USA**, 7/28/78, Williamsburg, PA, (193,153),
    size 6 3/4, wmk 47 ....1.00 | 1.00
☐   size 10, wmk 47 ....1.00 | 1.25
☐   size 6 3/4 window** ....10.00 | —
☐   size 10 window ** ....10.00 | —
☐ U587 15c **Auto Racing**, 9/2/78, Ontario, CA (209,147),
    size 6 3/4, wmk 49 ....1.00 | 1.00 | 14.00
☐   size 10, wmk 49 ....1.00 | 1.25
☐ U588 15c **on 13c Liberty Tree**, 11/28/78, Williamsburg, PA
    (137,500), size 6 3/4, wmk 47 ....1.00 | 1.00
☐   size 10, wmk 47 ....1.00 | 1.25
☐   size 6 3/4, window, wmk 47** ....10.00 | —
☐   size 10, window, wmk 48A** ....10.00 | —

1979-82

☐ U589 3.1c **(Non-Profit)**, 5/18/79, Denver, CO (117,575)
    size 6 3/4, wmk 48A ....1.00 | 1.00 | 10.00
☐   size 6 3/4, window, wmk 48 ....2.00 | 3.00
☐   size 10, wmk 49 ....1.00 | 1.25
☐   size 10, window, wmk 49 ....2.00 | 3.00
☐ U590 3.5c **(Non-Profit)**, 6/23/80, Williamsburg, PA, size 6 3/4,
    wmk 49 ....1.00 | 1.00
☐   size 10, wmk 48A or 49 ....1.00 | 1.25
☐   size 6 3/4, window ....1.00 | 2.00
☐   size 10, window ....1.00 | 3.00

SCOTT NUMBER	DESCRIPTION	UNCACH	CACH	CERM PROG
☐ U591	**5.9c (Non-Profit)**, 2/17/82, Wheeling, WV, size 6 3/4, wmk 47, 48A or 49 ....1.00		1.25	
☐	size 6 3/4, window, wmk 47 ....2.00		3.00	
☐	size 10, wmk 47, 48A or 49 ....1.00		1.50	
☐	size 10, window 2.00		3.00	
☐ U592	**(18c) "B" & Eagle**, 3/15/81, Memphis, TN (179,171), size 6 3/4, wmk 47, 48A, or 49 ....1.00		1.00	
☐	size 6 3/4, window, wmk 47, 48A, or 49 ....2.00		3.00	
☐	size 10, wmk 47, 48A or 49 ....1.00		1.25	
☐	size 10, window, wmk 47 or 49 ....2.00		3.00	
☐	3/15/81, San Francisco, CA, With Scott 1818-1820 on any of the above..1.50		2.00	
☐ U593	**18c Star**, 4/2/81, Star City, IN (160,439), size 6 3/4, wmk 47 or 49 ....1.00		1.00	
☐	size 10, wmk 47, 48A or 49 ....1.00		1.25	
☐	size 6 3/4, window 2.00		3.00	
☐	size 10, window 2.00		3.00	
☐ U594	**(20c) "C" & Eagle**, 10/11/81, Memphis, TN size 6 3/4, wmk 47 or 49 ....1.00		1.25	
☐	size 6 3/4 window 5.00		—	
☐	size 10, wmk 47, 48A or 49 ....1.00		1.50	
☐	size 10 window 3.00		5.00	
	Note: Window envelopes were sold and canceled with the "FDOI" cancel contrary to announced policy.			

1979

SCOTT NUMBER	DESCRIPTION	UNCACH	CACH	CERM PROG
☐ U595	**15c Veterinary Medicine**, 7/24/79, Seattle, WA (209,658), size 6 3/4, wmk 49 ....1.00		1.00	10.00
☐	size 10, wmk 49 ....1.00		1.25	
☐	size 6 3/4 window** 10.00		—	
☐	size 10 window** 10.00		—	
☐ U596	**15c Olympic Games**, 12/10/79, E. Rutherford, NJ (179,336), size 6 3/4, wmk 49 ....1.00		1.25	
☐	size 10, wmk 49 ....1.00		1.50	

1980

SCOTT NUMBER	DESCRIPTION	UNCACH	CACH	CERM PROG
☐ U597	**15c Bicycling**, 5/16/80, Baltimore, MD (173,978) size 6 3/4, wmk 49 ....1.00		1.25	10.00
☐	size 10, wmk 49 ....1.00		1.50	
☐ U598	**15c America's Cup Yacht Races**, 9/15/80, Newport, RI, (192,220), size 6 3/4, wmk 49 ....1.00		1.25	15.00
☐	size 10, wmk 49 ....1.00		1.50	
☐ U599	**15c Honey Bee**, 10/10/80, Paris, IL, (202,050) size 6 3/4, wmk 49 ....1.00		1.00	18.00
☐	size 10, wmk 49 ....1.00		1.25	

1981-82

SCOTT NUMBER	DESCRIPTION	UNCACH	CACH	CERM PROG
☐ U600	**18c Remember the Blinded Veteran**, 8/13/81, Arlington, VA (175,966), size 6 3/4, wmk 49 ....1.00		1.00	8.00
☐	size 10, wmk 49 ....1.00		1.25	
☐ U601	**20c Capitol Dome**, 11 /13/81, Los Angeles, CA, size 6 3/4, wmk 48A or 49 ....1.00		1.25	
☐	size 10, wmk 47 or 49, size 10 ....1.00		1.50	
☐ U602	**20c Great Seal**, 6/15/82, DC, (163,905), size 6 3/4, wmk 49 ....1.00		1.25	10.00
☐	size 10, wmk 49 ....1.00		1.50	

☐ U603	20c Purple Heart, 8/6/82, DC, (110,679), size 6 3/4,			
	wmk 49 ....1.00		1.25	10.00
☐	size 10, wmk 49 ....1.00		1.50	

1983

☐ U604	5.2c (Non-Profit), 3/21/83, Memphis, TN, size 6 3/4,			
	wmk 47, 48A or 49 ....1.00		1.25	
☐	size 6 3/4, window, wmk 49 ....2.00		3.00	
☐	size 10, wmk47 ....1.00		1.50	
☐	size 10, window, wmk 47 ....2.00		3.00	
☐ U605	20c Paralyzed Veterans, 8/3/83, Portland, OR,			
	size 6 3/4 ....1.00		1.25	6.00
☐	size 10 ....1.00		1.50	

1984

☐ U606	20c Small Business, 5/7/84, DC, (77,665) size 6 3/4 ....1.00		1.25	8.00
☐	size 10 ....1.00		1.50	

1985

☐ U607	(22c) "D" & Eagle, 2/1/85, Los Angeles, size 6 3/4, wmk 47,			
	48A or 49 ....1.00		1.25	
☐	size 6 3/4, window, wmk 47, 48A or 49 ....2.00		3.00	
☐	size 10, wmk 47, 48A or 49 ....1.00		1.50	
☐	size 10, window, wmk 47 ....2.00		3.00	
☐ U608	22c Bison, 2/25/85, Bison, SD, (105,271)			
	size 6 3/4, wmk 47, 48A or 49 ....1.00		1.25	
☐	size 6 3/4, window, wmk 47, 48A or 49 ....2.00		3.00	
☐	size 10, wmk 47, 48A or 49 ....1.00		1.50	
☐	size 10, window, wmk 48A or 49 ....2.00		3.00	
☐	DC, 11/4/86 (First Day sold) Precancelled, size 10			
	window, unwmk. 20.00		—	
☐ U609	6c U.S.S. Constitution, 5/3/85, Boston, MA, (170,425)			
	size 6 3/4, wmk 47, 48A or 49 ....1.00		1.25	8.00
☐	size 10, wmk 47, 48A or 49 ....1.00		1.50	
☐	size 6 3/4, window 2.00		3.00	
☐	size 10, window 2.00		3.00	

1986

☐ U610	8.5c The Mayflower, 12/4/86, Plymouth, MA (105,164),			
☐	size 6 3/4, wmk 48A, 49 or 50 ....1.00		1.25	
☐	size 6 3/4 with window, wmk 48A, 49 or 50 ....2.00		3.00	
☐	size 10, wmk 48A,49 or 50 ....1.00		1.50	
☐	size 10 with window, wmk 48A, 49 or 50 ....2.00		3.00	

1988

☐ U611	25c Stars, 3/26/88, Star, MS, (29,393) size 6 3/4 ....1.25		1.25	
☐	size 6 3/4, window 2.00		3.00	
☐	size 10 ....1.00		1.50	
☐	size 10 window 2.00		3.00	
☐	size 10 double window, wmk 50, (25,171),, 8/18/88,.1.25		1.50	
☐ U612	8.4c Sea Gulls & U.S. Frigate Constellation, 4/12/88,			
	Baltimore, MD, size 6 3/4 (41,420) 1.00		1.25	
☐	size 10 ....1.00		1.50	
☐	size 6 3/4, window 2.00		3.00	
☐	size 10, window 2.00		3.00	
☐ U613	25c Snowflake, 9/8/88, Snowflake, AZ, (32,601) wmk 50 1.25		2.00	

1989

☐ U614   **25c Stars in "perforated" square**, 3/10/89 Cleveland,
OH, (33,461) size 9, wmk 50......................................1.25   2.00   8.00

☐ U615   **25c Stars in circle**, 7/10/89, DC, size 9, unwmk 1.25   2.00
    FDOI cancellation at Washington, D.C., 12/29/89

☐   size 9 left window 3.00   7.50

☐   size 9 right window..3.00   7.50

☐ U616   **25c Love**, 9/22/89, McLean, VA (69,498), size 9, unwmk..1.25   1.50   6.00

☐ U617   **25c Space Station**, hologram, 12/3/89, DC, (131,245)

    size 9, unwmk...1.25   1.50   10.00

1990

☐ U618   **25c Football**, hologram, 9/9/90, Green Bay, WI
(54,589), size 10, unwmk...1.25   1.50

1991

☐ U619   **29c Star**, 1/24/91, DC, (33,025) size 6 3/4,
wmk 48A, 49 or 50 ....1.25   1.50

☐   size 6 3/4 window, wmk 48A, 49 or 50....................2.00   3.00

☐   size 10, wmk 48A, 49 or 50..................................1.25   1.50

☐   size 10 window, wmk 48A, 49 or 50 ....2.00   3.00

☐ U620   **11.1c Birds**, 5/3/91, Boxborough, MA, (20,720)

    size 6 3/4, wmk 48A, 49 or 50................................1.25   1.50   10.00

☐   size 6 3/4 window, wmk 48A, 49 or 50....................2.00   3.00

☐   size 10, wmk 48A, 49 or 50..................................1.25   1.50

☐   size 10 window, wmk 48A, 49 or 50 ....2.00   3.00

☐ U621   **29c Love**, 5/9/91, Honolulu, HI, (40,110)

    size 6 3/4, unwmk.......................................1.25   1.50

☐   size 10, unwmk..1.25   1.50

    exists on recycled paper, issued 5/1/1992, Kansas City, MO

☐ U622   **29c Magazine Industry**, 10/7/91, Naples, FL,

    size 10, unwmk..1.25   1.50   6.00

☐ U623   **29c Star**, 7/20/91, DC, (16,038), size 9 regular 1.25   1.50

☐   size 9 left window 2.00   3.00

☐   size 9 right window..5.00   10.00

☐ U624   **29c Geese**, 11/8/91, Virginia Beach, VA, (21,031)

    size 6 3/4, wmk 49 or 50 ....1.25   1.50

☐   1/21/92, size 10, wmk 49 or 50 (37,424)..................1.25   1.50

1992

☐ U625   **29c Space Station**, 1/21/92, Virginia Beach, VA, (37,646)

    size 10, unwmk..1.25   1.50

☐ U626   **29c Western Americana**, 4/10/92, Dodge City, KS, (34,268)

    size 10, unwmk..1.25   1.50

☐ U627   **29c Environment**, 4/22/92, Chicago, IL, (29,432) size 10,

    unwmk 1.25   1.50   22.00

☐ U628   **19.8c Bulk Rate Star**, 5/19/92, Las Vegas, NV,

    size 10, unwmk..1.25   1.50

☐ U629   **29c Disabled Americans**, 7/22/92, DC, (28,218)

    size 6 3/4, unwmk.......................................1.25   1.50

☐   size 10, unwmk..1.25   1.50   6.00

SCOTT NUMBER	DESCRIPTION	UNCACH	CACH	CERM PROG

1993-96

		UNCACH	CACH	CERM PROG
☐ U630	29c Kitten, 10/2/93, King of Prussia, PA, (49,406)			14.00
	size 10, unwmk	1.25	1.50	
☐ U631	29c Football, 9/17/94, Canton, OH, (44,711)			
☐	size 10, unwmk	1.25	1.50	
☐ U632	32c Liberty Bell, 1/3/95, Williamsburg, VA	1.00	1.25	
☐	size 6 3/4	1.25	1.50	
☐	size 6 3/4, window	2.00	3.00	
☐	size 10	1.25	1.50	
☐	size 10, window	2.00	3.00	
☐ U633	(32c) Old Glory, 12/13/94 size 6 3/4, 6 3/4 window, Cancel, released 1/12/95	1.00	1.25	
☐ U634	(32c) Old Glory 12/13/94, size 10, 10 window cancel, released 1/12/95	1.00	1.25	
☐ U635	(5c) Sheep, 3/10/95, State College, PA, size 6 3/4	1.00	1.25	
☐	size 6 3/4, window	1.00	1.25	
☐	size 10	1.00	1.25	
☐	size 10, window	1.00	1.25	
☐ U636	(10c) Eagle, 3/10/95, State College, PA, size 10	1.25	1.50	
☐ U637	32c Spiral Heart, 5/12/95, Lakeville, PA	1.25	1.50	
☐	size 10	1.25	1.50	
☐ U638	32c Liberty Bell, Security Size 9, 5/15/95, DC	1.00	1.25	
☐ U639	32c Space Hologram,(Legal size only) 9/22/95, Milwaukee, WI	1.25	1.50	
☐ U640	32c Environment, 4/20/96, Chicago, IL	1.25	1.50	8.00
☐ U641	32c Paralympics, 5/2/96, DC	1.25	1.50	10.00

UC1-7

UC14, UC18, UC26

UC16

UC25

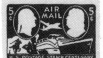

UC17

UC32

UC33-34

UC36

UC35

UC37

UC38-39

UC42

UC40-45

UC43

UC44-44a

AIR POST ENVELOPES & AIR LETTER SHEETS

1929

☐☐	UC1	5c Blue, 1/12/29, DC, size 13, wmk 28 ....35.00	—		
☐☐		2/1/29, DC, size 5, wmk 28 ....55.00	—		
☐☐		Size 8, wmk 28..................75.00	—		

1934

☐☐	UC3	6c Orange, 7/1/34, DC, size 8, wmk 33 ....25.00	100.00
☐☐		Size 13, wmk 33..................15.00	75.00

1932

☐☐	UC7	8c Olive green, 9/26/32, DC, size 8, wmk 30a..........35.00	—
☐☐		Size 13, wmk 30a..................20.00	—

1946

☐	UC10	5c on 6c Orange, 10/1/46, Aiea Heights, HI, size 13, die 2a, wmk 41** 100.00	—
☐	UC11	5c on 6c Orange, 10/1/46, Aiea Heights, HI, size 13, die 2b, wmk 41** 150.00	—
☐	UC12	5c on 6c Orange, 10/1/46, Aiea Heights, HI, APO & New York, NY, size 13, die 2c, wmk 41** 75.00	—
☐	UC13	5c on 6c Orange, 10/1/46, Aiea Heights, HI, size 13, die 3, wmk 41** 75.00	—
☐	UC14	5c Skymaster, 9/25/46, DC, size 13, wmk 41..............1.50	2.50

1947

☐☐	UC16	10c Skymaster Letter Sheet, 4/29/47, DC (162,802) ...3.00	5.00
☐☐	UC17	5c Stamp Cent. - Type I, 5/21/47, New York, NY size 13, wmk 41 ....1.25	2.50
☐	UC17a	5c Stamp Cent. - Type II, 5/21/47, New York, NY (421,232) size 13, wmk 41 ....1.25	2.50

Total for Scott UC17 and UC17a is 306,660.

1950

☐	UCl8	6c Skymaster, 9/22/50, Phila. PA (74,006), size 13, wmk 43 ....1.00	1.50	40.00

1952

☐	UC22	6c on 5c Carmine (UC15), die 2, 8/29/52, Norfolk, VA,** size 13, wmk 41 ....20.00	30.00

1956

☐	UC25	6c FIPEX, 5/2/56, New York, NY (363,239), size 13, wmk 45, with short clouds..................1.00	1.50
☐		Size 13, wmk 45, with long clouds 1.00	1.50

1958

☐	UC26	7c Skymaster, 7/31/58, Dayton, OH (143,428), size 6 3/4, wink 46, straight left wing..................1.00	1.00
☐☐		Size 6 3/4, wmk 46, crooked left wing..................1.00	3.00
☐☐		Size 8, wmk 46**..................35.00	—

SCOTT NUMBER	DESCRIPTION	UNCACH	CACH	CERM PROG
☐☐ UC32a	10c Jet Airliner letter sheet, Type I, 9/12/58, St. Louis, MO (92,400) 1.25		2.00	
☐☐ UC33	7c Blue, 11/21/58, New York, NY (208,980), size 6 3/4, wmk 46 ....1.00		1.25	35.00

1960

| ☐☐ UC34 | 7c Jet, carmine, 8/18/60, Portland, OR (196,851), size 6 3/4, wmk 46 ....1.00 | | 1.25 | 30.00 |

1961

| ☐☐ UC35 | 11c Jet Airliner letter sheet, 6/16/61, Johnstown, PA (163,460) (2 types)* ....1.00 | | 1.75 | 35.00* |

1962

| ☐☐ UC36 | 8c Jet, 11/17/62, Chantilly, VA (194,810), size 6 3/4, wmk 47 ....1.00 | | 1.25 | |

1965-67

☐☐ UC37	8c Jet Triangle, 1/7/65, Chicago, IL (226, 178) size 6 3/4, wmk 49 (2 types)* 1.00		1.25	25.00*
☐☐	1/8/65, DC, size 10, wmk 49** 10.00		20.00	
☐☐ UC37a	Jet Triangle, tagged, 8/15/67, Dayton, OH & DC, size 6 3/4, wmk 48** 3.50		5.00	
☐☐	Size 10, wmk 49** 3.50		5.00	

1965

| ☐☐ UC38 | 11c Kennedy letter sheet, 5/29/65, Boston, MA (337,422) .... 1.00 | | 1.75 | 15.00 |

1967

☐☐ UC39	13c Kennedy letter sheet, 5/29/67, Chicago, IL (211,387) 1.00		1.75	20.00
☐☐	5/29/67, Boston, MA** 5.00		7.50	
	Only exists with a normal cancel			
☐☐	5/29/67, Brookline, MA with # 1246 ....5.00		7.50	

1968

☐☐ UC40	10c Jet Triangle, 1/8/68, Chicago, IL (157,553), size 6 3/4, wmk 48 ....1.00		1.25	15.00
☐☐	1/9/68, DC, size 10, wmk 49** 4.50		7.50	
☐☐ UC41	8c + 2c Jet Triangle, 2/5/68, DC, size 6 3/4, wmk 49** 5.00		7.50	
	size 10, wmk 49** 5.00		7.50	
☐☐ UC42	13c Human Rights letter sheet, 12/3/68, DC (145,898) 1.25		2.50	18.00

1971

☐☐ UC43	11c Jet, 5/6/71, Williamsburg, PA (187,000), size 6 3/4, wmk 49 ....1.00		1.25	
☐☐	Size 10, wmk 49** 10.00		—	
☐☐ UC44	15c Birds letter sheet, 5/28/71, Chicago, IL (130,669) 1.00		1.25	18.00
☐☐ UC44a	15c Birds letter sheet, "Aerogramme" added, 12/13/71, Philadelphia, PA 1.00		1.25	
☐☐ UC45	10c + 1c Jet Triangle, 6/28/71, DC, size 6 3/4 wmk 47, 48A, or 49** 4.00		7.50	
☐☐	Size 10, wmk 49** 4.00		15.00	

1973

☐☐ UC46	15c Ballooning letter sheet, 2/10/73, Albuquerque, NM (210,000)	1.00	1.25	15.00
☐☐ UC47	13c Bird in Flight, 12/1/73, Memphis, TN (132,658) size 6 3/4, wmk 47	1.00	1.25	15.00
☐☐	12/28/73, size 10, earliest known use	15.00	—	

1974

☐☐ UC48	18c "USA" letter sheet, 1/4/74, Atlanta, GA (119,615)	1.00	1.25	
☐☐ UC49	18c NATO letter sheet, 4/4/74, DC	1.00	1.25	

1976

☐☐ UC50	22c "USA" letter sheet, 1/16/76, Tempe, AZ (118,303)	1.00	1.25	10.00

1978

☐☐ UC51	22c "USA" letter sheet, 11/3/78, St. Petersburg, FL (86,099)	1.00	1.25	10.00

1979

☐☐ UC52	22c Olympics letter sheet, 12/5/79, Bay Shore, NY (129,221)	1.00	1.25	

1980

☐☐ UC53	30c "USA" letter sheet, 12/29/80, San Francisco, CA	1.25	1.50	15.00

1981

☐☐ UC54	30c "USA" letter sheet, 9/21/81, Honolulu, HI	1.25	1.50	18.00

1982

☐☐ UC55	30c "USA" & Globe letter sheet, 9/16/82, Seattle, WA (209,210)	1.25	1.50	14.00

1983

☐☐ UC56	30c World Communications letter sheet, 1/7/83, Anaheim, CA	1.25	1.50	14.00
☐☐ UC57	30c Olympics letter sheet, 10/14/83, Los Angeles, CA	1.25	1.50	12.00

1985

☐☐ UC58	36c Landsat letter sheet, 2/14/85, Goddard Flight Center, MD (84,367)	1.25	1.50	8.00
☐☐ UC59	36c Urban Skyline letter sheet, 5/21/85, DC (94,388)	1.25	1.50	
☐☐ UC60	36c Comet Tail letter sheet, 12/4/85, Hannibal, MO (83,125)	1.25	1.50	10.00

1988

☐☐ UC61	39c Envelope letter sheet, 5/9/88, Miami, FL (27,446)	1.25	1.50	

1989

☐☐ UC62	39c Montgomery Blair letter sheet, 11/20/89, DC (48,529) (2 types)*	1.25	1.50	10.00*

1991

☐☐ UC63	45c Eagle letter sheet, 5/17/91, Denver, CO, blue or white paper	1.50	2.00	

UC46

UC47

UC48

UC49

UC52

UC53-54

UC58

UC59

UC50

1995

☐☐ UC64 50c Ballooning letter sheet, 9/23/95, Tampa, FL 1.50   2.00

OFFICIAL MAIL
1983

☐☐ U073 20c Eagle, 1/12/83, DC, size 10, wmk 47 ....1.25   1.50
☐☐   Size 10, window, wmk 47 ....2.00   3.00

1985

☐☐ U074 22c Eagle, 2/26/85, DC, (79,788)
       size 10, wmk 47, 48A or 49 ....1.25   1.50
☐☐   Size 10, window, wmk 47, 48A or 49 ....2.00   3.00

1987

☐☐ U075 22c Eagle, 3/2/87, DC, (34,799) savings bond size 2.00   3.00

1988

☐☐ U076 (25c)"E" Eagle, 3/22/88, DC, savings bond size...........1.25   1.50
☐☐ U077 25c Eagle, 4/11/88, DC, size 10, wmk 48A, 49 or 50...1.25   1.50
☐☐   Window, wmk 48A, 49 or 50 ....2.00   3.00
☐☐ U078 25c Savings Bond, 4/11/88, DC,
       savings bond size, plain back flap 1.25   1.50
☐☐ U078 25c Savings Bond, Washington, DC, 11/28/88,
       with printing on back flap (Legend 1) 1.50   1.75
       Total for Scott U077 and U078 was 12,017.

1990

☐☐ U079 45c Eagle, 3/17/90, Springfield, VA (5,956),
       passport size, Cerm. includes U080...........................1.50   2.00   6.00
☐☐ U080 65c Eagle, 3/17/90, Springfield, VA (6,922),
       passport size 1.75   2.25
☐☐ U081 45c Eagle, self-sealing, 8/10/90, DC (7,160),
       passport size 1.50   2.00
☐☐ U082 65c Eagle, self-sealing, 8/10/90, DC (6,759),
       passport size 1.75   2.25

1991

☐☐ U083 (29c) "F" Savings Bond, 1/22/91, (30,549)
       savings bond size, printing on backflap (Legend 2)...1.25   1.50
☐☐ U084 29c Eagle, 4/6/91, (27,841)
       size 10, wmk 48A, 49 or 50 ....1.25   1.50
☐☐   Size 10, window, wmk 48A, 49, or 50 ....2.00   3.00
☐☐ U085 29c Eagle, 4/17/91, savings bond size, wmk 51 ....1.25   1.50

1992

☐☐ U086 52c Consular Service, DC, 7/10/92, (25,563) passport size,
       logo on back at left, unwmk, heavy weight paper.....1.75   2.25
☐☐   3/2/94, passport size, logo on back at right, unwmk.6.00   7.50
☐☐ U087 75c Consular Service, 7/10/92, passport size, logo on
       back at left, unwmk, heavy weight paper..................2.00   2.50
☐☐   3/2/94, passport size, logo on back at right, unwmk.6.00   7.50

1995

☐☐	UO88	32c Eagle, 5/9/95, DC, size 10 ....1.25	2.00	
☐☐		size 10, window 2.00	3.00	

POSTAL CARDS
1873

☐☐	UX1	1c Liberty, 5/13/1873, Boston, New York or DC.........2250.

1875

☐☐	UX5	1c Liberty, unwmk, 9/30/1875 ....1200.

1910

☐☐	UX21	1c William McKinley, 2/13/10, any city....................250.00

1926

☐☐	UX37	3c William McKinley, 2/1/26, DC 200.00	—

1951

☐☐	UX38	2c Benjamin Franklin, 11/16/51, New York, NY	
		(170,000) 1.25	2.50

1952

☐☐	UX39	2c on 1c Thomas Jefferson (UX27), 1/1/52, DC.........12.50	25.00
☐☐	UX40	2c on 1c Abraham Lincoln, (UX28), 3/22/52, DC.......35.00	—
		Scott UX40 went on sale at the Philatelic Agency	
		3/22/52 and some were canceled that day. It is	
		believed that the 1/1/52 cancels are not legitimate.	
☐☐	UX43	2c Abraham Lincoln, 7/31/52, DC (125,400)................1.00	1.75

1956

☐☐	UX44	2c FIPEX, 5/4/56, New York, NY (537,474) 1.00	1.25	
☐☐	UX45	4c Statue of Liberty, 11/16/56, New York.(129,841) ...1.00	1.25	
☐☐	UX45 & UY16	4c Statue of Liberty and 4c Statue of Liberty		
		paid reply postal card (2 types)*...		60.00*

1958

☐☐	UX46	3c Statue of Liberty, 8/1/58, Philadelphia, PA		
		(180,610)...1.00	1.25	
☐☐	UX46a	Statue of Liberty "N God We Trust", 8/1/58,		
		Philadelphia, PA..175.00	250.00	

1961

☐☐	UX46c	Statue of Liberty, precanceled, 9/15/61,		
		Philadelphia, PA..50.00	—	

1962-66

☐☐	UX48	4c Abraham Lincoln, 11/19/62, Springfield, IL		
		(162,939)..1.00	1.00	
☐☐	UX48a	Abraham Lincoln, tagged, 6/25/66, Bellevue, OH **..25.00	30.00	
☐☐		7/6/66, DC**...1.50	2.50	
☐☐		Toledo, OH**...7.50	12.50	
☐☐		Overlook, OH**...4.50	7.50	
☐☐		Columbus, OH**...7.50	12.50	
☐☐		Bellevue, OH**...15.00	25.00	

SCOTT NUMBER	DESCRIPTION	UNCACH	CACH	CERM PROG
☐☐	Cleveland, OH**	6.00	10.00	
☐☐	Cincinnati, OH**	4.50	7.50	
☐☐	Dayton, OH**	3.50	6.00	
☐☐	Indianapolis, IN**	7.50	2.50	
☐☐	Louisville, KY**	7.50	12.50	

1963

☐☐	UX49	7c Map, 8/30/63, New York, NY	1.00	1.25	18.00

1964

☐☐	UX50	4c Flags, Map & "Customs," 2/22/64, DC (313,275)	1.00	1.25	20.00
☐☐	UX51	4c Social Security, 9/26/64, DC (293,650)	1.00	1.25	20.00
☐☐		with official government printed cachet	—	12.00	
☐☐		with blue hand cancel & government cachet	—	20.00	

1965

☐☐	UX52	4c Coast Guard Flag, 8/4/65, Newburyport, MA (338,225)	1.00	1.25	20.00
☐☐	UX53	4c Census Bureau, 10/21/65, Philadelphia, PA (272,383)	1.00	1.25	30.00

1967

☐☐	UX54	8c Map, 12/4/67, DC	1.00	1.25	15.00

1968

☐☐	UX55	5c Abraham Lincoln, 1/4/68, Hodgenville, KY	1.00	1.25	20.00
☐☐	UX56	5c Women Marines, 7/26/68, San Francisco, CA (203,714)	1.00	1.25	20.00

1970

☐☐	UX57	5c Weather Vane, 9/1/70, Ft. Myer, VA (285,800)	1.00	1.25	15.00

1971

☐☐	UX58	6c Paul Revere, 5/15/71, Boston, MA	1.00	1.25	12.00
☐☐	UX59	10c Map, 6/10/71, New York, NY	1.00	1.25	
☐☐		cerm. prog. includes UXC11			15.00
		Total for Scott UX59 and UXC11 is 297,000.			
☐☐	UX60	6c America's Hospitals, 9/16/71, New York, NY (218,200)	1.00	1.25	22.00

1972

☐☐	UX61	6c U.S. Frigate Constellation, 6/29/72, any city	1.25	1.50	
☐☐	UX62	6c Monument Valley, 6/29/72, any city	1.25	1.50	
☐☐	UX63	6c Gloucester, MA 6/29/72, any city	1.25	1.50	
☐☐	UX64	6e John Hanson, 9/1/72, Baltimore, MD (156,000)	1.00	1.25	12.00

1973

☐☐	UX65	6c Centenary of Postal Card, 9/1/73, DC(276,717)	1.00	1.25	20.00
☐☐	UX66	8c Samuel Adams, 12/16/73, Boston, MA (147,522)	1.00	1.25	12.00
☐☐	UX67	12c Ship's Figurehead, 1/4/74, Miami, FL (138,500)	1.00	1.25	
☐☐		cerm. prog. includes UXC15			15.00

UX1, UX3,
UX65

UX21

UX37

UX38

UX43

UX44

UX45, UY16

UX46, UY17

UX48

UX49, UX54,
UY19, UY20

UX50

UX51

UX52

UX53

UX56

UX58, UY22

UX62

UX63

UX67

HOW TO USE THIS BOOK
The number in the first column is its Scott number or
identifying number. Following that is the denomination
of the stamp, description, date of issue, and the value.

1975

☐☐ UX68 7c Charles Thomson, 9/14/75, Bryn Mawr, PA 1.00 1.25   10.00
      Total for Scott UX68 and UY25 is 321,910.
☐☐ UX69 9c John Witherspoon, 11/10/75, Princeton, NJ................1.00 1.25   10.00
      Total for Scott UX69 and UY26 is 254,239.

1976

☐☐ UX70 9c Caesar Rodney, 7/1/76, Dover, DE.............................1.00 1.25   10.00
      Total for Scott UX70 and UY27 is 307,061.

1977

☐☐ UX71 9c Federal Court House, 7/20/77, Galveston, TX
      (245,535)...1.00 1.25   20.00
☐☐ UX72 9c Nathan Hale, 10/14/77, Coventry, CT 1.00 1.25   10.00
      Total for Scott UX72 and UY28 is 304,592.

1978

☐☐ UX73 10c Cincinnati Music Hall, 5/12/78, Cincinnati, OH
      (300,000)...1.00 1.25   15.00
☐☐ UX74 (10c) John Hancock, 5/19/78, Quincy, MA 1.00 1.25   12.00
☐☐ UX75 10c John Hancock, 6/20/78, Quincy, MA 1.00 1.25
☐☐ UX76 14c U.S. Coast Guard Eagle, 8/4/78, Seattle,WA (196,400)1.00 1.25   10.00
☐☐ UX77 10c Molly Pitcher, 9/8/78, Freehold, NJ (180,280) 1.00 1.25   12.00

1979

☐☐ UX78 10c George Rogers Clark, 2/23/79, Vincennes, IN
      (260,110)...1.00 1.25   12.00
☐☐ UX79 10c Casimir Pulaski, 10/11/79, Savannah, GA (210,000) 1.00 1.25   18.00
☐☐ UX80 10c Olympic Games, 9/17/79, Eugene, OR 1.00 1.25   12.00
☐☐ UX81 10c Iolani Palace, 10/1/79, Honolulu, HI (242,804) 1.00 1.25   20.00

1980

☐☐ UX82 14c Winter Olympic Games, 1/15/80, Atlanta, GA
      (160,977)...1.00 1.25   15.00
☐☐ UX83 10c Salt Lake Temple, 4/5/80, Salt Lake City, UT
      (325,260)...1.00 1.25   15.00
☐☐ UX84 10c Landing of Rochambeau, 7/11/80, Newport, RI
      (180,567)...1.00 1.25   18.00
☐☐ UX85 10c Battle of Kings Mountain, 10/7/80, Kings Mountain,
      NC (136,130) 1.00 1.25   14.00
☐☐ UX86 19c Golden Hinde, 11/21/80, San Rafael, CA (290,547)...1.00 1.25   15.00

1981

☐☐ UX87 10c Battle of Cowpens, 1/17/81, Cowpens, SC (160,000).1.00 1.25   18.00
☐☐ UX88 (12c) Eagle, 3/15/81, Memphis, TN 1.00 1.25
☐☐ UX89 12c Isaiah Thomas, 5/5/81, Worcester, MA 1.00 1.25   8.00
☐☐ UX90 12c Nathaniel Greene, 9/8/81, Eutaw Springs, SC
      (115,755)...1.00 1.25   14.00
☐☐ UX91 12c Lewis & Clark Expedition, 9/23/81, St. Louis, MO....1.00 1.25   10.00
☐☐ UX92 (13c) Robert Morris, 10/11/81, Memphis, TN 1.00 1.25
☐☐ UX93 13c Robert Morris, 11/10/81, Philadelphia, PA...............1.00 1.25   10.00

HISTORIC PRESERVATION USA 10c
UX73

US Coast Guard Eagle USA 14c
UX76

USA 10c
Casimir Pulaski, Savannah, 1779
UX79

USA 12c
Lewis and Clark Expedition, 1806
UX91

USA 14c
Olympics 1980
UX82

USA 19c
Drake's Golden Hinde 1580
UX86

US
Domestic Rate
UX88, UY31

HOW TO USE THIS BOOK

The number in the first column is its Scott number or
identifying number. Following that is the denomination
of the stamp, description, date of issue, and the value.

1982

☐☐ UX94	13c Francis Marion, 4/3/82, Marion, SC (141,162)......1.00		1.25	12.00
☐☐ UX95	13c LaSalle Claims Louisiana, 4/7/82,			
	New Orleans, LA (157,691)................................1.00		1.25	10.00
☐☐ UX96	13c Philadelphia Academy of Music, 6/18/82,			
	Philadelphia, PA (193,089)...........................1.00		1.25	10.00
☐☐ UX97	13c Old Post Office, 10/14/82, St. Louis, MO 1.00		1.25	12.00

1983

☐☐ UX98	13c Oglethorpe, 2/12/83, Savannah, GA (165,750)......1.00		1.25	12.00
☐☐ UX99	13c Old Post Office, 4/19/83, DC (125,056)(2 types)*...1.00		1.25	8.00*
☐☐ UX100	13c Olympics (Yachting), 8/5/83,			
	Long Beach, CA (132,232) 1.00		1.25	10.00

1984

☐☐ UX101	13c The Ark and the Dove, 3/25/84,			
	St. Clement's Island, MD 1.00		1.25	8.00
☐☐ UX102	13c Olympics (Torch), 4/30/84, Los Angeles, CA 1.00		1.25	10.00
☐☐ UX103	13c Frederic Baraga, 6/29/84, Marquette, MI (100,156)1.00		1.25	8.00
☐☐ UX104	13c Historic Preservation, 9/16/84, Compton, CA 1.00		1.25	6.00

1985

☐☐ UX105	(14c) Charles Carroll, 2/1/85, New Carrollton, MD.....1.00		1.25	
☐☐ UX106	14c Charles Carroll, 3/6/85, Annapolis, MD.................1.00		1.25	6.00
☐☐ UX107	25c Clipper Flying Cloud, 2/27/85, Salem, MA (95,559)1.25		1.50	6.00
☐☐ UX108	14c George Wythe, 6/20/85, Williamsburg, VA 1.00		1.25	6.00

1986

☐☐ UX109	14c Settling of Connecticut, 4/18/86,			
	Hartford, CT (76,875)................................1.00		1.25	6.00
☐☐ UX110	14c Stamps, 5/23/86, Chicago, IL (75,548)..................1.00		1.25	8.00
☐☐ UX111	14c Francis Vigo, 5/24/86, Vincennes, IN (100,141) 1.00		1.25	6.00
☐☐ UX112	14c Settling of Rhode Island, 6/26/86,			
	Providence, RI (54,559)..............................1.00		1.25	6.00
☐☐ UX113	14c Wisconsin Territory, 7/3/86,			
	Mineral Point, WI (41,224)..........................1.00		1.25	6.00
☐☐ UX114	14c National Guard Heritage, 12/12/86, Boston, MA			
	(72,316)..................................1.00		1.25	6.00

1987

☐☐ UX115	14c Self-Scouring Steel Plow, 5/22/87, Moline, IL			
	(160,099)................................1.00		1.25	8.00
☐☐ UX116	14c Constitutional Convention, 5/25/87,			
	Philadelphia, PA (138,207)..........................1.00		1.25	6.00
☐☐ UX117	14c Flag, 6/14/87, Baltimore, MD...........................1.00		1.25	6.00
☐☐ UX118	14c Take Pride in America, 9/22/87, Jackson, WY			
	(47,281)..................................1.00		1.25	8.00
☐☐ UX119	14c Timberline Lodge, 9/28/87, Timberline Lodge, OR			
	(63,595)..................................1.00		1.25	8.00

1988

☐☐ UX120	15c Bison and Prairie, 3/28/88, Buffalo, WY (52,075).1.00		1.25	
☐☐ UX121	15c Blair House, 5/4/88, DC (52,188)..........................1.00		1.25	10.00
☐☐ UXI22	28c Yorkshire, Square-rigged Packet, 6/29/88,			
	Mystic, CT (46,505) 1.25		1.50	12.00

"Swamp Fox" Francis Marion, 1782
UX94

UX95, UY21

UX96

UX97

UX107

HOW TO USE THIS BOOK

The number in the first column is its Scott number or identifying number. Following that is the denomination of the stamp, description, date of issue, and the value.

		UNCACH	CACH	CERM PROG
☐☐	UX123 15c **Iowa Territory**, 7/2/88, Burlington, IA (45,565) 1.00		1.25	12.00
☐☐	UX124 15c **Settling of Ohio**, Northwest Territory, 7/15/88,			
	Marietta, OH (28,778) 1.00		1.25	12.00
☐☐	UX125 15c **Hearst Castle**, 9/20/88, San Simeon, CA (84,786) .1.00		1.25	10.00
☐☐	UX126 15c **The Federalist Papers**, 10/27/88, New York, NY			
	(37,661) 1.00		1.25	10.00

1989

		UNCACH	CACH	CERM PROG
☐☐	UX127 15c **Red-tailed Hawk** Sonora Desert, 1/13/89,			
	Tucson, AZ (51,891) 1.00		1.25	6.00
☐☐	UX128 15c **Healy Hall**, Georgetown University, 1/23/89, DC			
	(54,897) 1.00		1.25	6.00
☐☐	UX129 15c **Great Blue Heron**, Marsh, 3/17/89, Okefenokee, GA			
	(58,208) 1.00		1.25	6.00
☐☐	UX130 15c **Settling of Oklahoma**, 4/22/89, Guthrie, OK			
	(68,689) 1.00		1.25	
☐☐	UX131 15c **Canada Geese and Mountains**, 5/5/89, Denver, CO			
	(59,303) 1.00		1.25	6.00
☐☐	UX132 15c **Seashore**, 6/17/89, Cape Hatteras, NC (67,073) 1.00		1.25	6.00
☐☐	UX133 15c **Deer Beside Woodland Waterfall**, 8/26/89,			
	Cherokee, NC (67,878) 1.00		1.25	6.00
☐☐	UX134 15c **Hull House**, 9/18/89, Chicago, IL (53,773)................1.00		1.25	6.00
☐☐	UX135 15c **Independence Hall**, 9/25/89, Philadelphia, PA			
	(61,659) 1.00		1.25	
☐☐	UX136 15c **Inner Harbor Baltimore**, 10/7/89, Baltimore, MD			
	(58,746) 1.00		1.25	
☐☐	UX137 15c **59th Street Bridge**, 11/8/89, New York, NY (48,044)..1.00		1.25	
☐☐	UX138 15c **Capitol**, 11/26/89, DC (47,146).............................1.00		1.25	10.00
☐☐	UX139 15c **Independence Hall** 12/1/89, DC 2.00		3.00	12.00
☐☐	UX140 15c **Inner Harbor Baltimore**, 12/1/89, DC 2.00		3.00	
☐☐	UX141 15c **59th Street Bridge**, 12/1/89, DC............................2.00		3.00	
☐☐	UX142 15c **Capitol**, 12/1/89, DC...2.00		3.00	
	Scott UX135-UX138 have inscription and copyright symbol at lower left. Scott UX139- UX142 do not and are rouletted on 2 or 3 sides. `			
☐☐	UX143 15c **White House**, 11/30/89, DC (52,090) 1.25		1.50	10.00
☐☐	UX144 15c **Jefferson Memorial**, 12/2/89, DC (59,568) 1.25		1.50	10.00

1990

		UNCACH	CACH	CERM PROG
☐☐	UX145 15c **Rittenhouse Paper Mill**, 3/13/90, New York, NY			
	(9,866) (2 types)*..1.00		1.25	18.00*
☐☐	UX146 15c **World Literacy Year**, 3/22/90, DC (11,163) 1.00		1.25	6.00
☐☐	UX147 15c **Fur Traders Descending the Missouri**, 5/4/90,			
	St. Louis, MO (13,632)...1.25		1.50	6.00
☐☐	UX148 15c **Isaac Royall House**, 6/16/90, Medford, MA (21,708)..1.00		1.25	6.00
☐☐	UX150 15c **Quadrangle**, Stanford University, 9/30/90,			
	Stanford, CA (28,430)..1.00		1.25	6.00
☐☐	UX151 15c **Constitution Hall**, 10/11/90, DC (33,254) 1.25		1.50	6.00
☐☐	UX152 15c **Chicago Orchestra Hall**, 10/19/90, Chicago, IL			
	(28,546)..1.00		1.25	6.00

1991

		UNCACH	CACH	CERM PROG
☐☐	UX153 19c **Flag**, 1/24/91, DC (26,690) 1.00		1.25	
☐☐	UX154 19c **Carnegie Hall**, 4/1/91, New York, NY (27,063) 1.00		1.25	6.00

☐☐ UX155 19c "Old Red,"Univ. of Texas, 6/14/91,
    Galveston, TX (24,308) 1.00 1.25   6.00
☐☐ UX156 19c Bill of Rights, 9/25/91, Richmond, VA (27,457) 1.00 1.25   6.00
☐☐ UX157 19c Notre Dame, 10/15/91, Notre Dame, IN (34,325).....1.00 1.25   6.00
☐☐ UX158 30c Niagara Falls, 8/21/91, Niagara Falls, NY (29,762) .1.25 2.00
☐☐ UX159 19c Old Mill, Univ. of Vermont, 10/29/91,
    Burlington, VT (23,965) 1.00 1.25   6.00

1992

☐☐ UX160 19c Wadsworth Atheneum, 1/16/92, Hartford, CT 1.00 1.25   6.00
☐☐ UX161 19c Cobb Hall, Univ. of Chicago, 1/23/92, Chicago, IL ...1.00 1.25   6.00
☐☐ UX162 19c Waller Hall, 2/1/92, Salem, OR.................................1.00 1.25   6.00
☐☐ UX163 19c America's Cup, 5/6/92, San Diego, CA......................1.25 1.50
☐☐ UX164 19c Columbia River Gorge, 5/9/92, Stevenson, WA........1.00 1.25   6.00
☐☐ UX165 19c Great Hall, Ellis Island, 5/11/92, Ellis Island, NY....1.00 1.25   6.00

1993

☐☐ UX166 19c National Cathedral, 1/6/93, DC...............................1.00 1.25
☐☐ UX167 19c Wren Building, 2/8/93, Williamsburg, VA 1.00 1.25   6.00
☐☐ UX168 19c Holocaust Memorial, 3/23/93, DC 1.25 1.50   6.00
☐☐ UX169 19c Ft. Recovery, 6/13/93, Fort Recovery, OH 1.00 1.25   6.00
☐☐ UX170 19c Playmaker's Theater, 9/14/93, Chapel Hill, NC 1.00 1.25   6.00
☐☐ UX171 19c O'Kane Hall, 9/17/93, Worcester, MA.......................1.00 1.25
☐☐ UX172 19c Beecher Hall, 10/9/93, Chicago, IL...........................1.00 1.25   6.00
☐☐ UX173 19c Massachusetts Hall, 10/14/93, Brunswick, ME........1.00 1.25   6.00
☐☐ UX174 19c Lincoln Home, 2/12/94, Springfield, IL....................1.00 1.25   6.00

1994-96

☐☐ UX175 19c Myers Hall (Wittenberg Univ.) , 3/11/94,
    Springfield, OH...1.00 1.25   6.00
☐☐ UX176 19c Canyon de Chelly, 8/11/94, Chinle, AZ 1.00 1.25   6.00
☐☐ UX177 19c St. Louis Union Station,9/3/94, St. Louis, MO 1.00 1.25   6.00
☐☐ UX178-UX197 19c Legends of the West (20 different), 10/18/94,
    Laramie, WY, Lawton,OK, Tuscon, AZ, set of 20 ....20.00 35.00
☐☐ UX198 20c Red Barn, 1/3/95, Williamsburg, VA........................1.00 1.25
☐☐ UX199 (20c) "G" Old Glory, 12/13/94,cancel, released 1/12/95 .1.00 1.25
☐☐ UX200-UX219 20c Civil War, 6/29/95, Gettysburg, PA
    set of 20 ....20.00 35.00
☐☐ UX220 20c Clipper Ship,9/23/95, Hunt Valley, MD 1.00 1.25
☐☐ UX221-UX240 20c Comic Strips of 20, 10/1/95, Boca Raton, FL20.00 35.00
☐☐ UX241 20c Winter Farm Scene, 2/23/96, Watertown, NY..........1.00 1.25   8.00
☐☐ UX242-UX261 20c Olympics, Set of 20, 5/2/96, DC.................20.00 35.00
☐☐ UX262 20c St. John's College, 6/1/96, Annapolis, MD (8,793) ...1.00 1.25
☐☐ UX263 20c Alexander Hall, 9/20/96, Princeton, NJ (11,621) 1.00 8.00
☐☐ UX264-UX278 20c Endangered Species, set of 15, 10/2/96,
    San Diego, CA 20.00 35.00

1997

☐☐ UX280 20c City College of New York, 5/7/97, New York, NY.....1.00 1.25   8.00
☐☐ UX281 20c Bugs Bunny, 5/22/97, Burbank, CA 1.25 1.50
☐☐ UX282 20c Golden Gate (Day), 6/2/97, San Francisco, CA.........1.00 1.25   8.00
☐☐ UX283 50c Golden Gate (Night), 6/2/97, San Francisco, CA 1.25 1.50
☐☐ UX284 20c Fort McHenry, 9/7/97, Baltimore, MD 1.00 1.25
☐☐ UX285-UX289 20c Movie Monsters, 9/30/97, any card,
    Universal City, CA 1.75 2.00

1998

☐☐ UX290 20c **University of Mississippi**, 4/20/98, University, MS ...1.00   1.25
☐☐ UX291 20c **Sylvester & Tweety**, 4/27/98, New York, NY 1.75   2.00
☐☐ UX292 20c **Girard College**, 5/1/98, Philadelphia, PA.................1.00   1.25

REPLY POSTAL CARDS
1892

☐☐ UY1   1c + 1c **U.S. Grant** 10/25/92, any city 350.00

1926

☐☐ UY12 3c + 3c **William McKinley**, 2/1/26, any city ....250.00   —

1951

☐☐ UY13 2c + 2c **George Washington**, 12/29/51, DC (49,294).......1.25   2.50

1952

☐☐ UY14 2c on 1c + 2c on 1c **George Washington**, 1/1/52,**
       any city 50.00 75.00

1956

☐☐ UY16 4c + 4c **Statue of Liberty**, 11/16/56, New York, NY
       (127,874)...1.00   1.25
☐☐ UY16a 4c + 4c **Statue of Liberty**, message card printed on
       both halves, 11/16/56, New York,NY 75.00100.00
☐☐ UY16b 4c + 4c **Statue of Liberty**, reply card printed on both
       halves, 11/16/56, New York, NY 50.00 75.00

1958

☐☐ UY17 3c + 3c **Statue of Liberty**, 7/31/58, Boise, ID (136,768)1.00   1.25

1962-67

☐☐ UY18 4c + 4c **Abraham Lincoln**, 11/19/62, Springfield, IL
       (107,746)..1.00   1.25
☐☐ UY18a **Abraham Lincoln**, tagged, 3/7/67, Dayton, OH,
       earliest known use**..50.00   —

1963

☐☐ UY19 7c + 7c **Map**, 8/30/63, New York, NY 1.00   1.25

1967

☐☐ UY20 8c + 8c **Map**, 12/4/67, DC 1.00   1.25

1968

☐☐ UY21 5c + 5c **Abraham Lincoln**, 1/4/68, Hodgenville, KY 1.00   1.25

1971

☐☐ UY22 6c + 6c **Paul Revere**, 5/15/71, Boston, MA 1.00   1.25

1972

☐☐ UY23 6c + 6c **John Hanson**, 9/1/72, Baltimore, MD
       (105,708)... 1.00   1.25

UXC1 · UXC4 · UXC5, UXC8, UXC11 · UXC9-10 · UXC6 · UXC7 · UXC14 · UXC16 · UXC18 · UXC20 · UXC22

HOW TO USE THIS BOOK

The number in the first column is its Scott number or identifying number. Following that is the denomination of the stamp, description, date of issue, and the value.

1973

☐☐ UY24 8c + 8c Samuel Adams, 12/16/73, Boston, MA
(105,369) 1.00 1.25

1975

☐☐ UY25 7c + 7c Charles Thomson, 9/14/75, Bryn Mawr, PA 1.00 1.25
☐☐ UY26 9c + 9c John Witherspoon, 11/10/75, Princeton, NJ ...1.00 1.25

1976

☐☐ UY27 9c + 9c Caesar Rodney, 7/1/76, Dover, DE................ 1.00 1.25

1977

☐☐ UY28 9c + 9c Nathan Hale, 10/14/77, Coventry, CT 1.00 1.25

1978

☐☐ UY29 (10c + 10c) John Hancock, 5/19/78, Quincy, MA 1.75 3.50
☐☐ UY30 10c + 10c John Hancock, 6/20/78, Quincy, MA............1.00 1.25

1981

☐☐ UY31 (12c + 12c) Eagle, 3/15/81, Memphis, TN 1.00 1.25
☐☐ UY32 12c + 12c Isaiah Thomas, 5/5/81, Worcester, MA........1.00 1.25
☐☐ UY32a Isaiah Thomas, Small Die 3.00 5.00
☐☐ UY33 (13c + 13c) Robert Morris, 10/11/81, Memphis, TN 1.25 1.25
☐☐ UY34 13c + 13c Robert Morris, 11/10/81, Philadelphia, PA..1.25 1.25

1985

☐☐ UY35 (14c + 14c) Charles Carroll, 2/1/85,
New Carrollton, MD 1.25 1.50
☐☐ UY36 14c + 14c Charles Carroll, 3/6/85, Annapolis, MD.......1.25 1.50
☐☐ UY37 14c + 14c George Wythe, 6/20/85, Williamsburg, VA ..1.25 1.50

1987

☐☐ UY38 14c + 14c Flag, 9/1/87, Washington, DC, (22,314) 1.25 1.50

1988

☐☐ UY39 15c + 15c Bison and Prairie, 7/11/88, Buffalo, WY
(24,338)..1.25 1.50

1991-95

☐☐ UY40 19c + 19c Flag, 3/27/91, DC (25,562) 1.25 1.50
☐☐ UY41 20c+20c Red Barn, 2/1/95, Williamsburg, PA 1.25 1.50

AIR POST POSTAL CARDS
1949

☐☐ UXC1 4c Eagle in Flight, 1/10/49, DC, (236,620) 1.00 1.50

1958

☐☐ UXC2 5c Eagle in Flight, 7/31/58, Wichita, KS (156,474)......1.00 1.25 50.00

1960

☐☐ UXC3 5c Eagle in Flight, bi-colored border, 6/18/60,
Minneapolis, MN (228,500)......................................1.00 1.75 25.00
☐☐ With thin dividing line at top 2.50 5.00

1963

☐☐ UXC4 6c Bald Eagle, 2/15/63, Maitland, FL (216,203)...........1.00 1.25 20.00

1966

☐☐ UXC5 11c Flag & "VISIT THE USA", 5/27/66, DC (272,813)
(2 types)*...1.00 1.25 20.00*

1967

☐☐ UXC6 6c Virgin Islands, 3/31/67, Charlotte Amalie, VI,
(346,906)...1.00 1.25 20.00
☐☐ UXC7 6c World Boy Scout Jamboree, 8/4/67,
Farragut State Park, ID (471,585)...........................1.00 1.25 35.00
☐☐ UXC8 13c Flag & "VISIT THE USA", 9/8/67, Detroit, MI
(178,789) (2 types)*...1.00 1.25 15.00

1968-69

☐☐ UXC9 8c Eagle, 3/1/68, New York, NY.................................1.00 1.25 15.00
☐☐ UXC9a Eagle, tagged, 3/19/69, DC*.......................................10.00 15.00

1971

☐☐ UXC10 9c Eagle, 5/15/71, Kitty Hawk, NC, (167,000 est.) 1.00 1.25
☐☐ UXC11 15c Flag & "VISIT THE USA", 6/10/71, New York, NY 1.00 1.25

1972

☐☐ UXC12 9c Grand Canyon, 6/29/72, any city 1.00 1.25
☐☐ UXC13 15c Niagara Falls, 6/29/72, any city.............................1.00 1.25
☐☐ UXC13a Niagara Falls, address side blank.......................600.00 —

1974

☐☐ UXC14 11c Stylized Eagle, 1/4/74, State College, PA,
(160,500) 1.00 1.25 10.00
☐☐ UXC15 18c Eagle Weather Vane, 1/4/74, Miami, FL (132,114)..1.00 1.25

1975

☐☐ UXC16 21c Angel Weather Vane, 12/17/75, Kitty Hawk, NC
(113,191)..1.00 1.25 15.00

1978

☐☐ UXC17 21c Curtiss Jenny, 9/16/78, San Diego, CA (174,886)..1.00 1.25 10.00

1979

☐☐ UXC18 21c Olympics (Gymnast), 12/1/79, Fort Worth, TX
(150,124)..1.25 1.50 10.00

1981

☐☐ UXC19 28c First Transpacific Flight, 1/2/81, Wenatchee, WA...1.25 1.50 10.00

1982

☐☐ UXC20 28c Gliders, 3/5/82, Houston, TX (106,932) 1.25 1.50 8.00

SCOTT NUMBER	DESCRIPTION	UNCACH	CACH	CERM PROG

1983
☐☐ UXC21 28c Olympics (Speedskating), 12/29/83,
    Milwaukee, WI (108,397)........................1.25   1.50   6.00

1985
☐☐ UXC22 33c China Clipper Seaplane, 2/15/85,
    San Francisco, CA......................1.25   1.50

1986
☐☐ UXC23 33c Chicago Skyline, 2/1/86, Chicago, IL (84,480).......1.25   1.50   6.00

1988
☐☐ UXC24 36c DC-3, 5/14/88, San Diego, CA 1.25   1.50   6.00

1991-95
☐☐ UXC25 40c Yankee Clipper, 6/28/91, Flushing, NY (24,865)...1.50   2.00   6.00
☐☐ UXC26 50c Eagle, 8/24/95, St. Louis, MO................................1.50   2.00   8.00

OFFICIAL POSTAL CARDS
1983-96
☐☐ UZ2 13c Eagle, 1/12/83, DC 1.00   1.25
☐☐ UZ3 14c Eagle, 2/26/85, DC (62,396) 1.00   1.25
☐☐ UZ4 15c Eagle, 6/10/88, New York, NY (133,498) 1.00   1.25
☐☐ UZ5 19c Eagle, 5/24/91, Seattle, WA (23,097) 1.00   1.50
☐☐ UZ6 20c Eagle, 5/9/96, DC 1.00   1.50

PLATE NUMBER COIL FDC

Since early 1981, nearly all coil stamps issued by the United States have plate numbers printed on the stamps at regular intervals. The tiny digits printed in the stamps' bottom margins have given rise to the fastest growing area of modern United States stamp collecting — plate number coils (PNC).

Not all plate numbers exist on FDC's — only the Ones that are printed before the

stamp is issued or very shortly after the first day, during the grace period for submitting covers to be canceled.

Because some PNC first-day covers are scarce and expensive, and some forgeries have already appeared on the philatelic market, collectors are advised to have costly FDC's expertized.

SCOTT NUMBER	DESCRIPTION	PLATE NUMBER	PAIR VALUE	STRIP OF 3 VALUE
☐ 1891	18c Flag, 4/24/81	1	75.00	150.00
☐		2	225.00	425.00
☐		3	325.00	525.00
☐		4	200.00	350.00
☐		5	125.00	—
☐ 1895	20c Flag over Supreme Court, 12/17/81	1	20.00	40.00
☐		2	100.00	200.00
☐		3	200.00	400.00
☐ 1897	1c Omnibus, 8/19/83	1	9.00	13.00
☐		2	9.00	13.00
☐ 1897A	2c Locomotive, 5/20/82	3	12.00	20.00
☐		4	12.00	20.00
☐ 1898	3c Handcar, 3/25/83	1	10.00	20.00
☐		2	10.00	20.00
☐		3	10.00	20.00
☐		4	10.00	20.00
☐ 1898A	4c Stagecoach, 8/19/82	1	10.00	18.50
☐		2	10.00	18.50
☐		3	10.00	18.50
☐		4	10.00	18.50
☐ 1899	5c Motorcycle, 10/10/83	1	10.00	15.00
☐		2	10.00	15.00
☐		3	2,000.	—
☐		4	1,200.	1,800.

SCOTT NUMBER	DESCRIPTION	PLATE NUMBER	PAIR VALUE	STRIP OF 3 VALUE
☐ 1900	5.2c Sleigh, 3/21/83	1	15.00	30.00
☐		2	15.00	30.00
☐ 1900a	Sleigh, untagged (Bureau precanceled), 3/21/83	1	800.	800.
☐		2	800.	800.
☐ 1901	5.9c Bicycle, 2/17/82	3	15.00	25.00
☐		4	15.00	25.00
☐ 1901a	Bicycle, untagged (Bureau precanceled), 2/17/82	3	2,000.	2,000.
☐		4	2,000.	2,000.
☐ 1902	7.4c Baby Buggy, 4/7/84	2	10.00	20.00
☐ 1902a	Baby Buggy, untagged (Bureau precanceled), 4/7/84	2	2,000.	2,000.
☐ 1903	9.3c Mail Wagon, 12/15/81	1	20.00	40.00
☐		2	20.00	40.00
☐		3	2,000.	2,000.
☐		4	2,000.	2,000.
☐ 1903a	Mail Wagon, untagged Bureau precanceled), 12/15/81	1	2,500.	
	One cover known to exist			
☐	*One cover known to exist*	2	2,500.	
☐		3	2,000.	2,000.
☐		4	2,000.	2,000.
☐ 1904	10.9c Hansom Cab, 3/26/82	1	17.50	35.00
☐		2		350.00
☐ 1904a	Hansom Cab, untagged (Bureau precanceled), 3/26/82	1	2000.	2000.
☐		2	2000.	2000.
☐ 1905	11c Caboose, 2/3/84	1	15.00	35.00
☐ 1905a	11c Caboose, "B" Press, 9/25/91	2	-	350.00*
	*This price is for a cacheted cover with dial UO cancellation, there was no FDOI cancel although some exist where the stamps had been added to a postal card with the FDOI for the postal card. Also known on a Postal Bulletin with a FDOI cancel.			
☐ 1906	17c Electric Auto, 6/25/82	1	17.50	30.00
☐		2	17.50	30.00
☐ 1907	18c Surrey, 5/18/81	1	20.00	45.00
☐		2	20.00	45.00
☐		3	700.00	1500.
☐		4	700.00	1500.
☐		5	100.00	200.00
☐		6	100.00	200.00
☐		7	400.00	800.00
☐		8	100.00	200.00
☐		9	450.00	900.00
☐		10	450.00	900.00
☐ 1908	20c Fire Pumper, 12/10/81	1	75.00	150.00
☐		2	150.00	300.00
☐		3	15.00	40.00
☐		4	15.00	40.00
☐		5	100.00	175.00
☐		6	100.00	175.00
☐		7	1,000.	—
☐		8	1,000.	—
☐		10	2,500.	—

SCOTT NUMBER	DESCRIPTION	PLATE NUMBER	PAIR VALUE	STRIP OF 3 VALUE
☐	2005	20c Consumer Education, 4/27/82 1	25.00	40.00
☐		2	25.00	40.00
☐		3	25.00	40.00
☐		4	25.00	40.00
☐	2112	(22c)"D" & Eagle, 2/1/85 1	10.00	17.50
☐		2	10.00	17.50
☐	2115	22c Flag over Capitol Dome, 3/29/85 1	35.00	65.00
☐		2	15.00	25.00
☐		5		2500.
		One cover known to exist		
☐	2115b	22c Flag over Capitol Dome, inscribed "T" at bottom, 5/23/87 1		15.00
☐	2123	3.4c School Bus, 6/8/85 1	6.50	12.50
☐		2	6.50	12.50
☐	2124	4.9c Buckboard, 6/21/85 3	7.50	13.50
☐		4	7.50	13.50
☐	2124a	Buckboard, untagged (Bureau precanceled), 6/21/85 3	2,000.	2,000.
☐		4	2,000.	2,000.
☐	2125	5.5c Star Route Truck, 11/1/86 1	7.50	12.50
☐	2125a	Star Route Truck, untagged (Bureau precanceled), 11/1/86 1		40.00
☐	2126	6c Tricycle, 5/6/85 1	6.50	10.00
☐	2126a	Tricycle, untagged (Bureau precanceled), 5/6/85 1	—	—
		FDC's of the 6c Tricycle untagged are not believed to be legitimate, and are listed here for reference.		
☐	2127	7.1c Tractor, 2/6/87 1	—	12.50
☐	2127a	Tractor, untagged (Bureau precancel "Nonprofit Org."in black), 2/6/87 1		30.00
☐	2127a	Tractor, untagged (Bureau precancel), ("Nonprofit 5-Digit Zip + 4" in black), 5/26/89 1	—	10.00
☐	2128	8.3c Ambulance, 6/21/86 1	7.50	12.50
☐		2	7.50	12.50
☐	2128a	Ambulance, untagged (Bureau precanceled), 6/21/86 1	2,000.	—
☐		2	2,000.	—
☐	2129	8.5c Tow Truck, 1/24/87 1	—	10.00
☐	2129a	Tow Truck, untagged (Bureau precanceled), 1/24/87 1		15.00
☐	2130	10.1c Oil Wagon, 4/18/85 1	7.50	10.00
☐	2130a	Oil Wagon, untagged (red Bureau precancel), 6/27/88 2		8.50
☐	2131	11c Stutz Bearcat, 6/11/85 3	12.50	17.50
☐		4	12.50	17.50
☐	2132	12c Stanley Steamer, 4/2/85 1	7.50	12.50
☐		2	7.50	12.50
☐	2132a	Stanley Steamer, untagged (Bureau precanceled), 4/2/85 1	2,500.	—
		One cover known to exist		
☐	2132a	Stanley Steamer, B Press, untagged (Bureau precanceled) 1	2,000.	2,000.

The price is for the postally used EKU, prices for the covers with the Philatelic Center cancellation are $750.00
There was no official first day of issue for the B Press version of this

stamp. Cacheted covers exist canceled September 3, 1987, the date the stamp was placed on sale at the Philatelic Sales Unit in Washington, DC, currently the earliest known postmark. The stamp actually was placed on sale prior to that date at other locations, so there is a possibility of even earlier covers.

Scott	Description	Plate	Pair	Strip of 3
☐ 2133	12.5c Pushcart, 4/18/85 ....1.....................7.50			12.50
☐ 2134	14c Iceboat, 3/23/85 ....1.................15.00			20.00
☐		2.................15.00		20.00
☐		3.............................		2500.

One cover known to exist

| ☐ | | 4............................. | | 2,500. |

One cover known to exist

| ☐ 2134b | Iceboat, B Press, 9/30/86 ....2............................ | | | 2,000. |

There was no official first day of issue for the B Press version of this stamp. The earliest known use was September 30, 1986, but no cacheted covers are known.

☐ 2135	17c Dog Sled, 8/20/86 ....2............................—			10.00
☐ 2136	25c Bread Wagon, 11/22/86 ....1............................—			12.50
☐ 2149	18c George Washington, 11/6/85 ....1112.................20.00			35.00
☐		3333.................20.00		35.00
☐ 2149a	George Washington, untagged			
	(Bureau precanceled), 11/6/85 ......11121.................45.00			75.00
☐		33333.................45.00		75.00
☐ 2150	21.1c Letters, 10/22/85 ....111111.................15.00			25.00
☐ 2150a	21.1c Letters, untagged			
	(Bureau precanceled), 10/22/85 ... 111111.................35.00			65.00
☐ 2225	1c Omnibus, re-engraved, 11/26/86 ....1.....................7.50			12.50
☐ 2226	2c Locomotive, re-engraved, 3/6/87 ....1............................			8.50
☐ 2228	4c Stagecoach, re-engraved, 8/15/86 ....1............................			350.00

There was no official first day of issue for Scott 2228, but cacheted covers exist canceled August 15, 1986, the earliest known use.

| ☐ 2231 | 8.3c Ambulance, B Press, untagged | | | |
| | (Bureau precanceled), 8/29/86 ....1............................ | | | 1,000. |

There was no official first day of issue for the B Press version of this stamp, but cacheted covers exist canceled August 29, 1986, the earliest known use.

☐ 2252	3c Conestoga Wagon, 2/29/88 ....1............................			7.50
☐ 2253	5c Milk Wagon, 9/25/87 ....1............................			7.50
☐ 2254	5.3c Elevator, 9/16/88 ....1............................			7.50
☐ 2255	7.6c Carreta, 8/30/88 ....1............................			7.50
☐		2............................		1000.
☐ 2256	8.4c Wheel Chair, 8/12/88 ....1............................			7.50
☐		2............................		750.00
☐ 2257	10c Canal Boat, 4/11/87 ....1............................			8.50
☐ 2258	13c Patrol Wagon, 10/29/88 ....1............................			7.50
☐ 2259	13.2c Coal Car, 7/19/88 ....1............................			7.50
☐ 2260	15c Tugboat, 7/12/88 ....1............................			7.50
☐ 2261	16.7c Popcorn Wagon, 7/7/88 ....1............................			7.50
☐ 2262	17.5c Racing Car, 9/25/87 ....1............................			8.50
☐ 2262a	Racing Car, untagged			
	(Bureau precanceled), 9/25/87 ....1............................			10.00
☐ 2263	20c Cable Car, 10/28/88 ....1............................			7.50
☐		....2............................		60.00
☐ 2264	20.5c Fire Engine, 9/28/88 ....1............................			7.50

SCOTT NUMBER	DESCRIPTION	PLATE NUMBER	PAIR VALUE	STRIP OF 3 VALUE
2265	21c Railroad Mail Car, 8/16/88 1			7.50
	2			1,500.
2266	24.1c Tandem Bicycle, 10/26/88 1			7.50
2279	(25c) "E" & Earth, 3/22/88 1111			7.50
	1211			10.00
	1222			7.50
	2222			25.00
2280	25c Flag Over Yosemite, 5/20/88 1			10.00
	2			10.00
	3			150.00
	4			150.00
2280	25c Flag Over Yosemite, pre-phosphored paper, 2/14/89 5			20.00
	6			40.00
	7			8.50
	8			8.50
	9			60.00
	10			1,500.
2281	25c Honeybee, 9/2/88 1			10.00
	2			30.00
2451	4c Steam Carriage, 1/25/91 1			6.50
2452	5c Circus Wagon, engr., 8/31/90 1			6.50
2452B	5c Circus Wagon, photo., 12/8/92 ....A1			6.50
	....A2			8.00
2452D	5c Circus Wagon, SV, 3/20/95 ....S1			6.50
2453	5c Canoe, engr., 5/25/91 1			6.50
2454	5c Canoe, photo., 10/22/91 ....S11			6.50
2457	10c Tractor Trailer, engr., 5/25/91 1			6.50
2463	20c Cog Railroad, 6/9/95.............1			7.50
	2			25.00
2464	23c Lunch Wagon, 4/12/91 2			8.50
	3			7.50
2466	32c Ferry Boat, 6/2/95 2			7.50
	3			7.50
	4			15.00
	5			35.00
2468	$1 Seaplane, 4/20/90 1			10.00
2480	29c Pine Cone (self adhesive), 11/5/93 ....B1			10.00
2492	32c Rose (self adhesive), 6/2/95 ....S111			10.00
2495A	32c Peaches and Pears (self adhesive), 7/8/95 ....V11111			10.00
2518	(29c) "F", 1/22/91 1111			10.00
	1211			100.00
	1222			10.00
	2211			25.00
	2222			10.00
2523	29c Flag over Mt. Rushmore, engr., 3/29/91 1			7.50
	2			7.50
	3			7.50
	4			7.50
	5			7.50
	6			7.50
	7			7.50

SCOTT NUMBER	DESCRIPTION	PLATE NUMBER	PAIR VALUE	STRIP OF 3 VALUE
☐	2523A	29c **Flag over Mt. Rushmore,** photo., 7/4/91 11111		7.50
☐	2525	29c **Flower,** rouletted, 8/16/91 ....S1111		7.50
☐	2526	29c **Flower,** perf., 3/3/92 2222		7.50
☐	2529	19c **Fishing Boat,** 8/8/91 1111		7.50
☐		1112		15.00
☐		1212		7.50
☐		1424		250.00
☐	2529C	19c **Fishing Boat,** 6/25/94 ....S11		7.50
☐	2598	29c **Eagle** (self adhesive), 2/4/94...................111		10.00
☐	2599	29c **Statue of Liberty** (self adhesive), 6/24/94 ....D1111		10.00
☐	2604	(10c) **Eagle & Shield,** ABNC, 12/13/91 ....A11111		7.50
☐		....A11112		7.50
☐		....A12213		30.00
☐		....A21112		7.50
☐		....A21113		7.50
☐		....A22112		7.50
☐		....A22113		7.50
☐		....A32333		125.00
☐		....A33333		7.50
☐		....A33334		750.00
☐		....A33335		7.50
☐		....A34424		350.00
☐		....A34426		350.00
☐		....A43324		15.00
☐		....A43325		15.00
☐		....A43326		15.00
☐		....A43334		15.00
☐		....A43335		15.00
☐		....A43426		25.00
☐		....A53335		25.00
☐		....A54444		50.00
☐		....A54445		50.00
☐		....A77777		750.00
☐	2605	(10c) **Eagle & Shield,** BEP, 5/29/93 11111		6.50
☐	2606	(10c) **Eagle & Shield,** Stamp Venturers, 5/29/93 ....S11111		6.50
☐	2607	23c **Flag Pre-sort,** 9/27/91 ....A111		7.50
☐		....A112		250.00
☐		....A122		250.00
☐		....A212		7.50
☐		....A222		7.50
☐	2608	23c **Reflected Flag Pre-sort,** ABNC, 7/21/92 A1111		7.50
☐		....A2222		7.50
☐	2608A	23c **Reflected Flag Pre-sort,** BEP, 10/9/92 1111		7.50
☐	2608B	23c **Reflected Flag Pre-sort,** Stamp Venturers, 5/14/93 ....S111		7.50
☐	2609	29c **Flag over White House,** 4/23/92 1		7.50
☐		2		7.50
☐		3		7.50
☐		4		7.50
☐		5		7.50
☐		6		7.50

SCOTT NUMBER	DESCRIPTION	PLATE NUMBER	PAIR VALUE	STRIP OF 3 VALUE
☐		7		7.50
☐		8		1,000.00
☐	2799-2802 29c Christmas (self adhesive), 10/28/93	V1111111		10.00
☐	2813 29c Love (self adhesive), 1/27/94	B1		10.00
☐	2873 29c Santa (self adhesive),10/20/94	V1111		10.00
☐	2888 (25c) "G" Flag, 12/13/94	S11111		7.50
☐	2886 (32c) "G" Flag, (self adhesive), 12/13/94	V11111		7.50
☐	2888 (32c) "G" Flag, 12/13/94	S11111		7.50
☐	2889 (32c) "G" Flag, 12/13/94	1111		7.50
		2222		7.50
☐	2890 (32c) "G" Flag,12/13/94	A1111		10.00
☐		A1112		10.00
☐		A1113		10.00
☐		A1211		10.00
☐		A1212		10.00
☐		A1222		10.00
☐		A1311		10.00
☐		A1313		10.00
☐		A1314		10.00
☐		A1324		10.00
☐		A1417		10.00
☐		A1433		10.00
☐		A2211		10.00
☐		A2212		10.00
☐		A2213		10.00
☐		A2214		10.00
☐		A2223		10.00
☐		A2313		10.00
☐		A3113		10.00
☐		A3114		10.00
☐		A3314		10.00
☐		A3315		10.00
☐		A3323		10.00
☐		A3423		10.00
☐		A3324		10.00
☐		A3426		10.00
☐		A3433		10.00
☐		A3435		10.00
☐		A3536		10.00
☐		A4426		10.00
☐		A4427		10.00
☐		A4435		250.00
☐		A5327		10.00
☐		A5417		10.00
☐		A5427		10.00
☐		A5437		10.00
	Note: The full set of 36 ABN covers is valued at $1,000.00			
☐	2891 (32c) "G" Flag, perf., 12/13/94	S1111		10.00
☐	2892 (32c) "G" Flag, rouletted, 12/13/94	S1111		10.00
		S2222		10.00
☐	2893 (32c) "G" Flag, 12/13/94	A11111		10.00
		A21111		10.00

250

	SCOTT NUMBER	DESCRIPTION	PLATE NUMBER	STRIP OF 3 VALUE
☐	2902	(5c) Butte, SV, 3/10/95	S111	7.50
☐	2902B	(5c) Butte, SV, (self-adhesive), 6/15/96.	S111	6.50
☐	2903	(5c) Mountains, BEP, 3/16/96	11111	6.50
☐	2904	(5c) Mountains, SV, 3/16/96	S11	6.50
☐	2904A	(5c) Mountains, (self-adhesive),		
		6/15/96	V222222	6.50
☐			V333333	6.50
☐			V333323	6.50
☐			V333342	6.50
☐			V333343	6.50
☐	2905	(10c) Auto, 3/10/95	S111	7.50
☐	2906	(10c) Auto, (self-adhesive), 6/15/96	S111	6.50
☐	2907	(10c) Eagle & Shield, (self-adhesive),		
		5/21/96	S1111	6.50
☐	2908	(15c) Auto Tail Fin, BEP, 3/17/95	11111	7.50
☐	2909	(15c) Auto Tail Fin, SV, 3/17/95	S11111	7.50
☐	2911	(25c) Juke Box, BEP 3/17/95	111111	7.50
☐	2912	(25c) Juke Box, SV, 3/17/95	S11111	7.50
☐	2912A	(25c) Juke Box, SV, (self-adhesive),		
		6/15/96	S11111	7.50
☐	2912B	(25c) Juke Box, BEP, (self-adhesive),		
		6/15/96,	11111	7.50
☐	2913	32c Flag over Porch, BEP, 5/19/95	11111	10.00
☐			22221	15.00
☐			22222	10.00
☐			33333	10.00
☐			44444	10.00
☐			45444	35.00
☐			66646	35.00
☐	2914	32c Flag over Porch, SV, 5/19/95	S11111	10.00
☐	2915A	32c Flag over Porch, BEP, (self-adhesive),		
		5/21/96	55555	10.00
☐			66666	10.00
☐			78777	10.00
☐			87888	50.00
☐			87898	10.00
☐			88888	10.00
☐			88898	500.00
☐			89878	10.00
☐			89888	50.00
☐			89898	20.00
☐			97898	10.00
☐			99999	10.00
☐	2915B	32c Flag over Porch, SV, (self-adhesive),		
		6/15/96	S11111	10.00
☐	2915C	32c Flag over Porch, BEP, (self-adhesive),		
		5/21/96, serpentine die cut 11	66666	25.00
☐	3017	32c Christmas, (self adhesive)		
		9/30/95	V1111	10.00
☐	3018	32c Christmas Angel, (self adhesive)		
		10/31/95	B1111	10.00
☐	3044	1c Kestrel, 1/20/96	1111	6.50
☐	3053	20c Blue Jay, (self-adhesive), 8/2/96	S111	7.50

SCOTT NUMBER	DESCRIPTION	PLATE NUMBER	PAIR VALUE	STRIP OF 3 VALUE

OFFICIAL STAMPS

☐	O135	20c Official, 1/12/83 ....1..............30.00		75.00
☐	O139	(22c) "D" 2/4/85 ....1..............35.00		80.00

COMPUTER VENDED POSTAGE

☐	31	29c ECA GARD, 8/20/92 ....1..........................		7.50
☐	31	29c Variable Rate, 8/20/92, 1st print........1..........................		7.50
☐	31b	29c Variable Rate, 8/20/92, (2nd print) .....1..........................		25.00
☐	32	29c Variable Rate, 8/20/92 ....A11..........................		7.50

INAUGURATION, RESIGNATION, AND
DEATH IN OFFICE COVERS

All values given are for cacheted covers postmarked on the date of the presidents'
inauguration, resignation or death in office. Uncacheted covers sell for about one-half
of the catalogue value. Values for covers after 1945 are for unaddressed cacheted
covers. Addressed covers after 1949 sell for about one-half of the catalogue value.

☐   **McKinley** Mar. 4, 1901 ....1,500.
☐   **McKinley** Sept. 14, 1901, Assassination cover Death in Office ....1,500.
☐   **T. Roosevelt** Mar. 4, 1905 ....500.00
☐   **Taft** Mar. 4, 1909 ....250.00
☐   **Wilson** 1st Term Mar. 4, 1913 ....500.00
☐   **Wilson 2nd Term,** Mar. 5, 1917 ....450.00
☐   **Harding** Mar. 4, 1921 ....—
☐   **Harding** Death, Aug. 2, 1923 ....—
☐   **Coolidge** Inauguration, Aug. 3, 1923 ....400.00
☐   **Coolidge** 2nd Term, Mar. 4, 1925 ....—
☐   **Hoover** Mar. 4, 1929 ....200.00
☐   **F.D. Roosevelt** 1st Term, Mar. 4, 1933 ....50.00
☐   **F.D. Roosevelt** 2nd Term, Jan. 20, 1937 ....200.00
☐   **F.D. Roosevelt** 3rd Term, Jan. 20, 1941 ....200.00
☐   **F.D. Roosevelt** 4th Term, Jan. 20, 1945 ....150.00
☐   **F.D. Roosevelt** Date of Death, Apr. 12, 1945, canceled at Roosevelt, NY 65.00
☐   **Truman** 1st Term, Apr. 12, 1945 ....200.00
☐   **Truman** 2nd Term, Jan. 20, 1949 ....60.00
☐   **Eisenhower** 1st Term, Jan. 20, 1953 ....20.00
☐   **Eisenhower** 2nd Term, Jan. 21, 1957 ....20.00
         Note: 1/20/57 was a Sunday. However, some Artcraft and Fluegel
         cacheted covers do have the 1/20/57 cancel.
☐   With Artcraft cachet 35.00
☐   With Fluegel cachet 75.00
☐   **Kennedy** Jan. 20, 1961 ....20.00
☐   With Fluegel cachet 35.00
☐   **Kennedy** Assassination cover, Nov. 22, 1963 ....30.00
☐   **Kennedy** Assassination cover, Nov. 22, 1963, with FDC of
         Scott 1246 on May 29, 1964 ....50.00
☐   **L.B. Johnson** Jan. 20, 1965 ....10.00
☐   With Fluegel cachet 35.00
☐   **Nixon** 1st Term, Jan. 20, 1969 ....10.00
☐   **Nixon** 2nd Term, Jan. 20, 1973 ....8.00
☐   **Nixon** Announces resignation, canceled Aug 8, 1974 on same cover
         canceled Jan. 20, 1973 ....20.00
☐   **Nixon** Resigns to Congress, Aug. 9, 1974 ....8.00
☐   **Nixon** Resigns to Congress, canceled Aug. 9, 1974 on same cover
         canceled Jan. 20, 1973 ....10.00
☐   **Ford**, V.P. Dec. 6, 1973 ....8.00
☐   **Ford** Aug. 9, 1974 ....5.00
☐   **Carter** Jan. 20, 1977 ....4.00
☐   **Reagan** 1st Term, Jan. 20, 1981 ....3.00
☐   **Reagan** 2nd Term, Jan. 21, 1985 ....3.00
☐   **Bush** Jan. 20, 1989 ....3.00
☐   **Clinton** 1st Term, Jan. 20, 1993 ....3.00
☐   **Clinton** 2nd Term, Jan.20,1997...3.00

PATRIOTIC COVERS OF WW II

Listed below are significant World War II patriotic dates. Values are for related, printed-cacheted covers, canceled on the appropriate date. The listed values reflect the work of the following cachet makers: Crosby, Fidelity, Fleetwood/Knapp, Fleetwood/Staehle, Fluegel, Richardson/Knapp, Smartcraft, and Teixeria.

In addition, Minkus and several other cachet makers made a group of general purpose patriotic covers such as "Win the War" and "Sink the Japs". These covers generally have a value of $3.00 each, while uncanceled covers have a value of 75c each.

WWII COVERS DESCRIPTION	CACHETED SINGLE
☐ Pearl Harbor, 12/7/41	125.00
☐ U.S. Declares War on Japan, 12/8/41	75.00
☐ Germany and Italy Declare War on U.S., 12/11/41	75.00
☐ U.S Declares War on Germany and Italy, 12/11/41	75.00
☐ Churchill arrives at the White House, 12/22/41	60.00
☐ Manila and Cavite Fall, 1/2/42	60.00
☐ Roosevelt's Diamond Jubilee Birthday, 1/30/42	60.00
☐ Singapore Surrenders, 2/15/42	60.00
☐ Japan takes Java, 3/10/42	60.00
☐ Marshall Arrives in London, 4/8/42	60.00
☐ Dedication of MacArthur Post Office, 4/15/42	60.00
☐ Doolittle Air Raid of Tokyo, 4/18/42	60.00
☐ Air Raid on Tokyo by Doolittle, 4/18/42	60.00
☐ Fort Mills Corregidor Island Surrenders, 5/6/42	60.00
☐ Madagascar Occupied by U.S, 5/9/42	60.00
☐ Mexico at War with Axis, 5/23/42	60.00
☐ Bombing of Cologne, 6/6/42	60.00
☐ Japan Bombs Dutch Harbor, AK, 6/6/42	60.00
☐ Six German Spies Sentenced to Death, 8/7/42	60.00
☐ Brazil at War, 8/22/42	55.00
☐ Battle of El Alamein, 10/23/42	45.00
☐ Invasion of North Africa (Operation Torch), 11/8/42	45.00
☐ Gas rationing is Nationwide, 12/1/42	45.00
☐ The Casablanca Conference, 1/22/43	45.00
☐ The Casablanca Conference (You must remember this!), 1/22/43	40.00
☐ Point Rationing, 3/1/43	50.00
☐ Battle of the Bismarck Sea, 3/13/43	40.00
☐ U.S. Planes Bomb Naples, 4/5/43	40.00
☐ Bizerte & Tunis Occupied, 5/8/43	40.00
☐ Invasion of Attu, 5/11/43	40.00
☐ Sicily Invaded, 7/14/43	35.00
☐ Italy Invaded, 9/3/43	40.00
☐ The Quebec Conference, 8/14/43	45.00
☐ Italy Surrenders, 9/8/43	40.00
☐ Mussolini Escapes, 9/18/43	40.00
☐ U.S. Drives Germans out of Naples, 10/2/43	40.00
☐ Italy Declares War on Germany, 10/13/43	40.00
☐ Hull Eden Stalin Conference, 10/25/43	40.00
☐ U.S. Government Takes over Coal Mines, 11/3/43	40.00
☐ The Cairo Meeting, 11/25/43	35.00
☐ The Teheran Meeting, 11/28/43	35.00
☐ Roosevelt, Churchill, Chiang Kai-Shek at Cairo, 12/2/43	40.00

☐	FDR, Stalin, Churchill Agree on 3 fronts, 12/2/43	40.00
☐	Soviets Reach Polish Border, 1/4/44	30.00
☐	U.S Captures Cassino, 3/15/44	35.00
☐	Invasion of Dutch New Guinea, 4/24/44	35.00
☐	Rome Falls, 6/4/44	35.00
☐	D-Day Single Face Eisenhower, 6/6/44	125.00
☐	Invasion of Normandy D-Day, 6/6/44	35.00
☐	B29's Bomb Japan, 6/15/44	35.00
☐	Cherbourg Surrenders, 6/7/44	40.00
☐	Paris Revolts, 6/23/44	35.00
☐	Caen Falls to Allies, 7/10/44	35.00
☐	Marines Invade Guam, 7/21/44	35.00
☐	Yanks Enter Brest, etc., 8/7/44	35.00
☐	U.S. Bombs Philippines, 8/10/44	35.00
☐	Invasion of Southern France, 8/16/44	25.00
☐	Liberation of Paris, 8/23/44	30.00
☐	Florence Falls to Allies, 8/23/44	30.00
☐	Liberation of Brussels, 9/4/44	30.00
☐	U.S. Invades Holland, Finland Quits, 9/5/44	30.00
☐	Russians Invade Yugoslavia, 9/6/44	30.00
☐	Russians Enter Bulgaria, 9/9/44	30.00
☐	Liberation of Luxembourg, 9/10/44	30.00
☐	Albania Invaded, 9/27/44	35.00
☐	Philippines, We Will Be Back, 9/27/44	25.00
☐	Greece Invaded, 10/5/44	35.00
☐	Liberation of Athens, 10/14/44	30.00
☐	Liberation of Belgrade, 10/16/44	30.00
☐	Russia Invades Czechoslovakia, 10/19/44	30.00
☐	Invasion of the Philippines, 10/20/44	30.00
☐	The Pied Piper of Leyte-Philippine Invasion, 10/21/44	45.00
☐	Invasion of Norway, 10/25/44	25.00
☐	Liberation of Tirana, 11/18/44	25.00
☐	100,000 Yanks Land on Luzon, 1/10/45	25.00
☐	Liberation of Warsaw, 1/17/45	30.00
☐	Russians Drive to Oder River, 2/2/45	25.00
☐	Liberation of Manila, 2/4/45	25.00
☐	Yalta Conference, 2/12/45	25.00
☐	Budapest Liberated, 2/13/45	25.00
☐	Corregidor is Ours, 2/17/45	25.00
☐	Turkey Wars Germany and Japan, 2/23/45	25.00
☐	Yanks Enter Cologne, 3/5/45	25.00
☐	Cologne is Taken, 3/6/45	20.00
☐	Historical Rhine Crossing, 3/8/45	20.00
☐	Bombing of Tokyo, 3/10/45	25.00
☐	Russia Crosses Oder River, 3/13/45	25.00
☐	Capture of Iwo Jima, 3/14/45	20.00
☐	Battle of the Inland Sea, 3/20/45	20.00
☐	Crossing of the Rhine, 3/24/45	20.00
☐	Danzig Invaded, 3/27/45	25.00
☐	Okinawa Invaded, 4/1/45	25.00
☐	Japanese Cabinet Resigns, 4/7/45	25.00
☐	Liberation of Vienna, 4/10/45	25.00

☐	U.S. Invades Bremen etc., 4/10/45	25.00
☐	FRD Dies-Truman beomes President, 4/12/45	50.00
☐	Liberation of Vienna, 4/13/45	25.00
☐	Patton Invades Czechoslovakia, 4/18/45	25.00
☐	Berlin Invaded, 4/21/45	25.00
☐	Berlin is Encircled, 4/25/45	25.00
☐	GI Joe and Ivan Meet at Torgau-Germany, 4/26/45	25.00
☐	Mussolini Executed, 4/28/45	25.00
☐	Hitler Dead, 5/1/45	35.00
☐	Liberation of Italy, 5/2/45	25.00
☐	Berlin Falls, 5/2/45	25.00
☐	Liberation of Rangoon, 5/3/45	25.00
☐	5th and 7th Armies Meet at the Brenner Pass, 5/4/45	25.00
☐	Liberation of Copenhagen, 5/5/45	25.00
☐	Liberation of Amsterdam, 5/5/45	25.00
☐	Liberation of Oslo, 5/8/45	25.00
☐	Liberation of Prague, 5/8/45	25.00
☐	V-E Day, 5/8/45	35.00
☐	Atomic Bomb Test, 5/16/45	25.00
☐	Invasion of Borneo, 6/11/45	25.00
☐	Eisenhower Welcomed Home, 6/18/45	20.00
☐	Okinawa Captured, 6/21/45	25.00
☐	United Nations Conference, 6/25/45	25.00
☐	American Flag Raised Over Berlin, 7/4/45	25.00
☐	Big Three Meet at Potsdam, 8/1/45	25.00
☐	Atomic Bomb, 8/6/45	75.00
☐	Russia Declares War on Japan, 8/8/45	25.00
☐	Japan Capitulates, 8/14/45	25.00
☐	Japan Signs Peace Treaty, 9/1/45	50.00
☐	Liberation of China, 9/2/45	35.00
☐	V-J Day, 9/2/45	35.00
☐	Liberation of Korea, 9/2/45	25.00
☐	Flag Raising over Tokyo-MacArthur takes over, 9/8/45	25.00
☐	Gen. Wainwright Rescued from the Japanese, 9/10/45	25.00
☐	Nimitz Post Office, 9/10/45	25.00
☐	Marines Land in Japan, 9/23/45	40.00
☐	Nimitz Day-Wshington, 10/5/45	25.00
☐	War Crimes Commission, 10/18/45	25.00
☐	Premier Laval Executed as Traitor, 10/15/45	25.00
☐	Fleet Reviewed by President Truman, 10/27/45	35.00
☐	Trygve Lie Elected, 1/21/46	25.00
☐	2nd Anniversary of D-Day, 6/6/46	25.00
☐	Operation Crossroads, 6/3/46	100.00
☐	Bikini Atomic Bomb Test, 7/1/46	125.00
☐	Independence of the Philippines, 7/4/46	100.00
☐	Atomic Age, 7/10/46	25.00
☐	Victory Day, 8/14/46	25.00
☐	Opening of UN Post Office at Lake Success, 9/23/46	25.00
☐	Goering Commits Suicide, 10/16/46	40.00
☐	Opening Day of UN in Flushing, NY, 10/23/46	25.00
☐	Marshall is Secretary of State, 1/21/47	25.00
☐	Moscow Peace Conference, 3/10/47	25.00

SCOTT NUMBER	DESCRIPTION	SINGLE	PLATE BLOCK	CERM BLOCK	PROG
☐					
☐					
☐					
☐					
☐					
☐					
☐					
☐					
☐					
☐					
☐					
☐					
☐					
☐					
☐					
☐					
☐					
☐					
☐					
☐					
☐					
☐					
☐					
☐					
☐					
☐					
☐					
☐					
☐					
☐					
☐					
☐					

INDEX TO ADVERTISERS